# Zion's Dilemmas

A VOLUME IN THE SERIES

*Cornell Studies in Security Affairs*

Edited by Robert J. Art, Robert Jervis, and Stephen M. Walt

A list of titles in this series is available at www.cornellpress.cornell.edu.

# Zion's Dilemmas

*How Israel Makes National Security Policy*

CHARLES D. FREILICH

Cornell University Press

*Ithaca and London*

First published 2012 by Cornell University Press

Printed in the United States of America

*Library of Congress Cataloging-in-Publication Data*

Freilich, Charles D. (Charles David)
    Zion's dilemmas : how Israel makes national security policy / Charles D. Freilich.
        p.   cm.—(Cornell studies in security affairs)
    Includes bibliographical references and index.
    ISBN 978-0-8014-5104-1 (cloth : alk. paper)   1. National security—Israel—Decision
making.   2. Israel—Politics and government.   3. Israel—Military policy.
4. Israel—Foreign relations.   I. Title.   II. Series: Cornell studies in security affairs.
    UA853.I8F73   2013
    355'.03355694—dc23
    2012019706

Cornell University Press strives to use environmentally responsible
suppliers and materials to the fullest extent possible in the publishing
of its books. Such materials include vegetable-based, low-VOC inks
and acid-free papers that are recycled, totally chlorine-free, or partly
composed of nonwood fibers. For further information, visit our
website at www.cornellpress.cornell.edu.

Cloth printing   10 9 8 7 6 5 4 3 2 1

*To Lior and Tal, in the fervent hope that their children,
or at least grandchildren, may know peace and no longer
have to bear arms in Israel's defense*

# Contents

# Preface and Acknowledgments

Israel's history, its travails and accomplishments, especially in the area of national security, have been a lifelong passion. Having been born in the United States in the post–World War II era, following the Holocaust, I have always felt extraordinarily privileged to have been able to enjoy the magnificent freedoms and opportunities America affords and for which I bear an unabashed reverence. But for a geographic accident of birth, neither my family nor I might have been alive to share these blessings. After the Jewish people's two-thousand-year saga of exile, persecution, and achievement, I have always felt especially fortunate to have been born shortly after Israel's rebirth and that it was important that I make my life in Israel, participate in some small way in its stormy and dramatic history, and enjoy the freedoms and opportunities it, too, affords.

As such, this is a work of love, embedded in a lifelong commitment to Zionism, along with deeply felt frustration over Israel's shortcomings and failings, which I have long observed as a citizen, soldier, civil servant, and now scholar. This book is not part of the "revisionist history" popular in recent years among some Israeli scholars, whose often highly biased attempts to redress the biases of some of their predecessors have added little to our objective understanding of the Israeli experience. It is an attempt to describe Israel's national security decision-making processes as they truly are. I wish that the picture presented could have been far more positive and laudatory. I would have greatly preferred to extol than to criticize, but only a cold, unforgiving, and "objective" analysis, to the extent that I am capable of it, does justice to the importance of the subject and as such truly serves Israel's cause.

Perhaps the most frustrating part of my writing experience was to discuss my findings with former colleagues, senior officials, and academic experts and see them shrug their shoulders in a "so what else is new?" response. Indeed, many of the decision-making pathologies depicted in this book have long been known to those familiar with Israel. What is truly new, in addition to important specific observations and findings, is that the book constitutes the first attempt to set these pathologies out systematically and to submit them to rigorous analysis. To the extent that it contributes to our understanding of the problems and, I hope, to their partial alleviation, it will have more than justified the time and effort invested.

This book would not have been completed without the help of many others. First and foremost, I wish to express my deep thanks and admiration to the indomitable Professor Graham Allison, director of the Belfer Center for Science and International Affairs at the Harvard Kennedy School. In what was the shortest meeting I have ever had prior to being offered a position, Graham immediately understood the importance of this work and undertook to provide the Belfer Center's outstanding academic auspices as the home base for my work. He is one of the all-time political science greats, and working with him on the book and a variety of other areas has been a true pleasure. His insights have proved invaluable. The Belfer Center, under his direction, is one of the more intellectually stimulating places one could want to be.

Similarly, I thank Professor Steven Miller, director of the International Studies Program (ISP) at the Belfer Center, for being my direct host, for his warmth and support throughout, and for the numerous fascinating conversations we have had on a variety of issues. I have benefited greatly from Steve's encyclopedic knowledge and penetrating analyses.

My warm appreciation to Professors Robert Jervis and Richard Pious for nurturing a much earlier version of this work through a lengthy gestation period at Columbia University. I am indebted to Professor Jervis for opening up the world of decision-making theory to me, including his own outstanding works, and for facilitating this project in its final book form. Professor Pious's rapier Socratic teaching methods provided for the most challenging class of my life, not a few missed heart beats, and an unparalleled learning experience.

I am particularly indebted to Professor Robert Art of Brandeis University, who reviewed this book on behalf of the Cornell Security Studies series, for his truly extraordinary assistance. Bob is an author's dream. Not only does he immediately spot a manuscript's strengths and weaknesses, but also, and more important, he suggests how to build on the former and redress the latter. His comments were invaluable in strengthening the overall argument. I could have asked for no more. My thanks also to Roger Haydon, executive editor at Cornell University Press, for bringing this work to fruition, and to the copy editor, Julie Palmer-Hoffman.

Thanks also to Joshua Hantman, a former student at Harvard, for his critique of an early draft, and to Susan Lynch, ISP's miraculous administrator, who manages to create order and coherence in what would otherwise be chaos. Finally, let me note that an earlier version of Chapters 1 and 2 appeared in my 2006 article "National Security Decision Making in Israel: Processes, Strengths and Pathologies," *Middle East Journal*, October 2006, pages 635–663.

All of these special people share greatly in whatever merit this work may bear. I alone am responsible for its shortcomings.

I am deeply indebted to various people and foundations whose support enabled me to write this book. First of all, to Bette and Gene Kassanof. I have known Bette, with whom I share a birthday, since childhood, and the Kassanofs' support is very deeply appreciated.

My special appreciation to Lynne Schusterman and the dedicated staff of the Schusterman Foundation, Sandy Cardin and Lisa Eisen, as well as Dr. Mitchell Bard of their partner organization, the America Israel Cooperative Enterprise. Without their friendship and support, this project would not have been possible.

My thanks also to William Lee Frost, president of the Littauer Foundation, for its support, and to Haim and Edna Weizman, who started out as benefactors and in the process became friends. Many thanks also to Professor Shinasi Rama of NYU, whose friendship has proven invaluable. Much belated thanks to the Memorial Foundation for Jewish Culture and to the National Foundation for Jewish culture, which provided generous support for my doctoral dissertation on this same subject.

I have a lifelong debt of gratitude to Bruce Heiman, who has truly been a best friend, always there when needed, always the best guy around to talk to. My deepest thanks go to my parents, Anne and Ted Freilich, for whom education has always been a supreme value, as they have proved four times over, and, in that regard, to my three extraordinarily accomplished siblings, Shani, Dani, and Yael, for their love and for being there. Finally, to my children, Lior and Tal, who give new meaning to the words "parental love" and in whose lives and accomplishments I rejoice.

# Acronyms

| | |
|---|---|
| CAPS | Comprehensive Agreement on Permanent Status |
| CoS | Chief of Staff |
| DMP | decision-making process |
| DoD | US Department of Defense |
| DoP | declaration of principles |
| FADAC | Knesset Foreign and Defense Affairs Committee |
| FAPS | Framework Agreement on Permanent Status |
| FMM | Four Mothers Movement |
| FMS | foreign military sales (i.e., US military assistance funds) |
| GAO | US General Accounting Office |
| GWOT | global war on terror |
| IAF | Israel Air Force |
| IAI | Israel Aircraft Industries |
| IDF | Israel Defense Forces |
| INSC | Israel National Security Council |
| ISA | Israel Security Agency ("Shin Bet" or "Shabak") |
| LPA | Lavi Project Administration |
| MCoD | Ministerial Committee on Defense |
| MFA | Ministry of Foreign Affairs |
| MI | Military Intelligence |
| MK | Member of Knesset |
| MoD | Ministry of Defense |
| MoF | Ministry of Finance |
| NSA | National Security Adviser |
| NSC | National Security Council |
| NSU | National Security Unit |

ORBAT    Order of Battle (i.e., size and structure of military formations)
PA       Palestinian Authority
PLO      Palestine Liberation Organization
PMB      Prime Minister's Bureau
PMM      Prime Minister's Ministry
PR       proportional representation electoral system
SAM      surface-to-air missile
SLA      South Lebanese Army
UNIFIL   UN Interim Force in Lebanon
UNSCR    UN Security Council Resolution
VARASH   Committee of the Heads of the Intelligence Services

# Dramatis Personae

## (Primary Positions Held)

| | |
|---|---|
| Mahmud Abbas | Prime Minister of the Palestinian National Authority, 2003; Chairman of the PLO, 2004–present; President of the Palestinian National Authority, January 2005–present |
| Yasser Arafat | PLO Chairman, 1969–2004; President of the Palestinian National Authority, 1994–2004 |
| Moshe Arens | Defense Minister, 1983–1984, 1990–1992, and 1999; Foreign Minister, 1988–1990 |
| Bashar Assad | President of Syria, 2000–present |
| Hafez Assad | President of Syria, 1970–2000 |
| Aharon Barak | Legal Adviser to the Cabinet, 1975–1978; Chief Justice, 1995–2006 |
| Ehud Barak | Lt. General; Chief of Staff, 1991–1995; Foreign Minister, 1995–1996; Defense Minister, 1999–2001 and 2007–present; Prime Minister, 1999–2001 |
| Menachem Begin | Prime Minister, 1977–1983; Acting Defense Minister, 1980–1981 |
| Shlomo Ben-Ami | Professor; Domestic Security Minister, 1999–2001; and concomitantly Foreign Minister, 2000–2001 |
| Benjamin (Fuad) Ben-Eliezer | Brigadier General; Defense Minister, 2001–2002 |
| David Ben-Gurion | Prime Minister and Defense Minister, 1948–1954 and 1955–1963 |
| Meir Dagan | Major General; Head of Mossad, 2002–2009 |

| | |
|---|---|
| Moshe Dayan | Lt. General; Chief of Staff, 1953–1958; Minister of Defense, 1967–1974; Foreign Minister, 1977–1979 |
| Giora Eiland | Major General; Head of IDF Planning Branch, 2001–2005; National Security Adviser, 2004–2006 |
| Rafael (Raful) Eitan | Lt. General; Chief of Staff, 1978–1983; Minister of Agriculture, 1990–1991; Minister of Agriculture and the Environment and Deputy Prime Minister, 1996–1999 |
| Simcha Erlich | Finance Minister, 1997–1979; Deputy Prime Minister, 1997–1983 |
| Levi Eshkol | Finance Minister, 1952–1963; Defense Minister, 1963–1967; Prime Minister, 1963–1969 |
| Bashir Gemayel | Lebanese Phalangist leader; President of Lebanon, 1982 |
| Mordechai (Motta) Gur | Lt. General; Chief of Staff, 1974–1978; Deputy Defense Minister, 1999–1995 |
| Dan Halutz | Lt. General; IAF Commander, 2000–2004; Chief of Staff, 2005–2007 |
| David Ivri | Major General; IAF Commander, 1977–1982; Chairman of IAI, 1985; MoD Director General, 1986–1996 |
| David Levy | Foreign Minister, 1990–1992, 1996–1998, and 1999–2000 |
| Tzipi Livni | Justice Minister, 2005; Foreign Minister and Deputy Prime Minister, 2006–2009 |
| Shaul Mofaz | Lt. General; Chief of Staff, 1998–2002; Defense Minister, 2002–2006 |
| Yitzhak Mordechai | Major General; Defense Minister, 1996–1999 |
| Hassan Nasrallah | Hezbollah Secretary-General, 1992–present |
| Benjamin (Bibi) Netanyahu | Finance Minister, 1997, 1998–1999, and 2003–2005; Foreign Minister, 2002–2003; Prime Minister, 1996–1999 and 2009–present |
| Moshe Nissim | Finance Minister, 1986–1988 |
| Ehud Olmert | Finance Minister, 2005–2006; Prime Minister, 2006–2009 |
| Shimon Peres | Defense Minister, 1974–1977 and 1995–1996; Foreign Minister, 1986–1988, 1992–1995, and 2001–2002; Finance Minister, 1988–1990, Prime Minister, 1984–1986 and 1995–1996; President, 2007–present. |

| | |
|---|---|
| Amir Peretz | Defense Minister, 2006–2007 |
| Yitzhak Rabin | Lt. General; Chief of Staff, 1964–1968; Defense Minister, 1984–1990 and 1992–1995; Prime Minister, 1974–1977 and 1992–1995 |
| Chaim Ramon | Health Minister, 1992–1994; Interior Minister, 1996–1996 and 2000–2001; Minister without Portfolio, 1999–2000 and 2005 |
| Dennis Ross | US Middle East Envoy during Clinton and Bush administrations |
| Anwar Sadat | Vice President of Egypt, 1964–1970; President, 1970–1981 |
| Silvan Shalom | Deputy Defense Minister, 1997–1999; Finance Minister, 2001–2003; Foreign Minister, 2003–2006 |
| Yitzhak Shamir | Foreign Minister, 1980–1986; Finance Minister, 1990; Prime Minister, 1983–1984 and 1986–1992 |
| Ariel (Arik) Sharon | Major General; Defense Minister, 1981–1983; Foreign Minister, 1998–1999; Prime Minister, 2001–2006 |
| Gilad Sher | Prime Minister Barak's Chief of Bureau, 1999–2001 |
| Dan Shomron | Major General; Chief of Staff, 1987–1991 |
| Avraham Tamir | Major General; Head of the IDF Planning Branch, 1973–1978; Head of the National Security Unit, 1981–1983; Director General of the Foreign Ministry, 1984–1986 |
| Hassan Tohami | Egyptian Deputy Prime Minister under President Sadat |
| Mordechai Tzippori | Brigadier General; Deputy Minister of Defense, 1977–1981; Minister of Communications, 1981–1984 |
| Ezer Weizman | Major General; Commander of IAF, 1958–1966; Defense Minister, 1977–1980 |
| Moshe ("Bogie") Yaalon | Lt. General; Chief of Staff, 2002–2005; Deputy Prime Minister and Minister of Strategic Affairs, 2009–present |
| Yigal Yadin | Lt. General; Chief of Staff, 1949–1952; Deputy Premier, 1997–1981 |
| Dov Zakheim | US Deputy Under Secretary of Defense for Planning and Resources, 1985–1987 |

# Introduction

A country that sees itself living on the lip of a volcano, or inside the
eerie halls of Yad Vashem,* does not plan for the future and does not
think about bold initiatives. It only holds on for dear life.

—Tom Friedman, former *New York Times* Israel correspondent

Ever since Israel's establishment it has confronted an external environment
characterized by nearly overwhelming and unremitting hostility, punctuated in recent decades by periods of opportunity and hope. Repeated
wars, perpetual hostilities at lower levels, the failed peace processes with
the Palestinians and Syria, even the "cold peace" with Egypt and Jordan,
have all reinforced a sense of siege. Indeed, Israel's national security situation, according to former Premier Yitzhak Rabin, is one of "dormant warfare," which erupts into active conflict every few years.[1] As a result, national
security has been at the forefront of Israeli political life for over six decades.

Israel has responded to these circumstances by building a disproportionate defense capability designed to forestall the threats to its security and by
developing a "hunkering down" national security decision-making style.
Indeed, by the 1980s Israel's national security establishment had not only
earned a reputation for quality but had become one of the world's largest in
absolute terms. Ever since, it has continued to grow substantially, in size,
sophistication, and organizational complexity.

At the cabinet level, however, Israel has not developed a sophisticated
decision-making process (DMP) commensurate with the vital importance of
national security issues for the nation and with the quality and size of the
policy instruments it has developed. The process certainly served Israel well
in the early decades, when its national achievements were remarkable, in both
the domestic and national security areas, but today it is fundamentally flawed

---

* Yad Vashem is Israel's national Holocaust memorial.

and has a highly deleterious influence on Israel's conduct of policy and ability to achieve its objectives.

Indeed, it has become apparent in recent decades, to both practitioners and informed observers alike, that Israel's DMP is increasingly inadequate to the demands placed on it by the nation's extraordinarily difficult external circumstances. Consequently, we see a growing discrepancy between Israel's policy objectives, the resources it has devoted to national security, and the outcomes actually achieved. Although Israel has had numerous operational successes during these decades, some of them dramatic, it has not unequivocally won a major military confrontation since 1967 and has failed to achieve its objectives in most of the major diplomatic efforts it has undertaken as well—in some cases losing control over the process. These failures are particularly troubling because in many cases the initiative was largely in Israel's hands, and its ability to shape the course of events should have been far greater. If Israel has experienced an ongoing crisis of domestic governability, many believe that the costs associated with its national security failures have become untenable.

The literature on government and politics in Israel is extensive, though skewed in nature. Almost all studies have taken a historical approach, with virtually every incident and major event in Israeli history chronicled extensively. A fair amount of attention has also been given to the formal institutions of Israeli governance, to Israel's politics and its defense policy. Very little attention has been devoted, however, to the actual processes of Israeli national security decision making.

Brownstein's (1977) unfortunately brief article is an early exception to this rule. Brecher's works (1973 and 1977) were the first to deal with decision making in Israel in depth but did not provide an overall conceptual framework for understanding the process and are now dated. Ben-Meir's monograph on national security decision making (1986) was a major step forward and set out many of the issues of importance. His later work on civil-military relations (1995) is the seminal treatment of this dimension of Israeli decision making. Dror's works in 1989 and 1992 were breakthroughs in the more general study of Israeli decision making. All of Dror's work, including his most recent (2011), adds invaluable insights to the field. Other works of note include Peri (2006) and Maoz (2006), though both authors unfortunately allow personal biases to taint what are otherwise important contributions. This list, notably brief, covers the relevant works on the issue.

The present work seeks, for the first time, to present an overall characterization and model of national security decision-making processes in Israel. This model is structured around three primary causal factors, or independent variables, which result in five major decision-making pathologies, the dependent variables.

The first of these independent variables, described in detail in Chapter 1, is the uniquely harsh and dangerous external environment that Israel faces.

Characterized by extraordinarily rapid and sweeping change and only limited malleability, this highly compelling external environment greatly shapes and circumscribes Israel's national security choices.

Second is Israel's proportional representation system, which causes deep political fragmentation and a resulting need to govern through coalition governments. This has clear consequences for the roles of the premier, cabinet, and subcabinet forums and for governability generally.

Third, the decision-making capabilities and political and bureaucratic stature of the primary civilian national security organs (i.e., the ministries of foreign affairs and defense and the National Security Council) remain weak. This is particularly the case in comparison with the highly developed capabilities and stature of the Israel Defense Forces (IDF) and intelligence services.

The resulting five pathologies, presented in Chapter 2, form the dependent variables of the conceptual framework. The first of these is an unplanned process. Israel's national security DMP is marked by an overwhelming preoccupation with the present and immediate future, rather than the medium and long terms. Consequently, it is largely reactive in nature, though this study will argue that it has become more proactive in recent decades, and is characterized to an inordinate degree by an absence of sufficient forethought and policy planning. Its consequences include a failure to formulate clear policy objectives, priorities, and options; continual improvisation and crisis management; and sequential decision making.

Second, the DMP at the cabinet level is highly politicized. The need to maintain the coalition means that political considerations often reign supreme, with a focus on politics making, not policymaking. The basis for decisions is commonly "what will fly," that is, the minimum common denominator necessary for a cabinet majority, rather than what is truly needed. In these circumstances, the cabinet and Ministerial Committee on Defense (MCoD) are the foci of strident partisan debate, not serious policy deliberation; options are foreclosed or channeled in certain directions; and procrastination and even paralysis often result. To prevent issues from becoming politicized and thereby restricting their freedom of maneuver, premiers and ministers come to prefer ambiguity and refrain from clearly defining policy objectives and options. Public opinion has a major impact on the process.

Third, Israel's government is characterized by a degree of semiorganized anarchy. The premier has few formal prerogatives; his ability to govern is almost entirely dependent on his political skills and de facto power at any given moment. A powerful leader when in firm control of his party and coalition, the premier is often at their mercy, forced into endless political give and take. The cabinet has become dysfunctional due to its unmanageable size, politicized character, and dependence on policy advocates for information, options, and recommendations—a problem only partially alleviated by the establishment of the Israel National Security Council (INSC). Designed to deal with important national security issues discreetly and expeditiously, the MCoD suffers from most of the same problems as the cabinet plenum, and consequently most decision making is done in small, informal groups, leaving Israel without an effective statutory forum for policy formulation. In many areas, even the most important, there simply is no coherent policy, and the national security establishment has to "guesstimate" government policy. In a dysfunctional and politicized cabinet, leaks are rampant.

Fourth, although Israel is no longer a young state and the DMP has become increasingly institutionalized, it remains unusual for its informal character. Rather than rely on a formal policy-planning process, the DMP is highly idiosyncratic, with leaders' beliefs and preferences bearing an inordinate impact on the decisions made. This tendency is further reinforced by a limited culture of consultation and the inadequacy of institutional checks and balances. The process tends to be fluid, often changes from case to case, and is based to an unusual extent on personal ties and oral communications. Coordination and integration between the different ministries and agencies are insufficient, and there is often a disconnect between policy inputs and outputs (i.e., the information and assessments provided and the decisions made), including the allocation of resources.

Finally, the defense establishment, first and foremost the IDF, and defense considerations have an unusual degree of influence on the process, far beyond that typical of other Western democracies. The IDF has by far the most highly developed policymaking capabilities in Israel, at all stages: situational assessment, policy planning, and implementation. As such, it is the primary bureaucratic player, framing issues and presenting objectives, priorities, options, and recommendations. The IDF does not always prevail, indeed numerous major decisions have been made over its objections or even without its knowledge, but it is the single most powerful bureaucratic player. In fact, it is not the primacy of the IDF and defense establishment that is the problem—their capabilities are a national asset—but the weakness of the civilian national security agencies.

In analyzing the Israeli DMP this book focuses primarily on the prime-ministerial and cabinet levels and on their interaction with the organs of the national security establishment, though some mention is made of the latter's internal processes. Seven in-depth case studies are presented to substantiate the posited causal relationship between the independent variables and consequent pathologies, and numerous other cases are mentioned briefly to illustrate specific points. The seven cases are diverse and include three dealing with Lebanon (the invasion in 1982, unilateral withdrawal in 2000, and war in 2006), the peace processes with Egypt in 1977–1978 and with the Palestinians in 2000, the unilateral withdrawal from Gaza in 2005, and the development of the Lavi fighter aircraft in the 1980s.

These cases were chosen for several reasons. First, they cover many of the most momentous decisions Israel has faced in recent decades. With one exception, the Lavi, all dealt with historic issues of war and peacemaking, critical high-risk decisions involving fundamental political, ideological, and strategic considerations.

Second, although Israel was reacting to strong environmental pressures in all seven cases, those pressures were not so extreme as to compel decision makers to respond in a particular manner, and they consequently enjoyed the freedom to choose from a number of options. The Yom Kippur War, for example, a surprise attack, is not included.

To provide a current picture of Israeli decision making, relevant for policymaking purposes, all of the cases date from the Yom Kippur War, which marked a turning point in the size and sophistication of the national security establishment. Four cases are from the 2000s, only three earlier. Many of the secondary cases cited are far more recent.

The cases occurred under a variety of coalitions, Likud, Labor, and Kadima. In this manner, potential differences stemming from the character of a given coalition or party were at least partly neutralized, and a broader picture of the Israeli DMP emerges.

The case of the Lavi fighter was chosen precisely because it appeared, a priori, to be so different from the others, a case of cold calculation of financial, technological, and strategic factors, not highly charged ideological and political ones. If the pathologies found in the more charged cases also manifested themselves in the Lavi, this would add further credence to the findings. Similarly, issues such as Israel's settlement policy and the future of Jerusalem, which are so ideologically and politically driven as to make them aberrations in terms of overall Israeli decision making, were excluded, to demonstrate that the posited pathologies are not manifested just in extreme cases.

All but one of the case studies involved deeply flawed DMPs. The sole exception, the negotiations with the Palestinians at Camp David, entailed a comparatively "good" process but resulted in a failed outcome. Conversely, the peace talks with Egypt, a case of a successful outcome, had a deeply flawed process. The other five cases had both flawed processes and failed outcomes. The focus on unsuccessful cases risks introducing a methodological bias, and an attempt was thus made, with little success, to identify major cases characterized both by effective DMPs and by successful outcomes. The difficulty encountered in identifying such cases is itself an indication of the problems Israel faces, but should also be a focus of future research. It is important to note that the terms "successful" or "failed" do not reflect a subjective or normative judgment. Both terms, as herein used, refer solely to the degree to which Israel's policy objectives, as formulated by the decision makers themselves, were actually met in practice.

The case studies are intended not to be definitive histories but to illustrate how and to what extent the posited causal relationships were manifested. All of the cases have been chronicled extensively, but there is little doubt that when the archives are eventually opened, some of the details and contentions presented herein will prove to have been in error, while others will be substantiated. As long as the overall picture presented is accurate, this is sufficient for the purposes of the book.

No claim is made that the pathologies studied are unique to Israel. Indeed, it is assumed that observers of other governmental systems will find many, if not all, to be familiar. What is assumed to be unique are three factors: the fundamental nature or at least severity of the three independent variables noted above, the consequent intensity with which at least some of the pathologies are manifested, and given the threats Israel faces, the price it risks for its policy failures. The book's three parts are designed to substantiate this claim.

Part I provides an overview of the basic determinants of Israel's national security decision making, including its uniquely harsh external environment, the nature of its single-constituency PR system, and the formal structure and functions of the national security establishment, with its unusual influence on the national DMP. This section concludes with a broad characterization of how the process actually works in practice, the heart of the book. Part II presents the seven case studies and assesses the intensity with which the posited pathologies manifested in each. Part III presents a comparative summary of the findings in the case studies and past attempts to reform the process, with particular emphasis on the INSC. It argues that Israel can no longer afford its decision-making ills and concludes with a discussion of further reforms needed on both the institutional and electoral levels.

Given the focus on the Israeli DMP as it is today, the sources used come overwhelmingly from the 1990s and 2000s. While substantiated claims can thus not be made regarding the DMP during earlier decades, an overall familiarity with Israel suggests that a rigorous analysis would yield a similar picture. Furthermore, it appears that the processes depicted are typical of decision making in domestic affairs as well; if anything, the pathologies in this area are even more pronounced.

A word regarding some of the terms used throughout the book:

- *Incremental decision making* refers to cases where leaders formulate an overall strategy from the beginning, with a defined end-state, but pursue it in "increments." That is, they seek to achieve their goals through a step-by-step process, assessing their progress at each stage and deciding whether they can continue their pursuit of the predefined end-state.
- *Sequential decision making*, conversely, refers to situations in which the overall strategy and desired end-state have not been fully elucidated in advance. In this case, decision makers identify separate goals for each stage, or "sequence," but not an overall strategy; they assess their progress toward

achieving these goals; and then they decide on objectives and options for the next sequence.

- *National security policy* refers to foreign and defense affairs, as well as to those aspects of socioeconomic policy of relevance to national power.
- Reference is made at different times to Israel's *defense* or *national security* establishment. The former refers to the IDF, Ministry of Defense, and intelligence services. The latter is broader and includes the Foreign Ministry, National Security Council, and military industries as well.

Ideal academic models notwithstanding, in the real world there is no such thing as a "correct" process. No process ensures success, each must be suited to the demands and exigencies of the specific country, and reforms typically breed new pathologies. Indeed, flawed processes can at times result in positive outcomes, while good processes do not ensure success. Nevertheless, both the academic literature and the experience of nations around the word indicate that "better" processes will at least diminish the likelihood of failure. It is the conviction that this is the case, and not a view of decision-making reform as a panacea, that animates this work. The importance of the challenges Israel faces requires no less.

# I. THE SETTING

By wise counsel thou shalt make war and in a multitude of councilors there is victory.

—Proverbs 24:6

# CHAPTER ONE

# Constraints and Players

## The External Environment, Proportional Representation System, and National Security Establishment

The messiah arrived, gathered in Israel's exiles, triumphed over all the peoples around, conquered the Land of Israel . . . and then had to take a seat in a coalition.

> —An intimate of Ben-Gurion on the reasons for his resignation from the premiership

Israel is a nation without a memory. Memory, for most of us, is a luxury of societies that have the time to study their past, because their present is not pressing and their future is assured. Our history is written in the weekend newspaper magazines and goes to sleep with the fishes on Sunday morning.

> —Raviv Drucker and Ofer Shelah, Israeli journalists

Everything in Israel is political.

> —Minister Silvan Shalom

National security decision making in Israel takes place within the context of a uniquely harsh external environment, a proportional representation (PR) electoral system in which the entire country comprises one national constituency, and the structure of the national security establishment. These three factors, the independent variables presented in the Introduction, are set out in detail in the following.

This chapter is divided into three sections to more fully explore each of these variables. The first presents the basic characteristics of Israel's external environment, including extreme danger, the extraordinary rate and breadth of change, and an unusual degree of complexity and uncertainty. The second section discusses the primary characteristics of the PR system, including a fractious Knesset and cabinet, coalition-cabinet governance, and chronic instability. The final section sets out the formal structure of the organs involved in national security affairs. Together, the three parts serve as the basis for the overall characterization of the Israeli DMP developed in Chapter 2.

## Israel's National Security Environment

### EXISTENTIAL DECISION MAKING

From the pre-state days to the present, Israel's national security policy has been predicated on the assumption that the nation faces a realistic threat of both politicide (destruction of a state) and even genocide. Six wars, numerous major confrontations, and ongoing violence, from low-level terrorism to massive rocket attacks, have been basic features of Israel's external environment. A sense of nearly unremitting Arab enmity prevails, of a conflict of unlimited hostility and objectives. With multiple threats at any one time, the external environment is one of perpetual tension, punctuated by brief outbreaks of hostilities and a need for constant vigilance. Each war, and in the past every battle, was viewed as one of survival: Israel had to be prepared to fight and to win every time.[1]

The dangers posed to Israel's national security have few analogues in either magnitude or persistence.[2] Few states have faced, as Israel has, repeated wars and ongoing lower-level hostilities for decades. Although many states have faced threats of politicide, few, if any, have perceived a concrete threat of genocide. A nuclear holocaust could have erupted during the Cold War, but this was never intended and the actors avidly sought to avert it.

In these circumstances, national security issues in Israel are commonly addressed in existential terms. Defense Minister Dayan's infamous warning, during the bleak early days of the Yom Kippur War, regarding the possible "end of the Third Temple" is the most extreme expression of this deep-seated fear, but it has been manifested often, even when the dangers were far more limited, such as in the two Gulf wars. During the 2006 Lebanon War, Mossad Director Dagan went so far as to say that "if we do not win this war, the hourglass of our existence will start running (out)."[3] Iran is widely thought to pose an existential threat, and other players, such as Syria, Hezbollah, and Hamas, are also assumed to seek Israel's destruction, capability permitting. Experience has further demonstrated that national security decisions contain the potential to fundamentally transform the nation's course, even when they do not threaten its destruction, as happened following the Six-Day War and the Oslo Agreement. Decision making in Israel is thus uniquely critical and fateful.

In recent decades the threat of all-out conventional warfare has receded and Israel's overall strategic posture has improved greatly, although Iran and others potentially in pursuit of nuclear weaponry do represent a severe threat. This improvement notwithstanding, a "Masada Complex," or "Holocaust Syndrome," continue to color the perceptions of both leaders and the public alike. Public statements, even by younger, native-born leaders, such as Premier Netanyahu, are replete with references to the Holocaust. Both Holocaust Remembrance Day and the Memorial Day commemorations for fallen soldiers, observed one week apart, are poignant annual reminders of the dangers the nation continues to face. Countless offices are decorated with a famous picture of Israeli F-15s flying over Auschwitz. Each year, on Passover, virtually all of Israel's Jewish population recites the warning that "in every generation they have risen up against us to annihilate us." A centuries-old ritual this may be, but for much of Israel it strongly resonates with modern-day realities.

Israel does not have a formal national security doctrine, but most decision makers share a fairly coherent, if informal, "Operational Code,"[4] a series of basic strategic axioms and perceptional prisms. Central to this is the shared perception of fundamental Arab hostility, Israel's isolation, the Middle East's almost inherent volatility and uncertainty, the need for military activism in self-defense, and Israel's only limited capacity to materially affect its external environment.

Arab and other foreign observers often fail to comprehend Israel's national psyche, how a regional power with advanced conventional military capabilities, thought by many to be a nuclear state, can harbor such deep fears. Nevertheless, Israeli national security policy and decision making cannot be understood without comprehending this primal fear. Six decades after independence, Israel remains very much what the Bible refers to as "a nation dwelling alone," a latter-day heir to the scourges of Jewish history, destined to face new predators.

EXTREME UNCERTAINTY

Israel's national security environment is extraordinarily volatile, extreme in the breadth and frequency of change and in its level of uncertainty. Time and again, Israel has been forced to adapt to unexpected, sweeping changes in its external environment, requiring that it rethink basic concepts and gear up for new missions. It can be said, with only some hyperbole, that crises are the expected situation in Israel.[5]

The IDF responded to the Yom Kippur War fiasco, and huge Arab military buildup that followed, by transforming its capabilities. The postwar focus on revitalized military strength, however, was soon followed by the need for a historic change in outlook, with the 1977 Sadat initiative, and by 1982 the IDF had fully withdrawn from Sinai. In 1981 Israel was forced to confront an unprecedented strategic threat, in the form of Iraq's nuclear program, culminating in its attack on the Osirak reactor. The 1982 invasion of Lebanon led to the rise of Hezbollah and to a new and far more capable kind of guerilla warfare, which has continued intermittently to this day. In 1987 Israel again had to gear up for a new type of warfare, in the form of a violent civil uprising, the First Intifada. The Gulf War in 1991 posed unprecedented challenges, in terms of both the magnitude of the threat and Israel's potential responses, but was soon followed by the Madrid Conference, peace with Jordan, and negotiations with the Palestinians and Syrians. The Oslo Agreement transformed Israeli-Palestinian relations.

The negotiations with Syria in the 1990s forced Israel to confront the ramifications of a withdrawal from the Golan Heights, though its rejection of Israel's historic proposal at the Geneva Summit in 2000 forestalled this. The negotiations with the Palestinians reached a peak at the 2000 Camp David Summit and ensuing "Clinton Parameters," at which time Israel made dramatic concessions, including indicating its willingness to withdraw from most of the West Bank; what followed instead was the Second Intifada and unprecedented terrorism. In April 2000 Israel withdrew from Lebanon unilaterally, a concept that had previously been strategic anathema, and the second Gulf War again posed significant strategic quandaries for Israel. Sharon's belief that Israel did not have a Palestinian partner for peace led to a second unilateral withdrawal, from Gaza, in 2005. Olmert then declared his intention to withdraw unilaterally from most of the West Bank, a dramatic proposal derailed by events in Gaza and Lebanon in 2006. The Iranian nuclear program evolved during this period and came to be seen as the primary threat to Israel's security. In 2007 Israel reportedly destroyed a Syrian nuclear reactor, a newly disclosed part of a far more advanced Syrian nuclear program than had previously been known. In 2011 the Arab Spring overturned a decades-long regional order and led to fears regarding the future of the peace agreements with Egypt and Jordan.

A further manifestation of the problem of uncertainty is the extreme difficulty Israel faces in predicting the causal link between policy options and the actual outcomes achieved. For example, few observers would have predicted that Arafat would reject Barak's far-reaching proposals at Camp David and the Clinton Parameters, that Assad would reject the similarly dramatic proposal at the Geneva summit, or that Israel would face such difficulty in turning its military victories into diplomatic achievements.

## A COMPLEX ENVIRONMENT WORTHY OF A MAJOR POWER

A small nation, a virtual city-state by international standards, Israel faces numerous and complex national security "environments": diplomatic, military, economic, and technological. Although true to varying extents of all states, Israel is affected by changes in a far broader external environment than most and to a far greater degree. Indeed, by the 1990s, Israel's national security environment had come to extend far beyond its "natural" interests in the Middle East.[6] To illustrate:

- The WMD threats posed by Iraq and Iran joined the long-standing conventional threats on Israel's borders, presenting unprecedented challenges. It later turned out that both Libya and Syria were also pursuing nuclear programs.
- Ties with the United States grew even deeper, requiring new areas of expertise and ways of thinking. From a comparatively simple dependency relationship, bilateral ties now included cooperation in advanced weapons development and joint counterterrorism and counterproliferation programs; Israel even sought to become a "strategic partner." The continually deepening US role in the region meant a new set of considerations for Israel, for example, during the Gulf War, as did US global policies, which affected its views of Israel's ties with China and India.
- The European Union's regional role grew, and EU-Israeli relations took on a whole new range of issues, such as a significant upgrading of the relationship, even possible Israeli membership, and establishment of ties with the North Atlantic Treaty Organization (NATO). Relations with individual European states also expanded to include "strategic dialogues."
- The collapse of the USSR led to the establishment of relations with Russia, the arrival of a million immigrants in Israel, a change in Russia's role in the region, and a new need to take her interests into account.
- The Far East and subcontinent became an area of considerable Israeli interest as a result of North Korean and Pakistani proliferation in weapons of mass destruction (WMD); the establishment of relations with China, with whom economic ties expanded rapidly, but whose proliferation policies and problematic relationship with the United States were a source of friction; expanding ties with Japan; and a growing strategic relationship with India.
- For both economic and military reasons, Israel found it necessary to compete at the forefront of military technology and high tech generally. As Israel's economy advanced, its interest grew in international economic trends and organizations, such as the World Trade Organization (WTO) and the Organisation for Economic Co-operation and Development (OECD).

Growing environmental complexity led not just to new areas of geographic and functional interest but to far more complex decisions. The comparatively simple development of the Uzi submachine gun in the 1950s was succeeded by the development of the Lavi in the 1980s and the Arrow anti-missile system in the 1990s and 2000s. Israel's behavior in the 1991 and 2003 Gulf wars involved a complex web of regional and international considerations, with potentially global repercussions. Comparatively simple attempts to thwart Egyptian missile development efforts in the 1950s were succeeded by the intricate and conflicting array of US, Russian, European, Chinese, and global interests involved in the Iranian nuclear program.

### AN UNMALLEABLE ENVIRONMENT

Until the Sadat initiative in 1977, Arab hostility was considered so extreme as to preclude any Israeli ability to materially affect its strategic circumstances, diplomatically or militarily. Ever since, especially following the peace agreement with Jordan and negotiations with the Palestinians and Syria, Israel's strategic environment has come to be perceived as presenting far greater opportunities, major diplomatic initiatives have been undertaken, and the national consensus regarding the nature of the threats Israel faces has fractured.[7]

Conversely, the failure of the negotiations with the Palestinians and Syria, despite major Israeli concessions, and the "cold peace" with Egypt and Jordan have also served to reinforce the fundamental perception of incontrovertible Arab opposition to reconciliation, if not to Israel's very existence. A broad segment of the political spectrum continues to perceive an only limited range of military or diplomatic options, and many question the prospects of an end to the conflict. Few believe that there is anything Israel could do to diminish Iranian enmity, which reflects a theological opposition to Israel's existence, not concrete grievances, and the threats posed by Hezbollah and Hamas present a choice only between bad options. Moreover, Israel has been unable to transform its military victories into diplomatic gains, though they have ensured its existence. In these circumstances, many believe that Israel can take only limited steps to deal with immediate challenges but not fundamentally shape its environment.[8]

## The Proportional Representation System

The single most important domestic determinant of the Israeli DMP is the proportional representation (PR) electoral system and consequent need to govern through coalition cabinets. Under this system, Israel constitutes a single national constituency and parties are allotted seats in the Knesset (120 in all) based on their share of the overall popular vote.

### A FRACTIOUS KNESSET AND CABINET

With an extremely low threshold required for representation (1% of the vote until the 1990s, now 2%), Israel's PR system reflects the broad diversity of views prevalent in the country and ensures that the Knesset is split among a plethora of parties, most of which represent the ideological beliefs and interests of narrow constituencies. The Israeli system is extraordinarily democratic and virtually everyone is represented, but as will be seen, the consequence is a heavy price in terms of governability.

The party split in the Knesset is reflected in the cabinet, as no party has ever been able to form a government on its own without coalition parties. Until Labor's fall in 1977, Israel's coalitions were all centered around a loose alliance between Labor and the then moderate National Religious Party. Since then cabinet coalitions have become increasingly fractious and unstable, often with four or five coalition partners, six in Netanyahu's second term and even seven under Barak. Consequently, the degree of ideological congruence within the cabinet has decreased markedly, with some decidedly unusual coalitions of both the far right and far left, secular and orthodox. The one factor that has held them together has been a common desire to share in the spoils; only by participating in the coalition can a party have a significant impact on policies and budgets important to their constituencies.

## COALITION-CABINET GOVERNANCE

Under Israel's PR system, as in other parliamentary democracies, the executive branch (cabinet), by definition, almost always enjoys an automatic Knesset majority, in effect negating the separation of powers and denying the Knesset any significant power of oversight. When the coalition fails to command a Knesset majority, its tenure is short lived, and a new one must be formed or elections held. With the rare exception of issues of supreme importance and fundamental ideological or partisan discord—for example, the Camp David Accords—the Knesset's actual impact on national security policy is negligible.

The elementary fact of governance in Israel is that the Knesset is a nearly virtual legislative branch and the cabinet is the true locus of power. By law the cabinet plenum must declare war and, by convention, major operations as well. Typically, the cabinet authorizes the premier and defense minister to approve immediate military responses on their own recognizance, leaving a great deal of room for interpretation regarding the differences between "major" and "immediate" operations and "war."[9] The 2006 "war" in Lebanon, for example, was waged without a declaration of war, with the cabinet merely approving an "operation."

Neither the Knesset plenum nor the Foreign and Defense Affairs Committee (FADAC) have war powers of significance. The cabinet is required only to "inform" the FADAC of an impending war, though the committee does have to approve emergency mobilizations within fourteen days.[10] In the 2006 Lebanon war, which lasted over four weeks, the cabinet never declared a state of emergency, despite the large-scale mobilization, and FADAC authorization was never required.

Until 2006 the Knesset's "power of the purse" over the defense budget, in contrast with all other governmental budgets, was limited to authorization of its overall size. Since then, the defense budget has been submitted to the Knesset in two formats: a full classified version, with detailed line items, to a special, closed, joint forum of the FADAC and Finance Committee; and a partial, unclassified version, to the plenum. Until 2007, changes made to the budget were reported to the Knesset only at the end of each quarter, in effect relegating it to a position of post facto approval. Today changes above a certain sum require the joint forum's prior approval.[11]

## A "COLLECTIVE EXECUTIVE"

Ostensibly just "premus inter pares," first among equals, the statutory authority of the Israeli premier is highly circumscribed, and his or her actual power, even more than in other democracies, is a function of the premier's personality, political skills, and coalition exigencies. Neither commander in chief nor chief executive, as in the United States, the premier cannot issue directives, instead sharing responsibility with the other ministers on most matters, including national security. Indeed, the cabinet is considered a "collective chief executive," and the premier is subject to its decisions, albeit with the unique influence stemming from the centrality and prestige of the office.[12]

In recent decades, a number of attempts have been made to strengthen the premier's formal authority. In 1981 an amendment made ministers officially subordinate to the premier, who was given the authority to dismiss them, though for political reasons this has proven almost impossible in practice. A further amendment in 1991 officially made the premier the head of the MCoD.[13] A short-lived experiment with direct elections of the premier in the late 1990s was a further attempt to strengthen that power, as was the establishment of the INSC and its formalization in statute in 2008. A more detailed discussion of these and other past reforms appears in the final chapter, "Conclusions and Recommendations."

## THE "FEUDAL SPOILS SYSTEM"

Under the coalition-cabinet system, ministers are appointed primarily on the basis of their party's and their own political clout, rather than their professional expertise, managerial abilities, or personal inclinations. These other factors are generally taken into account, if at all, only after the ministries have been divvied up between the parties during coalition negotiations.[14] Until the appointment of Amir Peretz in 2006, the position of defense minister was an exception to this rule, remaining largely above politics, whereas the foreign, finance, and even justice ministers have long joined their fellow ministers as victims of the "spoils system."

As political figures in their own right, ministers do not serve at "the premier's pleasure" and are not necessarily beholden to the premier. Indeed, many, including the vitally important foreign and defense ministers, are the premier's primary intra- or interparty rivals,[15] for example, Likud Premiers Olmert and Netanyahu and Labor Defense Ministers Peretz and Barak, respectively. In reality, the cabinet is a conglomerate of semiautonomous ministerial fiefdoms, rather than an integrative decision-making forum, and ministers enjoy considerable autonomy in running them, both from other ministers and even the premier.

### CHRONIC POLITICAL INSTABILITY

One of the results of the PR system is chronic political instability. Between May 1948 and May 2006 Israel had seventeen Knessets and thirty-one cabinet coalitions, for an average of forty-three and twenty-three months, respectively. In the ten-year period 1996–2006, the average minister served just sixteen months, the nine foreign and finance ministers served even less, a mere fourteen months on average; and the six defense ministers during this period lasted an average of twenty-one months. These figures were paralleled by the short tenures of the various ministries' directors-general, the senior bureaucrat (akin to a British permanent secretary) who is supposed to provide professional continuity: the average director-general served twenty-one months in the foreign and finance ministries, twenty-five in defense, and just eighteen in the premier's ministry.[16] In short, ministers and directors-general are replaced at just about the time they have finally learned the ropes of their position, though at times they are reappointed.

## The National Security Establishment

### THE PREMIER'S MINISTRY (PMM)

Akin to the US Executive Office of the President, the PMM is responsible for assisting the premier in the conduct of domestic and national security duties and for interministerial coordination. The Mossad, ISA (Israel Security Agency), and Atomic Energy Commission are directly subordinate to the premier and are part of the PMM, in contrast to the IDF, which is subordinate to the defense minister.[17]

### THE PREMIER'S BUREAU (PMB)

Described as a "Byzantine court" by one observer,[18] the PMB is the premier's personal staff and the mechanism by which information is passed to and from the premier and the different ministries and agencies. In addition to political, media, and domestic affairs advisers, the PMB is composed of the following:

- The chief of bureau is the senior official in the PMB, usually the premier's closest and most trusted adviser, and is responsible for political affairs, scheduling, and the overall direction of the PMB. As such the chief of bureau is responsible for ensuring that issues are ready for presentation to the premier and often provides briefings in advance of meetings on the preparations conducted by the various agencies and prime-ministerial advisers. The chief of bureau is also responsible for maintaining ongoing contacts with counterparts abroad, for example, the White House chief of staff, and under some premiers has been the primary player in the national security field.[19]
- The military secretary is responsible for liaising with the IDF and intelligence communities and for updating the premier on defense affairs, on a real-time basis. Often the official with the most direct contact, typically the first and last to speak to the premier on any given day, the military secretary has instant access to the premier and accompanies the premier at all times, decides what national security materials the premier should see and often with whom he should meet, and participates in all of his defense-related meetings; the military secretary's summaries of those meetings are, in effect, directives, determining what the different ministries and agencies are to do. Though ostensibly just a liaison, the military secretary often serves as a senior adviser. It is a position, as one observer put it, of "zero authority and 100% influence." As a military officer the military secretary is subordinate to the IDF chief of staff (CoS), to whom he is beholden for his future career, and may face delicate situations of conflicting loyalties.[20]
- From the 1980s until recently, the foreign affairs adviser was a position of considerable influence, with a leading role in diplomatic affairs, such as the peace process and relations with the United States, Russia, Egypt, and other important international players. The foreign affairs adviser prepared and participated in the premier's meetings with senior foreign officials, often acted as a personal envoy or troubleshooter, and helped prepare talking points, speeches, and policy papers. With the strengthening of the role of the national security adviser following passage of the INSC Law in 2008, the stature of the foreign affairs adviser has been greatly downgraded, and it is unclear what the nature of this position will be in the future.
- First established in 1999, the INSC is modeled conceptually on the American National Security Council. Throughout its first decade, the INSC was sidelined by the premiers in office and, with few exceptions, had little impact on the work of the PMB or cabinet. A significant upgrade in the INSC's stature began with the recommendations of the Winograd Commission, established

to investigate the failings of the 2006 war in Lebanon, and especially follow-ing passage of the INSC Law. Unlike the other advisers in the PMB, the INSC has a professional staff capable of generating significant policy planning.

According to one view, the PMB actually consists of two warring factions whose relations have not yet been institutionalized: the military secretary, foreign affairs adviser, and chief of bureau, who have clout but not the staff needed for policy planning, and the INSC, which has the staff but was largely precluded from policy planning and is only beginning to achieve a position of influence.[21] We will return to the INSC in Chapters 2 and espe-cially in the final chapter, "Conclusions and Recommendations."

## THE MINISTERIAL COMMITTEE ON DEFENSE (MCOD)

Given the cabinet plenum's unwieldy size, a Ministerial Committee on Defense has usually been constituted to enable expedited and discreet de-liberations. Also known as the "Security Cabinet," it has existed in statute only since 1991,[22] though almost all cabinets since Israel's establishment have formed one. Its members include the premier, vice premier, and the ministers of defense, foreign affairs, and finance, with the premier autho-rized to appoint additional ministers up to a limit of half the size of the full cabinet. In practice, the MCoD, like the cabinet plenum, has become far too large to be a forum for expedited and discreet decision making

## KNESSET FOREIGN AND DEFENSE AFFAIRS COMMITTEE (FADAC)

Like the Knesset plenum, FADAC meetings tend to be raucous partisan debates rather than a locus of serious deliberation, and virtually everything leaks. Committee members are preoccupied with their personal political activities, which are the primary basis of their political advancement, and have little time, and even less incentive, to undertake the politically mixed task of trying to exercise serious parliamentary oversight of the national security establishment. Moreover, the FADAC lacks a staff of its own, mak-ing it almost entirely dependent on the national security establishment for information and assessments.

Given its dysfunctional nature and the fact that its composition inher-ently reflects the coalition majority, FADAC's impact on policy has been minimal. Ministry and agency presentations are typically designed to obfuscate rather than to illuminate, to minimize the committee's ability to delve into sensitive issues and reduce the danger of political manipulation and leaks.[23] Nevertheless, FADAC's oversight role has grown over the years. The premier, defense and foreign ministers, CoS, and heads of the various agencies appear before it regularly, more information is presented than in the past, and some substantive debate does take place, primarily in the closed subcommittees in which secrecy is generally observed. Sporadic attempts have also been made in recent decades to conduct more substantive policy work, including landmark reviews of Israel's defense doctrine and of Israeli intelligence's role prior to the 2003 war in Iraq.

## THE MINISTRY OF DEFENSE

The Ministry of Defense is responsible for arms procurement, the defense industries and arms exports, and, together with the IDF, the defense budget. The defense minister has virtually no staff, just a few aides, and the MoD has traditionally had only limited in-house assessment and planning capabilities, leaving it almost entirely dependent on the IDF for defense policy, force development, and in practice even the defense budget. In 2003, in recognition of the MoD's structural weakness and inability to fulfill a ministerial oversight role, a new Politico-Military Branch was established with responsibility for defense planning, relations with foreign defense establishments, including "strategic dialogues" with the United States and other countries, the peace process, arms sales policy, and various other strategic issues. In practice, the branch remains small, and its impact on the defense and national DMP has been mixed. Whereas it has played a central role in relations with Egypt, for example, it did not have a significant role in formulating Israel's policy during the 2006 Lebanon war. Two additional branches, dealing with defense-related economic and social affairs, were also established at this time, to provide the defense minister with greater policy planning capabilities in these areas.[24]

## THE ISRAEL DEFENSE FORCES

The IDF, not the MoD, is the dominant player in the defense establishment. Directly subordinate to the minister of defense, not to the ministry, which is neither authorized nor structured to exert supervision over it, the IDF has authority over all matters regarding the size and structure of its forces, operations, intelligence, strategic planning, training, doctrine, logistics, procurement plans (as opposed to actual procurement), and personnel.[25] The General Staff, unlike the American Joint Chiefs, is a unified military structure under the direct command of the chief of staff (CoS), who has clear and final authority in all areas.

The General Staff consists of the commanders of the staff branches (Operations, Intelligence, Planning, and more), services (Air Force, Navy, Ground Forces), regional commands (Northern, Central, and Southern), functional commands (Home Front and Training), three joint MoD-IDF branches (Coordinator of Government Activities in the Territories, R&D, Financial Adviser) and the legal adviser to the CoS. The MoD director-general, military secretaries to the premier and defense minister, and MoD comptroller are permanent participants in General Staff meetings. The roles of most of these officials are relatively self-explanatory; a few warrant special attention. Military Intelligence is presented in the next section, on the intelligence community.

The Planning Branch is responsible for military and politico-military planning, including the IDF force structure, defense budget, foreign military relations, and strategic affairs. It has been extensively involved in the peace processes with Egypt, Jordan, the Palestinians, and Syria, both through preparation of background and policy papers and active participation in the talks, and has produced numerous proposals for diplomatic initiatives over the years, whether of its own accord or at the request of the defense minister or premier. Other major areas of activity have included relations with the United States and issues of nuclear proliferation and terrorism. Interestingly, the Planning Branch has a standing order to develop an "exit strategy," that is, the politico-military criteria for ending hostilities, as soon as a significant military confrontation begins.[26]

Established following the 1973 Yom Kippur War and as one of the lessons drawn from Israel's failures at the time, the Planning Branch was the de facto National Security Council in Israel prior to the INSC's establishment and remains the most capable and influential strategic policy planning body. Although the Planning Branch has been involved in issues going far beyond what would normally be considered appropriate for a military body in a democracy, its nature as a military organization has imposed some limits on the issues it can cover and at times undoubtedly colors its approach to them. Facing enormous demands from the General Staff, defense minister, and premier, the branch suffers from severe work overload.[27]

The coordinator of government activities in the territories is responsible for civil administration in the West Bank (and Gaza, until 2005) and liaison with the Palestinian Authority. The coordinator's deep involvement in West Bank affairs affords him an influential advisory role in matters beyond his formal area of responsibility, such as how to deal with Palestinian violence and terrorism.

The legal adviser to the CoS is more than just the military advocate general but also a highly influential adviser on policy and legislation. The legal adviser's office has been extensively involved in the various peace talks, determination of the rules of engagement, especially since the Second Intifada, and approval of target lists during the 2006 Lebanon war and 2009 operation in Gaza. The legal adviser has also been involved in fundamental legislative issues, such as the nature of the relationship between the MoD and IDF, and has even appeared before the Knesset regarding the appropriate role of the cabinet in defense affairs.[28]

### THE INTELLIGENCE COMMUNITY

Military Intelligence (MI) is the primary arm of the intelligence community, responsible for intelligence collection and assessment in the political, military, and socioeconomic spheres, and is the only agency capable of integrative assessments in all three areas. It bears de facto responsibility for the Annual Intelligence Assessment and for early warning regarding possible outbreaks of hostilities and has provided extensive intelligence support for Israeli leaders and negotiators involved in the peace process. Focused primarily on Arab and Moslem actors, MI also provides assessments regarding the international community at large as well as economic issues, such as oil prices. MI's Research Division produces both daily assessments of ongoing developments and periodic in-depth reports. The head of MI presents regular weekly and special assessments to the premier and cabinet in all areas, many primarily diplomatic in nature.[29]

As an IDF officer, the head of MI is clearly subordinate to the CoS and defense minister, through whom and with whose approval he reports to the premier and cabinet. At the same time, established practice holds that the head of MI is also the senior intelligence adviser to the premier and cabinet and in practice has also served at times as a policy adviser. With few exceptions, such as the 1982 invasion of Lebanon, these potentially conflicting lines of authority have not proven problematic, and the head of MI has enjoyed unimpeded access and analytical freedom.[30]

Like the CIA, the Mossad (Institute for Intelligence and Special Operations) is responsible for covert intelligence operations abroad and official cooperation with foreign intelligence services. In addition to intelligence collection, Mossad operations include counterterrorism and the interdiction and thwarting of Arab arms programs, especially nonconventional ones. Under Sharon it was made the lead agency for Israel's efforts to thwart the Iranian nuclear program. As per the recommendations of the Agranat Commission of Inquiry following the Yom Kippur War, the Mossad established intelligence research divisions to end MI's monopoly and promote greater pluralism in intelligence assessment, but MI remains the primary player in this area.[31]

Akin to Britain's MI5, the Israel Security Agency (ISA, also known as Shin Bet or Shabak, its Hebrew acronyms) is responsible for all intelligence operations in Israel itself and in the West Bank, including counterintelligence, counterterrorism, and domestic subversion. It is also responsible for protecting senior officials and Israeli facilities abroad, such as embassies. Ever since the First Intifada in the late 1980s, counterterrorism has been the ISA's primary focus, and the very close collaborative efforts it has established with the IDF are largely responsible for Israel's success in confronting Palestinian terrorism. The ISA's research arm bears primary responsibility for assessments regarding the Palestinians.[32]

The Committee of the Heads of Intelligence Services (Hebrew acronym VARASH) is the senior forum for interservice coordination. Chaired by the director of the Mossad, committee members include the heads of MI and ISA, the premier's military secretary, and on occasion the premier himself.[33] Since 2008, the NSA has also been a statutory member.

## THE MINISTRY OF FOREIGN AFFAIRS (MFA)

The MFA is structured along both geographic and functional lines. The former include, inter alia, the Middle Eastern, North American, European, and East Asian divisions, responsible for relations with countries in these regions. The latter include the economic, media, legal, diaspora, research, planning, and strategic affairs divisions, which deal with issues of a cross-cutting nature or requiring particular expertise, such as nonproliferation.

The Center for Political Research (Hebrew acronym MAMAD) is the MFA's intelligence arm, akin to the US State Department's Intelligence and Research Division, and was established as part of the structural reforms following the Yom Kippur War. Although formally part of the intelligence community, the momentum behind its establishment dissipated within a few years and its bureaucratic fortunes waned. The intelligence agencies ceased sharing sensitive information with MAMAD out of fear of leaks, it no longer participated in the VARASH, and most of its work came to focus on short-term updates on current affairs, largely for internal ministry consumption. In recent years an attempt has been made to upgrade its capabilities and some improvement has taken place, but in the absence of appropriate research personnel, organizational clout, and interest on the part of senior ministry management, MAMAD remains underutilized, with only limited capabilities to conduct high quality and in-depth research.[34]

The Policy Planning Division was spun off from the MAMAD, which was originally responsible both for intelligence research and policy planning. Some foreign ministers and directors-general have made significant use of the Planning Division and appointed it to head interdepartmental MFA teams. Others have been loath to do so, out of concern that it might make recommendations at variance with their preferences. Like MAMAD, and for some of the same reasons, the Planning Division remains of limited importance in the MFA, among the other policy planning bodies and at the cabinet level.[35]

With the rising importance of politico-military affairs, especially WMD proliferation and terrorism, the MFA established the Strategic Affairs Division in the early 2000s, with three component departments: Arms Control, Terrorism, and Strategic Affairs. The new division provided the MFA with a more effective role in these areas, enabling it to prevent their complete takeover by the other agencies, though it suffers from problems of professional expertise and organizational clout.[36]

## ISRAEL ATOMIC ENERGY COMMISSION

Not formally part of the national security establishment, the Atomic Energy Commission advises the government on all matters related to nuclear research and development, policy, and priorities and is charged with implementation of governmental policies in this area. The Commission also represents Israel in international institutions dealing with nuclear issues, such as the International Agency for Atomic Energy, and has been involved in Israel's efforts to deal with the Iranian nuclear program.[37]

Having set out the formal institutions and roles of the Israeli national security establishment, we turn in Chapter 2 to a description of how the system actually works in practice.

# CHAPTER TWO

# The Decision-Making Process

## How the System Actually Works

> The Report's findings raise concerns regarding the quality of the decision-making process in the area of national security.
>
> —State Comptroller, *Report on the National Security Council*, September 2006

> I have never understood what hides behind the linguistic code word "staff work." . . . Should we assume a huge room with an oval table? And if we do it in a corner, with a low table, coffee and cookies, is this not staff work? Staff work is done through tens of daily phone calls and meetings and the premier sees the chief of staff at least twice a week.
>
> —Dov Weisglass, former bureau chief and senior adviser to Premier Ariel Sharon

The previous chapter presented the three independent variables held to be the primary determinants of Israeli decision making. This chapter shows how the process is affected by these variables, with a focus on five resulting pathologies, the dependent variables. A summary of the various pathologies and their subdimensions is presented in tabular form at the end of Chapter 3 (Table 2 on p. 99). The chapter concludes with an analysis of the strengths of the Israeli DMP.

## Pathology 1: An Unplanned Process

### FROM REACTIVE TO PROACTIVE DECISION MAKING?

Many observers of Israeli decision making have traditionally held that its most conspicuous characteristic is its essentially reactive nature. Since the external environment has long been perceived to be highly unmalleable yet extremely dangerous, many decision makers have largely come to accept

ability to foresee and shape it and have consequently adopted a re-
approach. Indeed, the persistent threat of imminent or actual hostilities has resulted in a nearly total preoccupation with the "thundering present,"[1] the here and now, and in the development of a DMP geared toward
ad hoc responses to immediate problems.

Given the constraints imposed by Israel's environment, many of the issues it faces truly present only a narrow range of options, typically all un-
satisfactory, and require immediate decisions in a highly uncertain and
pressured atmosphere. Taking one's time, seeing how things pan out, and
exploring different options as events unfold are not typically part of the Israeli experience. According to one former minister, "long term planning is
impossible. No one else plans and neither do you. In your subconscious
you do not prepare long term plans and if you do, nothing comes of it. . . .
All of the issues requiring long term planning are in a state of crisis."[2]

It has been suggested, only partly in jest, that Israel was taken completely
by surprise by the fiftieth anniversary celebrations in 1998 and by the mil-
lennium in 2000. How, indeed, could it have foreseen that they would occur
in those years of all times? In classic fashion, it was prepared for neither
and launched successful last-minute crash efforts to prepare for the celebrations.

To take a serious example, following the withdrawal from Lebanon in
2000, it was clear to Israeli decision makers that another "round" with Hezbollah was just a question of time, due to the organization's massive rocket
buildup and determination to challenge Israel. Israel, however, ultimately
responded only when a Hezbollah provocation became intolerable, not at
the timing of its choosing or by taking the diplomatic or military initiative.
Regarding the peace process, Israeli leaders have repeatedly stated over the
decades that the ball was in the Arab court and that there was little Israel
could do to change the situation.

This reactive characteristic is greatly exacerbated, both in reality and in
decision makers' subjective perceptions, by chronic political instability and
rapid coalition turnover and by the frenetic pace of change in the region.
Israel's only mixed success with past initiatives, both diplomatic and military, may have further reinforced its reactive tendencies. Although the Six-
Day War, attacks on the Iraqi and Syrian nuclear reactors, and other operations have been great military successes, other initiatives have left Israel's
leaders far less sanguine, inter alia, the Oslo Agreement, the Geneva and
Camp David summits in 2000, and repeated operations in Lebanon.

Nevertheless, in recent decades, as Israel has come to perceive its environment as being of at least somewhat greater malleability, a number of
radical departures have taken place in Israeli policy, demonstrating a proactive ability to take bold initiatives. Indeed, every premier from Yitzhak
Rabin until Benjamin Netanyahu (in his second term) has taken major diplomatic initiatives. They include Rabin's Oslo Agreement; Rabin's, Peres's,

and Netanyahu's (first-term) attempts to reach an agreement with Syria based on withdrawal from the Golan Heights; Barak's withdrawal from Lebanon and dramatic proposals at the Geneva and Camp David summits; Sharon's disengagement from Gaza; and Olmert's Consolidation Plan and far-reaching proposals to the Palestinians in 2008.

The tendency to react to events rather than shape them has traditionally led to both a budgetary and substantive emphasis on the intelligence and operational agencies—in other words tracking and responding to the other side—rather than on policy planning capabilities.[3] The desire to have a greater impact in shaping the environment may at least partially account for the growing number and importance of policy planning entities in recent years, especially the INSC.

## INSUFFICIENT POLICY PLANNING; FLAWED ELUCIDATION OF OBJECTIVES AND OPTIONS

The essence of systematic policy planning is a calculated assessment of policy objectives, priorities, and options under various scenarios, in order to ascertain the course of action likely to provide the greatest overall benefit. In Israel, however, policies are rarely formulated systematically, even on issues of great importance, let alone clearly articulated (publicly and/or internally). Often but imprecisely referred to as "staff work," the deficiency in systematic planning processes is held to be at the very heart of Israel's decision-making ills.[4]

Former national security adviser Giora Eiland bemoans the absence of almost any official position paper in any area of national security policy and maintains that "Most of Israel's politico-military initiatives have been taken without serious staff work. . . . [This] does not mean that thought was not devoted, nor that detailed discussions did not take place. It means that things were not done with the appropriate methodology."[5] In the absence of policy directives, the IDF faces great difficulty in understanding political leaders' policies and turning them into concrete terms. The solution, according to a former senior officer, is remarkable: senior officers simply listen to cabinet debates and then formulate strategic objectives based on their understanding thereof, turning to the premier for confirmation when necessary. A former head of the IDF Planning Branch notes that "we were asked to draw up strategic plans in the course of the peace talks without the political echelon being prepared to tell us explicitly what its policy was on territory. . . . We were forced to estimate, to guess, to make predictions of the leader's intentions."[6]

Hard to accept as it may be, on most issues there simply *is no official policy,* and senior officials, often the entire system, operate in ignorance thereof, relying on guesstimates of what they believe it to be. Typically reflecting the simple absence of a systematically formulated policy, only partially articulated positions, or the conflicting policies often enunciated by the premier and other ministers, this also results from a conscious decision on the part of premiers to keep it that way. Time and again, they have manifested a clear preference for "keeping their cards close to their chest"—so close at times, according to one minister, that even they cannot see them[7]—and to forgo the benefits of systematic policy planning because of the attendant politicization and loss of freedom of maneuver.

Menachem Begin attended the 1978 Camp David summit without the benefit of any substantive policy planning, including formulation of Israel's objectives, priorities, and fallback positions. He suppressed the one major study conducted by the IDF prior to the summit, as well as a prescient personal assessment by the head of MI, which concluded that peace would require a complete withdrawal from Sinai. A participant in the Oslo talks maintains that Rabin and Peres never gave negotiators clear directives regarding what was expected of them. During the first three years of the Second Intifada, the cabinet did not convene a single meeting on Israel's military objectives. Sharon decided on the Gaza Disengagement Plan without consulting the national security bureaucracy and also quashed a major new planning tool initiated by the INSC—an annual net assessment of Israel's strategic posture—apparently out of concern that its findings and recommendations would impose constraints on his freedom to maneuver. The failure to formulate clear objectives was at the heart of Israel's difficulties in the 2006 Lebanon war. The objectives of the 2009 Gaza operation were only formulated a few days after it began and became a source of contention among the primary decision makers.[8]

Three events illustrate the absence of systematic planning, indeed the haphazard nature of preparations generally, better, perhaps, than any other. Foreign Minister Moshe Dayan describes rising early on the morning of a vital meeting with his Egyptian counterpart, Deputy Premier Hassan Tohami—which set the stage for the entire peace process with Egypt—to handwrite the proposal he would present later that day, but because the proposal proved illegible to all but himself, he ended up having to read it to him out loud. Begin, on a day he felt ill, drafted the Autonomy Plan while on a stopover in London en route to a meeting with President Carter, and part of the plan was still handwritten when presented to the president. Numerous holes were found in the plan upon his return, and he was forced, unsuccessfully, to try to backtrack. During the early stages of the peace process with Jordan (the "London Agreement" in 1987), then Foreign Minister Peres asked his deputy, Beilin, to put their positions in writing for the first time while on a flight to meet with King Hussein, which Beilin, too, did by hand.[9]

Another manifestation of the absence of planning and consequently of coherent policy is that the Foreign Ministry rarely circulates policy papers or guidelines to its diplomatic staff; indeed, it issues few instructions on what they are expected to convey. Diplomatic cables typically pre positions expressed by foreign interlocutors in great detail, but savv lomats, cognizant of the absence of official policy and consequent political pitfalls, often make do with highly cryptic descriptions of how they presented Israeli policy, including the wonderfully enigmatic "I responded as required." Foreign embassies and officials in Israel, long aware of the absence of coherent policy, have consequently adopted a "polling" approach, that is, they canvass opinion among a comparatively large cross-section of agencies, officials, and ministers in the hope that the overall impression gained reflects actual policy directions.[10]

If systematic policy planning has been deficient in major strategic decisions, it is hardly surprising that this is also true for more mundane matters, such as preparation of the premier's meetings with various ministers and officials. Under Barak and Sharon issues for discussion in these meetings were frequently ill defined and the premier's interests and considerations were insufficiently elucidated. Moreover, most meetings, even those of high importance, were typically convened with no more than a few days' notice, a week at most, thereby making it hard for officials to prepare adequately.[11]

Preparations for meetings with foreign leaders were hardly better, typically consisting of just one or two meetings of the premier's staff with representatives of the various agencies. Background papers and talking points were prepared by the agencies on the basis of cursory directives from the premier's office, usually just a few lines, which did not provide any indication of the intended substance of the meetings or of the premier's priorities, goals, and areas of flexibility. Typically given notice of such meetings just days in advance, even when they had been scheduled months before, the different agencies had to prepare the various documents at the last minute, usually just updating laundry lists of issues they deemed important. As a result, insufficient time was left to integrate the numerous overlapping documents into a comprehensive position paper, and little use was actually made of all the work conducted. Conscious of the futility of their efforts, the agencies often downscaled them, while the expectations of the premier's staff were presumably scaled back as well.[12]

It is not that Israel's premiers do not feel the need for policy planning. Former CoS Moshe Yaalon, now a deputy premier, describes observing premiers "in distress, looking for options, grabbing at every phone call and iota of information that someone came up with," but, in the absence of an effective planning process, finding none. In 2003, he believes, Sharon faced a situation of this nature: his polls were falling, he faced serious legal problems, the talks with the Palestinians were stalled, and an unwanted international diplomatic initiative was in the offing. Sharon needed a way out and came up with disengagement from Gaza, without any advance planning and over the objections of the INSC and defense establishment.[13]

Premiers have undoubtedly been aware that information and options were usually presented to the cabinet and MCoD without systematic elucidation of objectives and options and solely by the policy advocates, but apparently they believed that the political costs attendant to this outweighed the benefits to be derived.[14] Had this been done, Rabin and Barak might have been forced to recognize that Yasser Arafat did not truly seek peace, at least on terms remotely acceptable to them or their coalitions, and thus that the very basis of their highly controversial policies at Oslo and Camp David was deeply flawed. Similarly, Sharon and Netanyahu might have had to accept the possibility that Syria was ready for a deal but that Israel would have to cede the entire Golan Heights and settle for a "cold peace." Right-wing premiers might have had to acknowledge that the settlement policy was diplomatically and demographically untenable; left-wingers, that viable options for talks with the Palestinians and Syrians did not exist at various points. The absence of systematic elucidation of objectives and options, however, enabled premiers to avoid what otherwise would have been repeated challenges to the future of their coalitions.

Policy proposals of an interministerial nature, typical of national security affairs, are poorly coordinated in advance by the different ministries and are typically presented solely by the specific policy advocate. Opposing policy options generated at the bureaucratic level tend to be ironed out prior to meetings of the cabinet, which as a result often remains unaware of the very existence of alternative policies.[15] One manifestation of the absence of options is the practice by which the defense minister presents the "defense establishment option," a joint MOD-IDF intelligence community position.

Former Finance and Foreign Minister Silvan Shalom maintains that only one option usually is—and should be—presented to the cabinet. After a minister has conducted often lengthy and complex processes of policy planning, it is simply impractical to reopen the entire issue before a large forum, such as the cabinet.[16] While Shalom's argument is well taken in regard to the cabinet, the situation has not been much better in the MCoD.

Until passage of the INSC Law in 2008, cabinet procedures did not require presentation of multiple policy options, and actual practice varied by cabinet and premier, though as a rule it was limited. In the absence of an "honest broker," policy advocates, unsurprisingly, usually presented just one favored option, which the cabinet could either accept or reject. Options for military action were often just variations on the same theme, that is, small, medium, and large versions of the same operation, as was the case in Lebanon in 1982 and 2006 and in the 2009 Gaza operation. In practice the IDF usually presents one clear preference and pushes for it forcefully.[17]

As will be seen in the final chapter, "Conclusions and Recommendations," the establishment of the INSC and passage of the INSC Law, which formalized its role in statute, have yet to have a fundamental impact on the policy process. Nevertheless, premiers appear today to be better prepared for meetings both with Israeli and foreign officials, and the policymaking process in the MCoD has improved somewhat, even if it remains too large to be an effective decision-making forum. The cabinet plenum and the informal ministerial forums premiers typically convene, such as Netanyahu's "Octet," which can have an important effect on the process by influencing the premier's thinking and setting the ground for MCoD meetings, have yet to come under the new, somewhat more systematic, procedures instituted.

Prior to the establishment of the INSC, in 1999, the relative absence of systematic policy planning could have been attributed, at least in part, to the absence of a formal institutional capability, but even then the means could have been found to ameliorate the problem had the desire existed. The premier has always had a number of aides and advisers who did at times engage in systematic planning, and the capabilities of the national security establishment were always at his disposal. The problem was thus more than structural and it remains so.

The case studies presented in Part II will further document the repeated failure in the Israeli government to formulate clear policy objectives, priorities, and options and at times even to engage in the most basic preparations. For now two caveats are in order, however. First, premiers have sometimes engaged in extensive planning: for example, Rabin, Barak, and Olmert established orderly negotiating teams for the talks with the Palestinians and conducted systematic preparations. The cabinet, however, was not privy to these processes, which were conducted by specially constituted forums and not part of an ongoing institutionalized process.

Second, the planning process within the defense establishment (but rarely the MFA) is highly developed, as evinced by the pivotal role played over the years by the IDF Planning Branch in the various peace processes, force development planning, and more. Indeed, painstaking formulation of objectives, priorities, and options is a hallmark of the Planning Branch. The defense establishment as a whole, from the operational organs up to the defense minister, engages in extensive planning. Defense Ministers Benjamin Ben-Eliezer and Shaul Mofaz, for example, convened weekly "Strategy Forums" with senior officials in which major issues were presented for discussion, followed by a "Defense Minister's Situational Assessment" and then an operational meeting in which all operations beyond Israel's borders were presented for approval.[18] The problem is that the highly structured process within the defense establishment usually ends once issues reach the cabinet level.

CRISIS MANAGEMENT AND "ILTUR" (IMPROVISATION)

Crisis management and improvisation, rather than forethought and planning, are the rule and to a large extent unavoidable outgrowths of Israel's national security environment, particularly in the early decades, when Arab hostility was at its height, resources scarce, and institutional capabilities and standardized procedures limited. For many Israeli leaders, decision making was all about immediate responses to military threats and staying alive to fight another day, while stitching together the resources needed through a variety of impromptu measures.

For a politically polarized nation facing fundamental questions regarding its future character and even survival, functioning in an extraordinarily volatile environment, improvisation has two important advantages: it enables action without a clear definition of policy objectives and options and facilitates flexible decision making in times of change and crisis. A necessary evil in the early years, crisis management and improvisation succeeded beyond any reasonable expectation and remain primary characteristics of Israeli decision making, indeed, a national hallmark, a sphere of excellence, and virtual faith. Deputy Premier Yaalon maintains that "we are experts at improvising."[19]

The West Bank security barrier, an immediate response to a vital need, which contributed significantly to the decrease in terrorism, was based on an only partial appreciation of the long-term consequences, both on the ground and for the future of the peace process, and has been caught up ever since in political and legal battles. Consequently, its delineation has been changed repeatedly, parts have been dismantled and rebuilt, and it has yet to be completed.[20] Olmert's dramatic Consolidation Plan in 2006, calling for withdrawal from some 90% of the West Bank, was conceived on the spur of the moment, only to be jettisoned a few months later when events intervened.

In recent decades, Israel's ability to improvise has decreased, as issues have become far more complex and the cost of error has grown, thereby requiring far more long-term and systematic planning. In too many areas, however, "firefighting" remains the norm, with policies attempted and abandoned as events develop, without sufficient forethought, systematic analysis, or a basic strategic framework.[21] Moreover, the development of a large and organizationally complex bureaucracy inherently reduces the latitude for improvisation.

The repeated collapse of the IDF's multiyear force development plans is an acute example of the need for careful, long-range planning, in which improvisation is entirely inappropriate. The possible deployment of Israeli forces "over the horizon" in Iraq, during the two Gulf wars, an operational and logistical operation of unprecedented complexity, required a degree of planning that was incompatible with traditional improvisation, as is development of a response to the Iranian nuclear threat. See also the comparisons in Chapter 1 of the Uzi and Arrow weapons programs.

To be fair, it must be stressed that even in the best of circumstances, Israel's highly compelling and volatile external environment would necessitate comparatively short-term perspectives and considerable improvisation. For the above reasons, however, the demands facing Israel's decision makers have changed, and the need for careful, long-term planning is critical.

## SEQUENTIAL DECISION MAKING

This book focuses on contemporary Israeli decision making, but perhaps the preeminent example of the improvisational and sequential character of the Israeli DMP is the Six-Day War and subsequent policies in the Occupied Territories. In what would be a defining event in the nation's history, Israel went to war in 1967 without an overall strategic plan. The need to deal with the massing of Egyptian forces in Sinai and blockade of Israeli shipping, long established casus belli, led to a prewar decision to eliminate the immediate threat. No decision had been made, however, to conquer all of Sinai, certainly not the West Bank, Gaza, and Golan.[22]

With the phenomenal success of the initial fighting, the conquest of all of Sinai was a case of the IDF "exploiting success." It was not a predetermined decision, but shelling by Jordan, which had concluded a military pact with Egypt that provided the pretext for the conquest of the West Bank, and the ongoing Syrian shelling of Israel's north paved the way for the attack on the Golan. Although each of the stages had a strategic rationale of its own, they were not part of a prewar plan but ad hoc responses to a developing situation. Little thought was given to the long-term ramifications of occupying the West Bank and Gaza, with their large Palestinian populations.[23]

The absence of a coherent strategy was especially pronounced in regard to the settlements. Prior to the war, and in its early aftermath, there was no intention to establish settlements on a massive scale, and Israel's thinking was focused primarily on the domestically consensual areas of East Jerusalem and the Etzion Bloc, open wounds from the War of Independence, and Rafah. Just days after the war, the cabinet formally announced Israel's willingness to withdraw from Sinai and the Golan Heights, in exchange for peace and security arrangements, though not from the West Bank, on which it was divided. Ten years later, when Likud assumed office in 1977 and fundamentally changed Israel's policies, the total number of settlers in the West Bank was still just a few thousand. As the years went by, the cabinet held numerous meetings on the West Bank and Gaza, but they were typically tactical, addressing day-to-day issues and whether to approve specific new settlements, not convened to develop an overall policy. Until 1993, the cabinet rarely, if ever, considered the fundamental issue of the future of the territories and of their impact on Israel. One former minister was particularly scathing, maintaining that for forty years Israel's leaders were incapable of adopting clear objectives regarding the foremost issue facing the nation, the future of the West Bank.[24]

Rabin's leadership of the Oslo process was also sequential in character. Lacking faith in Arafat's commitment to peace, Rabin preceded step by step, testing the waters, without formulating a clear endgame, even if its overall contours were generally understood. Sequentialism characterized both wars in Lebanon: in 1982 the cabinet had initially authorized just a limited operation but then successively expanded it; in 2006 the war plan was explicitly designed to be sequential in nature. The operation in Gaza in January 2009 was similarly sequential. The desired end-state was not predetermined—indeed, the objectives were formulated only after the fighting had begun.[25]

## "TACTICALIZATION OF STRATEGY" AND "DYNAMIC INCREMENTALISM"

In the relative absence of systematic policy planning, issues tend to be considered separately, in an "atomistic" fashion. Major policy is typically the cumulative, sequential, and often unintended outcome of a series of ad hoc responses to immediate needs, rather than a deliberately chosen course of action. Decision making is focused on the tactical and characterized by a form of "dynamic incrementalism," with Israel's basic policies and national security strategy rarely ever discussed.[26]

Begin made the critical decision on the Lavi engine, which ultimately led to the project's collapse, solely on the basis of the IAF's recommendation, without taking into account the overall consequences for the program and national budget. Israeli counterterrorism has been very successful tactically, but in the absence of an overall strategy has often led to unintended and counterproductive outcomes. For example, Israel destroyed the Palestinian Authority's security forces in response to gruesome terrorism but did not take into account the medium-term consequences, including a governmental vacuum that paved the way for the rise of Hamas in Gaza.[27] Fundamental aspects of the Gaza Disengagement Plan remained unresolved immediately prior to its final implementation, including the future of the Gaza-Egypt border and thus the entire security regime, raising questions regarding the basic decision to adopt the policy.

## SYSTEMIC OVERLOAD

Further contributing to the lack of planning is the tremendous pressure and stress under which the entire system operates, stemming from the discrepancy between the vast number of demands placed on it and the resources at its disposal. In these circumstances, the system naturally tends to concentrate on the immediate, at the expense of what may be truly important, especially if long term.

Despite the significant growth in the national security bureaucracies in recent decades, many capabilities remain greatly stretched. The state of nearly perpetual crisis means that both leaders and officials are typically juggling multiple issues at any given time and rarely have time to understand and deal effectively with one crisis before moving on to the next. Whereas critics of American decision making have called Washington a "one-crisis town," Israel typically faces a number concomitantly.

Mostly the problem is too few people facing far too many demands. In some areas, however, expertise is insufficient or lacking almost completely. The significant upgrading of Israel's relations with the EU and NATO in the late 1990s and early 2000s required new areas of expertise that simply did not exist in the Foreign Ministry, Defense Ministry, and IDF. The growing importance of the proliferation issue required that the national security establishment, as a whole, gear up accordingly.

## Pathology 2: A Highly Politicized Process

Israel constitutes a classic example of the "political process" or "bureaucratic politics" models of decision making.[28] The hierarchically arranged but unequal actors in the Israeli system engage in an ongoing process of political give and take, bringing their differing sources of influence to bear in the attempt to promote competing individual, party, and national agendas. In the absence of one clearly predominant actor, coalition politics are the mechanism by which the competing agendas are reconciled, with the final policy typically reflecting a compromise, as opposed to a coherent policy or any single player's preferences. The following section sets out the sources of Israel's highly politicized DMP.

### POLITICAL CONSIDERATIONS REIGN SUPREME

Because of Israel's PR system and the consequent need to achieve consensus both within the governing coalition and its component parties, the DMP is highly politicized.[29] To this one must add the unique circumstances of Israel's establishment, including the Holocaust, repeated wars, and ongoing security threats, and the fact that Israel remains deeply divided over fundamental issues of its national existence, first and foremost the future of the West Bank. Issues of national security are thus commonly argued in highly ideological and partisan terms and even in terms of national survival, despite the many cases where this has not truly been at stake.

Political and ideological considerations permeate the cabinet DMP, often superseding all calculations of strategic interest; indeed, parochial party views, rather than a broad conception of the national interest, are built into the coalition structure. Consequently, political and ideological considerations have an overwhelming influence on many issues of national security.[30] Politics are of course a major and legitimate consideration everywhere; it is the degree of politicization that makes Israel unusual.

Politicization has the practical effect of foreclosing options or channeling them in given directions. Olmert was forced to seek agreement with President Abbas on a postponement of talks on Jerusalem until the end of the negotiating process, out of fear that its political sensitivity would have led to the fall of his coalition.[31] Netanyahu similarly risked losing his coalition if he had agreed to extend a settlement freeze in 2009. Politicization, however, affects not just inherently charged ideological issues, such as the future of the West Bank and settlements, but even some ostensibly technological and financial decisions, such as the final decision to kill the Lavi jet fighter program, which was made on a purely partisan basis.

The defense budget is a further case in point. Once the annual process reaches the cabinet level, any semblance of substantive budgetary planning disappears and the whole issue becomes politicized, played out in the arenas of coalition politics and public opinion. The MoD proposes unrealistic increases, the MoF arbitrary cuts, both basing their positions on what they believe they can get away with, rather than on what is truly needed. The final outcome of this annual rite reflects the relative weight of the competing ministers, political considerations, and the issues on the national agenda at the time, rather than a systematic attempt to maximize budgetary alternatives.

In 2003 the MoD requested a budget of 39 billion shekels, warning that a shekel less would endanger the nation's security, whereas the MoF proposed 30.6 billion shekels, arguing that a shekel more would cause budgetary collapse. Premier Sharon intervened and a compromise of 32.6 billion shekels was approved by the cabinet, over the objections of other ministers who would have to absorb the increase. Two months later, however, the CoS met with Sharon to present the ramifications of this "irresponsible budget" to him; a "shocked" Sharon reconvened the cabinet and an increase of 4 billion shekels was approved.[32] In 2009 the MoF demanded a 3 billion shekel defense cut, whereas the MoD wanted an increase. In the resulting compromise, the MoD agreed to a two-year postponement of 1.5 billion shekels. Five months later, however, it demanded and received a 1.5 billion shekel supplemental budget. In 2010 the MoD demanded a 6.8 billion shekel increase over two years, but Premier Netanyahu intervened in the MoD-MoF battle and the increase was reduced to "just" 4.1 billion.[33]

Israel remains unusual, possibly unique, among democracies in the degree of ideological fervor that continues to pervade its politics,[34] even if the intensity of Zionist ideology has diminished over the decades. Israel's character as the nation-state of the Jewish people, a home, refuge, and at least partial protector for Jews worldwide, is not just a slogan but a fundamental commitment that colors foreign policy.

Yehezkel Dror, an eminent Israeli political scientist, stresses the im Zionist ideology on decision making in terms of "motivated irratio In some historical situations, he believes, careful and rational plann be counterproductive, leading to self-defeating prophesies and paralysis. Conversely, adherence to national dreams, to an "unattainable future," can make them possible. Israel's leaders, especially in the early years, were forced to make leaps of faith, basing their decisions on the force of will, intuition, a sense of national destiny, and a willingness to take the risks necessary to overcome objective assessments of Israel's capabilities. Dror believes that this early adherence to national dreams and resulting absence of rational planning were appropriate at the time and enabled Israel to overcome enormous obstacles. However, the belief in a national destiny and in the power of ideology to overcome the stubborn facts of reality remain pronounced to this day.[35]

A precarious balance between hard-headed realism and ideology is thus a basic feature of Israeli decision making. No one could have predicted that the 2003 war in Iraq would save Israel from an Iraqi WMD threat, which in the future potentially could have been coordinated with Iran's, Libya's, and Syria's WMD programs, or that the collapse of the Soviet Union would result in a nearly 25% increase in Israel's Jewish population and the realization of Ben-Gurion's dream of a population of five million Jews, which he believed would ensure the nation's existence. As one wag once put it, "anyone who does not believe in miracles in Israel is simply not a realist."

Israeli policy toward the Soviet Union and Russian Federation have been deeply affected by considerations of its Jewish population. The absorption of a million Russian immigrants during the 1990s, which imposed a huge burden on an already overtaxed national economy and infrastructure, was never an issue but an ideological commitment. Israel took extraordinary measures to bring Ethiopian Jews to Israel, helped Iranian Jews escape through various means, and worked long for the right of Syrian Jews to leave the country. In no area in recent decades has the ideological impact of Zionism been as pronounced as in matters affecting the future of the settlements and West Bank. Though supported by only a minority of Israelis, this has proved to be a wedge issue and has had an overwhelming influence on Israel's national security policy.

For most ministers, party politics are a primary focus of activity, demanding a disproportionate share of their time.[36] As political figures in their own right rather than professional or even political appointees, ministers must continually jockey to shore up their positions and ensure their political fortunes. Indeed, their future usually has far less to do with how effectively they run their ministries than with how successfully they pander to their party constituency and the media. With an extraordinarily frenetic 24–7 news cycle, volatile party politics, and electoral cycles, ministers have no choice but to devote time to intraparty politics and the next day's headlines, no less than to the affairs of their ministry and of state.

The premier, defense minister, and, in the past, foreign minister are expected to remain at least partially above the political fray and are held somewhat more accountable for the conduct of their ministerial duties. Though their positions inherently offer them greater opportunity for media coverage on weighty national affairs, they too must devote an inordinate amount of time and attention to party politics and the media. "Spin control," courting party activists, building a party base, and maneuvering to build party support for various policies, all consume an enormous share of their time. With what may be some hyperbole, one former senior official estimates that Israel's leaders are forced to spend 80% of their time on political survival, rather than policy, and that there were only three weeks during Sharon's entire tenure in which he was confident that his coalition would last to the end of that week. A different official was only slightly more restrained in his assessment of Olmert's tenure, stating that Olmert was never sure whether each quarter would be his last in office.[37]

Two important caveats have to be noted regarding the politicized nature of the process: with rare exception the DMP within the national security bureaucracy, unlike the cabinet, is strictly professional. Second, as the case studies in Part II will demonstrate, partisan politics appear to be far more limited in decisions on the use of force, for example, in the invasion of Lebanon in 1982 and war in 2006, though political maneuvering is extensive and public opinion has a significant role.

## THE COALITION ABOVE ALL — "BUT WILL IT FLY?"

Maintaining the coalition often becomes an end in itself, a nearly full-time preoccupation that supersedes strategic considerations. Coalition politics lead to a marked propensity for the cabinet to act as a forum for ironing out the differences dividing its party components, or for obfuscating them, rather than as an executive body. "What will fly" rather than what is needed is the true basis for decision making. In order to maintain the coalition, the premier is often forced to give priority to a coalition partner's preferences, over what he believes to be appropriate. Responding to coalition considerations, Netanyahu changed his position at least three times on the US effort to broker a rapprochement with Turkey, following the 2010 Gaza flotilla crisis, ultimately rejecting what the MFA and IDF considered an acceptable compromise.[38]

Furthermore, the need for compromise and consensus greatly limits the "search" for options and leads both to a marked decrease in attention to long-range and fundamental issues and to avoidance of policy planning processes. A strategy of procrastination, sequentialism, partial solutions, and paralysis is often the result, even on issues of grand strategy, and there exists a tendency to wait for issues to deteriorate into "no-choice" crisis situations, which require action and sudden improvisation. According to former Foreign Minister Shlomo Ben-Ami, Israel's "absurdly" proportional electoral system is no longer capable of producing working coalitions, with paralysis the result.[39]

The breakdown in the "national consensus" since 1967 on even the most fundamental issues (e.g., future of the West Bank and settlements) and pro-liferation of parties have further exacerbated the long-standing problem of governability.[40] Netanyahu's initial rejection of a two-state solution in 2009 is a recent example of the ongoing political stalemate over the West Bank, more than forty years after the Six-Day War and at least a decade since most of the Israeli political spectrum adopted this solution as the basis for negotiations.

Israel's coalition system produces strange and dysfunctional bedfellows. Rather than being the premier's appointees, ministers—even the foreign, defense, and finance ministers—are often his leading intra- and interparty rivals, continually vying to hasten his electoral demise and succeed him.[41] Although these rivalries are "part of the game," and ministers are often able to put them aside, it is clear that they do at times have a significant effect on the conduct of policy, even during crisis.

The legendary rivalry between Rabin and Peres, who served as each other's defense minister and in the latter's case as foreign minister, affected both the atmosphere and even the substance of the DMP preceding the Entebbe rescue operation.[42] Peres initially began the Oslo talks without Rabin's knowledge and later held a further round, despite the latter's request that it be postponed. In 1993 Peres made a successful end run around Rabin, convincing Secretary of State Warren Christopher to press him into accepting the participation of Palestinian leader Faisal Husseini in the talks. Rabin, no innocent certainly when it came to Peres, initially sought to keep him out of the peace process and on one occasion even phoned Christopher personally to make sure that Peres's account of the Oslo breakthrough was accurate. Rabin never told Peres about the "deposit" he gave the United States, in which he acknowledged his secret willingness to withdraw from the Golan.[43]

As foreign minister under Yitzhak Shamir, Peres was so concerned that he might derail the peace agreement he was trying to reach with Jordan in 1987 (the "London Agreement") if it was presented as his breakthrough that he asked the United States to present it to him as its own proposal. Shamir, for his part, was livid when Peres refused to give him a written copy of the draft agreement, reading it aloud instead and forcing him to turn to the US ambassador to obtain one. Shamir, like Rabin, believed that Peres repeatedly worked behind his back. "Everything he does," Shamir said, "is in the middle of the night. He wants to know what I am doing so he can sabotage it."[44]

In his first term Netanyahu had two Likud rivals as his foreign ministers, Sharon and David Levy. Barak had a Likud foreign minister, Levy. One observer commented that Barak's attitude toward his cabinet could be divided into three: those ministers he did not respect, those he could not stand, and those who fell into both categories.[45] Premier Sharon and Foreign Minister Silvan Shalom were rivals within Likud, while Defense Minister Yitzhak Mordechai was from Labor. Premier Olmert and Defense Minister Amir Peretz were the competing heads of the Likud and Labor parties. Tzipi Livni, Olmert's foreign minister, was at odds with him throughout much of their joint tenure, ultimately succeeding him as Kadima party leader. Netanyahu, in his second term, Defense Minister Barak, and Foreign Minister Avigdor Lieberman were the competing heads of Likud, Labor, and Israel Beitenu, respectively.[46]

Olmert decided to make Livni responsible for talks with the Palestinians in order to ensure that she would be committed to their success—and would bear responsibility for their possible failure. He had no intention, however, of allowing Livni to take credit for a breakthrough and so established a far more important back channel. Defense Minister Barak was less than forthright in implementing assurances Olmert had given the United States and Palestinians regarding the easing of transit limitations in the West Bank. Livni sought to establish a special team to provide staff support for Olmert, Barak, and herself, the three primary negotiators, but infighting prevented this. During the Gaza operation in January 2009, differences between Olmert, Barak, and Livni emerged by the second week, with the latter two advocating an early end to the fighting. Although some of this reflected legitimate policy differences, which should have been resolved in advance, the trio's abysmal relations clearly had an adverse impact on their ability to reach agreement.[47]

The ongoing inability to forge a consensus on a broad variety of issues means that the premier is hard-pressed to generate the political support necessary to lead the nation in clear directions. Where consensus does exist, usually in cases of decisions that are not ideologically and politically charged, the DMP is far more effective, for example, on the issue of the Iranian nuclear threat. However, this issue also became politicized in late 2011, when disagreements within the cabinet became known publicly.[48]

## PUBLIC OPINION

As befits a democracy, public opinion in Israel is an important player in the decision-making process. As such, it is a further contributing factor to the overall politicized nature of the DMP. Of the seven in-depth case studies in this book, public opinion had a decisive impact on two (the decisions to withdraw from Lebanon and develop the Lavi fighter) and a significant impact on the rest.

Barak commissioned over one hundred public opinion polls during his brief eighteen-month tenure as premier. Arriving at the Shepherdstown peace talks with Syria in 1999, Barak informed the US delegation that he could not go forward due to political problems at home. During the talks, Barak was shown a poll that led him to further harden his positions regarding withdrawal from the Golan Heights and possibly miss the opportunity for a deal. The following March he came to the conclusion that acceptance of Syria's demand for control of the northeastern corner of the Sea of Galilee, which was not part of its territory under the internationally recognized boundary, would be viewed by the public as a national humiliation and thus precluded any possibility of a successful national referendum on withdrawal. For domestic political reasons, especially with elections approaching, Olmert, Barak, and Livni did not wish to be seen as having favored an early end to Israel's operation in Gaza in January 2009, a factor that clearly contributed to its prolongation.[49]

## Pathology 3: Semiorganized Anarchy; or, Is Anyone at the Helm?

Israel's PR system and highly politicized DMP are the source of a growing crisis in governability. The premier is only partially in charge, and the cabinet and subcabinet committees are dysfunctional decision-making forums. Consequently, the government's ability to deal with the issues facing the nation is diminishing, at times bordering on paralysis.[50]

### THE PREMIER IS IN CHARGE, SOMETIMES

The premier's formal sources of authority, as noted in Chapter 1, are highly circumscribed. Neither the "chief executive" nor "commander in chief," the premier is just "first among equals" and requires cabinet approval for virtually all decisions, minor and major alike. With the exception of limited parameters approved by the cabinet, such as immediate responses to terrorist attacks, the premier cannot issue directives to the IDF and defense and foreign ministries, which are subordinate to their respective ministers, and is entirely dependent on the cooperation of these ministers. Independent political players in their own right, indeed, often the premier's leading political rivals, the defense and foreign ministers, as some observers have facetiously noted, do bear "some attachment and loyalty" to him.[51]

As in other countries, a premier's true ability to lead stems not from his statutory prerogatives but primarily from his de facto intra and interparty power, political skills, and an aptitude in wielding the prestige of office to generate support for preferred policies. Premiers such as Begin, who have had firm control of their parties and led relatively cohesive coalitions, have proven to be highly effective leaders, capable of dominating the political system and promoting controversial policies. Others, although always the hub of decision making, have been at the mercy of intraparty and coalition politics, their ability to promote preferred policies limited and their tenures often attenuated.

Many national security issues tend to be of a broad nature that does not fall within the clear purview of any one ministry or agency, thereby requiring the premier's involvement and facilitating his ability to gain control over them. Relations with the United States, the Iranian nuclear program, and the peace process are but a few examples. The premier's direct responsibility for the Mossad, ISA, and Atomic Energy Commission provides him with unique influence over the important issues they address.

One of the premier's primary formal sources of authority is the power to determine which issues will be placed on the cabinet agenda and when. If the premier does not want an issue to come up for discussion or a decision to be adopted, he can postpone discussion or refrain from placing it on the agenda. Conversely, he can give favored issues preferential and expeditious treatment. During the 2009 operation in Gaza, for example, Olmert refused to convene the MCoD in order to prevent a majority for what he considered to be a premature end to the fighting. The premier can also partly channel cabinet discussion in desired directions by giving the floor to preferred speakers.[52]

In some cases, premiers seek to keep issues from the cabinet for as long as they can and then simply try to tough it out and weather the political storm. Netanyahu presented the 1997 Hebron Agreement to the cabinet only at the last minute, after months of negotiations, but asked for approval that very day.[53] Despite repeated demands, Olmert agreed to hold an MCoD meeting on the 2007 Annapolis Conference just days before it was convened. Typically, however, delay is not feasible for long, at least on major issues, and cabinet debate is extensive—over two and a half years in the case of the Gaza disengagement. The cabinet debated the peace process with the Palestinians extensively under Barak, who lost his coalition majority and was forced to declare elections after just eighteen months.

Premiers also seek to "precook" many important decisions in advance of cabinet meetings, in informal consultations with relevant ministers and officials. During the 1991 Gulf War, Shamir opposed a military response to Iraq's missile attacks, favored by the defense minister and others, and thus "prepared" some ministers in advance, asking them to vote against the proposition. In the end, however, he refrained from calling a vote and closed the meeting on the dubious grounds that a majority did not exist for any decision, thereby achieving his objective by default.[54] "Precooking," however, has its limits and is inappropriate to many controversial decisions.

Conversely, premiers present some issues to the cabinet only after the fact, when it is too late to matter or when a contrary decision is no longer feasible in practice. Begin presented the Autonomy Plan and Camp David Accords to the cabinet only after Israel had already agreed to major concessions, thereby precluding any practical possibility that it would reject them. Rabin did the same with the Oslo Agreement, as did Sharon with agreements with the United States on the Gaza withdrawal.[55]

Prior to the Six-Day War (with one brief hiatus) and under Rabin and Barak since then, the premier also served as defense minister, thereby gaining control over the entire defense establishment and great influence. When these roles are separated—and this appears to be the likely trend in the future—the premier's power is greatly diminished.

All premiers are engaged in a never-ending, day-to-day process of political give and take, both with coalition partners and ministers from their own parties, in order to gain cabinet support for decisions. Indeed, on more than one occasion, premiers have had to rely on coalition partners and even opposition parties to pass historic legislation. Begin needed the then opposition Labor Party to obtain Knesset approval for the Camp David Accords. Sharon needed Labor, now a coalition partner, as well as opposition parties, to obtain approval for the Gaza Disengagement Plan. His ultimate success—which came at the price of the splintering of his Likud party—demonstrated both the strengths of a personally determined premier and the weakness of the office. Peres, Netanyahu (in his first term), and Barak saw their political support bleed away and the premature collapse of their governments. As a premier's tenure progresses and elections near, partisan politics heat up even further and his control of an increasingly fractious cabinet wanes.

Moreover, coalition politics even constrain the use of the premier's limited formal prerogatives. A delay or refusal by the premier to place an issue on the cabinet agenda risks a coalition crisis, as would an attempt to restrict ministers' right to address issues. Indeed, premiers often lean over backward to ensure ministerial goodwill by allowing them to speak freely. These prerogatives do nevertheless remain a means of encouraging ministerial reciprocity in the ongoing process of political give and take.

An inherent result of the coalition system, the weakness of the premier's office has been a growing problem in recent decades, as party coherence has further diminished and the overall politicization of the DMP has increased. This not only has led to repeated cabinet crises and attenuated terms of office but has even had an increasingly detrimental impact on the premier's ability to govern on a day-to-day basis, let alone chart a long-term course.

In short, Israeli premiers are in charge only part of the time. They can be strong leaders, capable of promoting dramatic policy departures, when they enjoy clear control of both their parties and coalitions. When this is not so, however, they are weak and limited in their ability to promote favored policies, as has typically been the case in recent decades.

## A DYSFUNCTIONAL CABINET

The cabinet and MCoD are the statutory forums for national security decision making, and all important decisions must be presented to them for approval. As a parliamentary system, the cabinet and its subforums are not just pro forma bodies, as in the United States, but the heart of the DMP. Ministers, however, are not truly the "lords of their (ministerial) manors." Although they are responsible for the ongoing operation of their ministries and enjoy influence stemming from their formal roles, they are subject to cabinet approval for important decisions. The defense minister, like the premier, cannot order the IDF into action on his sole recognizance, and the foreign minister, too, requires cabinet approval for major diplomatic initiatives.[56]

Partly a matter of leadership style, partly political belief, some premiers, Begin prominent among them, have attached considerable importance to cabinet discussion as a means of drawing ministers into the policy process and harnessing their support for preferred options.[57] Others have had little patience for the endless cabinet discussions and machinations. Because of the cabinet's dysfunctions, most premiers and ministers have come to view it as something "to get through alive," in order to obtain approval for their policy proposals, rather than as a forum for substantive policymaking. As a result, the last thing they usually want is true, open cabinet deliberation, with all objectives and options raised for consideration.[58]

The MCoD is usually the primary statutory forum for national security decision making, though there have been lengthy periods in which it was not convened regularly, or at all, and some major issues, for example, the 1982 invasion of Lebanon, have been debated solely in the cabinet plenum. When the MCoD has functioned on a regular basis, it has produced mixed results. In some cases, serious deliberations have been held, with in-depth consideration of objectives and options. In others, MCoD meetings have been more of a ritual, and in any event the MCoD has increasingly come to suffer from the same pathologies as the cabinet plenum, including problems of size, politicization, and secrecy. Furthermore, the MCoD has dealt mainly with military issues, not foreign policy. Given the IDF's predominance in the DMP, it is hardly surprising that MCoD discussion tends to focus on operational issues, rather than on diplomacy and overall strategy.[59]

Of the three major decisions Rabin made in his first year as premier in 1992–1993 (the expulsion of Hamas activists to Lebanon, closure of the West Bank and Gaza, and Operation Accountability in Lebanon), neither the cabinet nor the MCoD had significant influence. Rabin similarly astonished the assembled ministers with his announcement of the Oslo breakthrough, demanding and receiving approval that very day. Under Barak the MCoD did not play a substantive policy formulating role, though both he and Rabin sometimes presented military operations to it for serious consideration. Sharon viewed the cabinet and MCoD as forums for briefing ministers, rather than policymaking, maneuvering when possible to gain approval to act on his own recognizance.[60]

The cabinet and MCoD are thus not typically the loci of effective decision making. Indeed, their limitations have led to a growing propensity on the part of premiers to formulate policy on their own, or in small ad hoc forums, with only a few trusted confidantes and senior officials, and to then present decisions to the cabinet or MCoD on a take-it-or-leave-it, approve-or-reject basis. Rabin, Peres, and Shamir tended to work things out privately among themselves during the National Unity Government. Olmert convened a special "forum of former premiers" (with Peres and Netanyahu) and then a "Forum of Eight" during the 2006 Lebanon war. Netanyahu, in his second term, convened a "Forum of Six," ultimately eight.[61]

These informal forums are the true locus of decision making in Israel, and although they may have an advantage in terms of efficiency, only the cabinet and MCoD have statutory standing. With a premier of limited power and a dysfunctional cabinet, Israel simply does not have an effective statutory forum for decision making. The following explains why.

*Size, secrecy, and grandstanding.* The cabinet's size has become unmanageable, ranging from the lower to the entirely untenable upper twenties and even thirty in Netanyahu's second term, rendering it unable to hold effective deliberations. Size aside, cabinet meetings entail significant political grandstanding, rather than true policy deliberation, as many ministerial statements are made with an eye to media coverage and indeed are often designed to be leaked.

The ostensible solution to the problem of cabinet size and secrecy, the subcabinet MCoD, has been undermined by coalition parties' and individual ministers' insistence on inclusion in this politically prestigious forum, thereby negating its very raison d'être. The MCoD reached eighteen members under Barak, for example, and twenty-two under Netanyahu. Different premiers have thus devised various means of overcoming this problem by convening ad hoc forums for expedited and discreet decision making or at least consultations.

*Feudal fiefdoms.* The cabinet has become a conglomerate of semiautonomous ministerial fiefdoms, with the founding principle of "collective responsibility" no more than a vague memory. Given the minimal "political glue" holding coalitions together, ministries "belong" to the minister they are headed by. Rather than serving as members of an integrative body, ministers tend to be united by a common fear that if they delve too deeply into the affairs of their colleagues, the latter will "return the favor" and possibly stymie their attempts to promote preferred policies within their own ministerial purviews. A "live and let live" spirit of accommodation thus prevails, with each minister free to run his or her ministry with a high degree of autonomy, both from other ministers and even the premier, a particularly serious problem when interministerial coordination and integration are required. At times, different ministers work at cross-purposes. Under Barak, the minister of housing continued extensive settlement building at the same time that the premier was negotiating their dismantlement.[62] Foreign Minister Lieberman repeatedly made controversial statements that were at odds with Netanyahu's policy.

*"Pols," not decision makers.* Cabinet ministers are appointed primarily on the basis of their parties' and their own political clout and are typically not experts in their spheres of responsibility, nor in management, thereby raising questions of their basic competence to deal with the issues at hand.[63] Though generally highly experienced politically, some professionally as well, the cabinet is dysfunctional if for no other reason than the fact that the input of the ministers of agriculture and health, for example, is not needed on national security issues.

*Faulty information processing.* The cabinet does not have an independent capability to assess the information, objectives, and options presented by policy advocates.[64] The INSC, designed in part to address this problem, has alleviated it in the MCoD but not in the cabinet plenum and informal forums.

In these circumstances, intuition, hunches, and preconceptions often replace serious consideration, and ministers rely far too frequently on their general knowledge, personal, professional, and political connections, and the information they are able to glean from the media. One former minister speaks of the oft-repeated phrase "I am told" as a preface to ministerial questions, meaning that the source was a child, a relative, a friend in the IDF, a defense official, or a journalist. Another former minister describes a cabinet meeting regarding a possible IDF operation in Lebanon: having been briefed in advance by a senior official, he had the information necessary to ask probing questions, although other ministers, unaware of the background to his questions, viewed him as a "nudnik" (pest).[65]

Sharon was fond of telling a story about his days as minister of housing when he told an assistant, distraught at having brought the wrong maps to a cabinet meeting, to hang them anyway since the ministers did not understand topographical maps—and the proposal under consideration was, indeed, approved nevertheless.[66] As defense minister during the 1982 invasion of Lebanon, Sharon made good use of the ministers' lack of understanding of the maps presented, ultimately gaining approval for the expanded operation the cabinet had rejected.

Policy advocates do not usually present background and policy papers to the cabinet and MCoD, but when they do, it is often either during the meeting or immediately beforehand, thereby (not unintentionally) precluding formulation of substantiated counterproposals. Even more disturbing, ministers often do not read even those documents that are circulated in advance, thus necessitating recourse to lengthy, though far less precise, oral presentations and leaving the cabinet with insufficient time to consider the policy ramifications.[67]

*"Gabfest city."* Ministers are often unprepared for cabinet meetings, whether because no substantive support material was circulated in advance, because not all ministers (including members of the MCoD) are privy to all classified reports, or because they have not read materials that are circulated. Consequently, a significant portion of cabinet and MCoD meetings is devoted to situational briefings, not inconveniently leaving insufficient time for substantive policy deliberation, in contrast with political positioning, as virtually all ministers typically feel the need to expound on their views at length, largely for political reasons, and as these views are likely to be, or are intentionally, leaked. Even when fundamental issues are on the agenda, such as the annual intelligence assessment, little time is devoted to consideration of the policy implications.[68] This is not for lack of time—cabinet meetings are lengthy, often unbearably so—but because time is taken up by the oral briefings and lengthy ministerial statements.

To the ministers' credit, it must be noted that the reports reaching them are not always tailored to the cabinet's agenda and consequent need for certain kinds of information at specific times. The intelligence community, IDF, and defense and foreign ministries are often not fully apprised of Israel's own capabilities or policies and thus generate reports that can be of limited utility for policymaking purposes. Furthermore, a plethora of often overlapping assessments and position papers is generated, typically geared to immediate developments, without being integrated into systematic policy options. Many ministers thus have no recourse but to rely on the oral cabinet presentations and on informal talks with "informed" sources, within the government and without.

The cabinet devotes an inordinate amount of time to issues of dubious or secondary importance,[69] micromanaging details best handled by the professional bureaucracy and further reducing the time available for policymaking. Important issues are typically controversial, and premiers often prefer, if they can, to raise them in other forums, leaving the cabinet and MCoD to hold raucous but often ineffectual debates.

*Decision making by surprise attack.* Cabinet procedures require that agenda items for the weekly Sunday morning meeting be submitted by the preceding Wednesday at noon, that is, just one and a half work days ahead (the Israeli work week is Sunday through Thursday). As a result, ministers have virtually no time to study the proposals, let alone integrate policy with other ministries. In Israel's frenetic environment, frequent last-minute developments also require cabinet attention and ministers do not even have the minimal one and a half days to prepare. Moreover, some of the last-minute proposals, "surprise attacks" in the words of one observer, are not really unavoidable, urgent issues, but ones that could have been dealt with in advance, had they been addressed appropriately by the various bureaucracies.[70] This has been partly alleviated in recent years by a new decision-making protocol for meetings of the MCoD.

*Groupthink.* Group pressures toward solidarity and conformity are generally not a problem in the cabinet in Israel. Both bureaucratic pressures from the various ministries represented and, no less important, partisan political considerations typically far outweigh any such group pressures—if anything the problem is the opposite. There have, however, been exceptions. In 1982, during the crucial cabinet debate on the invasion of Lebanon, Deputy Premier Simcha Ehrlich became so unnerved that he inadvertently abstained in the mistaken belief that he was voting against the invasion, and many ministers were hesitant to voice reservations out of concern that they would undermine group solidarity. Regarding the 2006 war in Lebanon, Minister Ofir Pinnes-Paz stated, "I refrained from being the 'bad boy' in the MCoD because it was important to me to maintain internal and especially external cohesion during a time of war and so I made an effort not to stress disagreements."[71]

## LIFE IN A LEAKING POLITICAL FISHBOWL

It is commonplace today that everything in Israel leaks almost immediately. A standing joke among officials is that the only difference between information marked "top secret, for your eyes only" and media coverage is two days.[72]

In Israel's high-paced, cutthroat political environment, media coverage and the leaks central to it are the "political oxygen" that breathes life into ministers' political futures and ability to promote preferred policies. Media coverage is also commonly used as a means of "testing the waters," in terms of both substantive feedback on different policy options and, no less important, the domestic and international reaction to them. Furthermore, matters are often leaked prior to cabinet meetings in the attempt to affect the outcome. The result is that the cabinet and MCoD have become virtually open forums, precluding virtually any capability to conduct serious and discreet decision making.[73]

Everyone leaks, including the premier and his staff, who are am greatest leakers of all, and thus no one truly has an interest in cl down. Until Olmert came up with the novel idea of banning the us phones during cabinet meetings, ministers would commonly update reporters on what was being said as it happened, and radio and TV audiences could follow cabinet deliberations in real time. Needless to say, the ministers' accounts were not always totally accurate and were designed to affect the course of cabinet debate and how the public perceived both them and rival ministers. When this ban proved insufficient, Olmert then sought to bar ministers from stepping out of cabinet meetings to call reporters or to update their spokespeople so that they could do so. This, of course, had no effect on the long-established practice whereby ministers meet the throng of reporters waiting outside the cabinet building to interview them immediately after meetings.[74]

Leaks have become a seemingly unstoppable scourge of the Israeli DMP and have a significant impact on it. The problem is not just the sensitivity of leaks from a security or diplomatic perspective, but the loss of control over the issue once it gets out and becomes embroiled in Israel's fierce partisan politics. Consequently, premiers and ministers are reluctant to present sensitive information or their true positions to the cabinet and MCoD, to each other, and even to senior officials, and seek to avoid systematic elucidation of objectives and options. If at all, they are usually willing to do so only to a few trusted confidantes, in one-on-one meetings, very small groups, or the relatively closed confines of the defense establishment. The fear of leaks is so deep that they also commonly refrain from disseminating the substance of their talks with foreign leaders within the national security establishment, especially their own positions,[75] thereby denying officials engaged either in assessing the other side's policies or in formulating Israeli positions a full appreciation of the processes under way. The IDF and intelligence services, either at their own volition or the direction of the premier or defense minister, often refrain from presenting the true range of information and options to the cabinet and MCoD, saving this for the smaller and more discreet forums.[76]

Rabin feared that the "leaking disease" would even have an impact on issues of strategic importance and thus chose to conduct policy planning solely within the defense establishment, to minimize the danger. Premiers, however, rarely trust even the defense ministry fully, and Rabin himself kept the Oslo talks from it until a relatively advanced stage. Similarly, he refrained from telling the cabinet, including Foreign Minister Peres, about his conditional willingness to withdraw from the Golan (the "deposit"), out of fear that a leak of this concession, prior to conclusion of the final agreement, which would set out what Israel would receive in return, would lead to a political uproar and a collapse of the talks. Under Barak, an Israeli leak of the draft peace accord with Syria resulted in a suspension of negotiations.[77]

Sharon's bureau chief, Dov Weisglass, explained premiers' reluctance to fully open up even before senior defense officials, as follows: following meetings with the premier, each participant convenes his own senior staff and presents the premier's thinking to them. Each of these officials then updates his staff and the number of those "in the know" grows exponentially. As a result, premiers avoid putting themselves in this kind of situation without first considering the ramifications of a possible leak.[78] Weisglass notes: "Every premier's working assumption today is that not a single word said in his office [remains secret], except for maybe the most sensitive intelligence channels and special operations. . . . People who participate in military meetings [leak] the minute they leave. . . . An unfortunate phrase, a harmless joke, can result in a vote of no confidence . . . [or] an international uproar."[79] Weisglass himself was so afraid of leaks that he had the first draft of the Disengagement Plan typed by a secretary in his former law firm, over the weekend, rather than in the premier's office.

Barak was known to harbor a deep fear of leaks and to believe that the moment he said something he no longer had control over it. On important matters he therefore sought to minimize written documentation and avoided meetings, both large and small, preferring instead to consult with people on a one-to-one basis. By doing so, he could know who had leaked what and partly protect himself. Prior to the Camp David Summit, Barak was so afraid of leaks that he had a think tank, rather than a governmental agency, prepare a paper on Jerusalem, thereby preserving plausible deniability regarding his involvement. Olmert convened a closed meeting of ministers and defense officials on the anticipated ramifications of the Palestinian elections in January 2006, but instructed participants *not* to make recommendations out of fear that leaks would create the impression that Israel was considering intervening in internal Palestinian affairs. Sharon restricted intelligence briefings in MCoD meetings, whereas Mossad Director Efraim Halevy largely refrained from speaking in them and the head of the ISA simply chose not to attend some. A particular fear prevails of leaks from the sievelike MFA.[80]

In 2011, even the heretofore sacrosanct Iranian nuclear program became the subject of extensive leaks, as former Mossad Director Meir Dagan's opposition to an Israeli strike and the split within the cabinet on the issue became known.[81] Although "hard" information on Israel's capabilities and intentions did not leak, the very existence of such a deep debate within the Israeli leadership was undoubtedly of great interest to Iran.

## Pathology 4: An Uninstitutionalized Process

Whereas the true flow of power and decision making varies by leader and issue in all governments, time, experience, and tradition tend to produce accepted norms, practices, and standard operating procedures (SOPs). Though true, of course, to an extent in Israel as well, a primary characteristic of Israel's DMP is its comparatively uninstitutionalized nature.[82]

## IDIOSYNCRATIC DECISION MAKING

The personal policy preferences of the senior leaders, especially the premier and defense minister, often have an inordinate impact on the DMP. The problem is not the nature of the decisions made, nor the fact that they are often adopted over the opposition of a broad spectrum of the political leadership and national security establishment. It is that too many major decisions have been made largely on the basis of individual preference, without recourse to a systematic assessment of their ramifications.[83]

Sharon adopted highly ambitious objectives bordering on whim during the 1982 invasion of Lebanon, without submitting them to rigorous review, as did Barak in deciding on Israel's withdrawal eighteen years later. Begin, Rabin, Barak, Sharon, and Olmert adopted radically new positions on the peace process almost solely on their own recognizance. The Lavi case study will demonstrate the disproportionate nature of individual preference even on such technological and financial decisions as major weapons development plans.

Readers familiar with the US experience will not find this idiosyncratic dimension surprising. Indeed, the establishment of the US National Security Council, known at the time as "Forrestal's Revenge," was at least partially motivated by then secretary of the navy James Forrestal's desire to reign in what he considered to be a runaway presidency (that of Franklin D. Roosevelt).[84] The argument could be made that President Bush's decision to invade Iraq in 2003 was based on personal conviction and that no policy planning process could have dissuaded him from doing so. This may, indeed, be the case, but the fact remains that an extensive process did take place, flawed as some believe it to have been. The objective is thus not to prevent elected leaders from making decisions over the opposition of the professional bureaucracy but to minimize the impact of personal whim and reduce the frequency of errors by institutionalizing systematic processes.

The following factors at least partially explain the particularly pronounced idiosyncratic nature of Israeli decision making.

*Expertise and confidence.* The Israeli political system is such that by the time leaders reach the top positions they are generally highly experienced politically and have had extensive executive experience as well, including senior positions in the defense establishment and junior cabinet positions. As a result, they typically have long-standing familiarity with the primary national security issues and strongly held views.

Premiers Rabin and Barak were former chiefs of staff, Sharon a general, Peres had been defense minister, and Shamir a senior Mossad official. Defense ministers in recent decades, with the brief exception of Peretz, were also either former generals or long-time defense hands. Knowing what and whom to ask, they were confident of their capabilities and served as their "own staff," believing that their vast experience was such that their need for expertise and consultation was limited. Rabin, it is said, had no assistants or advisers, just subordinates, and tended to rely on his own experience. Asked about his leadership style, Rabin remarked, "Advisers? Okay, but they are not a channel you work with. I work by means of a military system. There are channels of command." At times this type of approach has bordered on hubris, as exemplified by Barak's public statement that "I do not need experts and I do not need advisers to know what Israel's defense needs are. I know that myself."[85] Furthermore, many premiers have come to office with a clear agenda and a belief that the question was not what to do, just how to best go about doing it.

Begin, similarly, is said to have simply trusted his own intellectual capabilities and experience and to have known what he wanted.[86] His defense minister, Ezer Weizman, provides the following glimpse into his leadership style:

> Leaders of his type need no advisers; they make do with aides. He is incapable of taking into account views or proposals that do not fit into his own basic philosophy. The people in Begin's immediate vicinity do not submit different proposals. . . . This is partly the result of past experience, which has taught them that such alternatives have no chance of being adopted, but mostly it is because Begin has chosen aides of a very specific human and political stamp. They think as he does. . . . Every now and then there was some microscopic signal that he was requesting advice. However, this was usually done with the aim of hooking the adviser into agreeing with a proposal that Begin had already put forward.[87]

In recent decades, as the issues facing Israel have become increasingly complex, going beyond the comparatively familiar ones of the Arab-Israeli conflict, decision makers' need for expert advice has grown greatly. North Korean, Pakistani, and even Iranian nuclear proliferation are cases in point, as are Israel's expanding relations with the European Union, China, and India. On the core issues of the conflict, however, the belief by leaders such as Rabin and Barak that their knowledge and experience far exceeded that of the ministers and officials reporting to them was not without considerable justification.

A US president with global concerns, by contrast, cannot possibly have a comprehensive grasp even of the primary national security issues he faces, experienced as he may be, and must rely to a far greater degree on advisers.[88] Cultural differences further accentuate the objective differences in the comparative need for policy planning and consultation. Israeli history celebrates the spirit of "can do" leaders (*bitsuistim*) who press forward without regard for constraints and expert opinion. Indeed, Israel itself is perceived as the victory of the determined few over insurmountable odds, as immortalized in a famous statement by Theodore Herzl, the founder of modern Zionism, which has become something of a national motto: "If you will it, it is not dream." Israel's spectacular successes in its early years further reinforced the sense that determined leaders could achieve almost anything.[89] Many decision makers have also internalized the defense establishment's highly mission-oriented ethos during long careers in it or, at a minimum, during compulsory military service.

"Experts," who tend to see shades of gray and to focus on complexities and constraints rather than simply getting on with it, have long been held in some contempt and accused of engaging in *palsaff*, that is, philosophizing, and the "culture of consultation" remains less developed than might otherwise have been the case. The Winograd Commission was highly critical of what it called the senior IDF command's anti-intellectual approach, which had spilled over into the senior leadership. Shimon Peres, ordinarily a sponge for information and new ideas, has said that he believes that "there are no experts on the future, only the past. Where were the Kremlinologists who predicted the fall of Communism?"[90]

This basic skepticism toward experts was best expressed by Ben-Gurion: "An expert must know the facts and figures. . . . He does not have to know people and is unlikely to have had much experience in political organization or leadership. A premier, on the other hand, has got there precisely through such experience. . . . If, allied to his judgment of people, he can also make wise assessments of situations, he can go ahead and set priorities with confidence, no matter what the experts say."[91]

In these circumstances, it may not be a coincidence that it was Netanyahu who finally established the INSC, decades after the concept was first broached. Arguably the least experienced of Israel's premiers when he first assumed office, but having grown up in the United States, Netanyahu was clearly more attuned to systematic policy planning processes. Olmert, the other "civilian" premier in recent years, also appears to have felt a greater need for expert advice, as evinced, inter alia, by his heavy reliance on the IDF during the 2006 war. Begin, conversely, felt no such compunctions.

*Limited institutional "checks and balances."* The Knesset plays virtually no oversight role, the MoD and MFA's policy planning capabilities remain circumscribed, the INSC's influence is limited, and the IDF Planning Branch is a clearly subordinate military unit. They thus lack the bureaucratic stature needed to serve as a curb against excessive haste or whim on the part of decision makers, and it is arguable whether this is an appropriate role for them to play in a democracy to begin with. The only institutionalized "checks and balances" are thus the political process itself and the judicial system. Both are often highly effective means of curbing excess but commonly come to bear only after the essential parts of a new policy have already been formulated and even implemented.

### ORAL AND PERSONAL COMMUNICATIONS

The DMP at the cabinet and senior official levels is based to an unusual degree on personal familiarity and oral communications. The senior leadership is small;* ministers and officials have usually known each other for years and share patterns of thought; and a highly effective informal flow of communications (or "old boys' network") exists. Phone calls between senior decision makers or one-time meetings with minimal preparation are often all that is needed to formulate positions. Even in meetings of the cabinet, cabinet subcommittees, and consultations held by the premier, presentations are typically made orally, with limited supporting documentation. Rabin and Peres met by themselves regularly, without benefit of a protocol, to discuss issues and make the most important decisions. The real decision to launch the war in 2006 was made in a phone call between the premier and CoS.[92]

The oral nature of senior communications has a number of detrimental effects, including submission of numerous issues to the cabinet that could have been dealt with at lower levels, had they been fully elucidated beforehand, and a lack of precision in the data presented. Oral presentations further contribute to the already intolerable length of cabinet meetings, in which perseverance and stamina are at least as important a source of policy influence as substance,† and thereby exacerbate the ongoing problem of insufficient time for policy deliberations, after most of the time allotted has been devoted to situational assessments that ministers could have read in advance. Most important, in the absence of in-depth supporting documentation, oral presentations typically do not reflect fully fleshed-out policy planning. Conversely, the oral character of communications does facilitate the speed and ease of decision making, especially in times of crisis.

### DISCONNECT BETWEEN POLICY INPUTS, PLANNING, AND IMPLEMENTATION

Israel's information-gathering capabilities (intelligence, Foreign Ministry, and other agencies) are widely considered to be highly developed, but there is often a fundamental disconnect between the information gener-

---

* According to one estimate, approximately one hundred people make 70%–80% of the decisions in Israel at any given time and only three to ten the most critical ones, though this number is held to be typical of other countries as well. Dror 2011, p. 7.

† The regular weekly cabinet meeting typically lasts some five hours, while meetings on important issues, or during crises, can last double that and even go through the night.

ated and the policies adopted by the cabinet. Cabinet meetings, for reasons mentioned earlier, are devoted in large measure to analyses of the situation—in other words to what is and was. The next and crucial stage in the DMP, that is, policy planning based on the picture presented, often does not occur, or occurs in a highly attenuated form, at times almost in total disregard of the information presented. Thus, options tend to focus on the short term and how to cope with the already evolving situation, rather than on trying to shape the future course of events over the long term.[93]

As will be seen in the case studies, a majority of the cabinet supported continuation of the Lavi project during the final debates, despite overwhelming information demonstrating that it was ruinously expensive and over the opposition of both the defense minister and IDF. In 2000 the cabinet voted for unilateral withdrawal from Lebanon despite various assessments indicating that Hezbollah attacks would continue nonetheless. The IDF repeatedly warned Sharon that disengagement would cause a deterioration in security, rather than the improvement he sought, and Sharon refused to even consider the alternative policy options presented to him. In 2006 the cabinet never knew that the IDF had concluded that Hezbollah's rocket arsenal could not be eliminated from the air, that even a major ground operation would not suffice, since Hezbollah could simply move the rockets further north, and that its strategy was thus essentially diplomatic, designed to lead to international intervention to change the situation in southern Lebanon.

In 2011 the defense establishment recommended that Israel continue monetary transfers to the Palestinian Authority, despite what was perceived as a provocative bid for UN membership, to ensure continuation of the effective counterterrorism cooperation then under way. It also recommended that Israel apologize to Turkey in order to restore relations badly harmed the previous year by the Gaza flotilla incident. In both cases the cabinet decided otherwise.[94]

In the absence of clearly defined policy objectives, insufficient attention is devoted to the relationship between ends and means, or objectives and policies. The embargo on Gaza may have helped reduce the flow of weapons and dangerous materials, but the reasons for imposing it blurred over time and the diplomatic price may have outweighed the benefits. None of Israel's diplomatic initiatives (Oslo, Camp David 1978 and 2000, disengagement from Gaza, and Olmert's proposals to Mahmoud Abbas in 2008) reduced international pressure to make further concessions to the Palestinians.

Furthermore, there is often only a loose connection between cabinet decisions and allocation of the resources needed for implementation. The budgetary process, a potentially powerful tool for policy planning, has become largely a matter of political give and take, rather than substantive consideration of alternative uses of resources. Despite its magnitude, complexity, and importance, the defense budget is not formulated on the basis of a systematic planning process, including an analysis of Israel's long-term strategic goals, cost-benefit trade-offs with social and economic needs, or the differing levels of security that could be derived from various budgetary levels. Indeed, the cabinet makes continual changes to the defense budget without elucidation of the budgetary, economic, and operational ramifications. In some cases, the cabinet has officially decided to cut the defense budget, while other decisions provided for exactly the opposite. Former Minister and CoS Amnon Lipkin-Shahak has called the cabinet meetings on the defense budget a disgrace, averring that the ministers simply have no idea what they are voting on. In 2007 the Brodet Committee recommended a variety of fundamental reforms in the budgetary process, which have led to some improvement.[95]

Many cabinet decisions are made for symbolic reasons or to pander to various political constituencies, and it is an open secret that a substantial portion is never implemented, with estimates ranging from 40% to 70%. Indeed, many decisions are adopted from the outset with no intention of actually implementing them.[96] One minister describes a November 2006 directive to the IDF to develop a comprehensive plan for ending rocket fire from Gaza as follows: "Did anyone think that there was a real plan such as this? Some miraculous trick that we had not yet tried? But it is good for the protocol."[97]

### INSUFFICIENT COORDINATION, FLEXIBLE SOPS

Problems of coordination and integration are a common pathology of governments everywhere. In Israel they are further exacerbated by the coalition structure, generally uninstitutionalized nature of decision making, the fear of leaks, and politicization.

As issues have grown in complexity over the years and the bureaucracy has grown in size, the need for more effective coordination has increased substantially, but the interagency machinery has not, and the cabinet and premier cannot adequately fulfill this function. The INSC, which was partly designed to alleviate this problem, has yet to tackle it in a meaningful way. It has been noted wryly that only the US ambassador, who usually has excellent sources of information in all branches of the Israeli government, actually knows what is going on and is thus capable of fulfilling the integrative function.[98]

When the premier has also served as defense minister, as in the case of Rabin and Barak, this has vitiated the need for a formalized definition of their respective roles and close cooperation. In recent decades, however, the positions have usually been separated, indeed, they have often been held by political rivals, and their relationship remains based to a large degree on personality and mutual political dependence. For the most part, they have managed to put rivalries aside on a day-to-day basis, but not always. Disagreement between Olmert and Barak during the 2009 Gaza operation had a significant impact on its conduct, and the 2006 Lebanon war witnessed an unprecedented, if brief, episode in which Defense Minister Peretz refused to convey the premier's orders to the IDF, a problem ultimately resolved informally by their staff. Problems of integration are particularly pronounced between the Foreign Ministry and defense establishment, often the premier as well.

In recent years premiers have increasingly adopted the time-honored tradition of leaders everywhere of making overlapping assignments, with ministers and officials often charged with tasks outside their areas of responsibility, or by going outside the system altogether. Rabin used former ISA official Yossi Ginossar as a go-between with Arafat. Sharon used his son. Netanyahu appointed Jewish American leader Ronald Lauder as an envoy to Syria. Barak appointed his domestic security minister as the chief negotiator with the Palestinians. All recent premiers have appointed their personal lawyers or confidantes as their chief of bureau, a position that has provided them with considerable influence on issues of national security, and have also used these same advisers as special emissaries or negotiators.

The plethora of ministries and agencies now involved in national security affairs further contributes to the problem of coordination. For coalition reasons, the Olmert and Netanyahu cabinets added a number of new ministerial inventions to the already large national security establishment, including ministers for strategic dialogues, strategic affairs, and intelligence. The deputy premier was also assigned responsibility for strategic issues.[99]

The Ministry of Finance takes a great deal of the blame for problems of interagency coordination, at least from defense officials, some of whom refer to it as the "counter-integrator." Others speak of its deleterious impact on multiyear planning, which is of particular importance in the defense area. Further criticisms are that it is almost single-mindedly focused on ensuring that expenditures remain within the approved budget, without regard to changing needs.[100] Needless to say, the MoF places the blame for the lack of integration on the defense establishment, charging it with a lack of budgetary transparency.

Over the years attempts have been made to improve policy integration and coordination by establishing formal interagency coordinating committees,‡ either on a permanent or ad hoc basis. Two apparently successful cases, at least in terms of longevity, are the Committee of the Heads of the Intelligence Services (VARASH; see Chapter 1) and the committee on Iran's nuclear program, headed by the Mossad. Most of the attempts to institutionalize such coordinating committees, however, have met with

‡ Known by the Hebrew acronym KABAM: *kvutzot avoda bein misradiot.*

y limited success, as the different agencies have fought to guard their organizational turf and limit the authority granted to others. It took years of bureaucratic warfare and a crisis with the United States before the MoD agreed to give the MFA a significant role in arms export licensing. An attempt in the early 2000s to improve interagency cooperation and integration, mandated by a ministerial committee, succeeded only in producing an interagency working group on interagency working groups and, not surprisingly, ultimately stalemated over the various agencies' jealousies and infighting.[101] The INSC has yet to succeed in establishing permanent interagency groups, the passage of the INSC Law notwithstanding. Numerous interagency committees exist at the working level, but they focus more on implementation than policy formulation, and their influence is limited.

A further example of problems of coordination is afforded by meetings between Israeli and foreign officials, both in Israel and abroad. Every minister, member of Knesset (MK), and senior (or not so senior) official demands to meet with the most senior foreign interlocutors possible, even when they are clearly not professionally or hierarchically appropriate counterparts.[102] For the MFA and PMB this has become not just a nightmare of coordination but a substantive problem, as each individual presents his or her viewpoint, often without regard to governmental positions. For the ministers, MKs, and officials, however, this is a matter of basic stature; in the ongoing competition over who succeeds in scheduling the most high-profile meetings, failure to do so can be an embarrassing indication of relative importance.

If the problem of interministerial coordination is significant, the defense establishment itself has a highly developed internal process. In meetings with the defense minister, the different defense chiefs, including those of the IDF, Mossad, and ISA, present the positions of their respective organizations. The defense minister then presents this to the premier and cabinet as the "defense establishment's position," one which carries great weight.[103]

## Pathology 5: Primacy of the Defense Establishment

Defense has been at the forefront of Israel's concerns from the prestate days, marshalling a disproportionate share of national attention and resources. A function of Israel's strategic circumstances, this unfortunate reality has had a clear impact on the way issues and priorities have been framed and on the development of national institutions. Foreign policy and, indeed, all areas of national endeavor have been subordinated to this one overriding consideration.

The IDF, consequently, is by far the biggest and most powerful bureaucratic player in Israel, and the defense establishment as a whole wields inordinate influence. The IDF's sources of influence, as elaborated below, are numerous, but it has also been the least reticent of the various agencies in adopting an aggressive approach to bureaucratic politics. Motivated by a deep commitment to its mission and a not unwarranted belief in its ability to handle most issues far more effectively than other governmental organs, the IDF has fought for control over a broad spectrum of national security issues. Although the other agencies, the MFA especially, are hardly innocent of engaging in bureaucratic politics, the primacy of the IDF is the story of bureaucratic politics in Israel.

The IDF's great influence notwithstanding, historic decisions have been made over its objections or even without its knowledge. Begin, known for his deep veneration of the IDF, did not inform it of the beginning of the peace talks with Egypt, nor did Rabin in the case of Oslo. Begin decided to attack the Iraqi reactor in 1981 over the objections of MI. Barak withdrew from Lebanon in 2000 despite IDF objections. Sharon decided to withdraw from Gaza without consulting the IDF and over its objections, as did Olmert regarding the West Bank Consolidation Plan. In recent years, the ISA's influence on Palestinian affairs has grown and its recommendations have been preferred to the IDF's on a number of occasions.[104] The IDF is thus not omnipotent, nor must it be so to substantiate its primacy in the DMP; IDF primacy is based not on "winning" every issue but merely on being the most important player in most.

The IDF is often a voice for moderation, stressing the importance of diplomatic rather than military options. Starting in the late 1980s, it was the IDF that urged that an effort be made to effect change in Israel's relations with the Arabs, and it has repeatedly supported peace agreements with the Palestinians and Syria, despite the concessions required. It was the IDF that concluded that only a political solution could bring an end to the First Intifada. When the Camp David Summit collapsed in 2000 and the Second Intifada erupted, the IDF quickly made a conceptual turnaround and adopted a more hard-line approach, but then concluded three years later that the conflict could not be ended without a political solution.[105]

With by far the most developed policy assessment, planning, and implementation capabilities in Israel, the IDF's strengths are a vital national asset. It is the weakness of the cabinet's policy formulation capabilities and of the civilian national security organs, primarily the MFA, MoD, and INSC, that is the true problem, providing the IDF with inordinate influence and skewing the DMP.[106]

By its very nature as a military organization, the IDF, including the Planning Branch and MI, cannot take the place of a robust and effective foreign ministry and INSC. As broad a national perspective as the Planning Branch seeks to take, it is inherently a subordinate IDF organ and views issues primarily through a military prism. Although the Planning Branch often recommends diplomatic options, military ones obviously receive great attention, and it can hardly be expected to weigh the defense budget in terms of overall national needs at the expense of the IDF's. Bound by the strictures of a military organization in a democracy, the Planning Branch is also limited in its ability to weigh social and economic issues that impact on defense policy, not to mention the political considerations that are an integral part of cabinet-level decision making. As the most influential bureaucratic player, it obviously cannot fulfill the interministerial-interagency integrative function the INSC ought to play.

The following section sets out the reasons for the defense establishment and IDF's great influence.

### PROFESSIONAL EXPERTISE

In many areas extending far beyond the accepted practice in most democracies,[107] the IDF is either the primary or sole entity capable of generating high-quality information, analyses, and policy advice for the premier, defense minister, and cabinet. No other institution can compete with the IDF Intelligence, Planning, and Operations branches' round-the-clock ability to generate rapid, sophisticated, and comprehensive policy planning.

According to the State Comptroller, decision makers typically view the IDF as the sole professional body in the field of national security. The CoS and other senior officers appear before the cabinet frequently and act as its advisers on both defense and foreign affairs. It was the IDF, for example, not the MFA, that first presented the cabinet with an assessment of the US "roadmap for peace," a diplomatic issue clearly within the MFA's purview. MI or the defense minister usually present the situational assessment in the MCoD, often on issues of a clearly diplomatic nature, such as developments in the Security Council. Whereas numerous defense officials have always participated in MCoD meetings, the MFA's director-general was included only after repeated bureaucratic battles.[108]

Unlike other ministries and agencies, which are often not even invited to cabinet or MCoD meetings or the premier's informal consultations, the IDF is almost always represented—and in "military proportions." Former CoS Moshe Yaalon speaks of there being "far too many people in uniform and not enough civilians" in various senior forums, though he bemoans the fact that the civilians do not come nearly as well prepared, thereby enabling the IDF to set the agenda and largely determine the outcome.[109] Former head of MI Amos Malka describes cabinet meetings in similar terms (albeit prior to the establishment of the INSC): "The political echelon usually comes to these meetings as if it is coming for a visit. . . . It has no staff, no one to prepare papers, preparatory meetings are not held, it arrives at a meeting which is run, more or less, by the army (IDF). The army comes and says what its assessment is, the intelligence assessment, and what the possibilities are, option A, option B, option C."[110]

Minister Dan Meridor, a highly respected expert on defense affairs, stresses the great impact the IDF has on cabinet meetings, in which "half-a-dozen" generals present a very well prepared and unified position, argued in authoritative tones. Former NSA Ilan Mizrahi speaks of the cabinet's "worshipful" attitude toward generals and of their decisive influence on it.[111]

The clear primacy of MI and the Planning Branch in the intelligence and policy areas, respectively, including the frequency of their cabinet presentations, has an important impact on how issues are framed and decisions made. As a military organization, MI tends to focus on potential threats and generally takes a worst-case approach. Its assessment in September 2000, that the Intifada had been premeditated by Arafat,[112] greatly colored Israel's thinking at the time and had a decisive impact on the forceful response adopted. In 2006, after the war in Lebanon, the IDF began speaking of a renewed confrontation with Hezbollah as early as the following summer, and possibly with Syria, too, coloring the national debate on what had happened during the war and the resources needed to rectify its failings.

## THE "CLOSED CIRCLE"

The IDF is usually the primary player at all stages of the DMP: situational assessment, policy planning, and implementation:

- *Intelligence assessment:* The intelligence community, especially MI, has a virtual monopoly over information provided to decision makers. MI is responsible for the National Intelligence Assessment and is the only service capable of generating comprehensive political, military, and socioeconomic assessments, in all areas, 24–7. None of the other services' research capabilities, nor the MFA's, have made serious inroads into its primacy.[113]
- *Strategic planning:* The Planning Branch, similarly, remains the most important strategic planning entity, with by far the best developed capabilities.[114]
- *Diplomacy in uniform:* From the Armistice Agreements in 1949 to the present, the IDF has played a major role in diplomatic contacts with Arab and other states and in the various peace talks. Military-to-military relations have also been an important means of fostering relations with foreign countries, including Jordan, India, and Turkey. The MoD, too, has played an important diplomatic role, chairing strategic dialogues with the United States and other countries and bearing primary responsibility for managing relations with Egypt.[115]
- *Military government:* The IDF's responsibility for civil administration in the West Bank (and Gaza in the past) provides it with great influence over the entire range of issues involved, many of a largely civilian and particularly sensitive character.[116]

- *Policy implementation:* With so much of Israeli national security policy conducted on the military level, the IDF has been the primary instrument of policy implementation.[117]

### THE IDF AS A POLICYMAKER

The IDF's control of the "Closed Circle" provides it with considerable sway over policy. Moreover, the highly general and often deliberately vague nature of ministerial and cabinet decisions, designed to bridge or obfuscate policy disagreements rather than clarify them and chart a clear course, leaves considerable room for IDF discretion and further increases its influence over policy. This has been particularly true in the many cases in which the cabinet has failed to formulate clear objectives, leaving the IDF to make what are, in effect, its own policy decisions—as, for example, over how to respond to terrorism and violence in the West Bank.[118]

Speaking in regard to the Intifada, but indicative of the general state of civil-military relations, a former head of the Central Command (responsible for the West Bank) maintains that the IDF was never given clear directives from the political leadership. Similarly, after being instructed by the defense minister to "ease up" on restrictions imposed on Gaza, the general in command asked the CoS what he was to do; the CoS, presumably equally perplexed by the vague nature of the directive, replied laconically "do what you understand"—and in the end nothing was done.[119] For years the cabinet never clearly decided what to about "illegal" outposts, leaving it for the IDF to decide, or in this case often not decide, what to do. In the absence of clear political guidance, it was usually the IDF that was left to draw up proposed withdrawal maps during the various negotiating processes. Former Deputy Foreign Minister Yehuda Ben-Meir maintains that the political leadership's repeated failure to adopt clear objectives constitutes an abdication of its responsibilities.[120]

In Israel's informal, close-knit environment, senior officers are expected to openly express their professional views before political leaders—indeed, doing so is considered a fundamental responsibility. Following the 1982 invasion of Lebanon, the Kahan Commission of Inquiry found the head of MI derelict of duty and forced his resignation on the grounds that he had refrained from presenting his dissenting assessments to the defense minister after concluding that they were leading to his marginalization. Once a decision has been made, however, IDF officers are expected to faithfully implement policy, regardless of their own positions.

In 1991, CoS Dan Shomron, who strongly opposed Defense Minister Moshe Arens's support for a military response to Iraqi Scud attacks, met privately with Shamir prior to the crucial cabinet meeting and ultimately prevailed. CoS Mofaz publicly dissented from Barak's plan for unilateral withdrawal from Lebanon, demurred from his initial efforts to expedite the peace process, and openly called the cabinet's acceptance of the Clinton Parameters a danger to Israel. CoS Yaalon expressed public dissent over Sharon's Gaza Disengagement Plan, while both he and other senior officers pressed the premier to respond favorably to Syrian peace overtures. The commander of the Central Command, facing growing pressure from the premier and defense minister to remove checkpoints in the West Bank, responded that he would obey orders, of course, but that the responsibility for terrorist attacks would be on their shoulders; not surprisingly, the directive was "postponed." CoS Gabi Ashkenazi and Mossad chief Dagan were known for their opposition to a possible attack on Iran's nuclear program. In 2011 Netanyahu allowed the CoS to present his opposition to defense cuts to the cabinet.[121]

One observer describes the following scene, just minutes before the signing of the Oslo Agreement:

> The Commander of the IDF Central Command, Ilan Biran, entered President Clinton's office and launched into a stormy debate with Premier Rabin. The commander argued that Rabin must not agree to the new deployment lines in Hebron. . . . Rabin embarked on a long, vociferous debate with the general, while the rest of us, including the president, had to wait. . . . We were astonished. In our wildest dreams we could not have imagined that such a situation could occur between any premier and one of his generals. And all this at the White House, in front of the president.[122]

Some thus speak of a "partnership" between the political and military leaderships in Israel, and they do undoubtedly enjoy an unusually open and close relationship, with the political leadership highly reliant on the IDF. It is, however, an entirely lopsided relationship, in which the IDF's subordination has never been in question. There has never been a case of the IDF refusing or knowingly failing to obey an order, though there have been occasions where military leaders have gone beyond their orders (e.g., reaching the Suez Canal in 1967, the strong initial response to the Second Intifada), permission was obtained only after the fact, or of bureaucratic foot-dragging (e.g., easing up on security measures in the West Bank and Gaza).[123]

## THE IDF AS A PRESSURE GROUP

The IDF's institutionalized role in the DMP, as well as the high access afforded it by its close ties with the political leadership, makes it a highly influential pressure group. Furthermore, virtually all ministers have served in the IDF, many are former senior officers or defense officials, and the "old boys' network" is nearly all pervasive. As such, many ministers and premiers tend to "feel at home" working with the defense establishment, sharing a "common language," norms, and work procedures.[124]

Until 1967 no more than two former defense officials served in the cabinet concomitantly, but this number has risen consistently since, reaching an average of six to seven from the mid-1980s on. Three of Israel's twelve premiers were former generals and all but four of the eighteen former chiefs of staff as of the mid-2000s have gone into politics, ten becoming ministers. At least twenty generals have become ministers and many other senior officers and defense officials have become MKs, averaging 10%–12% of the Knesset, in parties spanning the political spectrum.[125]

The IDF's public stature is greatly enhanced by its image as the guarantor of the nation's existence, role as the national melting pot, and popular association with much of what is successful in Israel. As a consequence, the IDF has a huge impact on public opinion, which attributes far greater veracity to its statements than to political leaders. Given its popular prestige, turning to the public, whether on the record or through leaks, at times over the heads of the political leadership, is a highly effective means by which the IDF affects policy.[126]

Each year, the MoD and IDF mount a public relations campaign, at times bordering on scare tactics, to generate public support for the defense budget. This "softening up" process is then followed by cabinet meetings in which "twenty senior officers" present indigestible mounds of data and frightening maps, with red arrows pointing directly at the heart of the country, from Iran, Syria, Lebanon, and the Palestinian Authority. It is all designed to scare, dazzle, and cajole the ministers; and if the budget is not approved, they warn, the cabinet will bear responsibility for the consequences.[127] Following the 2006 Lebanon war, the IDF warned that a failure to approve its budget would leave it unable to replenish emptied stores, procure vital new weapons systems, and improve training. The CoS stated that he could make do with less, if necessary, but that this was the premier's decision, for which he could not bear responsibility. At the same time, the defense establishment began warning of a possible war with Syria the following summer, raising the specter of five thousand rockets and missiles being fired at Israel. No one could stand up to its arguments, and as invariably occurs, the cabinet gave in, approving its budget request.[128]

Furthermore, a disproportionate share of the national labor force is employed by the defense establishment, making it a major economic player, especially in the high-tech sector, one of the primary drivers of the national economy. The defense establishment is one of the largest customers in Israel and in the mid-2000s controlled some 50% of Israel's land resources, with defense products comprising 32% of all industrial exports. Defense retirees head major public institutions and commercial enterprises.[129]

## LEGITIMACY: THE TRUTH FACTOR

In a highly charged political environment, in which every word and policy preference is presumed to reflect partisan calculations, the defense establishment, first and foremost the IDF, is considered the only reliable, professional, and "objective" source of information and policy recommendations. Consequently, the IDF is the only entity that virtually all players trust and are willing to work with, attaching great importance to its assessments and recommendations, and it enjoys a unique legitimizing role. In presenting his dramatic proposal for peace with the Palestinians to Secretary of State Condoleezza Rice in 2008, Olmert stated, "I can sell this deal, but not if the IDF says that it will harm security."[130]

## UNITY OF COMMAND

The IDF General Staff is a unified military structure under the direct command of the CoS, who has final authority in all areas. Although senior officers differ frequently on policy issues and bureaucratic politics are prevalent within the IDF, it does not appear to be plagued by the degree of interservice rivalry common in the United States, for example. For the most part, but with important exceptions, such as in the debate over the Lavi program, the positions of the CoS reflect the collective judgment of the senior military leadership and it typically presents a united front to the political leadership.[131]

## ABSENCE OF EFFECTIVE OVERSIGHT

The cabinet, MoD, and Knesset do not have the capability to exercise effective oversight over the IDF and other defense agencies.[132] The cabinet rarely discusses basic defense policy, focusing primarily on the here and now, and does not determine budgetary priorities, leaving it to the IDF to decide on the appropriate strategies and allocation of resources. Moreover, follow-up on policy implementation is limited. The Knesset and FADAC have virtually no practical role in providing legislative oversight either. Unlike the budgets of other ministries and agencies, the defense budget does not require line item approval by the Knesset and until 2005 was not subject to the supervision of a Finance Ministry–appointed comptroller.[133]

The absence of cabinet and Knesset oversight does have the important benefit of at least partially isolating defense policy and budgets from partisan politics, by leaving defense officials to decide how best to utilize resources. The IDF, however, is understandably loath to cut important programs, usually preferring to stretch cuts out over years, thereby often negating their economic rationale, or to adopt cuts that it knows will cause a public outcry and lead to pressures to increase the budget.

The nature of the division of authority between the IDF and the MoD is a further source of IDF primacy. Instead of the IDF being subordinate to the MoD, the division is in fact a complementary one, with the IDF by far the stronger player, and over the years it has further encroached on the MoD's already limited areas of responsibility, for example, arms procurement and exports. Even in areas of ostensibly joint responsibility the MoD is the junior partner. The financial adviser to the CoS, responsible for the defense budget, doubles as head of the MoD Financial Branch. Usually an IDF officer, the financial adviser's staff consists mostly of IDF personnel, with a few civilians from the MoD, thereby providing the IDF with decisive influence over budgetary matters and eliminating the MoD's ability to conduct one of the most effective sources of policy oversight: budgetary supervision. The R&D division is also a joint IDF-MoD unit.[§]

Moreover, the IDF is directly subordinate to the defense minister, not the MoD, which is neither authorized to exercise oversight nor structured to do so. Attempts have been made in recent years to strengthen the MoD's policy planning capabilities, with the establishment of the Politico-Military Planning Branch as well as two additional branches in the areas of defense-related economic and social affairs. Interestingly, former CoS Dan Halutz agreed that the IDF's influence in the national DMP was too strong and supported efforts at the time to strengthen the Politico-Military Branch.[134]

### ABSENCE OF BUREAUCRATIC COMPETITION

The primacy of the IDF is further reinforced by the absence of significant "bureaucratic competitors." Neither the MoD Politico-Military Branch nor the INSC can challenge its primacy in policy planning, and the MFA is clearly a secondary player, lacking in professional and bureaucratic clout. Over the years, the MFA and defense establishment have pulled apart, working in partial isolation from each other.[135]

Life in the shadow of the defense establishment and PMB, which have gradually encroached on the MFA's areas of responsibility, has led to the MFA's growing marginalization. The premier has largely taken over issues of importance pertaining to relations with the United States, Russia, Egypt, and Jordan, to the peace process, and more. The IDF, too, plays a major role in the peace process and, given the importance of Israel's defense ties, has spearheaded relations with strategically important countries, such as the

---

[§] Because of the increasingly sophisticated nature of weapons systems, the MoD no longer has sufficient professional expertise to identify procurement sources on its own or, more important, to analyze the costs and benefits of different procurement options. Similarly, the MoD has become dependent on the IDF's better professional understanding of potential clients for Israeli defense exports.

United States, Russia, India, and Turkey, and initially took a lead role in establishing relations with China. The MoD has played a major role in relations with Egypt. The Mossad was given responsibility for coordinating policy regarding the Iranian nuclear program, including the extensive diplomatic activity this required, and the Atomic Energy Commission has also been deeply involved. The Ministries of Finance and of Commerce and Trade have taken the lead on these respective issues in the international arena, as has the Atomic Energy Commission in its area of expertise.

In these circumstances the MFA typically finds itself left with responsibility for those issues in which other players are not interested, or relegated to the role of a "spokesperson," presenting and explaining Israeli policy abroad, with limited involvement in its formulation.[136] It has also been excluded from important meetings and processes in areas for which it ostensibly bears responsibility. The MoD, IDF, Mossad, and ISA all make regular presentations to the MCoD, whereas the MFA has not always been present. Until the 2000s, the director-general of the MFA, unlike the MoD's and the CoS, was not a regular participant in MCoD meetings, and even after the initial precedent was established, the battle had to be waged once again when a new director-general was appointed. MI, not the foreign minister, makes the weekly politico-military presentation to the MCoD, including on purely diplomatic affairs, such as developments in the Security Council.[137]

Despite the clear diplomatic ramifications, the MFA did not participate in the DMP leading to the attack on the Iraqi reactor in 1981 or the invasion of Lebanon in 1982, and it played only a marginal role in the Gaza disengagement. In 2006, Foreign Minister Livni found it necessary to request a clear division of responsibilities with the premier, that they meet at least once a week, and that she participate in the premier's meetings on defense and foreign affairs.[138] Under Lieberman, after 2010 the MFA was almost completely sidelined.

The deterioration in the MFA's stature is certainly not for lack of qualified people. Recruitment of foreign-service officers is contingent on successful completion of a highly demanding selection process and professional training course. Over time, however, the motivation and performance of MFA personnel tend to deteriorate and the sum total of the ministry's capabilities is far less than that of its staff as individuals.

A former MFA director-general claims that new personnel are "the best and the brightest" but that they are simply not challenged or expected to deliver results. As young officials become increasingly aware of the ministry's marginalization, the drive to be involved diminishes and demoralization and inertia set in.[139] They soon learn that "not rocking the boat" is of the essence; dynamic or ambitious officials who seek to make a difference and promote various issues find the ministry unresponsive and discouraging, at times outright hostile. Obstructionism is common both internally and externally, the latter from other ministries and agencies seeking to preserve or expand their own prerogatives.

Overall demoralization in the MFA has been further exacerbated since the 1980s by the repeated appointment of foreign ministers primarily for reasons of coalition politics, most notably Levy and Lieberman. With limited interest in ministry affairs, other than as a means of advancing their political agendas, or lacking the necessary qualifications, some ministers left the ministry's affairs largely in the hands of their directors-general, further contributing to its marginalization

It is thus hardly surprising that the MFA lacks a mission-oriented organizational culture. Over time it has come to be viewed, and to view itself, as an auxiliary instrument for the day-to-day conduct of relations with foreign countries, rather than as a locus of policy formulation. In the early 2000s, recognition of this reality led to attempts, over considerable internal resistance and with only partial success, to develop annual work plans, by organizational unit and individual, with defined objectives and measures for assessing performance.[140]

The MFA's problems, however, go beyond understandable demoralization, for even when it does have the lead or a chance to play a significant role, it often fails to live up to its responsibilities. Officials, including at the highest levels, consistently come to meetings without sufficient preparation, lacking familiarity with basic issues and having failed to even try to work out a coordinated position among the MFA's warring divisions. The MFA's inability to conduct essential staff work on matters under interagency review, or actually implement them once decided upon, is a source of deep frustration for officials from other agencies. Typically far better prepared and capable of carrying out agreed tasks, these officials have found their own work undermined by the MFA's ennui. The never-ending leaks from the MFA further add to other agencies' reluctance to work with it.[141]

Most MFA officials have not sought service in the Policy Planning Division, which was not considered a route for rapid promotion, and the MFA has not developed a cadre of policy planning specialists. Planning documents are often produced in the context of immediate needs and problems or independently of the operational divisions' needs, not as part of an integrated and systematic approach. In 2009 Foreign Minister Lieberman put an end to an important innovation begun by his predecessor, an annual policy assessment and planning process, subsequently reinstituted, apparently to prevent the ministry's professional staff from recommending initiatives he opposed.[142]

The rapid turnover of directors-general is also a problem for the MFA: those holding the position averaged just twenty-nine months between 1990 and 2001 and even less since then. The turnover rate for MFA officials generally is also rapid,[143] and the promotion system has had a highly injurious impact on organizational morale and proficiency. Both the "employees' committee" (an internal "union") and the Foreign Minister's Bureau play a central role in appointments and promotions, and bureaucratic politics have become as important as professional accomplishment. In 2006 the backlog in the appointment process left over one hundred officials, more than 20% of the Foreign Service staff, without assignments, idling away their time at home for months and in some cases even years.[144]

The MFA's weakness as a bureaucratic player has not moderated its sensitivity to issues of turf and stature. To the contrary, it is continually engaged in efforts to protect its prerogatives from others, often in petty matters of status and at the expense of policy. Both as a result of the Byzantine appointment and promotion system and out of a desire to preserve their turf in a continually shrinking "organizational pie," bureaucratic politics within the MFA are never ending, a seemingly almost all-consuming preoccupation of officials at all levels. Ties between many officials, including at senior levels, are badly strained.[145] Although the Winograd Commission recommended that the MFA be strengthened organizationally and that its role in the national DMP be upgraded, so far this has come to little avail.

## Something Must Be Good: Strengths of the Israeli System

As would be expected, not all is bad. The above pathologies notwithstanding, the Israeli DMP does have a number of strengths, as follows.

### RAPID, FLEXIBLE, AND CREATIVE RESPONSE

The unplanned and improvisational nature of the Israeli DMP are among its primary pathologies. Given, however, that Israel's environment is extraordinarily frenetic, necessitating frequent and rapid changes in policy, the ability to change gears and rapidly adapt to new circumstances is also a vital strength. In other words, if a high degree of adaptability and even improvisation are essential for objective situational reasons, not just subjective national style, it is imperative that they be done very well and this has, indeed, become a sphere of national excellence. The severity of the threat also stimulates a tendency to creativity in the formulations of options, particularly at the operational level. At the same time, the mixed result achieved in Lebanon in 2006, for example, also shows the growing limitations of improvisation.

### PRAGMATIC, NONIDEOLOGICAL DECISION MAKING

Although political discourse in Israel is highly charged ideologically and politically, the national security establishment itself takes a distinctly pragmatic, problem-solving approach.[146] For the most part, it focuses strictly on the professional ramifications of issues, including options for peace agreements, has generally been a force for moderation in the peace process, has taken a pragmatic approach to administering the West Bank (and in the past Gaza), and has done its utmost to avoid being drawn into the public debate on politically charged issues.

Moreover, if one looks beneath the veneer of rhetoric and party politics, dynamic and pragmatic decision making, not rigidity and ideological conviction, typify many Israeli leaders. Begin withdrew from Sinai; Rabin and Peres negotiated the Oslo Agreement and sought to reach a final agreement entailing Palestinian statehood. Barak and Netanyahu pursued a peace agreement with Syria based on full withdrawal from the Golan Heights, and the former withdrew unilaterally from Lebanon and made dramatic proposals at Camp David. Sharon withdrew unilaterally from Gaza, and Olmert proposed a settlement with the Palestinians that went even further than the concessions proposed by Barak. Olmert and Barak were willing to divide Jerusalem. In recent decades, only Shamir, and to a lesser extent Netanyahu, truly tended toward ideological rigidity, though Shamir manifested considerable pragmatism at times—for example, in refraining from responding to Iraqi missile attacks during the Gulf War. Clearly, the West Bank, settlements, and some other issues are at least partial exceptions to the general rule of pragmatism.

## SMALL, TIGHTLY KNIT ESTABLISHMENT, EASE OF COMMUNICATIONS

Israel's national security establishment, at least at senior levels, is comparatively small, most officials know each other personally, and the old boys' network facilitates development of a common understanding of issues. Moreover, it enables ease and speed of communications through informal ties, which cut through various areas and layers of authority. New issues tend to "percolate" quickly, there is usually little difficulty in bringing issues to decision makers' attention, and the comparatively small size of the establishment makes it easier to identify both those responsible for, and capable of, dealing with an issue.[147] As a former US official noted, "in Israel you can accomplish with one phone call what would require two weeks of memo writing in the US."[148]

## LIMITED RANGE OF ISSUES

Israel's national security environment has grown significantly in recent years, in both breadth and complexity. Nevertheless, many of the basic national security issues that have been a major part of national life since the early decades remain so to this day. As such, most of the major issues are clearly defined and are well known to decision makers, and a compara-

tively high degree of expertise prevails, thereby mitigating the pit.
the DMP itself.[149]

## HIGHLY POROUS BOUNDARIES

The Israeli national security establishment, like all organizations, has its own codes, axioms, and ways of thinking. It is, however, very much *not* a closed elite, removed from broader trends in Israeli and international society. Indeed, civil-military borders are highly porous. In the virtual absence of closed military living quarters and with a largely conscript and reservist force, the IDF's regular elements have lives that are fully integrated within the general population.[150]

National security officials are in frequent contact with civil, political, and business leaders, which further increases their exposure to outside influences, as does extensive travel abroad, both professional and private. Moreover, turnover is high, with most officers retiring at relatively young ages, thus facilitating the flow of new ideas and helping reduce the danger of long established mind-sets. Particularly sensitive agencies, such as the intelligence community, run a greater risk of isolation, but here too this does not appear to be a significant problem.

## JUDICIAL, MEDIA, AND PUBLIC REVIEW

Israel's judiciary intervenes in national security affairs as do few, if any, others in the world, setting the parameters for what can and cannot be done. IDF actions are repeatedly challenged and various policies and operational practices have been amended or overturned by the courts. Israel is reported, analyzed, and often skewered by both the domestic and international media, and the national security establishment is engaged in an ongoing exchange with the international community at all levels and on all issues. Indeed, exchanges with the United States are so extensive that American policymaking capabilities almost become a de facto extension of Israel's. "What the Americans think" is the single most important consideration in virtually all policy deliberations, exposing the system to additional insights, approaches, and limits. Short-term difficulties aside, Israel enjoys the fundamental strengths of a vibrant democracy, in which judicial review, media coverage, and domestic and international opinion serve as important policy inputs and "reality checks," which may not prevent errors but do help "straighten the politicians out" in the long term.[151]

## HIGH MOTIVATION AND QUALITY OF PEOPLE

If the DMP itself is faulty, this is partly offset by the quality of the people involved at all levels and their deep motivation, based on a shared sense of threat, belief in the fundamental righteousness of the cause, and consequent commitment to common goals. Interpersonal and bureaucratic infighting aside, long years of experience with the primary national security issues help overcome the failings of the process.[152]

## CENTERS OF EXCELLENCE

If the DMP at the cabinet level remains fundamentally dysfunctional and the national security bureaucracy suffers from structural weaknesses, it nonetheless has a number of centers of excellence, such as the intelligence agencies, Planning Branch, Air Force, and various other units. For the most part, however, this is largely operational excellence, not cabinet-level policymaking, which is the primary problem.[153]

## GROWTH IN SIZE AND SOPHISTICATION OF THE NATIONAL SECURITY ESTABLISHMENT

Notwithstanding the various pathologies described, the national security establishment has grown tremendously in recent decades, in size, organizational complexity, and sophistication. New organizational structures have been added, existing ones greatly expanded, and staff work within the various agencies has improved markedly. To cite just a few examples, the IDF Planning Branch has become a primary player, both within the IDF and at the cabinet level; the intelligence community grew greatly in size and capabilities; the Mossad, ISA, and Foreign Ministry all established new research divisions; the Atomic Energy Commission expanded its research and policy planning capabilities; and the INSC and MoD Politico-Military Branch were established.

This chapter has presented a first-of-its-kind attempt to depict the overall character of the Israeli DMP, centered around five primary pathologies and a number of strengths. Prior research on decision making in Israel took an overwhelmingly historical nature and was, in many cases, conducted too early to enable an attempt to draw such broad conclusions. We now turn to Part III, the case studies, to assess the degree to which these overall characterizations actually hold in practice.

# II. THE CASE STUDIES

*It is not true that Israel's cabinets never make the right decisions. They often do, but usually only after trying everything else.*

—Abba Eban, former Israeli foreign minister

Part II presents the seven case studies. Each study is structured around the five pathologies held to be characteristic of Israeli decision making, as described in the preceding chapter. As could be expected, the intensity with which the pathologies were manifested varies by case. Some prove stronger across all of the cases and have greater explanatory power; others, less so, as will seen in the comparative analysis in the final chapter, "Conclusions and Recommendations."

The case studies include many of the most momentous decisions Israel has faced in recent decades, focusing primarily on the critical high-risk issues of war and peace, with all of the fundamental political, ideological, and strategic considerations they entail. The cases include two decisions to go to war, in Lebanon in 1982 and 2006; two attempts to make peace, with Egypt in 1977–1978 and the Palestinians in 2000; and two lesser but nevertheless crucial strategic decisions, the unilateral withdrawals from Lebanon in 2000 and Gaza in 2005. The final case, the development of the Lavi combat aircraft program, is an "outlier," seemingly just a matter of cold financial, technological, and strategic considerations, not highly charged political and ideological ones. If it, too, is found to manifest pathologies similar to those in the other cases, this will further substantiate the study's findings regarding the posited nature of the DMP.

The cases occurred under a variety of coalitions and thus at least partly discount potential differences stemming from the character of a given coalition or party. Environmental pressures, while significant in all of the cases, were not so extreme that Israel was compelled to act in certain ways, and its leaders had the freedom to choose from a number of policy options. All seven cases were selected because the initiative was at least partially in Israel's hands, thereby precluding the possibility that the unplanned nature of the process and other decision-making ills were the result of overwhelming environmental pressures, which did not leave Israel with much room to choose between policy options.

Each case begins with an overview of the strategic setting in which the specific DMP took place, that is, the first of the three independent variables set out in the analytical model presented in the Introduction. It is important to note that the strategic overviews are designed not to be comprehensive portrayals of events, but to describe the forces that shaped the decisions of Israel's leaders during the periods under discussion. The other two independent variables, the nature of Israel's PR electoral system and the relative weakness of the civilian national security organs, remained fundamentally unchanged throughout the period under discussion and are thus not addressed in the cases.

Table 1 presents a summary of the five pathologies and their subdimensions. Readers may find it of use in following their presentation in the case studies, which follows the same order. It should be noted that almost all of the subdimensions presented in Chapter 2 are analyzed in the case studies and thus appear in the table, with a few exceptions, either because the information available was insufficient to sustain a rigorous analysis, such as the posited oral nature of Israeli decision making, or, in one case, the question of its proactive or reactive nature, because the case studies, as noted above, were intentionally chosen for their at least partially proactive character. A comparative table, showing the intensity of the pathologies manifested in all seven cases appears in the "Conclusions and Recommendations."

## Table 1 Pathologies and Subdimensions

| Pathology | Subdimensions |
| --- | --- |
| **Unplanned Process** | Deficient policy planning: absence of or avoidance of systematic policy formulation; ineffective formulation of objectives, priorities, and options; faulty or insufficient preparatory staff work<br>Improvisation<br>Sequential decision making |
| **Politicized Process** | Politics reign supreme: focus on politics and consensus building, not policy; politics affect process; political grandstanding; time devoted to party and media; rivalry between premier and ministers<br>Coalition maintenance above all: compromised policy; "what will fly"; minimum consensus necessary; procrastination<br>Public opinion affects process |
| **Semiorganized Anarchy** | The premier is in charge sometimes: premier's control of party and coalition and ability to realize desired policies; degree of political give and take; costs of obtaining policy approval<br>Dysfunctional cabinet and MCoD: not true locus of decision making; absence of substantive policy debate; "precooking" of issues; ineffective preparation; absence of effective decision-making forum<br>Leaks: affect process; avoidance of presenting true positions in cabinet, MCoD, and ministerial forums; work just with trusted confidantes, small groups, or in defense establishment |
| **Uninstitutionalized Process** | Idiosyncratic decision making: personal preferences as primary policy driver, not systematic policy planning; limited culture of consultation<br>Disconnect between policy inputs and formulation: absence of proactive efforts to turn information into policy and allocation of resources to policy decisions; decision makers unaware of or ignore information; symbolic or declaratory policy<br>Insufficient policy coordination and integration: relevant players involved; interministerial coordinating meetings and papers; clear division of labor |
| **Primacy of Defense Establishment** | IDF/defense establishment primary source of expertise: "closed circle"<br>IDF and defense agencies are primary bureaucratic player: frame issues; present objectives, options, and recommendations; responsible for implementation<br>Defense minister/IDF positions prevail; centrality of defense considerations |

# CHAPTER THREE

# Camp David I: Making Peace with Egypt, 1977–1979

The trials of peace are better than the scourges of war.

—Menachem Begin

This case study focuses on the period from the initial diplomatic contacts prior to Egyptian president Anwar Sadat's visit to Israel in November 1977 and the Camp David Summit in September 1978. Six more months of intensive negotiations would be required before the peace treaty was concluded, but the major principles had been worked out by the summit's end.

## The Strategic Setting

When President Sadat stunned the world with the announcement of his willingness to visit Israel and begin negotiations, he found an Israel avid for peace but unsure how to respond to this unexpected reversal of the thirty-year-long Arab policy of total hostility. Israel was still reeling at the time, militarily, economically, and psychologically, from the devastating effects of the Yom Kippur War.

In the interim, Arab petro-power, then at its height, together with effective diplomacy and public relations on the part of the Arab states and PLO, had led to a severe deterioration in Israel's international standing concurrent with a growing recognition of the Palestinian cause.[1] In 1975 the General Assembly invited PLO chairman Arafat to address it and adopted a resolution equating Zionism with racism (ultimately revoked). Saudi Arabia was no longer the focal point for the Moslem faithful alone; world leaders also now paid homage to it, closely following every word and deed of the petroleum superpower. Sadat's signing of the 1974 Disengagement Agreement and 1975 Interim Agreement had transformed Egypt's international standing and made him one of the world's more popular leaders, long before his dramatic peace initiative turned him into a global hero.[2]

Egypt had long been by far the most powerful of Israel's enemies, fighting four major wars and one limited one in just twenty-five years. In 1977 a massive Egyptian and Arab arms buildup threatened to raise arms levels in the region to unprecedented heights and to alter the military balance. Israel thus had an overwhelming strategic interest in peace with Egypt, both in its own right and because it had long been assumed that the other Arab states would not have a viable military option without it.[3]

In the years following the 1967 and especially the 1973 wars, Israel became highly dependent on the United States. Emergency assistance during the 1973 war and a multibillion-dollar aid program in the years thereafter became primary determinants of Israel's national security. Isolated internationally, the United States was also Israel's sole important source of diplomatic support and a buffer before unwanted international initiatives. Moreover, the United States had played a key role in achieving the partial postwar agreements with Egypt and Syria, which began the "peace process" and gave Israel time to recover. For these and other reasons, American policy now became a preeminent Israeli strategic consideration.

President Carter brought a new approach to the peace process with him when he entered office in 1977, becoming the first president to speak of a Palestinian "homeland." Instead of the old "step-by-step" approach, Carter sought to bring the PLO and Syria into the process, as part of an attempt to reach a "comprehensive settlement."[4] Even Carter's approach toward Israel's security was a source of disquiet in Jerusalem, as he began speaking of the 1967 borders as "secure and recognized ones." A US military relationship with Egypt and Saudi Arabia also began during this period, presenting Israel with the danger of having to confront both advanced Soviet and Western weapons. In 1978 the administration even made the provision of combat aircraft to Israel contingent on congressional approval of the sale of aircraft to Egypt and Saudi Arabia.

In October 1977 the United States and the USSR placed a bombshell at the door of Middle Eastern diplomacy, in the form of a Joint Communiqué. After striving for years to minimize Soviet influence in the region, the United States now granted Moscow equal standing in the peace process and agreed both to reconvene the Geneva Conference, the multilateral peace conference convened following the 1973 war, which Israel considered a hostile forum, and to adopt controversial new language, including a call for a "comprehensive settlement," the participation of "all parties concerned," and recognizing the Palestinians' "legitimate rights." Although this was counterbalanced by calls for peace, the Communiqué was viewed in Israel as a "catastrophe." Coming on top of Carter's other changes, it appeared that a severe deterioration in US policy had occurred.[5]

Foreign Minister Dayan met with Carter following the Communiqué and described their talks as "brutal," saying that Israel preferred a rupture with the United States to establishment of a Palestinian state. The meeting did, however, produce movement on both sides. In a major departure, Dayan now agreed to Palestinian participation in negotiations over the West Bank, as long as Palestinian representatives were not avowed members of the PLO, while Carter agreed that the Palestinians would not be represented separately at Geneva and that the Palestinian issue would not be raised. The statement issued at the end of the Carter-Dayan talks created the impression that Carter had backed away from the Communiqué.[6]

The common view of Sadat's decision to visit Israel just weeks later is that it was designed to derail the renewed Soviet role provided for by the Joint Communiqué. Conversely, W. B. Quandt maintains that it was Sadat's belief that the Carter-Dayan statement indicated that Washington was backing away from the Communiqué, rather than a desire to derail it, that was the catalyst.[7] Either way, the surprising change in US policy led to an even more surprising one in Egypt's. Israel's elation during Sadat's visit was tempered by a fear of increased diplomatic isolation, US pressure, and heightened risks of renewed warfare, were it to end in failure.[8]

Notwithstanding the dramatic breakthrough to direct negotiations, both Israel and Egypt rapidly concluded that continued US mediation remained crucial. Indeed, both sides competed for US support throughout the peace process and negotiated with it, to gain support for their positions, no less than they did with each other. In July 1977 Premier Begin had met with Carter for the first time and presented the outlines of an Israeli peace plan. In December the race for American support got under way in earnest. Begin again presented Israel's plan for a Sinai withdrawal to Carter, now adding a new component designed to address the Palestinian issue, the autonomy proposal, even though the Egyptians had reacted coldly when Foreign Minister Dayan informally raised it before them.[9]

In January 1978, however, Carter and Sadat issued the "Aswan Declaration," which spoke of "solving the Palestinian problem in all its aspects" and "recognition of the legitimate rights of the Palestinian people." In February Carter publicly declared that Security Council Resolution 242 applied to all fronts, that peace was impossible without resolution of the Palestinian problem, and that Israeli settlements were illegal and an obstacle to peace.[10] These statements demonstrated that US policy was far more in tune with Egypt than with Israel—indeed, they marked the beginning of a period of ongoing US-Egyptian collaboration designed to change Israel's positions, especially on the issues of the Sinai settlements and the West Bank. Carter and Sadat adopted a coordinated negotiating strategy, whereby Sadat would intentionally take hard-line positions, to the point of creating crises, at which time the United States would step in and submit "bridging" proposals. Sadat would then moderate his positions and enable the United States to press Israel to compromise. The strategy was only partially implemented, but it substantiated Israel's concerns regarding US-Egyptian intentions.[11]

Begin and Carter next met in March 1978, with the latter reiterating his support for the Egyptian position and calling on Israel to accept the Aswan Declaration. The Sinai settlements would have to be dismantled, though one airbase might remain. Carter demanded that Begin accept the applicability of Resolution 242 to all fronts and raised the possibility of holding a referendum on the West Bank to determine its final status. Begin rejected Carter's demands, describing the talks as "the hardest in my life."[12]

In May Carter submitted a humiliating "questionnaire" to Israel on the nature of the final agreement, along with "suggested" responses. Israel gave an only partially positive response and Egypt announced that it would not renew talks. The United States then began efforts to "save" the peace process.[13]

The United States played a vital role at the Camp David Summit, without which an agreement would not have been reached. Partly a neutral intermediary, the US role went far beyond that, as it submitted proposals of its own and demanded that the sides make concessions to it, if not to each other. The Americans cajoled, argued, and at times exerted massive pressure, threatening Begin with economic and military sanctions. They also provided vital economic and military assistance to both sides and undertook to rebuild the Sinai airbases in Israel, thereby greatly easing the latter's decision to dismantle them.[14]

Israel feared that Sadat's true objective at Camp David was a collapse of the negotiations, for which it would be blamed and which would result in a severe deterioration in US-Israeli relations. Begin thus resolved that preserving relations with the United States would be one of his basic considerations at the summit. His fears were not eased by American behavior; indeed, Carter laid down the law in their very first meeting. "We must leave the summit with an agreement," he stressed before delivering the following punch line: "reconciliation between Israel and Egypt is even more important to me than my own political prospects."[15]

On the tenth day Carter threatened to state publicly that whereas he had reached full understanding with Sadat, Begin's refusal to dismantle the Sinai settlements and recognize the applicability of Resolution 242 to the West Bank had prevented agreement. American pressure came to a head on the twelfth and penultimate day, as Carter threatened direct sanctions: "I will not be able to turn to Congress and say 'continue providing Israel with assistance' when I am not sure that you really want peace." It was at this meeting that Begin finally conceded on the settlements and Palestinian clauses. He would later tell the Knesset: "there was the possibility of saying no to President Carter and the Camp David Summit would have blown up that very day. . . . I knew that Israel would not be able to withstand it . . . not in the US, not in Europe, not before the Jews of the United States. . . . Israel could not have stood . . . facing the (entire) world."[16]

## Pathology 1: An Unplanned Process

In the days prior to Sadat's visit, MI conducted a new assessment of Egyptian policy toward peace with Israel. In contrast with a previous assessment just two months earlier, it now concluded that Sadat was, indeed, interested in peace but that he would insist on far-reaching concessions, including complete withdrawal from Sinai and establishment of a Palestinian state. MI further concluded that the impact of Sadat's visit would be such that Israel would be forced to withdraw from all of Sinai.[17] In an unprecedented violation of MI's analytical independence, Begin directed that the assessment be recalled from those who had already received it, on the grounds that the possibility of a complete withdrawal simply did not exist and that MI should not be dealing with political matters (even though it always had and still does).[18]

In addition to the official assessment, the head of MI, Shlomo Gazit, prepared a personal position paper recommending Israeli positions. During the week before Sadat's visit, Gazit called Begin's office twice daily, inquiring of the premier when he intended to hold a preparatory meeting, but to no avail. His paper was returned by the premier's office with acerbic comments, including a rhetorical question asking when MI had begun dictating cabinet policy.[19] Finally, on the morning before Sadat's arrival, Begin summoned Gazit and other senior officials to a meeting to address Deputy Premier Yigal Yadin's fear that the visit was a ruse for a surprise attack and recommendation that the IDF be mobilized immediately. The others disagreed strongly and Begin postponed the decision on mobilization. With that, remarkably, Israel's policy planning in preparation for Sadat's momentous visit ended. Not a single cabinet meeting was held, nor were policy papers prepared.[20]

Begin's two historic concessions during the visit—full withdrawal from Sinai and the still embryonic concept of Palestinian autonomy—were presented on his own recognizance, with no input from the national security establishment, just informal consultations with Dayan. Begin's subsequent attempts to back off from a full withdrawal and retain control of the settlements and air bases are indicative of the absence of systematic planning. No protocol was made of Begin and Sadat's private talks during the historic visit, nor did Begin dictate the essential points afterward. Following the visit, Dayan publicly called for a review of Israeli policy toward the West Bank. A seemingly eminently reasonable idea following a historic change in the course of the entire conflict, the proposal caused a political uproar and Dayan never made another public suggestion of this sort.[21]

The MoD and MFA did set up task forces in preparation for the Cairo Conference, to which Sadat invited Israel shortly after the visit. In the end, however, the delegation was not provided with new guidelines, and was once again given the same plan Begin had presented to Carter the previous July, despite the historic developments in the interim.[22]

During the month between Sadat's visit and the presentation of Israel's peace plan to Egypt, Begin became further convinced of the need to bridge two seemingly conflicting objectives: Israel's desire to conclude a "separate peace" with Egypt, independent of the Palestinian issue, versus Sadat's need to demonstrate to the Arab world that he had not betrayed the Palestinian cause. The autonomy plan still appeared to provide the best answer, but once again Begin conducted no policy planning and did not consult with the defense establishment, nor did he even consider the options it had prepared on its own. Only Dayan, Cabinet Legal Adviser Aharon Barak, and his closest confidantes were let in on his thinking. In the absence of substantive preparations, Dayan rose early on the morning of his historic meeting with the Egyptians and wrote out the autonomy proposal by hand, on the basis of his talks with Begin. As the proposal proved nearly illegible, he ended up having to read it aloud to the Egyptians.[23]

Following Dayan's talks with the Egyptians, Begin made a number of amendments to the plan and presented it the MCoD for the first time. Begin only drafted the actual plan the next day, during a stopover on a flight to Washington, on a morning when he felt ill. Parts of the proposal were thus still in handwritten form when presented to Carter, and Begin, having only just drafted it, was unable to answer some of the president's probing questions. After his return, Begin now presented the proposal to the full cabinet, which found it to have numerous flaws, and corrections were urgently cabled to Washington. Israel's first peace proposal, both to the greatest of its enemies and the greatest of its friends, was presented in this haphazard way.[24]

In late December Begin met with Sadat in Ismailia and officially presented Israel's peace plan for the first time, including both the autonomy proposal and Sinai withdrawal, stressing that the settlements would remain. Weizman "presumed" that this was Begin's extreme position and that he would be willing to compromise, but in the absence of preparations was not familiar with his true thinking.[25]

For a change, preparations for the meeting of the Military Committee in January 1978 were significant. Two working groups were established, one under the head of the Planning Branch, Avraham Tamir, and the other in the Operations Branch. Drawing on extensive work the Planning Branch had conducted on possible peace settlements, Tamir's group prepared various options for the final borders in Sinai and the stages of the withdrawal. Begin convened a meeting on the different plans and directed that Tamir's proposal be adopted. The preparations for the meeting of the Political Committee later that month were far less extensive.[26]

An interministerial working group was set up in preparation for the Camp David Summit, coheaded by the director-general of the Premier's Ministry and Tamir. Whereas Tamir insisted that the final document, the "Blue Book," covered all of the outstanding issues and that many of its recommendations ultimately served as the basis for the agreements reached, Dayan and Barak maintained that it provided no new information of use to anyone fully immersed in the negotiations.[27]

Begin, in any event, directed that the Blue Book be distributed to the cabinet in preparation for a meeting on the summit, but no meeting was ever held and the cabinet never discussed Israel's negotiating positions. Dayan, who sought to preserve the negotiators' flexibility, requested that Begin drop a proposal to have guidelines drafted for the delegation, and Begin and the other ministers agreed. Instead, the cabinet merely authorized the negotiators to present once again the plan Begin had submitted to Carter six months earlier, along with leeway to make limited changes, provided that they did not violate the spirit of the plan. More fundamental changes were to be subject to cabinet approval. As of just a few days before Camp David, Begin, Dayan, and Weizman had still not found time to meet in preparation.[28] Thus ended the preparations for one of the most momentous events in Israel's history.

Because no policy planning had been conducted, Israel's objectives and priorities had not been defined, nor had agreed-upon fallback positions been prepared, and a coordinated negotiating strategy did not exist. In these circumstances, members of the Israeli delegation began pressing Begin to compromise as soon as the summit began.[29] Both Dayan and Weizman believed prior to Camp David that the negotiations would revolve primarily around the West Bank, but whereas Dayan maintained that Israel should seek to channel the talks to the Sinai withdrawal, on which there was considerable agreement, and only turn to the Sinai settlements and West Bank issues if the first issue was successfully concluded, Weizman believed that the talks should begin with the latter. This disagreement surfaced again during Camp David, with Weizman unaware that Begin and Dayan had privately agreed to begin with the withdrawal.[30]

On the first day of the summit, Sadat submitted a document so extreme that the Israelis feared that the talks would collapse immediately. The United States also submitted a document of its own. Only then and for public relations purposes, to prevent Israel from being blamed for the talks' failure, was a statement of its positions prepared, with Begin rising at 5:30 a.m. to dictate it to an adviser.[31]

Throughout the process, neither Begin nor Dayan made use of advisory teams, merely consulting with each other and occasionally with trusted individuals, though Weizman did make use of the extensive policy planning conducted by the IDF. All three actively sought out various options at different points—as, for example, in their repeated attempts to find a formula that would enable Sadat to conclude a separate peace—but this was done almost entirely on their own. Indeed, all three appear to have formulated their positions primarily on the basis of what they learned firsthand during the negotiations and given their personal assessments of what was achievable.

These findings indicate an at least tacit understanding between Begin and Dayan on the desirability of systematic policy planning, or, more correctly, the lack thereof. If policy planning is designed to force officials to clarify objectives, priorities, and options and to smoke out differences, this is precisely what Begin and Dayan did not want. Similarly, the last thing they would have wanted was an "honest broker" giving the cabinet the full range of options. Obfuscation, the antithesis of systematic policy formulation, was the primary means they had to protect their flanks politically and gain the flexibility they required—and such an approach paid off. Once agreement had been reached at Camp David and the cabinet and Knesset were faced with the option of "taking peace or leaving it," the decision almost became moot.

Paradoxically, "proper" policy planning might have made it even harder, possibly impossible, to reach agreement. Had a policy paper been drafted in advance of the Camp David summit, for example, envisaging that Israel would ultimately have to cede the Sinai settlements and air bases, accept the Palestinian clauses (recognition of "legitimate rights," "resolution of the Palestinian problem in all its aspects," and resolution of the "final status" of the West Bank), and agree to an exchange of letters on Jerusalem, it is likely that the political uproar, within the cabinet and public at large, would have precluded agreement. Moreover, had the ultimate price been clear in advance, Begin and Dayan themselves might not have been psychologically capable of making the necessary concessions. The outcry caused by Dayan's public call for a review of Israeli policy toward the West Bank following the Sadat visit is highly indicative of this.[32]

Modifying one's positions in response to the other side is the essence of negotiations, and feelers, ploys, even improvisation, are part of the "game." As such, Israel's positions could reasonably have been expected to evolve over time—and they did. Some positions were deeply felt, others more flexible, and the participants themselves may not have always known which were truly inviolate and which would ultimately prove negotiable. Even if Begin and Dayan did have a relatively clear endgame in mind—that is, a "separate peace"—the exigencies of the negotiating process would require numerous changes in Israel's positions and concessions.

Begin launched his pursuit of a peace agreement with Egypt on the very night of his election, in May 1977, publicly calling on Sadat and other Arab leaders to come to the negotiating table. It was the first in a series of signals he would send to Sadat of his interest in talks.[33] In July Begin presented the outlines of an Israeli peace plan to Carter, and in August he met with

Romanian president Nicolae Ceausescu, who conveyed Begin's willingness to compromise on Sinai and the premier's wish to meet to Sadat. Days later Dayan met secretly with Moroccan king Hassan, who promised to try to arrange direct contacts with Egypt.[34]

These initial contacts led to a secret meeting in September between Dayan and Sadat's personal envoy, Hassan Tohami, who demanded a complete withdrawal from all of the territories as a precondition for further talks. Dayan stated that "everything was open for discussion and maybe Sadat will convince Begin to withdraw from Sinai." In effect, he was probing to see whether Sadat really meant all Arab territory or just Egyptian territory, which would provide an opening for the separate agreement that both he and Begin pursued throughout the negotiations. According to other accounts, Dayan merely reiterated what Begin had presented to Carter, that is, a willingness to withdraw from most but not all of Sinai.[35]

In November 1977 Sadat's announcement of his visit took Israel completely by surprise. Even Begin and Dayan, who had been deeply involved in the initial contacts, did not at first believe that Sadat was serious. The intelligence agencies, which were unaware of the secret contacts and still had the trauma of the Yom Kippur War uppermost in their minds, maintained that Israel ought to prepare for the possibility that Sadat's announcement was really a strategic deception, aimed at lulling Israel into a false sense of security prior to a surprise attack. Indeed, an assessment of Egypt's approach toward peace with Israel, which MI had just completed two months earlier (and, as noted, subsequently revised), concluded that a fundamental change had not occurred and that Egypt might even initiate hostilities within months. So great were the fears, that CoS Motta Gur publicly warned that Israel would not be taken by surprise and the IDF was placed on alert. Once it became clear that Sadat truly intended to visit, a new fear arose, that his real objective was to drive a wedge between Israel and the United States.[36]

During Sadat's visit Begin made a historic concession, offering to "restore all of Sinai to Egyptian sovereignty," but rejected Sadat's two primary demands: withdrawal to the 1967 borders on all fronts and establishment of a Palestinian state. Begin's distinction between restoration of "sovereignty," as opposed to "control," was apparently lost on Sadat, who understood that the entire Sinai territory would be returned to Egypt, whereas Begin still hoped to retain control of Israel's settlements and air bases. Begin made a second major concession when he also broached the concept of Palestinian "autonomy" in the West Bank and Gaza, thereby indicating that Israel would not insist on sovereignty over these areas.[37]

In December 1977 Dayan again met with Tohami and described Israel's proposals in greater detail, stressing that they had not yet been presented to the cabinet and were intended to sound out Egypt's response. If favorable, they would be presented to the cabinet for approval and then be resubmitted to Egypt formally. Dayan proposed that Sinai be fully restored to Egypt and divided into three zones; one with limited Egyptian military forces, a demilitarized zone, and a zone in which the Israeli settlements and Etzion air base would remain under UN supervision. As for the Palestinians, Dayan stated that a detailed separate proposal was being formulated based on the concept of autonomy. He repeatedly tried to seek Tohami out on the possibility of a separate peace.[38]

Having taken Israel by surprise with his visit, Sadat now did so once again, with an invitation to attend a Cairo Conference in mid-December. Begin instructed the delegation to explore Egypt's willingness to conclude a separate peace, while avoiding any discussion of future borders and a Palestinian state. In reality, the Israeli delegation was actually playing a holding game, while Begin prepared for talks with Carter some days later. During this meeting Begin presented the plan Dayan had already outlined to Tohami, despite the latter's rejection thereof.[39]

In late December Defense Minister Weizman returned from a meeting with Sadat convinced that agreement could be reached only if the settlements and air bases were dismantled. A few days later Begin, Weizman, and Dayan met with Sadat in Ismailia. Begin now officially submitted his peace plan, including both the Sinai withdrawal and autonomy proposal, but stressed that the settlements would remain in place.[40]

In contrast to Israeli expectations, Sadat focused at Ismailia almost solely on the Palestinian issue, to the near exclusion of Sinai. The summit ended in agreement on Begin's proposal to establish two working committees, but little else. A military committee would deal with the Sinai withdrawal and a political committee with the Palestinian issues. Some of the Israeli participants in Ismailia, Weizman among them, believed at this time that Sadat merely sought a Palestinian "fig leaf," in the form of a "declaration of principles" (DoP), and that the price Israel would have paid for peace would have been much lower had it agreed to this. Begin believed otherwise, that Sadat would insist on withdrawal on all fronts and on a declaration on the Palestinian issue, which would have been unacceptable to Israel.[41]

In January 1978 the Military Committee reached considerable agreement on the division of Sinai into the three zones as proposed, though Egypt again rejected the possibility of the settlements and air bases remaining under UN administration. The Political Committee achieved progress on the wording of a Palestinian DoP, but Sadat surprised Israel by breaking off the talks, in effect manufacturing a crisis in order to compel US intervention.[42]

In late January the Military Committee reconvened in Cairo and achieved further progress on the security arrangements in Sinai. Weizman continued to explore Egyptian willingness to make do with a face-saving arrangement on the Palestinians, as well as a practical solution for the settlements: Israel would announce its willingness to withdraw from all of Sinai "in principle," while a separate agreement would provide for them to remain in place until the issue was reconsidered in 2000.[43]

In March Begin met with Carter and again presented the plan he had proposed four months earlier, in effect seeking to ascertain whether there was any room for US and Egyptian flexibility on the West Bank. Weizman met with Sadat later in the month, further probing the possibilities for a separate peace. In April Dayan met with Secretary of State Cyrus Vance on the future status of the West Bank and Palestinian participation in the talks and suggested that if the administration backed off from its demand for a referendum on the "final status," it would be possible to reach agreement on a DoP.[44]

In May, in response to Carter's "questionnaire" and "suggested" responses on the "final status," weeks of fierce cabinet debate elicited a creative improvisation, designed to prevent both a coalition crisis and a rift with the United States. Israel would agree to discuss its "future relations" with the West Bank, after a transition period, but not its "final status" as Washington proposed.[45]

At the Leeds Conference in July, Dayan sought to recharge the moribund talks with two concessions: Israel would accept the principle of territorial compromise on the West Bank and, contrary to its official response to the "questionnaire," would be willing to discuss "final status" following a transition period, but without forgoing its right to claim sovereignty at that time.[46] Sadat rejected the Israeli concessions, and Leeds ended in renewed impasse, with Carter growing concerned that Sadat might abandon the talks entirely. The president thus concluded that only a dramatic step could lead to a breakthrough, and invitations were issued a week later to a summit at Camp David in September.[47]

Begin's strategy at Camp David was to postpone major concessions until Sadat compromised on the Palestinian issues. Some claim that he contemplated an eventual concession on the settlements from the beginning, but the practical result of this approach was to make them the pivotal issue on which the summit's outcome hinged.[48] By midsummit, Weizman and Dayan had concluded that Israel had to make a historic choice between settlements and peace and now advocated their dismantlement. Begin himself would later say that he could not have allowed the summit to fail because of the settlements. Prior to the summit, it was decided that if Egypt insisted on dismantlement of the air bases, Israel would demand a ten- to fifteen-year postponement on the most important one, Etzion. In practice, Begin and Dayan focused at Camp David almost solely on the settlements, and once the United States eliminated the air base problem by undertaking to rebuild them in Israel, the Israeli delegation readily acceded to their dismantlement.[49]

Begin made the final concessions, which enabled the breakthrough, when he agreed to a series of Palestinian clauses that he had previously rejected, including "the legitimate rights of the Palestinian people," "Palestinian participation in determining their future," and "resolution of the Palestinian problem in all its aspects." The Palestinians would have "full" autonomy, but it would be limited to a period of five years, pending negotiations on "final status," which would begin within three years. The IDF would withdraw some forces and the remainder would "redeploy in specified security locations."[50]

At the last minute, when the talks had seemingly come to a successful conclusion, the Egyptians again raised the issue of Jerusalem and the summit teetered on the verge of collapse. A solution was found in the form of an exchange of letters, in which the sides reiterated their long-standing (and conflicting) positions. Even mention of this disagreement was a painful concession for Begin, for it implicitly acknowledged that Jerusalem had become a subject of negotiation.[51]

Some members of the Israeli delegation believed that at "Camp David we founded the Palestinian state." Begin, conversely, believed that the agreement saved Judea and Samaria, the West Bank. Although he had been forced to accept a two-pronged agreement, one on the Palestinian issues, the other on Israeli-Egyptian peace, their implementation was not mutually dependent and he had thus successfully found a mechanism that enabled Egypt to conclude what was, in essence, a separate peace. Moreover, the United States and Egypt were now co-signatories to an agreement recognizing that Israel had a legitimate stake in any future resolution of the West Bank issue.[52]

The posited unplanned nature of the process was partially substantiated. Policy planning was grossly deficient, indeed, the most basic preparations were not conducted even at critical junctures, and the formulation of objectives and options was clearly flawed. The improvisational nature of the process was partly immanent in the nature of the negotiating process, but also reflected the lack of systematic planning and was thus only moderately substantiated. Begin and Dayan did, however, have an overall strategy that they pursued assiduously, that is, a separate peace agreement with Egypt, and the process was thus more incremental than sequential.

## Pathology 2: A Highly Politicized Process

Public opposition to the cabinet's conduct of the peace talks was extensive, from both the left and right. In March 1978, 348 reserve officers wrote to Begin calling up him to show greater flexibility. Within a month, ten thousand people had co-signed the letter and forty thousand rallied in Tel Aviv in support. The Peace Now movement was established in early 1978, and a hundred thousand people signed a petition it initiated. Left-wing pressure reached its height on the eve of the Camp David summit, with mass demonstrations.

Right-wing pressure coalesced primarily over the Sinai settlements. In January 1978, for example, Weizman was "almost certain that the government would not survive if it were to cede the settlements."[53] Gush Emunim (the West Bank settlers' movement), the Sinai settlers, other extraparliamentary groups, and right-wing MKs, conducted a myriad array of demonstrations and political moves to sway the cabinet, ultimately even trying to physically prevent the settlements' dismantlement.[54]

Begin was keenly aware of domestic and coalition politics and bowed at times to pressure; for example, he placated the right wing by appointing his director-general, not Dayan, to head the delegation to the Cairo Conference. He presented the autonomy plan to Carter even before submitting it to the cabinet, in an attempt to marshal support for what he knew would be a difficult political battle. He virtually implored the president to say something positive about it, almost anything, making much ado over Carter's less than enthusiastic public characterization of the plan as "favorable." The cabinet's January 1978 decision to establish new settlements near the Egyptian border, which created a firestorm in Egypt, the United States, and Israel itself, was partly a display of defiance in response to the US-Egyptian Aswan Declaration, but it was also an attempt to placate growing right-wing opposition. Although the cabinet was forced by US pressure to back away from this decision, new reports of settlement activity surfaced immediately. In August 1978, party pressure forced Begin to promise that the Sinai settlements would not be dismantled, a promise he violated at Camp David just weeks later.[55]

Politics played an important role during the critical closing days at Camp David. At Dayan's instigation, General Tamir called Ariel Sharon (then minister of agriculture) from Camp David, apprised him of the impasse over the settlements, and suggested that he phone Begin and express the view, as a recognized military authority and known hawk, that there was no military justification for refusing to dismantle them. It was a fateful conversation. With Sharon's right-wing legitimization, Begin took the historic step that clinched the summit's success, agreeing to submit the issue to the Knesset.[56]

Partisan politics and coalition maintenance thus had a clear impact on the nature of the DMP. Through adroit political maneuvering, however, Begin was able to prevent them from having a decisive influence on the substance of the negotiations and their outcome. The practice of keeping as much information secret as possible, of "keeping his cards close to his chest," was his primary means of addressing the political challenges. If neither the cabinet nor the public really knew what was going on, fewer demands could be made of him and he could conduct the negotiations in relative safety, presenting matters for cabinet and Knesset approval only once they had largely become faits accomplis.[57] In Israel's leak-prone environment, this approach also suited the needs of the negotiating process itself.

Begin's decision to make the Camp David Accords contingent on Knesset approval—peace with Egypt in exchange for a full withdrawal from Sinai, dismantlement of the settlements, and Palestinian clauses—was a master stroke. By placing the onus on the Knesset, in effect saying "peace is in your hands," he circumvented what would have otherwise been an extraordinarily divisive and possibly insurmountable challenge. As it was, he barely carried his own party, and the Accords would not have been passed without opposition support (Labor).

Three factors greatly strengthened Begin's ability to withstand the political pressures. First, most of the opposition in the Knesset at the time was considerably more moderate than Begin's Likud and supported his efforts, if anything pressing for greater flexibility. Right-wing opposition in the Knesset was limited.

Second, Begin enjoyed nearly unchallenged control of his party and coalition throughout most of the process. The hard-liners did raise objections, and the Likud's Knesset faction and party organs became scenes of raging debate, as did the cabinet. Begin was forced to make occasional rhetorical concessions and engage in political maneuvering, including the critical decision to place final responsibility on the Knesset. His overall control of the party and coalition, however, was such that the problem was manageable most of the time.[58]

Finally, Israel was united, from left to right, by the desire for peace with Egypt, and disagreement, extensive as it was, was over the extent of the concessions to be made, not the principle. The Sadat initiative had transformed public expectations in Israel, and the cabinet enjoyed broad public support throughout the process. In late July 1978, for example, after months of stalled talks, when the prospects for success appeared bleakest, 60% approved of its conduct of the negotiations.[59] Opposition to the final agreement was thus partly tempered by a shared recognition of its vital importance. The right, too, sought peace and did not wish to bear public blame for preventing it.

Politicization, coalition politics, and public opinion thus had a strong impact on the nature of the decision-making process, but not on its substance, nor on the outcome of the negotiations. The posited pathology was thus manifested at only a moderate level.

## Pathology 3: Semiorganized Anarchy

The cabinet and MCoD met extensively throughout the negotiating process but with rare exception were not the true locus of decision making, nor did they constitute effective forums for policy debate. Indeed, they were was kept in the dark throughout much of the negotiations, and most issues of importance were brought before them only after the fact, once it was too late to adopt alternative policies or meaningfully shape events. Begin and Dayan's reporting to the cabinet was selective, incomplete, and untimely, designed to present just that part of the picture that suited their negotiating needs and to isolate themselves from the political pressures that threatened to derail the talks.

In the atmosphere of historic anticipation that engulfed Israel after Sadat announced his visit, it would have been reasonable to presume that the cabinet would have conducted extensive deliberations in preparation for the talks. In fact, *no* cabinet discussions were held, with the exception of the supremely important issue of whether to permit the then opposition leader Shimon Peres to address the Knesset after Sadat and Begin. Weizman, at the time in the hospital, described his dismay upon discovering that the cabinet had not devoted a single meeting to substantive discussion of the impending visit. Both of Begin's historic concessions during Sadat's visit—withdrawal from Sinai and West Bank autonomy—were made solely on the basis of consultations with Dayan, who opposed the latter, and were presented to the cabinet as faits accomplis. Neither Weizman nor even Dayan were confident that Begin fully briefed them on the substance of his talks with Sadat.[60]

Dayan's second round of talks with Tohami in December 1977, in which he presented a more fleshed out autonomy proposal, was held, as with the first round, without the cabinet's knowledge. During the MCoD meeting following the talks, both Dayan and Begin insisted that no changes could be made to the plan, even though Dayan had told Tohami that it was subject to cabinet approval, on the grounds that Sadat had already accepted it as a basis for negotiations. Begin presented the proposal on a take-it-or-leave-it basis and stated that he was leaving the very next day to present it to Carter. The ministers protested that one meeting was insufficient to consider such a major departure and that Begin was confronting them with no choice at all, but with Begin leaving for the United States, their hands were tied and the proposal was approved unanimously. Upon his return, Begin first presented the plan to the full cabinet. He opened the meeting by stressing, once again, that no substantive changes were possible, this time because the plan had already been presented to Carter.[61]

By March 1978 significant differences had emerged between Begin and Dayan on one side and Weizman on the other, with the latter threatening to resign over the new settlements being established in Sinai.[62] The close relationship Weizman had developed with Sadat also became a source of distrust in the cabinet. Begin and Dayan feared that Weizman's enthusiasm for the peace process enabled Sadat to take advantage of him, and as a result they often excluded him from their sensitive consultations, including those prior to and during Camp David.[63]

Carter's questionnaire and "suggested" responses on the final status of the West Bank, in May 1978, elicited three weeks of fierce debate in the cabinet, during which Begin, Dayan, and Weizman each threatened to resign on one or more occasions. At the cabinet meeting of June 12, a clear majority coalesced in favor of a positive response to the United States, but Begin was adamant, staking his leadership on the issue, and a vote was postponed. In the end, with three threatened resignations hanging in the air, a compromise was reached and the cabinet decided on a partially favorable response.[64]

The cabinet learned of the two major concessions Dayan made at Leeds in July (i.e., acceptance of the principle of territorial compromise on the West Bank and willingness to discuss its "final status"), in contravention of its decisions, only after his return. However, having originally decided otherwise only because of Begin's stance, it now approved the new proposals, this time with the premier's support.[65]

Begin accepted the American invitation to Camp David immediately, without waiting for cabinet approval or even consulting with Dayan. As with the Sadat visit the previous year, the cabinet did not hold any substantive meetings prior to the summit, and when Begin submitted the Camp David Accords to it for approval, the ministers were thunderstruck. They were united in the fear that Begin had begun a process that not only had resulted in the dismantlement of the Sinai settlements but would undermine Israel's control of the West Bank.[66]

Begin, however, was firmly in charge. His control of the cabinet was nearly complete, and with the exception of the Israeli response to Carter's questionnaire, he did not encounter significant difficulty in gaining cabinet approval at any point. Ministers who disagreed with him often found it prudent to support him openly; Weizman, who was more confrontational, found himself partly sidelined. Begin would update the cabinet as he deemed appropriate, but when pressed to do so at inopportune times, he would typically reply that he had nothing new to report, since he was "operating within the framework of the cabinet's Basic Guidelines" (the largely pro forma coalition agreement). Remarkably, he even used this justification on the eve of Sadat's visit, when virtually all of Israel's positions had been thrown into flux by this historic development. Even Dayan was never sure that Begin had fully briefed him. Other ministers were "starved for information."[67]

Dayan and Weizman did, at times, go beyond Begin's positions on a number of occasions. Weizman suspected that Begin used them to do the "dirty work," that is, make any concessions that were flagrantly in contravention of Likud ideology, while he ostensibly remained loyal to it. Dayan, for the most part, played the role of loyal subordinate, adhered to his positions publicly, and then worked behind the scenes to adapt them to the evolving negotiations. Usually Begin would come around and these occasions would prove to be turning points in the negotiations.[68]

Begin had to maneuver extensively to obtain cabinet and Knesset approval at the different stages of the process, but he was very much in charge, thereby disproving this part of the posited pathology. The dysfunctional nature of the cabinet, conversely, was fully substantiated. The data on leaks were insufficient to substantiate a claim.

## Pathology 4: An Uninstitutionalized Process

In May 1977, following twenty-nine years in opposition, Begin led the Likud to its first electoral victory. The most reviled figure in Israeli political history, a pariah from his days as the leader of a pre-independence underground movement, Begin finally had his chance for national power and the opportunity to sweep away all of the old humiliations and gain his rightful place among Israel's founding fathers.

The Sadat visit and peace process provided the setting. The hawk known for his hard-line approach would show that he, too, was capable of grand measures. "For twenty-eight years they said that if elected I would bring catastrophe upon the state, but see what happened once I was given the chance," Begin would later say. Whereas Ben-Gurion had led the armed struggle for independence, Begin would begin the process of reconciliation with the Arabs and sign Israel's first peace treaty.[69]

Begin believed that the step-by-step approach, which had been the basis of the peace process up to that time, weakened Israel by requiring incremental concessions, without providing the true payoff it sought—peace—and that this approach had run its course. Always a leader of sweeping vision, Begin sought to transform Israel's circumstances radically, by achieving full peace treaties.[70] Throughout his life, however, Begin had maintained an uncompromising commitment to the indivisibility of the Land of Israel, and retention of Judea and Samaria and their ultimate annexation were his foremost political objectives. In pursuit of this end, there is broad consensus that he was even willing to cede Sinai in exchange. Begin thus sought to reach a separate peace with Egypt, independent of the Palestinian issue, throughout the negotiations.[71]

Dayan believed that Begin had a broad and long-standing view of the Arab-Israel conflict and of the means of addressing it, which precluded a need for policy planning and into which he was able to incorporate the events under way, despite his full appreciation of their historic significance. Begin's refusal to meet with Head of MI Gazit, to discuss the position paper the latter had drafted prior to the Sadat visit, lends credence to this conclusion.[72] In pursuit of his objectives, however, Begin was capable of conceptual flexibility, and he began adapting his positions immediately following Sadat's historic visit. The autonomy plan is a primary example, as were the major concessions he made at Camp David, including on heretofore unacceptable Palestinian clauses.

In 1977 Dayan was a man in distress. Hero of the Sinai Campaign and even more so the Six-Day War, darling of the Israeli and international media, Dayan had been excoriated in Israel since the Yom Kippur War debacle. Falling from the heights of public adulation, he was reviled for the military disarray that had cost thousands of lives and endangered Israel's very existence. With Labor's defeat in May 1977, it appeared that his public career was over and with it the prospects of easing the agony of 1973.[73] It thus must have seemed to Dayan like a heaven-sent opportunity when Begin, to the consternation of all, asked him to join his government as foreign minister. Though Dayan would prove the most skeptical of the three lead negotiators, becoming convinced of Egypt's sincerity only after nearly a year of talks, the diplomatic creativity he demonstrated was crucial to the talks' ultimate success.

Weizman completed the negotiating triumvirate. A flamboyant former pilot, Air Force commander, and chief of the Operations Branch, Weizman had been a primary architect of Israel's crushing victory in 1967. He was also the architect of the Likud electoral victory in 1977 and was widely perceived as the leading candidate to succeed Begin. Weizman threw himself into the peace talks with all of the unbridled energy for which he was known, as well as with the drive of a father whose son had been severely wounded in battle and whose personal agony was manifest.[74] His enthusiasm and the special relationship he forged with Sadat helped ensure the talks' continuation and ultimate success.

The Sadat visit and subsequent negotiations were a psychological earthquake for all three, transforming peace from a distant dream into a tangible reality. Begin was in a state of emotional anxiety in the days preceding the visit, imbued with a sense of mission, his speeches replete with biblical and other historic images. The sense of historic mission, fully shared by Weizman and Dayan, continued throughout the process, as did Begin's tendency to withdraw psychologically at times of importance, for example, before proposing the autonomy plan.[75]

Begin clearly engaged in "cognitive restructuring" behaviors, such as denial and bolstering, on a number of occasions, especially in his justifications of Camp David's Palestinian clauses. Although part of this may have been tactical, as a means of "marketing" the more controversial parts of the agreement, Begin apparently believed some of his own rhetoric, for example, that the agreement ensured future Israeli control over Judea and Samaria. Weizman and Dayan approached the talks with greater pragmatism, but all three were caught up in a great historical drama and emotion played an important role.

Dayan and Weizman, career officers and defense leaders, had spent a lifetime viewing Egypt in military terms, as a series of targets to be destroyed. Weizman stressed the wrenching emotional experiences all three of them underwent throughout the talks, portraying the challenges to their psychological predispositions as the greatest they faced. Dayan described Camp David as "an agonizing psychological and ideological crisis" in which long and deeply held views had to be abandoned. For Begin, the impassioned visionary, all of Israel's adversaries conjured up past visions of Jewish persecution.[76]

It was thus hardly surprising that many of the informal exchanges they held with their Egyptian interlocutors revolved around past battles. With five wars behind them, especially the still fresh Yom Kippur War, it was not easy for the Israeli leaders to begin thinking of Egypt in terms of peace. The wounds and experiences of a lifetime were still raw and the past continually intruded on their attempts to forge the future. Moreover, the subjects under negotiation, particularly the Sinai settlements and future of the West Bank, were emotionally and ideologically charged issues, which had occupied all three throughout their lives. The negotiations' outcome would also have an important, possibly decisive, impact on their political fortunes.

A clear disconnect existed between the extensive information and assessments generated by the system and the absence of virtually any policy planning by Begin, Dayan, and to a lesser extent Weizman. All three relied primarily on what they learned from their personal involvement in the talks, rather than on input from the national security agencies. Begin had MI's assessment prior to Sadat's visit recalled, and no use was made of the Blue Book prior to Camp David.

Not only did Begin and Dayan keep the different ministries and agencies out of the process and in the dark regarding developments, thereby precluding appropriate interagency coordination, but policy integration and coordination was limited even within the negotiating triumvirate. Dayan did not believe that he was fully briefed by Begin, even though they consulted with each other extensively, and both partly sidelined Weizman. Astonishingly, the triumvirate did not even meet in preparation for Camp David.

Lacking Begin's ideological bona fides and political mastery, arguably no one else could have made the concessions needed to reach agreement. At a minimum, the nature of the process was very much a function of Begin the man and leader and would have been very different in his absence. Dayan and Weizman, too, made important personal contributions. The highly idiosyncratic nature of decision making was thus manifested to a high degree. The data regarding policy disconnects were insufficient to enable a conclusion. The information regarding policy integration and coordination was also limited but supports a conclusion that it was deeply flawed.

## Pathology 5: Primacy of the Defense Establishment

In a highly centralized process in which Begin and Dayan were the locus of decision making, the IDF and defense establishment as a whole were the primary source of expertise and bureaucratic player nonetheless. The fact that Begin sought so assiduously to keep the IDF and other agencies out of the DMP is, in itself, an indication of his concern regarding their possible influence had they been involved and adopted contrary positions.

The defense establishment's actual impact on the talks, however, was surprisingly limited. From the initial secret contacts up to Camp David, Begin and Dayan made most of the decisions on their own. Major concessions, such as the withdrawal from Sinai and the Palestinian clauses at Camp David, were made without even consulting the IDF and other agencies, in some cases even without their knowledge. Begin made little use of the policy papers prepared by the IDF and paid little heed to CoS Gur's objections. Though the negotiations had enormous defense ramifications, Begin clearly believed that the decisions to be made were political and the defense establishment's role was limited.

This was true of Defense Minister Weizman as well. Of the three chief Israeli negotiators, he was clearly the junior one, with Begin and Dayan making the real decisions and often excluding him. This unusual state of affairs—the defense minister and establishment are almost always far more influential than the MFA—did not, however, translate into increased influence for the latter. Dayan's role in the talks was personal, not institutional, and the ministry remained largely uninvolved.

The posited pathology was thus only partially substantiated. The IDF and defense establishment were the primary sources of expertise and bureaucratic player, but their impact on the substance of the talks was limited.

**Table 2 Manifestation of Pathologies in Camp David I**

| Category | Manifestation | Rating |
|---|---|---|
| Unplanned Process | Absence of Policy Planning, Objectives, and Options | High |
| | Improvisation | Mod. |
| | Sequential Decision Making | Low |
| Politicized Process | Politics Reign Supreme | Mod. |
| | Coalition Maintenance | Mod. |
| | Public Opinion | Mod. |
| Semiorganized Anarchy | Premier Not in Charge | Low |
| | Dysfunctional Cabinet | High |
| | Leaks | ID |
| Uninstitutionalized Process | Idiosyncratic | High |
| | Policy Disconnects | ID |
| | Insufficient Coordination and Integration | High |
| Primacy of Defense Establishment | Primary Source of Expertise | High |
| | Primary Bureaucratic Player | High |
| | Positions Prevail | Low |

Mod. = Moderate
ID = Insufficient data

# CHAPTER FOUR

# The Makings of a Young Lion

## The Lavi Combat Aircraft, 1980–1987

> When the Americans went to the moon, it was not just the moon that
> was their goal. The goal was . . . the scientific and technological
> development along the way. Maybe if we just produced chocolates
> it would be cheaper. . . . But it would not provide any real scientific
> achievement. For that, you must take real risks.
>
> —Shimon Peres, July 1986

> "Israel," it seems, is simply the first word in "Israel Aircraft
> Industries."
>
> —*Jerusalem Post* editorial, August 21, 1987

In 1974 Israel Aircraft Industries (IAI) stood both at the pinnacle of success
and at the edge of an industrial abyss. Following years of development, the
Kfir, an upgraded version of the French Mirage fighter, entered production.
For a nation as small as Israel, production of a modern combat aircraft was
a signal technological achievement. With the Kfir in the production stage,
however, IAI no longer had a major, future-oriented project to serve as a
focus of organizational drive. The desire to preserve this unique technological capability and to avoid the need to lay off the highly skilled Kfir
development team was the primary motivation behind IAI's interest in
producing an entirely self-developed aircraft.[1]

If IAI's interests were self-evident, Israel's were not. Only a handful of
nations, all major powers, are capable of producing combat aircraft, and in
the 1980s even Britain and Germany found it prudent to engage in coproduction. Israel's decision to produce the Lavi ("Young Lion") was thus either
a case of overwhelming strategic imperative or folly.

## The Strategic Setting

The origins of the Lavi lie in the French arms embargo of 1967. France had been Israel's leading ally and primary source of arms up to that time, and its stunning reversal of policy was viewed in Israel both as a betrayal and as a grave threat to Israeli security. The deep national trauma it caused led to a firm resolve to reduce Israel's dependence on foreign weapons suppliers.[2]

The idea of weapons self-sufficiency was certainly not new—indeed, it had been an article of faith from the pre-state days, when Israel first began establishing domestic arms industries. Nevertheless, the shock and fear caused by the embargo led to a change in the guiding concept: from a focus on smaller systems with unique Israeli applications or on weapons that simply could not be procured abroad, Israel would now also produce major weapons, including tanks and aircraft.[3]

As this new policy was taking form, the nascent Israeli-American military relationship was also emerging. From today's vantage point it may be hard to remember, but Israel's overall relationship with the United States was limited until the late 1960s and Israel had received its first American aircraft and tanks only a few years earlier, following difficult and protracted negotiations. It was only after the 1973 war that this military relationship became institutionalized and came to be viewed by both sides as a virtual American commitment.

The mammoth Arab arms buildup in the years following the 1973 war made the need for large-scale Israeli armament a moot point, especially in the air. A race was on, and with the Yom Kippur War debacle in the background, Israel had no alternative but to compete. The Israel Air Force (IAF) had long been the spearhead of the entire IDF and an area of clear supremacy, which enabled Israel to counter the Arabs' quantitative advantage.[4]

The accepted wisdom in Israel was that self-produced weapons were usually considerably cheaper than those procured abroad, and as long as this was the case, Israel had a clear strategic interest in self-sufficiency. The Lavi's unique operational capabilities were also an important consideration. Unlike all other IAF aircraft, the Lavi would be the only one that Arab air forces did not fly as well, thus providing an element of operational surprise. Moreover, the Lavi was the embodiment of the lessons the IAF had learned from the 1973 war, when it lost 20% of its aircraft to surface-to-air missile (SAM) defenses, and was tailored to its combat requirements. Whereas all other Western aircraft at the time were primarily air-superiority fighters, the Lavi was designed primarily for ground attack, with high SAM survivability. Israel's F-15s and F-16s would be deployed against Arab air forces, the Lavi against missile defenses and ground forces.[5]

The United States did not doubt Israel's need for new aircraft; indeed, in the mid-1980s it considered the need for three hundred new aircraft, over twenty years, to be a given.[6] Israel, however, was never fully confident of the US commitment to supply advanced aircraft, especially in a timely fashion. The Nixon administration had delayed the sale of aircraft during the 1969–1971 War of Attrition and of arms generally during the early days of the 1973 war. The Ford administration conducted a half-year-long "reassessment" of US policy toward Israel, during which it refused to sign new arms agreements, whereas the Reagan administration temporarily suspended shipment of F-16s to Israel on three occasions. As Ariel Sharon put it, "I always regarded aircraft as a political weapon. Every time somebody wanted to threaten or pressure us, the first step was to stop selling planes."[7]

Repeated American rejections of Israel's requests to coproduce F-16s in the late 1970s and early 1980s were the decisive factor behind the decision to pursue self-sufficiency. It rapidly emerged, however, that self-development would not greatly diminish Israel's dependence on the United States. The decision to develop the Lavi in 1980 was predicated on American willingness to supply the engine, by far the most complex and expensive component of a combat aircraft. The decision in May 1981 to change the engine, a fundamental conceptual redesign, again required US agreement, and by 1983 it had become clear that Israel did not have the financial wherewithal, or in some areas the technology, to develop a frontline aircraft on its own. Israel's request to utilize US military aid to fund development of the Lavi, first made in 1980 and approved in late 1983, was the ultimate proof of its dependence on the United States, even for this "self-sufficiency" motivated project.[8]

In 1983 Congress authorized $550 million in annual Foreign Military Sales (FMS) funds for the Lavi, of which $250 million, later increased to $300 million, could be spent in Israel. FMS funding transformed the project and changed Israel's strategic calculus. For all practical purposes, the Lavi became a joint project and for the first time now had a sound financial basis on which to proceed.[9] Paradoxically, US funding also became an obstacle to the project's termination, since it would result in the "loss" of the annual $300 million allocated for expenditure in Israel. Moreover, having fought for FMS funding and having already spent $800 million in US aid on the Lavi by the end of 1984, Israel was hardly in a position to say the equivalent of "sorry, we blew it" and cancel the project. The blow to its credibility would have been severe.

In 1984 the Department of Defense (DoD), now that it was funding the Lavi, began taking a harder look at the project and concluded that it was an inefficient use of US assistance funds, given the option of procuring American aircraft. Whereas the "American factor" had been a major reason behind the original decision to build an Israeli aircraft and American aid had subsequently become a financial prerequisite for the project's continuation, the United States now became the driving force for termination.[10]

In late 1984 Defense Minister Rabin decided to reassess the project, at least partly in response to DoD data that showed that development costs had been seriously underestimated. In late 1985 the United States submitted the "Zakheim Report,"[11] which received vast press coverage in Israel and caused a severe shock. Although it substantiated the operational concept behind the Lavi, the report's cost estimates were completely at odds with Israel's. Whereas the Ministry of Defense (MoD) had estimated per-unit costs at $15.2 million, Zakheim estimated $22.1 million, a whopping gap of 45%, while his estimate of the total life-cycle costs was 40.1% higher. Moreover, Zakheim found that an annual budget of $937 million would be required during the development stage, whereas Rabin had set an annual cap of $550 million. The findings were so extreme that they set a process of reassessment in motion in Israel.[12]

Almost at the same time as the Zakheim Report began changing Israel's fundamental perception of the project, Congress lifted the restriction that limited use of the $300 million annual allocation for expenditure in Israel to the Lavi. In so doing, it in effect eliminated the economic motivation for the project's continuation—the loss of the FMS funds—and provided supporters of termination with a decisive card in their favor. From this point on, debate in Israel was no longer framed in terms of the project's termination and consequent loss of FMS funds but rather in terms of possible alternatives.[13]

In an attempt to reach an impartial assessment of the project's costs, Congress commissioned the General Accounting Office (GAO) to conduct a comparative analysis of the MoD and Zakheim estimates. The GAO report significantly narrowed the gap but did not change the overall picture. According to the GAO, the per-unit costs (assuming three hundred aircraft) would be $17.8 million, compared with MoD's $15.2 million and Zakheim's $22.1. If this was a partial vindication for those who claimed that Zakheim's figures were inflated, the GAO was even more extreme in its estimate of the total annual expenditures required. Whereas Israel had set a cap of $550 million and Zakheim estimated that nearly $1 billion would be required, the GAO estimated that this might reach $1.4 billion.[14]

Throughout 1986, following the Zakheim and GAO reports, the United States increased pressure on Israel to terminate the project. The secretaries of defense and state both sent letters to Premier Peres, Defense Minister Rabin, and Foreign Minister Shamir in which they urged termination. During visits to Washington, both Peres and Rabin were officially requested to scrap the project and buy F-16s instead. The Pentagon began bureaucratic foot-dragging, intentionally delaying licenses IAI needed in order to sign contracts with American subcontractors.[15]

In late 1986, a year after the Zakheim Report, the United States submitted the "Zakheim options," possible alternative uses of US aid, which further strengthened the Lavi's opponents. Of the five options proposed, Israel considered two worthy of serious consideration (partial coproduction of F-16s or coproduction with Israeli avionics). An analysis of Zakheim's data by the Lavi Project Administration (LPA) now showed that Israel would be able to buy no more than one hundred Lavis, but the project would be economically viable only if a minimum of two hundred were ordered. This was a drastic decrease from the original plan for four hundred, subsequently reduced to three hundred and then to 210, and cast serious doubts about the entire project.[16]

In June 1987 Rabin obtained US agreement to allow continued expenditure of the FMS funds in Israel, thereby making the decision to terminate easier. Some time earlier, the United States had already agreed to use FMS assistance to cover termination costs. After three years of equivocation, stemming largely from his fear of the termination costs and loss of FMS funds, Rabin now had the wherewithal to take a clear stand and terminate the project.[17]

## Pathology 1: An Unplanned Process

As a weapons development program, the considerations involved in the Lavi process should have been essentially technological, operational, and financial, not ones of deep political or ideological conviction, as in all of the other case studies in this book. As such, they lent themselves to quantification and to decision making under circumstances of comparatively low uncertainty, especially after US willingness to supply a new aircraft had been assured. For example, the contention that development of a combat aircraft would be an engine of growth for the entire national economy could have been compared with other investments, with reasonable accuracy, to ascertain their relative utilities. Moreover, the Lavi DMP lasted over thirteen years, from the early designs until the project's termination in 1987, or six and a half years from the decision on the Lavi configuration itself. Time constraints were thus not of great importance and in-depth systematic planning could have been conducted. Reality was different.

Numerous options were explored by the defense establishment and MoF throughout the Lavi process. During Weizman's meeting on February 8, 1980, for example, in which he approved the Lavi, three options for coproduction with the United States were considered, along with three options for self-development. The MoD financial adviser's review of the project in January 1982 studied four different options.[18] These options were not presented, however, to the cabinet and MCoD, which were repeatedly given binary "take it or leave it" choices. When the Lavi was first presented to the MCoD in February 1980 and again five years later, in July–August

1985, no other options were submitted and it was merely asked to approve the project.

During the final cabinet meetings in 1987, numerous options were initially presented, but the entire process rapidly deteriorated into a political squabble, as the cabinet sought to avoid what was essentially a painful choice between two bad options: continuation, despite ruinous costs and strong American opposition, or termination. The options raised toward the end were absurd, with both Peres and Shamir proposing production of just seventy-five Lavis, which would have made it the most expensive aircraft of its kind in history, and the former even proposing the "Lavi 2000," a ludicrous plan to develop a "next-generation" aircraft but never actually manufacture it. The "IDF option," the ostensible alternative proposed at the end (which prescribed termination of the Lavi, purchase of one hundred F-16s without coproduction, and utilization of the large remaining budget of $3.5 billion for IDF modernization projects), was hastily devised, to provide the cabinet with a face-saving means of voting for termination.[19]

The failure to systematically formulate policy objectives was no less egregious than the faulty definition of options. The IAF and IAI were charged with formulating the aircraft's operational specifications, but Israel's overall strategic objectives were never considered, certainly not by the MCoD or cabinet. Employment was a primary motivation, but a cost-benefit comparison of the Lavi and other possible projects was never conducted. Self-sufficiency was also a primary motivation, but Israel's dependence on the United States for the engine, funding, and certain technologies should have negated it.

The improvisational and sequential character of the Lavi DMP was apparent from the start. In 1974, with the Kfir in production, IAI began considering designs for a new aircraft. In the absence of any official specification of its intended capabilities or of the strategic purpose it was to serve, IAI presented a number of options to Defense Minister Peres, who approved limited funding for continued design work. Concomitantly, the IAF conducted a study of its requirements and concluded by 1975 that its next aircraft would be a dual-engine attack fighter, equal to or better than the F-15 and F-16.[20]

During this early stage, which lasted until Weizman's formal decision to produce the Lavi in February 1980, the IDF, IAF, and MoD were lukewarm toward the idea of a self-developed aircraft, preferring procurement of American F-15s and F-16s. In 1978 IAF commander Ivri stated that he did not consider self-development a top priority and would even be opposed if it was funded by the defense budget. He further stressed that the IAF could not forgo even part of its procurement plans during the anticipated eight-year development period and would decide whether to purchase the new aircraft only after development had been completed.[21]

Weizman, appointed defense minister in May 1977, devoted little attention to the issue during his first eighteen months in office. Even then, he
engaged only in response to heavy pressure from IAI, which sought to
put the project on a more permanent footing by obtaining cabinet approval for a formal budget. Weizman, however, preferred to act on his
own recognizance and authorized IAI to employ two hundred engineers to
study possible configurations.[22]

In 1979, at Weizman's direction, work on the project swung into high
gear. The IAF was again directed to specify its future requirements, and
IAI was tasked with developing options to meet them. In September Weizman met with Secretary of Defense Harold Brown and presented three
options: procurement of American aircraft with partial coproduction in
Israel, full coproduction, or production of an Israeli aircraft. Weizman
sought to convince Brown that it was in the US interest that Israel develop
aircraft of its own, instead of antagonizing the Arab world by supplying
them to Israel. Brown received the idea coolly, stressing US willingness to
provide aircraft to Israel. The meeting ended with agreement on a US assessment of the IAF's future procurement plans, including options for coproduction.[23]

On February 8, 1980, without waiting for the American assessment, Weizman convened the decisive meeting on the new aircraft. Both CoS Rafael
Eitan and IAF commander Ivri favored American aircraft modified to meet
Israel's needs or coproduced in Israel. The MoF opposed self-development,
on the grounds that it would not be economically viable, since the United
States was unlikely to approve exports, and because coproduction would
significantly reduce development risks. IAI, conversely, pressed the case for
self-development and made it clear that it would "shake the heavens" if the
decision was made to opt for coproduction, unless Israel (i.e., IAI) gained
the right to produce most of the future aircraft.[24]

Weizman opted for self-development. The Lavi was to be an inexpensive
single-engine "workhorse," designed primarily for ground attack missions,
to complement the air-superiority role of the frontline F-15s and F-16s. The
decision envisaged a future force of four hundred Lavis, together with one
hundred frontline American aircraft, with estimated development costs of
$750 million, plus $200 million for the engine. The type of engine was not
specified but was "presumed" to be the F404, with American willingness to
supply it a prerequisite for the entire project. Beyond this, however, the
Lavi was still largely an unknown quantity, and Weizman instructed the
IAF and IAI to jointly formulate its intended operational roles and specifications. In reality, then, the decisive February 8 decision was just a general
directive providing for the design of an Israeli aircraft. The details remained
to be worked out.[25]

On February 20, 1980, Weizman presented the Lavi program to the MCoD
for the first time. Approval was granted that very day, over the renewed

objections of the CoS and IAF commander. To placate the minister of finance, who was adamantly opposed, the MCoD made its approval contingent on the outcome of a joint MoD-MoF assessment of the project's economic ramifications, but it was never carried out and the project went ahead nonetheless.

The United States approved the sale of the F404 engine a few weeks later, before the IAF and IAI had time to carry out Weizman's directive that they further refine the plane's operational roles and specifications. The vitally important decision on the engine was thus made by default.[26]

Weizman's resignation in May 1980 provided the IAF, which had been opposed from the beginning to his concept of an inexpensive "workhorse," with a new opportunity. Although it could not officially overturn the decision, it now set about designing the Lavi in such a way that it came close to being the frontline aircraft it preferred, which would require a far more powerful engine, the PW1120. During the meetings on the engine, the IAF disagreed openly with the IDF, to which the former is subordinate. IAF commander Ivri argued that the "Big Lavi" (with the PW1120) was the optimal option, since the "Small Lavi" (with the F404) did not meet the IAF's operational requirements, while CoS Eitan continued to express the IDF's opposition to self-development and preference for procurement of F-16s.[27]

On May 29, 1981, Premier Begin, now also the acting defense minister, convened the decisive meeting on the engine. The MoF adamantly opposed the Big Lavi, arguing that the decision was not really about the engine, but the future of the entire national budget and the relative shares of the defense establishment and IAF therein. Begin, however, accepted the IAF's recommendation and decided that the Lavi would be equipped with the PW1120.[28] The decision fundamentally altered the entire operational concept behind the Lavi, turning it from an inexpensive workhorse into a frontline aircraft, which was beyond Israel's resources and ultimately sealed the project's fate.

Sharon was appointed defense minister in September 1981 and announced a review of various projects, for budgetary reasons, including the Lavi. The IDF continued to favor procurement of F-16s, arguing that this would tie up fewer resources and leave greater latitude for the purchase of weapons for the ground forces. The MoF proposed that Israel seek US agreement to co-produce the F-16 or F-18 and rejected Sharon's request for special supplemental funding for the Lavi. The IAF continued to press for the Big Lavi. Faced with this conflicting advice, Sharon announced a project "freeze" pending completion of the review. The final decision, he stated, would have a critical impact on Israel's defense and economy for twenty-five years and would thus have to reflect its overall military needs.[29]

Sharon ultimately decided on continuation for two primary reasons, having little to do with budgetary or operational factors. One was political:

Sharon retorted to the MoF's objections to the project that "the premier wants this plane and none of your games will help." The other was strategic: the Reagan administration had temporarily suspended the supply of F-16s to Israel, in response to Israel's bombing of the Iraqi reactor, which rekindled fears of dependence on foreign weapons suppliers.[30]

The price Sharon paid for continuation was heavy. The Lavi would be financed by the defense budget, not by the special supplemental budget he sought, and an attempt would have to be made to find an American partner, to reduce development costs and risks. Sharon was in a bind; he had an aircraft but not the funds to develop it. A steering committee was established to propose means of financing the project, but it disbanded without finding a solution. Sharon ostensibly intensified Israel's efforts to find an American partner but never truly pursued this.[31] His involvement in the preparations for the imminent invasion of Lebanon, in June 1982, may partly account for this.

In 1983, Moshe Arens, Sharon's successor, succeeded in obtaining US agreement to fund the project through American military assistance (FMS). This crucial breakthrough provided it with a clear budgetary basis and appeared at the time to have ensured the project's future.[32]

Rabin succeeded Arens in 1984. Although he had been opposed to self-development from the beginning, Rabin now maintained that circumstances had changed. Development was being funded by the United States, the FMS funds earmarked for expenditure in Israel would be "lost" if the project was terminated, and Israel's credibility in the United States would be severely undermined. Rabin thus maintained that the Lavi had passed the "point of no-return." He stipulated, however, that continuation would remain contingent on US agreement to fund 50% of the production stage, as well as development, and that the total annual expenditure on the project would not exceed $550 million, even during production.[33]

Rabin's decision was actually a "punt," which allowed the project to muddle along for three more years. By that time, even IAF support had grown weak, and Rabin, after considering the "Zakheim options," finally forced a decision on termination. He still feared the political ramifications of this highly unpopular decision, however, and referred it to the cabinet, to avoid having to bear sole responsibility.[34]

A special IDF task force was set up at this time to reexamine its priorities. Rabin decided that if the cabinet rejected the "IDF option"—that is, the task force's ultimate recommendation—only 150 Lavis would be produced, down from the 210 he had decided on the year before and the initial plan for four hundred.[35] In August 1987, with development now largely complete, the cabinet voted for termination, but only after considering a variety of outlandish proposals to save the project.

The posited unplanned, improvisational, and sequential nature of the process was substantiated to a high degree. In the early pre-Lavi years, the entire process was a "shoestring" operation, but matters did not substantially change even after Weizman made the formal decision to develop the Lavi. The engine and other crucial design elements were not specified and the sources of funding were unclear. Begin later changed the operational concept completely. The endgame, a self-developed plane, was clear, but not much beyond that was, and it became evident, almost from the start, that the objective of self-sufficiency would not be achieved. What might have been a cautious incremental approach, had Weizman's decision been pursued, devolved into sequentialism.

## Pathology 2: A Politicized Process

Until 1987 the Lavi was almost entirely an internal defense establishment matter and even the few cabinet meetings held on the project were perfunctory. Consequently, it was largely immune during this period from partisan politics and issues of coalition maintenance. Events changed dramatically during the final series of cabinet meetings in the summer of 1987.

The meetings were held in an atmosphere of intense political pressure. The three leading candidates to succeed Shamir as premier (Levy, Arens, and Sharon) exerted heavy pressure in favor of continuation, with Arens, Shamir's closest ally, even threatening to resign. The Likud Party convention voted in favor of continuation, in an attempt to influence the cabinet. Minister Yitzhak Modai, a strong opponent of the project ever since his tenure as finance minister, reversed himself when his rival, the current finance minister, proposed termination.[36]

Shamir and Peres initially coordinated positions and even agreed to postpone the decision when it appeared that the cabinet might support termination. As pressure for termination grew, however, they began scrambling to find means of placing the blame on the other side. Shamir directed IAI to formulate a new plan to cut development costs by almost half, through wage cuts and greater efficiency, and to reduce manufacturing costs by producing just seventy-five Lavis.[37] The idea of producing just seventy-five aircraft had first been raised by Peres a few months earlier, as a means of keeping the Lavi alive and maintaining IAI's industrial capabilities. With Shamir now supporting this as well, Peres, not to be outdone, proposed a tax increase to finance the budgetary shortfall and ultimately even proposed the preposterous idea of the "Lavi 2000."[38]

Toward the end of the series of cabinet meetings, any semblance of bipartisanship ended. The Likud, whose defense ministers (Weizman, Begin, Sharon, and Arens) had made the decisions to develop the Lavi, in contrast to the only limited design activities authorized by Peres and Rabin's decision to seek termination, accused Labor of trying to kill "the

Likud's plane." For the Likud the project was an excellent issue over which to wage the upcoming elections; indeed, most Labor ministers also remained in favor until the last minute, supporting Rabin and Peres's call for termination only when the Labor leaders exerted extreme pressure. Had they been allowed to vote freely, a majority would have supported continuation.[39]

The final cabinet vote was split along straight party lines: all Labor ministers voted for termination; all Likud ministers, with the sole exception of Finance Minister Nissim, for continuation. The final count was eleven for the Lavi, twelve against. In what was the equivalent of a cabinet dogfight, rather than serious policy deliberation, Labor "shot down" the Likud.

To truly understand the Lavi DMP, it must be placed in the broader context of Israel's national character. Established following the Holocaust and at war for survival for decades, the IDF and everything that went into making it a strong military force took on overwhelming importance for the public. Moreover, the public viewed the IDF not just as the guarantor of its security but as a primary focus of individual identification with the state, an important unifying factor in a society of highly diverse immigrants. IAI was considered a vital part of Israel's defense capabilities, and its achievements were a focus of great attention and pride. IAI was not "just another factory," and the Lavi was not "just another aircraft"—they belonged to the nation. From the time the Lavi's development became publicly known, the entire nation followed with rapt attention.[40]

To the "security conscious" element of Israel's character one has to add the somewhat messianic nature of the Zionist movement generally, as well as the sense, prevalent at the time, that the nation had been floundering in recent years. Tom Friedman, then the *New York Times*'s Israel correspondent, eloquently captured the spirit of Israel and the Lavi project:

> In Israel there is a cherished notion that the nation can always accomplish the impossible, no matter what the odds. The Lavi had its roots in the basic philosophy of Zionism: "If you will it, it is not a dream." This national motto came to mean that nothing was too large, audacious or inventive, including a fighter jet at a time when only major powers have the resources for them.[41]
>
> At a time when the Zionist revolution seems to be drifting at middle age, the Lavi has come to symbolize for many Israelis the old audacious spirit of striving and achieving far beyond their means, something that seemed to be a hallmark of Israel in its youth. The Lavi is to Israel what the Mercury space program was to America—a national project that justifies itself more in terms of pride and innovation than in pure economics.[42]

The Lavi swept the nation's collective imagination. Polls conducted in May 1987, on the eve of the final cabinet meetings, showed that 80% favored continuation and 67% were even willing to help pay for the Lavi through increased taxes. In August, at the end of the series of cabinet meetings, after months in which the media had been flooded with compelling reasons for termination, a full 63% still supported continuation.[43] No politician anywhere could take such sentiment lightly.

The Lavi also touched on Israel's national penchant for technology and the popular belief, fostered by the statist economic policies pursued during the early decades, that grand government-inspired projects could propel development of the economy and society as a whole. As a rapidly modernizing nation that sought to attract immigrants (and minimize emigration), Israel had long pursued a policy of broad governmental intervention in the economy, designed to promote employment and industrialization, especially in advanced areas. Development of a modern combat aircraft, it was argued, although a mammoth undertaking by Israel's standards, would greatly accelerate achievement of these goals and do so in the strategically important area of defense industries.[44] The Peres epigraph that began this chapter captures this best, as does a statement by a senior IAI official: "We must decide what kind of future we envision. . . . Do we intend to compete with Taiwan in the manufacturing of shirts, or will we produce sophisticated products? The Lavi will advance all of Israel's industry, which will achieve a technological breakthrough."[45]

Adding to the project's importance, IAI was the largest company in Israel, both in terms of employees and export earnings, and the Lavi was the largest project ever undertaken in Israel's history. By 1984, three thousand people were working on the Lavi at IAI alone, and this became a clear factor behind Rabin's decision to continue the project. By 1987, this number had risen to five thousand at IAI, there were a further five thousand in more than a hundred other firms, and this number was expected to rise greatly once the actual production stage began. Unsurprisingly, Israel's powerful trade unions fully supported the Lavi.[46]

Economics, however, also had an adverse impact on the Lavi's future. In 1984 Israel's economy was in a severe crisis. Inflation was skyrocketing, spurred by the ruinous economic mismanagement of the previous years and subsequently the costs of the 1982 invasion of Lebanon, ultimately reaching nearly 500%. Rabin's "reassessment" of the Lavi in late 1984 stemmed at least partly from the economic crisis. The emergency economic measures adopted in July 1985, including a 20% cut in the defense budget, turned the IDF decisively against the project. Even IAF support grew soft.[47]

Although some Israeli leaders, Arens most prominently, took a "Lavi at all costs" approach, it could not have been pursued over time in the absence of US financial assistance. The weight of budgetary constraints was such that Israel would ultimately have had no choice but to terminate the project (possibly only in the early production stage) or risk collapse of the IDF force structure.

The posited highly politicized nature of the process was incompletely substantiated. The final cabinet debates were highly politicized and public opinion played a major role in the process. The Lavi did rock the coalition, but because it presented no threat to the future of the politically deadlocked "National Unity Government" then in office, it did not require extraordinary efforts to preserve it.

## Pathology 3: Semiorganized Anarchy

The Lavi was Israel's foremost defense project for the better part of a decade, with vital ramifications for its defense posture, its relationship with the United States, and the economy. Its great importance notwithstanding, the premier became intensively involved in the issue only at the very end of the process, during the final cabinet debates on termination, and the cabinet's treatment of the issue was entirely dysfunctional.

The Lavi first reached the cabinet level in February 1980 in a meeting of the MCoD. The Lavi's missions and operational capabilities, engine requirements, and costs were not spelled out; no other options were raised; and the MCoD was not informed that both the CoS and IAF commander were opposed. Approval was nevertheless given that very day, but because Finance Minister Yigael Hurwitz adamantly insisted that the project's economic ramifications had not been fully considered, this approval was made contingent on the outcome of a joint MoD-MoF assessment.[48]

Both the rapidity and highly general character of the MCoD's decision are indicative of the "depth" of its deliberations. The idea of an Israeli-made aircraft was popular politically and so the MCoD was more than ready to give approval. None of the ministers, with the exception of Hurwitz, ever expressed concern over the fact that the joint assessment never took place.[49]

Over five and a half years passed before the next cabinet-level meetings on the Lavi were held, in 1985. The MCoD met twice and approved continuation with a degree of alacrity similar to its initial decision in 1980. Eight of the ten ministers voted in favor, including Premier Peres, Foreign Minister Shamir, and Defense Minister Rabin. The sole dissenters were Weizman, who correctly maintained that the Lavi had become an entirely different aircraft from the one originally approved, and the new finance minister, Modai, who was concerned that the treasury, not the MoD, would ultimately have to foot the project.[50]

In January 1986 the MCoD briefly returned to the Lavi. Weizman once again favored termination, but Peres refused on the grounds that it had just been reapproved half a year earlier. In contrast with his usual enthusiasm for the Lavi, however, Peres spoke in guarded terms and agreed with

Rabin's fatalistic contention that it was simply too late to stop it. In May 1986 the MCoD again reaffirmed its support.[51]

The first substantive cabinet deliberations on the Lavi took place only in 1987, seven years after the project's initial approval, by which time the issue had become its possible termination. Shamir, now premier, was cognizant of the political sensitivity of the issue and decided that it would be raised this time in the cabinet plenum, not the MCoD. Between May and August the cabinet held a series of eight marathon meetings, during which all of the relevant agencies presented data and assessments and all twenty-four ministers expressed their views at length, on one or more occasions. It was a bitter and drawn-out fight, culminating in the base political squabble between the Likud and Labor described earlier. The final decision was purely partisan, not a function of the overwhelming information presented.[52]

Leaks were not a problem in the Lavi case. The Lavi's general character was known to the public, and the development process and cabinet meetings received massive media coverage. The sensitive information, however, was in the Lavi's detailed operational capabilities, and they were carefully safeguarded, the vast media coverage notwithstanding.

The posited pathology regarding the semianarchic nature of the DMP was only partially substantiated. Shamir was unable to obtain approval for continuation during the final cabinet meetings, but since the Lavi had been dealt with only intermittently at the prime-ministerial level until that time, this in itself is insufficient evidence to support a conclusion that the premier was not in charge. Leaks were not an issue. The cabinet's treatment of the issue, conversely, was highly dysfunctional throughout, whether in its perfunctory initial approval of the project, its subsequent reaffirmations, and especially the farcical final debates on termination, thereby fully substantiating this dimension of the posited pathology.

## Pathology 4: An Uninstitutionalized Process

Four premiers, six defense and seven finance ministers, four chiefs of staff, and numerous senior officials were involved in the lengthy Lavi DMP.* All had their own strategic views, ideological beliefs, priorities, and personal styles, and all had an impact on the DMP, at times major. Although these differences were legitimate, the absence of a consistent long-term approach is deeply inimical to the development of major weapons systems, where periods of a decade or more between the initial design and actual deployment are common.

* Including the early pre-Lavi stage, prior to the official decision to develop it in 1980.

Weizman, appointed defense minister in May 1977, had formerly been IAF commander and was later the head of the IDF's Operations Branch during the 1967 war. An enthusiastic supporter of weapons self-sufficiency, he nevertheless believed that US aircraft were too expensive for Israel and that their procurement would require either an increase in the defense budget or a cut in the IAF force structure. Weizman thus favored an aircraft "mix," the Lavi for simpler ground attack missions and a limited number of advanced American aircraft for purposes of air superiority. This simpler concept would also have the advantage of reducing development risks, by tying up development funds for fewer years, thereby providing greater budgetary flexibility. Moreover, it would generate significant employment earlier than the more advanced options, since the production stage would be reached sooner, while still promoting a significant leap in Israel's industrial capabilities. In February 1980 Weizman thus decided on the Lavi, over the objections of the CoS and IAF commander.[53]

Begin, who succeeded Weizman as acting defense minister, was long known for his deep veneration of Israel's military leaders, whom he viewed as the new "fighting Jews," as opposed to the weak and oppressed ones of the Diaspora of his youth. As acting defense minister, Begin presided over the crucial meetings in which the decision to develop the Big Lavi, with the PW1120 engine, was made. During the final meeting on the issue on May 29, 1981, following months of deliberations, Begin was clearly irked by the MoF's request that the decision be postponed once again, rejecting its arguments out of hand:

> In operational matters it is not possible to act like Hamlet, to get up on the stage and talk; just words, words, words. We need deeds. This matter has been studied for four months and a decision will be reached today. . . . The problem we face is not economic or social [but operational]. Of course, everything is involved . . . [but] if the IAF Commander says that in his view it is preferable that we choose a certain engine, can we allow ourselves to reject his view?[54]

By approving the IAF's request for the Big Lavi, Begin completely overturned Weizman's original concept of a workhorse, turning it into a frontline aircraft. Since the IAF force structure would now be composed primarily of expensive aircraft, this also required a reduction in the planned number of Lavis from four hundred to three hundred. Moreover, Begin's decision meant that the developmental risks would be far greater, the timetable for delivery would be lengthier, and Israel might have to purchase advanced US aircraft just to tide the IAF over until the Lavi entered service.[55]

MoF director-general Sadan, who participated in some of the meetings Begin chaired on the engine, charged that the premier "was incapable of seeing mere civilians. . . . If you did not wear a uniform it was as if you were not in the room," and that "it was impossible to conduct a rational discussion with Begin on the Lavi." Be that as it may, Begin does not appear to have fully appreciated that the issue was not truly about the engine but a fundamental strategic decision that would affect Israel's military posture and economy for decades. The State Comptroller (a government watchdog agency) found that Begin's narrow approach stemmed from "euphoria" over his dual position as premier and defense minister, much like Ben-Gurion in his heyday, and his weakness for senior brass.[56] Clearly, Weizman, and presumably Rabin, would have made different decisions.

Sharon was the first defense minister to conduct a serious financial and strategic review of the Lavi. He did not follow through on the logical conclusions, however, largely due to his reluctance to oppose Begin on something the latter so greatly favored, and Sharon therefore did not have a major imprint on the project.

Arens succeeded Sharon as defense minister following a highly regarded tour as ambassador in Washington. A former professor of aeronautical engineering and a vice president at IAI, Arens had been one of the earliest and most vociferous supporters of self-development, and he remained an ardent champion of the Lavi long after the project's termination, which he considered "a tragedy of historic proportions." Arens's reasons for supporting the Lavi were nearly all encompassing: self-sufficiency; cost; prevention of a brain drain; encouragement of immigration; the Lavi's operational capabilities, which he continually referred to as the most advanced of their kind; and the huge boost it would give to Israel's industrial capabilities. For Arens the Lavi was not merely an aircraft but a "vision, ideology and obsession."[57]

Arens became intensively involved in the project immediately upon his appointment. One of his first decisions was to cancel a study then under way regarding the possible incorporation of Lavi technology in F-16s, thereby neutralizing pressure to procure F-16s with Israeli components. He also directed that the development of the Lavi proceed as rapidly as possible and that it remain immune to budgetary cuts. Arens's primary contribution to the project was the budgetary breakthrough he achieved by obtaining US funding for it. His unbridled enthusiasm was such that he personally spent entire days pouring over the designs.[58]

Peres, as MoD director-general in the 1950s, was one of IAI's founding fathers. Known for his belief in the importance of rapid technological and industrial development and in weapons self-sufficiency, Peres remained an avid IAI enthusiast. As defense minister in the 1970s, he had given IAI approval for the initial design activities, over the objections of then Premier Rabin,[59] but as premier from 1984 to 1986 he did not play a major role in the Lavi, leaving it to Rabin, now defense minister. During the final months prior to the program's termination, however, as foreign minister and Labor Party leader, Peres played a central role in the attempt to keep the project alive, with his outlandish proposals to produce just seventy-five Lavis and then the "Lavi 2000." By this time, though, it was clear that he was no longer truly in favor of the project and was merely playing political damage control. In the end, he was a full partner to Rabin's politically courageous decision to terminate the project.

Rabin recognized the importance of weapons self-sufficiency but believed it more important that the IDF be equipped with the most advanced weaponry possible, at the earliest date, regardless of where it was produced. As premier in the mid-1970s, Rabin had thus favored procurement of F-16s, rather than self-development, but acquiesced to Peres's decision to conduct initial design work. During FADAC hearings on the issue in 1978, Rabin was one of only two members to oppose self-development, but chose to absent himself from the final vote, presumably to avoid having to vote against a popular project.[60]

As defense minister, Rabin allowed the project to muddle along for nearly three years before finally taking a decisive stand and forcing a cabinet vote on termination. In so doing, his actions did not reflect a fundamental change of views, so much as an attempt to wait for the situation to "gel" in a way that would make it politically feasible for him to press for termination. This did not happen until 1987, after the Zakheim, GAO, and State Comptroller's reports had presented a clear-cut case against the Lavi, the new CoS had come out decisively against it, and the necessary trade-offs had been obtained from the United States.[61] Arguably, no one else would have had the defense reputation and political clout to press successfully for termination, and as it was the vote was carried by a majority of one.

The discrepancy between policy inputs and outputs was more glaring in the case of the Lavi than any other in this book, beginning with Weizman's original decision to approve it in February 1980. The State Comptroller was scathing in its criticism of the decision, charging that it was not based on an appropriate analysis of the different options, multiyear budgeting considerations, prospects for achieving arms self-sufficiency, and impact on Israel's industrial capabilities. Moreover, the decision was made despite the fact that American coproduction proposals, which were expected at any time, might have changed the entire decisional calculus. Perhaps most damning was the finding that the decision to produce four hundred Lavis was unrealistic at the very moment it was made, due to already known budgetary constraints.[62]

Later that month, when the Lavi was first presented to the MCoD, the committee was not informed that the CoS and IAF commander were opposed, and its directive that a joint MoD-MoF assessment of the project's economic ramifications be conducted as a condition for final approval was never carried out. The United States approved the sale of the F404 engine before the IAF and IAI had time to carry out Weizman's directive that they further refine the Lavi's specifications, and this vitally important decision was thus made by default.[63]

Sharon approved continuation of the project even though he knew that a new US proposal for coproduction of the F-16 was expected within days. Once submitted, the American proposal was never seriously considered by the MoD, nor was it brought to the MoF's attention.[64]

The State Comptroller was deeply critical of Begin's decision on the engine, charging that the IAF, Planning Branch, and other entities of the General Staff did not adequately consider the various options' economic and operational ramifications. Although there was a "general understanding" that the far more expensive Big Lavi would come at the expense of other defense needs, the impact was not fully elucidated to decision makers.[65] Most important, Begin simply refused to take the MoF's objections into account, basing his decision solely on the IAF's operational preferences. The cost increases stemming from the decision to develop the Big Lavi were a primary reason for the project's ultimate collapse.

The final cabinet meetings were the ultimate manifestation of the policy disconnect. The Zakheim, GAO, and State Comptroller reports had all clearly established that the Lavi was ruinously expensive. The defense minister and IDF were unequivocally opposed to the project, and the United States had agreed to supply Israel with advanced aircraft, cover termination costs, and permit ongoing use of FMS funds in Israel. Nevertheless, an overwhelming majority of the cabinet supported the Lavi and the Labor ministers voted for termination only under duress.

Policy coordination and integration were clearly flawed throughout the process. The MoD kept the MoF at arm's length, and when in April–May 1981 the MoF almost begged Begin to postpone the decision on the engine until the joint MoD-MoF assessment was carried out, the request was to no avail. The MoD continued working on the project on its own and the MoF was asked to participate only in the final meeting Begin held, not in the crucial working-level ones preceding it.[66]

Even within the defense establishment policy integration was flawed, with the IDF, IAF, and IAI at loggerheads at numerous points. The IAF, which had initially—and ultimately—opposed the project, went along when it appeared that it had become a done deal, seeking to make the best of an unwanted situation. In response to charges that the Big Lavi was too expensive for Israel, IAF commander Ivri took the surprisingly narrow view that "my job is to take care of the IAF. Responsibility for the economy as a whole is in the hands of others."[67] The IDF was opposed throughout, though it chose to mute its opposition at times. IAI consistently pressed for the Lavi at all costs.

From the early pre-Lavi designs beginning in 1974 until the formal decision to develop the Lavi in February 1980, not a single cabinet meeting was held on the fundamental strategic question of whether Israel should develop a combat aircraft or pursue weapons self-sufficiency generally. The final cabinet debates had nothing to do with strategy and policy integration, everything to do with partisan politics.

The posited uninstitutionalized nature of the process was thus substantiated to a high degree. Personal preference, rather than systematic policy-making, played a decisive role, the policy disconnect was severe, and policy coordination and integration were flawed.

## Pathology 5: Primacy of the Defense Establishment

The IDF and IAF were responsible for specifying Israel's requirements and remained deeply involved in the DMP throughout, but once the decision had been made to explore possible designs for an Israeli aircraft and subsequently to develop one, IAI was the primary source of expertise. Numerous agencies were involved in cost estimates over the years, but only IAI, as the sole manufacturer of aircraft in Israel, could provide data on such critical issues as per-hour labor costs, a primary factor in developing and manufacturing a modern aircraft. Even "small" differences in estimates translated into total development and production costs varying by hundreds of millions of dollars.

Weizman's original decision to produce the Lavi in February 1980 was based on IAI's estimated development costs of $710 million. Over the course of the Lavi's lifetime, however, IAI "updated" its estimates six times, with the final one 250% higher than the original. Part of the increase was beyond IAI's control, owing, for example, to design changes and foreign currency fluctuations; part may have been typical of any major project; but much was clearly the result of the biased estimates made by a highly interested party, the contractor. Rabin eventually became so disillusioned with IAI estimates that he demanded independent ones, declaring in August 1987 that "I no longer believe IAI data. Let someone else put his signature on the cost (estimates) IAI submitted."[68] An expression of such total lack of faith in a governmental body, by the minister directly responsible for it, was certainly rare.

The defense establishment was the primary source of expertise and in control of the "policy circle," in the sense that the IDF and IAF determined the needs, and IAI, a part of the defense establishment, provided the solution. In fact, however, IAI acted as an independent commercial entity, pursuing its own interests.

IAI was also the primary bureaucratic player, indeed the driving force, behind the Lavi throughout. IAI was both the sole manufacturer of aircraft in Israel and the largest company generally and was thus an inherently influential body, enjoying a pivotal position vis-à-vis the MoD, to which it is ostensibly subordinate. To this one must add IAI's unique role in Israeli life, as an industrial and technological spearhead of the defense establishment, and the consequent evolution of a broad IAI constituency. Israel's small size and the closed nature of the military and political elites greatly facilitated the effectiveness of the IAI lobby.

In the mid-1980s, IAI mounted the largest and most professionally orchestrated lobbying campaign in Israeli history, certainly up to that time. Virtually anyone of influence was invited to visit IAI and given the grand tour. Ministers, MKs, government officials, reporters, businessmen, trade union leaders, and academics were all assiduously courted. During eighteen months in 1985 and 1986 alone, over one thousand "public opinion molders" were given the IAI treatment. No one could remain immune to the technological marvels shown and the patriotic pride they evoked, even if not all were fully converted to the cause.[69]

The general public was also targeted with great effectiveness. IAI was never tired of expounding on the Lavi's technological prowess, which invariably outstripped that of all competitors, its inexpensive cost, and the employment opportunities it generated. The unending flow of favorable media coverage, "fly-bys," and open-house visiting days at IAI facilities all had an enormous affect. The Lavi's first test flight in January 1987, which received vast coverage—one week before the "Zakheim options" were presented—was clearly timed by IAI. On Independence Day in 1987, on the eve of the final cabinet meetings, 100,000 people came to see the Lavi perform, which amounted to nearly 3% of Israel's Jewish population at the time.[70]

If the above reflects a "positive approach," IAI was not above scare tactics. In the later stages, as opposition grew, it began warning of massive layoffs—two thousand, four thousand, eventually six thousand—many of whom, IAI ominously added, would emigrate. IAI itself would "collapse"; one hundred additional firms, with five thousand employees, would be hard hit; and project termination costs alone would add up to $1.4 billion (the MoD estimated this at $400 million). Most dangerously, the IAF, Israel's frontline of defense, would be severely weakened.[71]

IAI's work force was a further weapon in the lobbying campaign. In the weeks prior to the final decision on termination, IAI workers held numerous demonstrations (five thousand demonstrated outside the cabinet office on one occasion) and did everything possible to exert pressure on the ministers, making use of the extensive links between IAI labor leaders and the two coalition parties (Labor and Likud). The head of the workers' committee publicly warned the two parties about the political clout wielded by IAI's employees and their dependents, estimated to be the equivalent of five or six seats in the Knesset.[72]

The IDF had been less than enthusiastic about the Lavi from the outset, believing that it was motivated primarily by economic considerations rather than military ones. Until Rabin's appointment in August 1984, however, the defense ministers in office were clearly in favor of the project and to oppose it was to go against ministerial policy. The IDF thus preferred to play a "holding" and "damage control" role, to minimize the effects on its broader interests. As time passed, however, IDF sentiment hardened, even within the IAF, and with Rabin expressing only lukewarm support, it finally felt free to press for its position. Moreover, the cuts in the defense budget, following the emergency economic plan of July 1985, forced the IDF to conduct an in-depth analysis of its future force structure, which concluded that the Lavi's share would be untenable.[73]

The crucial turning point came with Dan Shomron's appointment as CoS in early 1987. Shomron had been one of the earliest and most vociferous opponents of the Lavi, preferring coproduction of F-16s. Rabin must have taken this into account in appointing him; indeed, he probably viewed Shomron's opposition as a "military fig-leaf" that would bolster his own position in the upcoming political battle. Shomron, in any event, together with the head of the IDF Planning Branch, Avihu Ben-Nun, a renowned fighter pilot who also strongly opposed the Lavi, set out to kill it once and for all.[74]

The Shomron–Ben-Nun axis was important, for the Lavi's supporters were hard-pressed to advocate a major weapons system that virtually the entire IDF now opposed. During the final cabinet debates, Shomron and Ben-Nun aggressively pressed the IDF's case against the Lavi. When Shamir and Peres raised the possibility of increasing the defense budget by $150 million, the shortfall needed to continue the project, Shomron made it clear that his opposition was fundamental and would not be changed by budgetary increases.[75]

The posited centrality of the defense establishment was thus substantiated only to a moderate degree. The IDF, normally the most powerful bureaucratic player in Israel, was caught between strong contending forces and unable to make its preferences prevail until the very end. IAI was the primary source of expertise and the most powerful bureaucratic player for many years, utilizing its considerable political clout to force a project on the IDF that it did not wish. Indeed, Israel entered and continued the project for years largely due to IAI pressure and domestic politics. Conversely, the defense ministers, until Rabin, were committed to the project and managed to promote it despite serious obstacles and heavy MoF pressure, demonstrating the power of the defense establishment. Moreover, Rabin and the IDF achieved what they wanted in the end and the project was terminated, but the final decision was not truly about defense considerations, in which case their preferences would have prevailed easily, but partisan politics.

**Table 3 Manifestation of Pathologies in Lavi Case**

| Process | Manifestation | Rating |
|---|---|---|
| Unplanned Process | Sequential Decision Making | High |
| | Improvisation | High |
| | Absence of Policy Planning, Objectives, and Options | High |
| Politicized Process | Public Opinion | High |
| | Coalition Maintenance | Low |
| | Politics Reign Supreme | High |
| Semiorganized Anarchy | Leaks | Low |
| | Dysfunctional Cabinet | High |
| | Premier Not in Charge | ID |
| Uninstitutionalized Process | Insufficient Coordination and Integration | High |
| | Policy Disconnects | High |
| | Idiosyncratic | High |
| Primacy of Defense Establishment | Positions Prevail | Mod. |
| | Primary Bureaucratic Player | Mod. |
| | Primary Source of Expertise | Mod. |

Mod. = Moderate
ID = Insufficient data

# CHAPTER FIVE

# The Invasion of Lebanon, 1982

> All of Sharon's reports to the cabinet were submitted under duress. . . .
> Sharon drew maps for us with all sorts of unacceptable situations, so
> that if we had refused to approve some move he proposed, we would
> have been responsible for numerous casualties. . . . This did not leave
> us with much choice. We could not check every move and inch of
> ground. Even so, he complained that we were persecuting him with
> a ruler.
>
> —Minister Zvulun Hammer

On June 5, 1982, Israel invaded Lebanon. Initially planned as a limited operation, both in duration and scope, Israel ultimately remained mired in Lebanon for eighteen years. The invasion commanded resounding public support during its early stages but later became the only war in Israel's history to generate significant public opposition. This chapter focuses on the DMP during the period prior to the invasion and until shortly after the conquest of Beirut, by which time the primary political and military stages had been completed.

## The Strategic Setting

The invasion of Lebanon was directed against two distinct enemies, Syria and the Palestine Liberation Organization (PLO), although the strategic rationale for attacking each differed. Whereas the PLO was an irregular force, whose acts of terrorism could not pose a major military threat to Israel, anguishing though they were, Syria had long been Israel's most implacable enemy and after the 1978 Camp David Accords actually become the most dangerous. In 1982 Israel and Syria were locked in a battle for influence in Lebanon.

The strategic reasoning behind Israel's efforts to prevent Syrian hegemony in Lebanon was straightforward. From 1949 on, Lebanon had been the only one of Israel's neighbors that had refrained from hostilities against it. Northern Lebanon, however, had been occupied by Syria ever since its intervention in the civil war in 1976 and were Syria to gain control over all of Lebanon, it too would become an active part of the Arab-Israeli conflict.

In April 1981 Syria deployed surface-to-air missiles (SAMs) in southern Lebanon, during a battle with Lebanon's Christians in Zahlah.* In so doing, Syria not only posed a challenge to Israel's freedom of aerial maneuver over Lebanon, essential to the battle against PLO terrorism from that country, but was in effect extending its control to the south. Israel had thus sought to destroy the missiles from the time they were first deployed, only to have the operation delayed by US pressure and diplomacy. Throughout 1981 and early 1982, Israel repeatedly informed the United States that it would give diplomacy only limited time and that it would deal with the missiles militarily if diplomacy failed. Syria's deployment of ground forces in the area further exacerbated the situation.[1]

As events unfolded in Lebanon, Syria was nearing its long-sought goal of "strategic parity" with Israel, that is, the ability to wage war against it on its own, without Egypt. To this end, Syria had conducted a massive arms buildup, which according to an MI assessment would be completed in 1982. This alone might have been cause for Israeli preemption, but the situation was actually far more ominous. With "strategic parity" near, MI's assessment was that there was a "high probability" that Syria would initiate hostilities during 1982, possibly during the summer. If hostilities were inevitable, better to preempt on a limited scale in Lebanon, than await an all-out conflagration on the Golan Heights.[2]

From the beginning of PLO terrorism in the late 1960s until 1982, some 700 Israelis were killed and nearly 4,000 wounded. The PLO was thus a serious threat to Israel, not in the conventional military sense, but to its ability to live a normal life.[3] Israel had long faced this reality and learned to cope with it through defensive and limited offensive operations.

In July 1981, however, the situation changed and the PLO became an actual military threat for the first time. During a ten-day period it bombarded Israel's north with over a thousand rockets and artillery shells, disrupting life in an entire region of the country. In Kiryat Shmonah, the largest northern town, 40% of the population fled, an unprecedented event, which had a shattering public effect. Elsewhere, the population lived in shelters, as the IDF proved incapable of stopping the bombardment, short of launching a ground operation to push the PLO out of range.[4]

---

* The missiles themselves were deployed after Israel downed two Syrian helicopters ferrying troops to the battle in Zahlah; however, the necessary emplacements had been prepared beforehand, in anticipation of a decision to install them.

Contributing to this picture was the long-term transformation of the PLO from lightly armed irregulars into a standing force, with regular formations and heavy weaponry. Indeed, the PLO had taken advantage of the year-long cease-fire, following the July 1981 bombardment, to build up its arsenal, which more than doubled in some areas. Furthermore, MI concluded that the PLO intended to employ its new capabilities to attack the north once again and even overrun an entire town. Had it succeeded, even briefly, the impact on Israeli public opinion would have been calamitous.[5] Creation of a security zone along the border, the invasion's stated objective, or some other means of protecting the north, was thus a strategic imperative.

The 1979 peace treaty with Egypt marked a turning point in Middle Eastern history, with the most powerful of Israel's neighbors renouncing the use of force. Israel feared, however, that Egypt's commitment to peace might wane after it withdrew from Sinai in April 1982. If an operation against the PLO and Syria was in the offing in any event, it was argued, better to act before April and put Egypt to a test. If found wanting, Israel would at least be able to retain the remaining half of Sinai. An alternative approach, conversely, advocated waiting until after April, when Egypt, having received its territory, would be hard-pressed to justify active opposition to an Israeli move in Lebanon.[6] The essential point, in either case, was that Israel could probably count on a quiet Egyptian front.

A second change in the regional balance of power also served to ease Israel's decision to invade. Following the 1973 war, Israel had come to view Iraq as a primary threat, but Iraq was now deeply embroiled in a war with Iran and its abysmal military performance exposed capabilities far less threatening than those feared.[7] Moreover, in June 1981 Israel destroyed the Iraqi nuclear reactor, further reducing its threat perception. With Jordan also expected to sit out any hostilities, the regional balance of power appeared quite favorable.

The "missile crisis" of April 1981 began a period of intensive US-Israeli contacts, lasting until the invasion over a year later. Defense Minister Sharon believed that American acquiescence was essential if Israel was to launch an invasion, but that an overt "green light" could simply not be expected from a superpower. Conversely, he believed that a sense of inevitability and resignation could be fostered in Washington and that once it took hold, the United States would seek to make the best of an unwanted situation. He thus adopted a policy of gradually familiarizing the administration with his thinking and the justification of Israel's impending actions.[8]

By December 1981 Sharon's familiarization approach was paying off, at least in regard to Secretary of State Haig, who came to the conclusion that an Israeli operation was inevitable and thus merely sought to limit its scope and possible consequences. In February 1982 Haig insisted that only "a strictly proportional response to an internationally recognized provocation" would be acceptable, but what this constituted was not defined.[9]

In April 1982 the United States renewed its diplomatic efforts to fore-stall an Israeli operation, but Israel warned that it would be forced to act if PLO attacks continued. In May, after a number of further attacks, Israel informed the United States that it would respond if just one more violation of the cease-fire took place. Sharon met with Haig and presented two pos-sible military options: one, a limited operation to pacify southern Lebanon; the other, a large-scale invasion to restructure Lebanon politically and put the Christian Phalangists in charge. Haig maintained that an Israeli attack would have a devastating effect unless perceived to be a justified response, but he acknowledged Israel's right to self-defense and refrained from any ulti-matums. In emphasizing that that the circumstances would determine the US position, Haig in effect left it to Israel to define them. Sharon chose to interpret this as acquiescence to a limited operation, provided that it was swift, circumscribed, and launched with sufficient pretext. As far as he was concerned, he had received the necessary "amber light."[10]

Haig's own actions lend credence to Sharon's impressions. Immediately following their meeting, Haig's advisers convinced him to send a follow-up letter to Premier Begin, to ensure that Israel did not misconstrue what he had said and draw far-reaching conclusions. The letter indeed backed away from some of what Haig had said but did not contradict the essence of his words and in practice served to create the impression of a pro forma expression of American reservations. Later in May Haig further strengthened Israel's sense of American acquiescence when he stated that US troops could be deployed in a buffer zone, if Israel cleared a 25-mile-wide area of PLO positions.[11]

With the US position seemingly assured, the cabinet barely discussed the potential American response during the June 5 meeting, in which the deci-sion to invade was made. Indeed, during the invasion's early days, before Israel had attacked the Syrian missiles and it had become clear that the actual objective was Beirut, the United States did not press for a cease-fire. In a press conference on June 9, Haig made a highly revealing slip of the tongue: referring to Israeli combat losses, he spoke of the losses that *"we suffered."* Only on June 10, in the wake of a sharp Soviet demand that Washington restrain Israel, did the United States begin calling for a cease-fire.[12]

In fact, the US position was moving closer to Israel's. On June 16 the United States stated that it recognized the need for a "period of stabiliza-tion" in Lebanon and no longer favored an immediate Israeli withdrawal. Haig stated publicly that there was considerable justification for Israel's in-vasion and privately that Israel ought to complete the effort and destroy the PLO in west Beirut, though it was preferable that this was done by the Phalangists. Reagan stated that the United States favored the withdrawal of all foreign forces (i.e., the PLO and Syrians too), establishment of a stable government in Beirut, and means of guaranteeing Israel's security. The United States also moved toward the Israeli position regarding the appoint-ment of Bashir Gemayel, the Phalangist leader, as president of Lebanon.[13]

The threats to Israel's northern border in June 1982 presented a strategic imperative that would likely have led any Israeli government to take military action against the PLO,[14] and possibly Syria too. A favorable US position and regional environment greatly eased Israel's decision to invade.

## Pathology 1: An Unplanned Process

By the time of the invasion in June 1982, the Syrian missiles had already been in Lebanon for fourteen months and the PLO bombardment had taken place nearly a year earlier. Some PLO violations of the cease-fire had occurred but were not of a magnitude that required immediate or massive retaliation. Nevertheless, the missiles and bombardment constituted severe changes in Israel's external environment, which would have necessitated a commensurate response at some point. In pursuit thereof, Israel had all of the time necessary to conduct systematic policy planning.

Sharon began planning the invasion immediately upon his appointment in September 1981, and on December 20 Begin submitted the plan, code-named "Oranim" (Pines), to the cabinet for the first time. The plan provided for an invasion up to the Beirut-Damascus highway, with the conquest of Beirut itself to be left to the Phalangists. The PLO's capabilities in Lebanon would be destroyed and the stage would thereby be set both for its expulsion and for the Phalangists to take control of the government. To avoid a clash with Syria, whose forces were deployed in the central and eastern parts of southern Lebanon, the IDF would advance along western axes.[15] To Sharon and Begin's dismay, the cabinet rejected the "Big Oranim" plan, due not to differences over its basic objectives, but to concern that it would lead to war with Syria and because of the costs entailed.[16]

In December 1981 Israel formally annexed the Golan Heights, concentrating forces in the north to deter a possible Syrian retaliation. Unlike previous cases of tensions with Syria, however, this time Israel's forces were not redeployed after the tensions had subsided, instead remaining in the area throughout the half year leading to the invasion. In fact, their continued presence was part of a strategic deception plan, designed to lull the PLO and Syria into a sense of complacency while keeping sufficient forces in the area to begin a "rolling" campaign into Lebanon.[17]

During the months following the cabinet's rejection of Big Oranim, Begin and Sharon presented a number of more limited options for invasion. In January 1982 they proposed that Israel respond to a new PLO terrorist attack by bombing PLO positions in Lebanon. A majority of the cabinet remained opposed, out of concern that the true aim was to draw the PLO into shelling the north, thereby providing the pretext for Big Oranim. In April, following the murder of an Israeli diplomat, Begin and Sharon again requested authorization for an invasion, but only air strikes were approved. On May 10, for the first time a small majority voted in favor of a "little" Oranim plan, but Begin concluded that cabinet support was still insufficient. On May 16 the cabinet decided that a further act of terrorism would lead to an immediate and large-scale response. The attempted assassination of the Israeli ambassador in London on June 3 was the final straw and on June 5 the cabinet finally approved an invasion. Sharon had worked for nine months to convince the cabinet to act. "I knew I would break them in the end," he said.[18]

The invasion planning process was deeply flawed, for a number of reasons. First, the extensive planning conducted by the defense establishment never fully reached the cabinet. Indeed, once the cabinet rejected Big Oranim and the various scaled-down options, Sharon and Begin no longer apprised it of their thinking, including the invasion's true objectives.

Second, the cabinet was never presented with discrete policy options at any point. From the time the Big Oranim plan was first presented in December 1981, until the crucial vote on June 5, 1982, all of the options submitted were merely scaled-down variants thereof, not alternative policies. In all cases, including on June 5, the cabinet was presented with just one option, which it could accept or reject, without alternatives.

Third, even some of the invasion's formal objectives, as approved by the cabinet on June 5, were either poorly elucidated or unrealistic. These included the following:

- creation of a "security zone" by pushing PLO artillery out of range;
- conclusion of a peace treaty with Lebanon;
- creation of a "new political order" in Lebanon;
- avoiding a confrontation with Syrian forces, unless attacked first.[19]

The cabinet was never informed of the security zone's precise delineation but was "given to understand" that it would be approximately 25 miles. It rapidly turned out, however, that Sharon's "understanding" was different, indeed, that he had expanded the operation most of the way to Beirut. The cabinet did not know that MI had warned in advance that the Phalangists would not fulfill their commitment to conclude a peace treaty and that the objective of creating a "new political order" in Lebanon was probably unattainable. The character of this new order, in any event, was never elucidated before the cabinet. MI's pre-innovation assessment, shared by others as well, was that it would inevitably result in a clash with Syria.

Fourth, Begin's and especially Sharon's true objectives, as opposed to those presented to the cabinet, envisaged sweeping historic regional changes, going way beyond the Lebanese theater (see Pathology 4). Israel's ability to achieve these objectives was dubious at best, if not fanciful.

Finally, policy planning was flawed even within the defense establishment, the extensive work conducted notwithstanding. Sharon set up his own "personal" planning unit, the Unit for National Security (UNS), as a means of circumventing opposition to his aims from within the IDF, thereby biasing the process and precluding consideration of dissenting inputs.

The invasion was sequential from the outset. Israeli forces advanced beyond the 25-mile line approved by the cabinet on the very first day, a matter raised in the cabinet the following day. Sharon explained that he had meant 25 miles from the northernmost point, not from all points along the border. The practical result of his delineation was that the operation's outer limits now reached over halfway to Beirut.[20]

On June 7 Sharon proposed that the IDF open a new axis of advance, ostensibly designed to outflank the Syrians and avoid a clash with them. The cabinet approved the request, thereby giving the first official sanction to the move beyond the 25-mile limit, while also reiterating its previous decision to avoid a confrontation with Syria. Later on the 7th, however, a Syrian tank column threatened the Israeli flanking force, and the cabinet acceded to Sharon's request to attack it. Syria responded by sending in further reinforcements and SAMs.[21]

On June 8 Sharon requested approval to "improve positions" and advance on the Beirut–Damascus highway, to increase pressure on Syria to expel PLO forces from the areas under its control. Also on the 8th, Gemayel was informed that Israeli forces would soon link up with the Phalangists and that he should prepare to take Beirut and establish a new government.[22]

On June 9, with Israel's flanking force encountering heavy resistance, Sharon's entire strategy (Big Oranim) was at stake. In order to overcome Syrian resistance and protect Israeli forces, Sharon asked for approval to attack the Syrian SAMs. Although many of the ministers felt uncomfortable with the request, they were unable to refuse "the boys" the protection they "deserved." The missiles were destroyed that day, before the United States even had a chance to convey the cabinet's previous decision to avoid a clash with the Syrians to them.[23]

On June 10 Sharon requested approval to take the Beirut–Damascus highway, explaining that this was essential to deny Syria control of Lebanon. By severing its contact with Beirut, Syria would no longer be able to dictate developments in Lebanon. The IDF encircled Beirut the following day and entered east Beirut on June 12, even though the cabinet had not approved this and despite Sharon's assurances that it would not enter Beirut. Even Begin was taken by surprise. On June 15 the cabinet specifically resolved not to enter west Beirut but ended up doing so on the 24th. For all practical purposes, it had now approved all of the elements of the Big Oranim plan it had rejected in December.[24]

Sharon's strategy began unraveling the moment the Israeli and Phalangist forces met outside Beirut. The Phalangists reneged on their commitment to sign a peace treaty with Israel and to use their forces to take west Beirut, two of the primary reasons for the invasion's advance that far north, and Sharon now decided that Israel would do so itself.[25] The PLO was expelled from Lebanon, a major achievement, but in September the Syrians assassinated Gemayel and Israel's entire strategy collapsed, with Syrian forces remaining in Lebanon. Israel's eighteen-year-long Lebanese quagmire had begun.

In reality, Israel launched two different invasions in June 1982: the large-scale invasion that actually took place and the limited one officially approved by the cabinet. The first, the product of extensive planning carried out by the defense establishment under Sharon's guidance, reflected a comprehensive, if controversial, strategic construct. The second, the result of the cabinet's repeated refusal to approve the "big" plan, was manipulated by Begin and Sharon in order to turn it into the invasion they had wanted to begin with. Although it could be argued that a plan thus existed at least at the defense establishment level, the formulation of objectives and options by the cabinet was clearly flawed and the unplanned nature of the process was thus manifested at a high level. The posited improvisational and sequential nature of the DMP was also substantiated to a high degree. By means of improvisation and sequential decision making, without elucidation of the overall strategy and endgame, the cabinet was led, step by step, to approve essentially all of the components of Big Oranim.

## Pathology 2: A Politicized Process

Partisan politics were not a significant factor during the pre-invasion period and the early weeks. The cabinet's rejection of Big Oranim and the smaller subsequent variants was substantive, not partisan, and once the invasion was launched it enjoyed strong support from both the cabinet and opposition. Begin and Sharon were thus able to make the crucial early decisions largely free of political considerations. Moreover, the invasion's initial successes, especially the attack on the Syrian missiles,[26] gave Sharon's position in the cabinet (and public) an early boost.[27]

The situation began changing in early July, when a number of ministers banded together in opposition to the entry into west Beirut and the National Religious Party even threatened to leave the coalition, which would have led to its fall. Begin was forced to temporarily backtrack on this and two further occasions in which the cabinet voted against the entrance into Beirut. Only in August, as it became clear that Sharon's strategy was collapsing, did partisan politics truly become an issue of significance. By that time, however, the invasion's military objectives, including the conquest of Beirut, had largely been completed.[28]

If partisan politics were not a major factor, coalition maintenance was. From the moment the cabinet rejected Big Oranim in December 1981, the entire nature of the process changed. The cabinet came to be viewed by Begin and Sharon as an adversary to be overcome. Cabinet meetings now became all about "what would fly," not what was truly necessary, with Begin and Sharon seeking to build the minimum consensus necessary for an operation, almost any operation. Once approved, they would turn it into the large one they wanted. A process of political give and take, compromise and deception, not policy, became the order of the day.

The cabinet's inner balance also played a role. The leading moderates in Begin's first cabinet (Weizman, Dayan, and others), who had exerted a moderating influence on him, including his willingness to make painful concessions to Egypt, were replaced by hawks such as Sharon and Foreign Minister Shamir. By spring 1982, moreover, Sharon was the most influential minister in the cabinet, and he and Begin together constituted a formidable alliance. Sharon had worked tirelessly to cultivate a close relationship with Begin, who became almost completely dependent on Sharon for defense affairs, allowing his other sources of information and advice to be largely severed.[29]

Public opinion was very much a factor behind the invasion, beginning with the "missile crisis" in April 1981. Begin repeatedly threatened to destroy the missiles if Syria did not remove them, going so far as to turn this into a campaign pledge during the June 1981 elections. At US insistence, Begin agreed to defer the operation as long as diplomacy appeared to bear some chance of success, but having pledged that they would be destroyed, the missiles' ongoing presence posed a challenge to his political credibility.[30]

Events became even more problematic in July 1981, with the PLO bombardment of the north, which led to heavy public and Knesset pressure for action; Begin now declared that "not one more Katyusha [rocket] will fall on Kiryat Shmonah." Coming on top of the US failure to secure a withdrawal of the missiles, the bombardment placed Begin in an untenable political position and an attack largely became a question of when, not if, while the IDF's inability to counter the rocket and artillery threat through limited military means convinced Begin that a large-scale ground operation was the only viable option. Some believe that it was at this point, July–August 1981, that he opted for war and thus decided to appoint Sharon to execute his plans.[31] If public opinion was thus a major factor in the decision to launch the invasion, the public remained highly supportive of the invasion during the early weeks and contributed significantly to the cabinet's willingness to take the risks involved and further expand it.

The posited politicized nature of the process was largely substantiated. Partisan politics had a moderate effect, but both coalition maintenance and public opinion played a central role and were manifested to a high degree.

## Pathology 3: Semiorganized Anarchy

Begin was a full party to the original Big Oranim plan and to the invasion's objectives as adopted by the cabinet. Moreover, he was presumably aware that preparations for Big Oranim were continuing even after having been rejected by the cabinet, was complicit in Sharon's piecemeal effort to lead the cabinet to the "big" operation, and provided full backing for Sharon's moves, well past the conquest of Beirut. Although he was clearly uninformed at times and may have chosen to allow Sharon to take the lead (and blame) for political reasons, a portrayal of the invasion as "Sharon's war" would do Begin's role an injustice. Indeed, it is highly unlikely that he would have allowed Sharon to continue pressing for a policy of which he did not approve, or that it would have been repeatedly discussed in the cabinet, had he not so wished.[32]

Begin's role in the decisions to attack the Syrians and conquer Beirut is less straightforward. It is unclear whether he truly believed that a clash with Syria could be avoided, even if this was the view he espoused.[33] Given his personal commitment to the destruction of the Syrian missiles and overall familiarity with the military planning, it is more likely that he supported the strike and merely chose to allow Sharon to bear the brunt of the criticism.

As for Beirut, Begin informed the cabinet on June 5 that it would be convened if it became necessary to take the city, thereby indicating that he did not preclude this. On June 12 he enthusiastically supported the move into west Beirut and attempted to devise ways to overcome cabinet opposition, for example, by convening it late at night. Conversely, Begin was clearly surprised by the IDF's entrance into east Beirut. In a radio interview he denied that the IDF had done so, only to have his statement contrasted with a live broadcast describing the movement of IDF forces in the city. In a meeting with a US diplomat, Begin was again put in an embarrassing position when the latter replied to his assertion that the IDF would not enter Beirut by retorting that it had already done so.[34]

Begin ultimately overcame cabinet opposition and achieved what he wanted: a large-scale invasion. Conversely, between December 1981 and June 1982 Begin was unable to obtain approval for an operation on five occasions and he was at least partially misled by Sharon.[35] As such, he was truly only partially in charge.

In contrast to the DMP in virtually all other military operations in Israel's history, Begin chose to conduct invasion decision making in the cabinet plenum, not the MCoD or some other subcabinet forum. The cabinet held extensive deliberations on the invasion during the months preceding it and met daily during the early weeks. Put bluntly, however, the cabinet simply did not know what was going on and the real decision making was done elsewhere, in the defense establishment or in meetings between Begin and Sharon.

Paradoxically, it was the cabinet's firm stand in rejecting Big Oranim, as well as the scaled-down versions presented over the following months, that led to its circumvention by Sharon and, to a lesser extent, by Begin, too. From this point on, Sharon no longer presented the cabinet with a full elucidation of his thinking, choosing to gradually overcome its resistance through selective reporting of events and planning. The information provided was incomplete and highly biased, tailored to lead the cabinet to the "appropriate conclusions," and only those defense officials who agreed with Sharon's views were allowed to appear before the cabinet. The ministers did not have an independent ability to assess the situation and the prospects of achieving the invasion's stated objectives, and there was simply no one, other than the policy advocates, to provide authoritative analyses.[36]

Nevertheless, it was clear to some of the ministers during the June 5 cabinet meeting that the limited operation they had approved was merely the beginning of a far broader invasion. As one minister explained: "We had said no so many times. Now, faced with this global drama and the premier's stormy emotional state, we could no longer stand firm. . . . We were not enthusiastic, but we understood that the snowball could not be stopped any longer."[37]

Cabinet deliberations did not even approximate the degree of sober, in-depth, and open deliberations to be expected. None of the ministers objected to the war's objectives as defined by Begin and Sharon on June 5, and only Minister Mordechai Tzippori, a former general, voiced any hesitations regarding the assumption that a clash with Syria could be avoided. He, too, voted in favor of the invasion.[38]

On June 5 Sharon informed the cabinet that the operation would last up to forty-eight hours at most. He made no mention of a possible advance beyond the 25-mile security zone, of a link-up with the Phalangists in the north, or of his true assessment, that the goal of "creating a new political order" in Lebanon (i.e., helping engineer Gemayel's election as president) would require that the IDF remain there for a period of three to six months. As for Beirut, Sharon stated that it was "out of the picture. We must not enter an Arab capital." He similarly assured the cabinet that the IDF would do its best to avoid a clash with Syria.[39]

Sharon's cabinet assurances notwithstanding, the IDF was given very different instructions. During the months preceding the invasion, while the cabinet was busy debating a limited operation, Sharon directed the IDF to prepare for Big Oranim, as he did again, in operational terms, on June 5. On the first day of the invasion, Sharon told IDF officers that an attack on the Syrian missiles would be necessary but did not mention this when briefing Begin on the meeting. On a different occasion he told military commanders that it was unclear what the cabinet would decide regarding the Syrians and that they should therefore move against them gradually "without creating the impression of a big war."[40] Sharon appears to have known that his flanking move on June 7, ostensibly to avoid a clash with the Syrians, would actually force them to respond and thereby provide him with a pretext for attacking them. Needless to say, Sharon did not express this assessment to the cabinet.[41]

Within days of the invasion, a number of ministers began to realize that Sharon's moves, even if ostensibly related to operational developments, appeared to be leading to the "big" plan the cabinet had rejected. Sharon's request on June 10 for approval to advance on the Beirut–Damascus highway and subsequent entry into Beirut marked the turning point in the cabinet's attitude toward him. Some ministers concluded that they had been lied to and circumvented and grew increasingly unwilling to accept Sharon's requests without careful examination. The invasion's initial success was such that weeks would still go by before they spoke out against Sharon openly, but the mood in the cabinet had become one of distrust.[42]

By August 7 even Begin was beginning to show displeasure. He criticized Sharon in the cabinet that day by noting that he was "the cabinet's representative to the army, not the army's representative to the cabinet." On August 12 Sharon found himself entirely isolated. Following the renewed bombing of west Beirut earlier that day, in violation of the cabinet's decision to the contrary, it now suspended Sharon's unilateral authority to order the Air Force into action. The decision, in which Begin concurred, was an unprecedented limitation of the defense minister's authority and marked the final turning point in the cabinet's attitude toward Sharon.[43]

During the early days of the invasion, the cabinet clearly manifested attributes of groupthink. Conformity with the emerging consensus, rather than agreement on the merits of the issue, led to the suppression of dissenting views and to an illusion of unanimity, greatly eased by the weakness of many of the ministers, particularly Tzippori and Deputy Premier Ehrlich.[44] The pressures for conformity also led to an overestimation of Israel's prospects of success and a consequent deterioration in reality testing, with ministers withholding judgment and giving Sharon the benefit of the doubt in the hope that he could "pull it off." Premature cognitive closure led to flawed analyses of available information, policy options were restricted to those preferred by the policy advocates, Begin and Sharon, and only proponents of their preferred policies were heard. Indeed, many of the decisions were close to what they would have been had they been made solely by Begin and Sharon.[45]

The claim that the cabinet was led astray by Sharon is only partially acceptable. The cabinet was deeply involved in the process from the beginning, approved the initial objectives, and continued approving each additional step. Indeed, as Sharon disingenuously claimed, the invasion of Lebanon was given greater cabinet approval than any previous war in Israel's history. Cognizant of the cabinet's skeptical attitude toward him, Sharon made sure to receive approval for virtually every step he took, even if he did not fully apprise the cabinet of the consequences, requested approval only after the fact, or engineered events so that it was left with little choice. Although the ministers' lack of military expertise prevented them from fully understanding each of Sharon's moves, the overall direction should have been clear—and was to some—particularly since he had spent the preceding half year trying to convince them that his was the best approach. The cabinet was misled, but more important, it preferred to hide behind a cloak of ostensible ignorance in the hopes that Sharon could "pull it off." If the invasion was a success, the cabinet would share the glory; failure would be Sharon's alone.[46]

The posited pathology was only partially substantiated. Begin was ultimately able to get what he wanted, a large-scale invasion, but only by misleading the cabinet, and he at least partially lost control of the DMP to Sharon once the invasion began. The premier was thus only moderately in control. The cabinet was not the true locus of decision making, was in the dark about most of what was happening both before and during the invasion, and allowed itself to be swept along, thereby fully substantiating the dysfunctional dimension of the pathology. Insufficient data were available to substantiate the pathology in regard to leaks.

## Pathology 4: An Uninstitutionalized Process

The cataclysmic theme of the Holocaust and Israel's rebirth were the seminal events in Begin's life, pervading his thinking, perceptions of the world, and actions as premier. For Begin, the PLO was a direct descendant of the Nazis, similarly bent on the destruction of the Jewish people. Attainment of a preponderance of military force, to ensure Jewish survival, was the logical outcome of this outlook. "Our fate in the Land of Israel," Begin stated, "is that we have no choice but to fight with selfless dedication. The alternative is Auschwitz."[47]

By 1978 Begin was dismayed by reports from Lebanon, fearing a Christian collapse. As a small and embattled religious minority, Lebanese Christians' plight evoked associations similarly found in Jewish history, and Begin expressed fear of a Christian "holocaust," an unconscionable prospect for him. A deep moral commitment thus served as the initial basis for the alliance with the Phalangists, which later took on politico-strategic dimensions as well. By December 1980 Begin had provided the Phalangists with a guarantee of Israeli intervention on their behalf, if Syria used its air force against them, and by 1982 Israeli assistance totaled hundreds of millions of dollars, including tanks, artillery, and training.[48]

For Begin, however, the ultimate issue facing Israel, the one by which history would judge him, was the future of Judea and Samaria (the West Bank). Begin feared that once Israel completed its withdrawal from Sinai in April 1982, the United States and Egypt would launch a diplomatic initiative designed to end Israeli control over this area. Staving off this eventual-

ity was his primary goal as premier and was in itself at least a
fication for a significant operation against the PLO in Lebano'
Begin went to war on June 5 convinced of the righteousn(
sion. Though his aims were less grandiose than Sharon's, Beg..
vinced that the invasion would lead to Israel's second peace treaty, the ⌐
struction of the PLO, and prolonged quiet in the north. By expelling the
PLO from Lebanon he would finally be rid of the Palestinian problem, or at
the very least the momentum of Palestinian nationalism would stall, and
the possibility of Judea and Samaria ever being severed from Israel would
greatly diminish. Begin sought to achieve what no previous premier ever
had, a knockout blow, which would enable Israel to dictate terms to the
Palestinians.[50] His role in achieving cabinet support for the invasion was
crucial.

Sharon believed that Israel had taken an overly narrow approach toward
Lebanon in the past, focusing on the immediate threats, rather than a fundamental resolution of the overall Lebanese problem, which would entail
the destruction of the PLO's political and military presence and withdrawal
of Syrian forces. Were this to happen, the way would be open for the establishment of a legitimate government in Beirut that was willing to make
peace with Israel. To this end, Sharon advocated providing Phalangist
leader Gemayel with all of the assistance necessary to ensure his election as
president.[51]

These objectives, of major importance in themselves, were only stepping-
stones to the even broader transformation of the Middle East that Sharon
envisaged. For him, the most serious dangers Israel faced were not military
but political, stemming from the growing international recognition of the
Palestinian cause. Sharon had long been an advocate of the "Jordan is Palestine" thesis, which favored establishment of a Palestinian state in place of
Jordan, in which Palestinians were already then nearing a majority. Were
this to happen, the Palestinians could no longer claim that their right of
national self-determination was being denied, and pressure on Israel to relinquish the West Bank would diminish.

The PLO's quasi-independent status in Lebanon, however, posed a major
obstacle to Sharon's vision, and he thus sought to destroy its military capabilities and bring about its expulsion from Lebanon. With the PLO in ruins,
moderate Palestinian leaders would rise to power and have little alternative but to conclude an autonomy agreement with Israel and to realize their
national aspirations in Jordan. A process leading to the overthrow of King
Hussein would ensue and result in the establishment of the Palestinian
state in Jordan. Concomitantly, the invasion would force Syria to withdraw
from Lebanon, at least from the Zahlah-Beirut area, and the growing threat
it posed to Israel would be greatly reduced. By significantly weakening Israel's two primary enemies, Sharon sought to end any possible challenges
to its control of the West Bank.[52]

Over time Sharon had become the most influential minister in Begin's cabinet, largely because of his ability to formulate practical strategies for implementing Begin's political and ideological commitments and for resolving the primary strategic challenges he faced. Upon his appointment, for example, he took on the politically thankless task of completing the withdrawal from Sinai. He also negotiated a new Memorandum of Strategic Cooperation with the United States, thereby raising bilateral relations to a new level. Above all, Sharon formulated a practical plan for ending the Syrian and PLO threats in Lebanon, with their wider ramifications for the Palestinian issue, Begin's foremost concern.[53]

Former premier Rabin believed that the invasion went awry because of the character of the decision makers involved, primarily because Begin did not know how to control the defense establishment and thus Sharon was able to "pull one over" on him. Former foreign minister Abba Eban believed that Sharon's role was decisive and that the invasion would not have taken place if someone like Rabin, Weizman, or even the hard-liner Arens had been defense minister.[54] Be that as it may, Begin and Sharon had an inordinate influence on the invasion DMP, in terms of both the objectives they set and their role in obtaining cabinet approval for the invasion.

The policy input-output disconnect was far deeper in this case than the usual failures of omission. Indeed, the cabinet was intentionally misled by Sharon, with Begin's at least partial complicity, in order to lead it to decisions that it would not have otherwise adopted. Both Begin and Sharon told the cabinet far less than they knew, and both had severed highly important sources of information and advice of their own—Sharon because he "knew what he wanted" and was unwilling to hear contrary views, and Begin by allowing himself to become totally reliant on Sharon. With the exception of Foreign Minister Shamir, none of the other ministers had independent sources of information.[55]

The cabinet was not fully apprised of the depth of Israel's cooperation with the Phalangists, nor was it aware that MI had repeatedly warned Sharon that the invasion planning was based on deeply flawed assumptions. According to MI, the Phalangists could not be relied on to live up to their commitments to Israel, including the promised peace treaty and conquest of Beirut; they were actively seeking to draw Israel into a war for their own purposes; and they would abandon Israel for Syria once the former had achieved their desired aims for them. MI further warned that the Phalangists did not have sufficient strength to take control of Beirut, as intended, that Israel would be caught in the Lebanese quagmire if it sought to do so itself, that the invasion's objectives could not be achieved in the short period envisioned, and that an attack on Syrian targets would result in the escalation the cabinet had specifically proscribed. All of these assessments proved prescient, as did MI's updated assessment on the eve of the invasion, which found its long-term goals to be almost unattainable.[56]

MI head Yehoshua Saguy continued to express opposition to the invasion planning as long as he felt that his voice had some impact. Sharon, however, who must have viewed Saguy as a threat to his ability to sway the cabinet, blocked Saguy's access to it, and Begin was unwilling to hear any of the voices of opposition emanating from the intelligence community. In early 1982 Saguy thus appears to have concluded that further opposition was futile and to have retreated into an acquiescent silence. Although he continued to participate in all cabinet meetings prior to and during the war, he became a silent partner to Sharon's deception. Possibly for the first time in Israeli history, MI was largely excluded from the DMP leading to a major military operation.[57]

In March 1982 both the IDF's primary pre-invasion war game and a second lower-level one reached similar conclusions: the invasion's outcomes would diverge widely from those intended, a clash with Syria could not be avoided, the Phalangists would not live up to their commitments, and Israeli casualties would far exceed those anticipated. The cabinet, including Begin, was never informed of these findings and did not know that the IAF commander and commander of the Northern Front had reservations regarding the missile strike and that the deputy CoS opposed some of Sharon's proposed ground operations.[58]

In April the Mossad joined MI in warning against the feasibility of the plan to install Gemayel as president and withdraw within weeks. In contrast with MI, the Mossad had previously considered the Phalangists to be reliable partners, but it, too, now expressed doubts regarding their military capabilities, ability to take control of Lebanon, and the invasion's overall prospects. There is no indication that any of this was known to the cabinet. Like Saguy, Mossad director Yitzhak Hoffi refrained from expressing his true assessments, in this case at least partly out of concern that Begin would suspect that they were colored by his long-standing rivalry with Sharon.[59]

Policy coordination and integration were deeply flawed throughout the process. The MFA played no role in the pre-invasion planning and, unusually, policy coordination and integration were flawed even within the defense establishment. In order to circumvent opposition to his plans from within the IDF, Sharon cut it off from important information and decisions both he and the cabinet made. He even established a special entity to conduct invasion planning, the UNS, thereby sidelining the IDF Planning Branch.[60] The intelligence community's access to the cabinet was restricted, and within the cabinet discussion was not about substantive differences over policy, which might have contributed to coordination and integration, but about power politics, how Begin and Sharon could force their preferences on the recalcitrant ministers.

The posited uninstitutionalized character of the process was substantiated at a high level. The nature of the process was highly idiosyncratic, as both Begin's and Sharon's personal preferences had an inordinate influence, at the expense of the formal process. The policy input-output disconnect was severe and policy coordination and integration flawed.

## Pathology 5: Primacy of the Defense Establishment

The IDF and intelligence agencies were the primary sources of information and expertise throughout the invasion process and the primary bureaucratic actors. The roles played by Foreign Minister Shamir and the MFA, as a whole, were notable only for their insignificance. Shamir, a lifelong hawk, viewed his role as foreign minister as that of implementing Begin's policies, and he fully supported Big Oranim from the time it was first presented.[61]

To CoS Eitan's way of thinking, Israel's War of Independence had not yet ended and the invasion of Lebanon was "part of the battle for the Land of Israel that has already lasted 100 years."[62] Eitan believed that that there was a military solution to both the terrorist and diplomatic threats posed by the PLO and that a decisive military blow would enable Israel to conduct negotiations on its own terms. He thus fully supported the invasion—indeed, it was Eitan who convinced Sharon that the "big" plan should include all of southern Lebanon, not just the western sector, as initially conceived. In any event, Eitan believed that the "difference between a small operation and a large one is only how it starts, because the operation will continue and turn into a large one."[63]

Eitan's strategic priorities, however, differed from Sharon's. Whereas Sharon aspired to sweeping regional changes, Eitan was narrowly focused on the PLO. Eitan also feared that a clash with Syria, as Sharon intended, would lead to international pressure for an early cease-fire and thereby deny Israel a victory even over the PLO. He had thus initially favored only limited operations against Syria, but later acceded to their expansion out of concern that the advances against PLO positions would also be endangered. Eitan was a full partner to Sharon's efforts to mislead the cabinet, if only through omission. When asked questions, he answered fully but did not volunteer information and chose not to participate in cabinet meetings during the first week of the invasion, when the critical decisions were made, to avoid exposing his differences with Sharon.[64]

With control of the "policy circle" (intelligence, policy recommendations, and implementation), Sharon as the driving force, and the premier's support, the primacy of the defense establishment was clear. In Israel of 1982 there were no other power centers in the field of national security. The INSC did not yet exist, the MFA did not play a role, and dissenting voices within the defense establishment were denied access to the premier and cabinet. Indeed, by June 1982 an atmosphere had been created in which senior officers were reluctant to turn to the cabinet with their knowledge of the distorted information presented to it. Some leaked to the media, others met informally with senior leaders, a majority went along, and most sincerely supported the operation's stated objectives.[65]

The posited centrality of the defense establishment was largely but not completely substantiated. The fact is that the combined power of Begin and Sharon was insufficient to obtain cabinet approval for the invasion for half a year and even then they were authorized only to conduct a limited operation. Conversely, the cabinet went along with Sharon during the early weeks, and he was able to turn the invasion into the one he wanted, before the cabinet eventually turned against him. In conclusion, then, the posited role of the IDF and defense establishment as the primary source of expertise and bureaucratic actor was fully substantiated, but their influence on the actual policy outcomes was only moderately so.

**Table 4 Manifestation of Pathologies in the Invasion of Lebanon**

| Category | Manifestation | Rating |
|---|---|---|
| Unplanned Process | Absence of Policy Planning, Objectives, and Options | High |
| | Improvisation | High |
| | Sequential Decision Making | High |
| Politicized Process | Politics Reign Supreme | Mod. |
| | Coalition Maintenance | High |
| | Public Opinion | High |
| Semiorganized Anarchy | Premier Not in Charge | Mod. |
| | Dysfunctional Cabinet | High |
| | Leaks | ID |
| Uninstitutionalized Process | Idiosyncratic | High |
| | Policy Disconnects | High |
| | Insufficient Coordination and Integration | High |
| Primacy of Defense Establishment | Primary Source of Expertise | High |
| | Primary Bureaucratic Player | High |
| | Positions Prevail | Mod. |

Mod. = Moderate
ID = Insufficient data

# CHAPTER SIX

# Leaving Lebanon

## The Unilateral Withdrawal, 2000

[A unilateral withdrawal from Lebanon would] "endanger Israel's
security, endanger the security of the residents of the north and
strengthen Hezbollah. To initiate this would be to demonstrate
public irresponsibility.

—Ehud Barak, 1998

On March 6, 2000, the Barak cabinet decided that Israel would withdraw
from Lebanon unilaterally, if negotiations then under way with Syria,
which was in de facto control of Lebanon, failed to yield an agreed withdrawal by July. In April, at the Geneva Summit, Syrian president Hafez
Assad rejected a dramatic Israeli proposal to withdraw from the Golan
Heights, presented to him, at Barak's behest, by President Clinton, and
Barak concluded that an agreed withdrawal from Lebanon would not be
feasible by the July deadline. The withdrawal was carried out unilaterally
on May 23, in a hasty and disorderly fashion, under Hezbollah fire, with
the IDF leaving behind equipment, weapons, and Israel's longtime proxy,
the South Lebanon Army (SLA), to finally collapse.

Hezbollah triumphantly claimed credit for having driven Israel out of
Lebanon, an assessment many in Israel bleakly shared.[1] On this ignomini-
ous note, Israel's eighteen-year-long presence in southern Lebanon came to
an end.

## The Strategic Setting

Although the case study in Chapter 5 ended with the completion of the primary military stages of the 1982 invasion, this proved to be just the beginning of Israel's Lebanese saga. In 1983 Israel forced the Lebanese government

to fulfill its pre-invasion promise to sign a bilateral peace treaty, one of Israel's primary war objectives. By the following year, however, Syria had reasserted its control over Lebanon and compelled it to abrogate the treaty, ending Israel's already fraying alliance with the Maronites and leaving the invasion strategy in ruins. In January 1985 Israel withdrew from most of Lebanon, retaining a 3- to 12-mile-wide "security zone" along the border, designed to protect its northern population from cross-border terrorist and rocket attacks.

The Israeli invasion, rise of the Islamic regime in Tehran, and long-standing Shiite grievances led to the establishment of Hezbollah, which would prove to be the most determined and effective of Israel's adversaries. Careful and deliberate in both planning and action, Hezbollah steadily built up its military capabilities, inflicted ongoing casualties on Israel, and withstood all of Israel's attempts to deter and defeat it. By 2000, with Syrian and primarily Iranian assistance, Hezbollah had an arsenal of some seven thousand rockets, capable of blanketing northern Israel.[2]

To Israel, Lebanon was a failed state in which some semblance of order was maintained only by the Syrian occupation, which had begun in 1976 following the outbreak of the civil war. Syria, it believed, was in firm control of most events of a political and military character in Lebanon and that Hezbollah, too, could take little action without Syrian approval, or at the very least acquiescence.[3]

Hezbollah fired some four thousand rockets at Israel between 1985 and 2000. The number of civilians killed was small, just seven all told, but many were wounded and the disruption to civilian life was significant, with the public repeatedly forced into shelters, at times for days. On Israel's election day in June 1999, Hezbollah made it a point of firing around fifty Katyushas at Israel. January 2000 was one of the worst months, with approximately forty Hezbollah attacks, of various kinds, each week. Just weeks before the decision to withdraw, a major Hezbollah attack forced 300,000 people into shelters. Forty percent of the residents of Kiryat Shmona, the largest town in the north, fled their homes,[4] much as had happened in July 1981, greatly contributing to Israel's decision to launch the invasion at the time.

Militarily, the security zone proved a mixed bag: highly successful in preventing cross-border infiltration but too narrow to prevent rocket fire. During the fifteen years in which the security zone existed, the IDF lost a total of 256 soldiers on the Lebanese front, an average of seventeen annually,[5] a large number for Israel.

Over the years the IDF had responded to Hezbollah attacks with ongoing, often round-the-clock operations. Mostly limited in nature, consisting largely of air strikes (numbering twenty to twenty-five a month in the years before the withdrawal) and small-scale ground operations, IDF efforts occasionally flared up into major confrontations. Although they presumably reduced the number and effectiveness of Hezbollah attacks, these opera-

tions failed to weaken its determination to continue attacking Is'
prevent the long-term buildup of its military capabilities. In
pressure and the limited efficacy of the IDF's military operation
led to their early termination, before Israel was able to achieve its obj.
tives. Two major operations, Accountability in 1992 and Grapes of Wrath in
1996, ended badly for Israel, with Hezbollah able to continue operating
from populated areas, whereas Israel's freedom of maneuver was limited
by the terms of the cease-fire agreements.[6]

In 2000 Israel thus had a clear interest in preventing or minimizing the
Hezbollah threat, which was increasingly eroding both the public's sense
of confidence and quality of life and Israel's deterrent posture. Indeed,
virtually all prior experience indicated that Israel would adopt an offensive posture. Instead, it chose an unprecedented policy of unilateral withdrawal.

As initially conceived, the withdrawal was meant to be not unilateral
but part of a peace agreement with Syria, with whom negotiations were
then under way. Given its choke hold over Lebanon, Syria had long made
progress in the Lebanese-Israeli negotiations contingent on a Syrian-Israeli
agreement. With Israel now indicating its willingness to cede the Golan
Heights, however, it hoped that Syria would reign in Hezbollah—Israel's
gesture was a means of further inducing Syria to do so—and ultimately
permit progress on the Lebanese-Israeli track.

Moreover, Israel knew that Syria deeply feared a unilateral Israeli withdrawal from Lebanon and hoped that this would constitute a further incentive for it to reach an agreement with Israel.[7] Though placed in the ludicrous position of opposing an Israeli withdrawal from "occupied Arab
land," Syria had two good reasons for doing so. First, Syria had long made
use of Hezbollah as an indirect means of exerting pressure on Israel to
make concessions on the Golan Heights, through an ongoing "bloodlet-
ting" in Lebanon designed to sap its internal resilience. Having been "badly
burned" by its experiences in the 1967 and 1973 wars, Syria sought to avoid
a direct conflict on the Golan, which would play to Israel's military
strengths, but viewed Lebanon as a relatively risk-free battleground. Were
Israel to withdraw from Lebanon, Syria would lose this important source of
leverage. Second, Syria presciently feared that an Israeli withdrawal would
undermine the justification for its own occupation of Lebanon, from which
it derived great benefit, and set in motion a process that would force it, too,
to withdraw, as indeed happened in 2005.[8]

Israel's attempt to wield the "unilateral card" was thus not without
foundation, even if it ultimately failed to yield the desired change in Syria's positions. Syria simply refused to take any action to encourage an Israeli withdrawal, preferring to acquiesce to its unilateral actions in Lebanon. The Arab world and the international community were also put on
the defensive, initially opposing the Israeli move but then forced to accede

to it. Once Israel resolved that it would withdraw from Lebanon, regardless of the ramifications, the unilateral card was a win-win diplomatic strategy.

A more fundamental question was the military logic behind the concept of unilateral withdrawal. Could the north be defended from the border, as Barak now averred, as effectively as from the security zone? The new approach, he argued, would ensure Israel's security by bestowing a mantle of international legitimacy on it. By completely withdrawing to the international border and thereby fully implementing Israel's obligations under UN Security Council Resolution (UNSCR) 425, an "invisible wall of legitimacy" would be created and would deny Hezbollah the domestic, regional, and international justification necessary for continued attacks.[9]

To buttress this newly gained international legitimacy, Israel also announced that it would adopt a policy of massive retaliation in the event that Hezbollah continued to attack it after the withdrawal. The potential cost to Lebanon, it believed, would prompt other Lebanese actors to press Hezbollah into refraining from further provocations, so that Lebanon, weary after twenty-five years of war, would not be forced to pay the price of its actions. Hezbollah, lacking legitimization for additional attacks and not wishing to be blamed for the further destruction of Lebanon, would be forced to focus primarily on political and socioeconomic affairs. It would not change its fundamental aims and occasional incidents might still take place, but Hezbollah's freedom of maneuver would be constrained and over time its weapons would hopefully "rust" from disuse. Having fully implemented Resolution 425, the international community would have to support Israel if Hezbollah conducted further attacks.[10]

Moreover, the withdrawal from Lebanon was part of a dramatic attempt by Barak to change the entire course of the Middle Eastern conflict. In the space of just a little over a year, Barak sought to achieve peace with both Syria and the Palestinians, culminating in the Geneva and Camp David summits, respectively, and as part of this to end the conflict on the Lebanese border, preferably as part of an agreement with Syria. When the Geneva Summit failed, however, he decided to withdraw from Lebanon unilaterally, to clear the way for the Camp David Summit, which took place just two months later.

Subsequent events at least partly bore out Barak's strategy. During the years following the withdrawal Hezbollah did find itself in a bind, pressed by Arab countries and especially Lebanese domestic opinion to curb its attacks against Israel and focus on the domestic arena, but unwilling to forego its jihadi identity and the battle against Israel. It thus pursued a middle of the road approach, designed to address these conflicting considerations, by repeatedly conducting limited attacks against Israel that were insufficient to justify a major retaliation and overly anger Lebanese opinion, but enough to keep the pressure on and ultimately lead to the desired escalation, as happened in 2006. The international community did demonstrate somewhat greater understanding of Israel's policy in Lebanon, as evinced by its comparatively muted response during the 2006 war, though this did not extend beyond the early limited operations and, in any event, did not ultimately affect Hezbollah behavior.

One of the primary reasons for the ultimate failure of the withdrawal strategy was a major development that could have been—and was—largely foreseen: the outbreak of the Palestinian Intifada just four months later. The Intifada rapidly became an all-absorbing preoccupation for Israel and created a situation in which it was unable to carry out the declared retaliatory policy, thereby emboldening Hezbollah to further increase its attacks. The priority Israel was compelled to accord to the Palestinian front thus undermined one of the withdrawal's primary strategic pillars, the massive retaliation policy, from the outset.

## Pathology 1: An Unplanned Process

Following the withdrawal of Israeli forces to the security zone in 1985, Israel remained in a primarily reactive mode, responding to Hezbollah attacks while occasionally undertaking more significant offensives. The unilateral withdrawal, in contrast, was a major initiative, indeed, a fundamental change in all Israeli strategic thinking up to that time, which had heretofore viewed unilateral concessions, as opposed to negotiated agreements, as anathema.

Upon his election in 1999, Barak explicitly stated his intention to withdraw from Lebanon, preferably as part of an overall agreement with Syria but unilaterally if this did not prove feasible. A basic incremental decision-making strategy was thus in place, but for all practical purposes, no substantive discussion of Israel's objectives and options ever took place. The decision to withdraw had been a campaign pledge and there is no indication that Barak, or the cabinet, ever seriously considered Israel's objectives or additional options. Possible alternatives, such as a major change in the IDF's deployment in Lebanon or in its operational approach, were not discussed, nor, initially, were options for international involvement, though this came up at a later stage. According to one minister, "everything had been decided upon by Barak before he submitted it to the cabinet for discussion. No options were presented."[11] The IDF sought to propose variations on the basic concept, such as retaining some outposts just over the border, but these were minor tactical changes.

In fleshing out the initial withdrawal concept and turning it into reality, the process was characterized by considerable improvisation and sequentialism. If changing considerations, conceptual zigzags, and conflicting decisions are typical of many major DMPs everywhere, in this case, however, they *followed* the decision to withdraw, rather than being part of the preparatory process leading to its adoption. Five primary issues demonstrate the improvisational and sequential nature of the process: whether it would be negotiated or unilateral, the line to which Israel would withdraw, the desired international role, the future of the SLA, and the timing of withdrawal. We now turn to each.

First, despite Barak's explicit intention to withdraw unilaterally, if necessary, IDF planning was conducted on the assumption that an agreed withdrawal would be reached. Its withdrawal plan, first presented to Barak in late 1999, referred only to this option and Barak himself still spoke in terms of an agreed withdrawal in February 2000. The failure of the Geneva Summit in March, however, ended Barak's hopes that agreement could be reached and led to the decision to withdraw unilaterally. For both operational reasons and to clear the way for the Camp David Summit just weeks later, the decision was then made to withdraw in May, six weeks earlier than originally planned, and the IDF was forced to conduct crash operational planning in preparation.[12] In the end, the withdrawal was hastily devised, disorderly, and humiliating, undermining Israel's deterrent posture.

Second, Barak announced from the outset that Israel would withdraw to the international boundary, without knowing the full ramifications of this decision. In early 2000, however, a study of the Israeli-Lebanese border prepared by the IDF Mapping Unit found that some 60% of the line was still in dispute, either because its demarcation had never been agreed to begin with or in some cases because Israel had encroached on Lebanese territory.[13]

The biggest issue, which remained unresolved until just weeks before the withdrawal, was whether to withdraw completely and thus dismantle every Israeli border outpost or to deploy along the existing border fence. The latter option would mean that a few encroachments, up to a few hundred meters in depth, would remain, but that Israel would be able to retain some of the outposts. As late as March 2000, Barak still hoped to retain the important outposts, on the assumption that this would satisfy the international community that Israel had, for all intents and purposes, withdrawn fully. A further option considered was to declare that the remaining outposts were temporary and would be dismantled if and when negotiations with Syria led to a breakthrough. By April, however, it transpired that only a complete return to the international border, confirmed by a special UN cartographic team, would satisfy international opinion and the decision was made to withdraw completely.[14]

Third, in early 2000 the MFA recommended that the withdrawal be made contingent on UN recognition that it would constitute fulfillment of Israel's obligations under UNSCR 425 (i.e., withdrawal to the international border). In so doing, pressure would be placed on Lebanon, Syria, and Hezbollah to uphold their obligations under the resolution as well (in other words, restoration of order and security in the south, withdrawal of Syrian forces, and dismantlement of Hezbollah), the withdrawal would gain further international legitimacy, and Israel would be in a position to demand international support if future violations by Hezbollah necessitated Israeli retaliation.[15]

Adoption of the MFA's recommendation fundamentally changed the nature of the withdrawal, which in effect now became an agreed one, even if Israel's quid pro quo would be provided by the international community, rather than the local actors. Moreover, the recommendation reversed a decades-long policy of keeping the UN and international community, other than the United States, at arm's length from Israel's affairs and provided them with a key role in the withdrawal process; only with UN approval would Israel be able to claim that it had fully withdrawn and thus that there was no justification for further Hezbollah attacks. Over the next weeks Israel also raised a number of additional options for international involvement, including the possibility that UNIFIL (the UN force stationed in Lebanon) would take control of the border, redeploy along it, or take responsibility for the safety of SLA soldiers. The possibility of establishing a new international force was also first raised at this late date.[16]

Fourth, it was clear from the beginning that the withdrawal would seal the fate of the SLA, which Israel had equipped, trained, and fought alongside for decades, indeed, which it had helped establish as a semi-independent mini-state in southern Lebanon. For both strategic reasons, such as Israel's credibility toward potential future allies, and moral ones, Israel could not just walk away from the SLA—and Hezbollah made the mortal consequences of doing so clear. Conversely, if Israel was to gain international recognition of the withdrawal, its ties with the SLA would have to be severed.

In practice, almost nothing was done to prepare, and the SLA collapsed in the final weeks prior to the withdrawal. Many of its members sought to cut deals with Hezbollah, such as handing over weapons and providing information on Israel, in exchange for shortened jail terms or to save themselves from an even worse fate. In the final hours of the withdrawal, hundreds frantically converged on Israel's closing gates, seeking entry. Although unprepared, Israel took emergency steps and shelter was provided.[17]

Fifth, Barak had publicly pledged to withdraw within one year of his cabinet's formation, that is, by July 7, 2000. In reality, the year-long interval reflected his wish to deflate public pressure for an immediate withdrawal and to use the time gained to "threaten" Syria with a unilateral withdrawal. Following a Hezbollah escalation in February 2000, however, which caused comparatively heavy casualties, pressure for an immediate withdrawal grew once again, both at the public and cabinet levels, but Barak still wanted to give more time to the talks with Syria in the hopes of reaching an agreed withdrawal. In April, following the failure of the Geneva Summit, it was decided to move up the withdrawal timetable to May.[18]

The three dimensions of Pathology 1 were thus substantiated at a moderate to high level—to be conservative, let us say moderate. An overall endgame existed from the start, but a fully fleshed out strategy did not, and the formulation of objectives and options was minimal. Important modifications and additions were made to the plan over time, leading to its essentially improvisational and sequential character.

## Pathology 2: A Highly Politicized Process

The unilateral withdrawal from Lebanon was the result, above all, of grassroots public pressure. Over time the concept gained broad support across the political spectrum, and thus neither partisan politics nor coalition maintenance were an issue in the withdrawal process.

The number of Israeli civilians killed in the north was small, but the number of soldiers was not, and together with the ongoing disruption to civilian life, there was a grinding, cumulative effect that eroded public support for Israel's presence in the security zone. Hezbollah's continual and increasingly sophisticated attacks, including ambushes, suicide bombings, and rocket fire, created a popular perception of a seemingly unending stream of casualties, a sense of never ending tension, and fatigue.[19]

For reasons of operational secrecy, the public had only limited knowledge of the IDF's constant, often heroic efforts to prevent Hezbollah attacks, whereas every failure was given disproportionate media coverage. The government's fear of casualties often led to limitations on offensive operations, further strengthening the image of the IDF as a heavy and ineffectual conventional army, compared with Hezbollah's agile guerilla tactics.[20]

Until 1997 a clear majority of the public supported Israel's presence in the security zone, but two tragic events that year caused a decisive change. The first was a midair collision between two IAF helicopters ferrying troops into Lebanon, in which seventy-three soldiers were killed, a devastating number for Israel. The second was a deep raid into Lebanon by Israeli naval commandos, who were ambushed by Hezbollah, with twelve soldiers killed.[21] From an annual average of seventeen soldiers lost in previous years, the number peaked in 1997 at over a hundred.

Coming on top of popular dissatisfaction with Israel's involvement in Lebanon generally, the two accidents had a galvanizing effect and led to the rise of a number of protest movements. The most noteworthy, the Four Mothers Movement, was the creation of the mothers of four combat soldiers then serving in Lebanon and it rapidly gained political attention through a broad and effective lobbying and media campaign. It gained further influence with the rise of additional opposition groups that were closer to the "establishment." In 1997 the Council for a Peaceful Exit from

Lebanon, composed of former MFA officials, academics, and a few left-wing MKs, was formed. In 1998 the Council for Peace and Security, a prestigious group of former defense officials, came out in favor of unilateral withdrawal, thereby providing the concept with legitimacy from within the heart of the defense establishment. Public support grew commensurately, from 41% in 1997 to 55% in 1999 and fully 62% in 2000.[22]

The concept of unilateral withdrawal was thus not new. Indeed, it had been first considered by the National Unity Government in 1984 and was raised once again toward the end of the Netanyahu government, largely at the unlikely initiative of Ariel Sharon. As minister of infrastructure in 1998 and foreign minister in 1999, Sharon repeatedly proposed that Israel conduct a graduated unilateral withdrawal if Netanyahu's efforts to engineer an agreed one did not reach fruition.[23]

For Netanyahu, the question was no longer whether to withdraw from Lebanon but how to do so in a way that minimized the dangers. He initially believed that only an agreed withdrawal would ensure Israel's security, but by early 1999 he too had come around to supporting a unilateral one. Conversely, Defense Minister Mordechai favored an agreed withdrawal based on Resolution 425, which would entail disarmament of Hezbollah and security measures by Lebanon, not just an Israeli move. The cabinet supported Mordechai's approach. With Sharon's right-wing approval, however, as well as Netanyahu's and Mordechai's more centrist support, the basic concept of withdrawal from Lebanon had now become a legitimate part of Israeli political discourse, including that of the hawkish Likud.[24]

During the 1999 elections Barak was running a close tie with Netanyahu. Previously on record as strongly opposed to unilateral withdrawal (see the chapter epigraph) but now in search of popular issues with which to set himself apart, Barak's polls showed that withdrawal from Lebanon, even unilaterally, was a winning platform. Both he and Netanyahu, as well as Mordechai, now head of a new party, vied over who could best resolve the Lebanon issue. Netanyahu even sought to implement a partial unilateral withdrawal prior to the elections but was stymied by the opposition of now defense minister Arens and the IDF. Barak's victory, based at least partly on his explicit campaign promise to withdraw within one year, made the withdrawal a matter of his personal credibility.[25]

When Barak assumed office in July 1999, the unilateral withdrawal issue had thus been fully framed and enjoyed broad support, from left to right. By the time of the cabinet vote in March 2000, even heretofore opponents, such as Minister Lipkin-Shahak, a former CoS, concluded that once Israel had decided to withdraw, there was no point in prolonging the process and suffering additional casualties. Support came from the right as well, with Sharon, now an opposition leader, calling for an immediate unilateral withdrawal.[26] The cabinet approved the proposal unanimously.

Substantiation of Pathology 2 was thus mixed. The posited impact of partisan politics and coalition maintenance was not substantiated, the impact of public opinion highly so.

## Pathology 3: Semiorganized Anarchy

Barak was clearly in charge throughout the process. The cabinet, however, was largely relegated to the background.

Unilateral withdrawal had been a central Labor Party campaign platform during the 1999 elections and thus enjoyed considerable support in the Labor-led cabinet from the outset. The IDF, however, was strongly opposed, meaning that cabinet approval would not be trivial nevertheless. Moreover, as conceived by Barak, the withdrawal was to be not a stand-alone decision, which commanded wide public support, but part of a broader peace agreement with Syria, which would entail an extremely unpopular withdrawal from the Golan Heights. Barak handled these contradicting considerations through the time-honored approach preferred by many premiers of keeping his cards close to his chest and the cabinet at arm's length.

Barak was intensively involved in the Lebanese issue from day one, devoting forty-one meetings to it during his first eight months in office alone and many more over the following months.[27] Nevertheless, he only convened the first cabinet meeting on withdrawal on February 27, 2000, almost eight months after taking office. Even then, his immediate objective was to deflect cabinet pressure for an immediate withdrawal, following a major Hezbollah escalation that month, and to shore up support for his phased approach (an agreed withdrawal if possible, unilateral if not), rather than to engage the cabinet substantively.[28]

Eight hours were devoted to the February 27 cabinet meeting, but not all of the ministers had the opportunity to speak and debate continued the following week. In the end, the cabinet unanimously approved Barak's proposal. Just three more cabinet-level meetings were convened throughout the withdrawal process, including a largely technical MCoD meeting to assess the IDF's preparations and a cabinet plenum on May 22, which gave largely pro forma final approval to actually carry out the withdrawal.[29]

Leaks, for the most part, were not an issue in the withdrawal from Lebanon. Barak explicitly stated his intentions and strategy from the outset, little changed over the course of time, and the cabinet was involved only on a handful of occasions. On May 22, however, in order to prevent leaks that might have enabled attacks against the withdrawing troops, Barak requested that the cabinet give its final approval for the withdrawal only *in principle* and that he (Barak was also defense minister) and the CoS be authorized to decide on the precise timing.[30]

Pathology 3 was therefore only partly substantiated. Barak was firmly in control, thus disproving this part of the posited pathology. The cabinet DMP was not dysfunctional in itself, as in the other cases studied in this book, but the cabinet was circumvented by Barak, who made all of the decisions on his own, and was not the locus of decision making, thereby at least moderately substantiating the posited pathology. Leaks were not an issue.

## Pathology 4: An Uninstitutionalized Process

The withdrawal process, as with most of Barak's decisions, was a one-man show. By the spring of 2000, however, the concept of unilateral withdrawal had largely become a consensual issue and was thus not a case of idiosyncratic decision making, even if Barak's style had an effect on the nature of the process.

Conversely, a disconnect existed between some of the policy inputs of the national security establishment and the policies adopted by the cabinet. An IDF simulation exercise conducted two to three years earlier had concluded that unilateral withdrawal would leave Israel with insufficient military depth and undermine its security. In what would sound prophetic in the summer of 2006, then CoS Lipkin-Shahak summed up the exercise by warning that if Israel withdrew from Lebanon unilaterally, the IDF would ultimately have to enter southern Lebanon once again. In June 1999, just one month before Barak's cabinet was formed, an IDF position paper concluded that unilateral withdrawal would not prevent continued Hezbollah attacks and that it was the worst of the options Israel faced. From the time Barak assumed office until the actual withdrawal, the IDF repeatedly expressed opposition to its unilateral nature. The IDF and MoD coordinator for Lebanon also rejected Barak's contention that Israel's newly gained international legitimacy would provide it with the diplomatic leeway necessary to carry out the intended massive retaliation policy.[31]

With Barak serving as both premier and defense minister, the need for policy coordination and integration was somewhat more limited than might otherwise have been the case. The MFA did, however, make an important contribution with its recommendation that Israel present the withdrawal as the fulfillment of its obligations under Resolution 425 and thereby seek international legitimacy for its actions.

Pathology 4 was partially substantiated. The posited idiosyncratic nature of the process was not substantiated and the policy disconnect moderately so, though the information available is limited. The information available regarding policy coordination and integration is insufficient to draw even a tentative conclusion.

## Pathology 5: Primacy of the Defense Establishment

The defense establishment was united by a broad, if not unanimous, consensus, firmly opposed to a unilateral withdrawal, though not to a negotiated one. Beginning with the Netanyahu cabinet's early consideration of this option and especially once Barak took office, the IDF did its best to convince the cabinet of the negative consequences it foresaw.[32]

The IDF argued that Hezbollah would view a unilateral withdrawal as a victory, which would undermine Israel's deterrence and lead to a further deterioration in the security situation. The SLA would collapse and with it the buffer provided by the security zone. Moreover, the new situation would increase the danger of escalation with Syria, for whom Lebanon had constituted an arena for limited conflict with Israel and which might now have no recourse other than to engage in direct hostilities on the Golan Heights.[33]

In a highly unusual step, Barak did not invite IDF officers or other senior officials to the crucial February 27 and March 6 cabinet meetings in which the withdrawal was approved in principle, explaining that this was to ensure that they would be truly "strategic" discussions rather than narrowly focused military ones—as if the IDF did not regularly participate in all such meetings. It is far more likely that he simply feared the impact that the IDF's firm opposition to unilateral withdrawal would have had on the cabinet, had it been present.[34]

IDF opposition to unilateral withdrawal continued virtually up to the last minute, even while it was busy making the final preparations necessary to carry it out.[35] If the IDF and defense establishment generally have been said to wield excessive influence, this was certainly not true of the withdrawal from Lebanon. Despite the IDF's best efforts, the cabinet voted for the withdrawal unanimously.

Neither the MFA nor the newly established INSC played a discernible role in the withdrawal process, with one important exception: the MFA's recommendation, in early 2000, regarding the presentation of the withdrawal as the implementation of Resolution 425, was a major change in the withdrawal concept, which helped Israel gain international support for it.

Pathology 5 was largely substantiated. The IDF was the primary source of expertise and bureaucratic player, as posited, and though its positions had no effect on the policy outcome, those of the defense minister prevailed. This dimension of the posited pathology was thus moderately manifested.

**Table 5  Manifestation of Pathologies in the Withdrawal from Lebanon**

| Category | Manifestation | Rating |
|---|---|---|
| Unplanned Process | Sequential Decision Making | Mod. |
| | Improvisation | Mod. |
| | Absence of Policy Planning, Objectives, and Options | Mod. |
| Politicized Process | Public Opinion | High |
| | Coalition Maintenance | Low |
| | Politics Reign Supreme | Low |
| Semiorganized Anarchy | Leaks | Low |
| | Dysfunctional Cabinet | Mod. |
| | Premier Not in Charge | Low |
| Uninstitutionalized Process | Insufficient Coordination and Integration | ID |
| | Policy Disconnects | Mod. |
| | Idiosyncratic | Low |
| Primacy of Defense Establishment | Positions Prevail | Mod. |
| | Primary Bureaucratic Player | High |
| | Primary Source of Expertise | High |

Mod. = Moderate
ID = Insufficient data

# CHAPTER SEVEN

# Camp David II

## The Israeli-Palestinian Negotiations, 1999–2000

> Tell the Palestinians discreetly that we Israelis are built for a settle-
> ment "in one fell swoop," all the issues, all the subjects, all the pain.
> As a people and society we are not built for agreements in stages, in
> which we will have to make continual political down payments.
>
> —Ehud Barak to his chief negotiator, May 2000

## The Strategic Setting

When Premier Ehud Barak took office in 1999 he inherited a mixed bag. Six years after the Oslo Agreement launched Israeli-Palestinian negotiations, the Palestinian Authority (PA) was in control of most of the Palestinian population, most of the territory of Gaza, and nearly half of the West Bank. Israel had recognized the PLO as the sole legitimate representative of the Palestinian people and agreed to negotiations designed to lead to a final agreement within five years. Terrorism, following the horrific spring of 1996, was comparatively low, Israel's economy was booming, and the severe do-mestic tensions produced by the peace process, culminating in Rabin's assas-sination in 1995, had subsided. The year 2000 promised to be—and was—an even better one economically, with the highest growth rates in decades both in Israel and the PA.

By the late 1990s, however, many in Israel felt a growing sense of urgency regarding the conflict with the Palestinians. Even on the right many were coming to share the left's long-standing fear that the Palestinians' high birth-rates posed an inexorable threat to Israel's Jewish character. "Demography" became the driving force in Israeli politics and national security thinking, and an increasingly broad part of the political spectrum viewed withdrawal from the West Bank and Gaza not as a threat but as an Israeli interest.

Moreover, the preceding Netanyahu years had been a period of considerable foreign policy adversity for Israel. The dramatic steps Israel had taken for peace under Rabin and Peres and the ongoing Palestinian violence notwithstanding, the international community placed the primary onus for the failure of the peace process on Israel, and its international stature plummeted. In May 1999 "Oslo's" five-year deadline for an agreement expired and Israel feared that a unilateral Palestinian declaration of statehood—their stated intention, unless agreement was reached by September—would be recognized by the vast majority of the world, including the United States, which would greatly exacerbate Israel's isolation.[1] Barak's determination to transform the situation of Israel's own accord provided him with a brief "honeymoon" with the international community, but heavy pressure was just around the corner.

The beginning of Barak's premiership in July 1999 was marred by terrorism, seven attacks in the first half of August alone, which continued throughout the negotiations. Security was thus a paramount consideration and Israel sought agreement on a variety of security arrangements, such as demilitarization and early warning sites. Much attention has been devoted to the question of Palestinian leader Yasser Arafat's complicity in the outbreak and continuation of the Intifada (uprising) in September 2000. One thing is clear. By February, eight months earlier, Israeli intelligence had already predicted, accurately, that mass Palestinian violence was likely to erupt later that year, especially if the peace process failed. In a chillingly prescient assessment on the eve of the Camp David Summit (July 12–25, 2000), Barak warned the cabinet that the summit's failure would lead to thousands of casualties.[2]

The year 1999 was also one of growing concern in Israel over the broader trends in the region. Iraq appeared to be emerging from the international sanctions and inspections regime imposed on it, and its WMD capabilities were a source of great concern, as was Iran's nuclear program. Both threats added a measure of urgency to Israel's fundamental interest in peace with the Palestinians and Syria, in the hope that agreements could be reached before Iraq and Iran had gone nuclear. Israel's security zone in southern Lebanon was increasingly viewed as a burden rather than a strategic asset, as Hezbollah engaged in a large-scale arms buildup and claimed a growing number of Israeli casualties. Pressure for a withdrawal from Lebanon, as noted in the preceding chapter, was growing.

If regional trends were a source of concern, the timing nevertheless appeared to be propitious for negotiations. Agreements with the Palestinians and Syria were thought to be more likely while their aging leaders, Arafat and Assad respectively, were still in power. Both were considered powerful leaders, capable of "delivering" on an agreement, whereas it might take years before their successors had the political clout to make the concessions required for peace.[3] Arafat, at the apex of his leadership, had the opportunity to finally lead the Palestinians to statehood and, having built a close relationship with President Clinton, after decades of US ostracism, would not want to jeopardize this strategic achievement. With Barak willing to put everything on the table, Arafat would not be able to refuse.

Barak devoted great attention to the Palestinian track from day one but preferred a "Syria first" strategy and subordinated the negotiations with the Palestinians to those with Damascus. Syria, unlike the Palestinians, constituted a severe military threat, and peace with it would fundamentally alter Israel's military circumstances. The outlines of an agreement with Syria had emerged during the negotiations under Rabin and were relatively clear-cut, painful though they were. Moreover, Syria was a state, whose leader had a record of fulfilling agreements.[4] The prospects for an agreement with Syria thus appeared far more favorable than with the chaotic Palestinians, with whom a deal would require concessions affecting Israel's fundamental character. Moreover, a Syria-first agreement would increase the pressure on the Palestinians to make concessions, so as not to be left in the position of "last man out" after Egypt and Jordan had already made peace, and would facilitate the Israeli withdrawal from Lebanon, which Barak had promised to complete by July 2000. Syria, in de facto control of Lebanon, had the ability to ensure peace on the Israeli-Lebanese border following the withdrawal, but had made Israeli-Lebanese negotiations contingent on the outcome of its own negotiations with Israel.[5]

From November 1999 until the collapse of the talks with Syria at the Geneva Summit in March 2000, Barak thus focused primarily on Syria and then turned to the withdrawal from Lebanon in April and May. Only then did he turn his full attention to the Palestinian track.[6]

The failure of the talks with Syria had important consequences for the Palestinian track. Assad's rejection of the dramatic deal Clinton proposed in Geneva, at Barak's behest, in which Israel offered to withdraw from virtually 100% of the Golan Heights, demonstrated that one could say no to the US president without fear of consequences. Furthermore, Assad's refusal to compromise on territory, rejecting the deal over tens to hundreds of meters, reaffirmed the principle of the sanctity of the 1967 borders. If Egypt had received 100% of its territory and Assad had been so steadfast, Arafat, the embodiment of Palestinian aspirations, could not settle for less.[7]

Israel's unilateral withdrawal from Lebanon in May 2000 was viewed by the Arab world as a historic victory, the first time Israel had been compelled to withdraw from territory by force, and Hezbollah was considered a model to be emulated. Arafat shared this assessment, but Hezbollah's very effectiveness placed him in an awkward position. How could he, leader of the Palestinian struggle for decades, now engage in negotiations that would require major concessions, when a mere five hundred Hezbollah fighters had driven the IDF out of Lebanon? For Arafat, what had happened in Lebanon was a humiliation, which hardened his positions.[8]

The United States played a central role throughout the negotiations, providing both sides with both positive and negative inducements to compromise. The true negotiations often took place between the United States and each of the sides, no less than between the sides themselves, as both vied for US support. Unlike the negotiations with Egypt, however, US-Israeli coordination was very close this time, on both the substantive and tactical levels. Indeed, Barak had made full coordination with the United States a primary concern, beginning his premiership with a series of extended talks with Clinton designed to cultivate a close relationship, and he continued to meet and conduct endless phone calls with him throughout the process, as well as with Clinton's senior advisers.

From the outset Clinton was deeply impressed by Barak's determination to forge dramatic breakthroughs with Syria and the Palestinians and to withdraw from Lebanon, and with Barak intent on going far beyond what the US president had expected, Clinton was happy to let him take the lead. The failure of the summit with Assad in Geneva, for which Barak had pressed hard, dampened Clinton's enthusiasm for Barak's headlong attempts to reach rapid breakthroughs, and he imposed conditions before again agreeing to risk presidential prestige at Camp David.[9] Barak, however, was clearly an audacious leader, worthy of US support, and after decades of involvement in the peace process the United States could hardly refuse to help him reach an historic breakthrough.

The US role throughout the negotiations proved to be a mix of intensive intervention, along with repeated failures to bring the full brunt of American influence to bear. Clinton and his senior advisers made tireless, round-the-clock efforts at Camp David and at times exerted heavy pressure. During the first nine days of the summit, Clinton held twelve meetings each with Barak and Arafat, one joint meeting, and one with each of the negotiating teams.[10] An endless array of additional meetings was also held by the other US officials, in a variety of settings and formats.

American pressure grew as the summit turned sour. On July 16 National Security Adviser Sandy Berger warned Barak that if he did not demonstrate further flexibility, Berger would change his focus from what was best for the talks to "protecting the president" (from the consequences of failure). On the 17th Clinton yelled at Arafat, demanding that he finally provide clear answers and threatened to call off the summit. On the 19th Clinton told Arafat that "you are leading your people and the entire region to a catastrophe. I am very disappointed, you are about to lose my friendship and to miss the opportunity to reach an agreement for many years."[11]

Conversely, when both sides objected to an American working paper on the first day of the summit, which set out the premises and guidelines for the negotiations, the United States pulled it. Both sides similarly rejected the first American position paper, submitted on the 13th, and from this point on the US team did not present any further position papers of its own, though it did submit bridging proposals.[12]

Though ostensibly a "lame duck," Clinton was intensively involved in the negotiations until the very end of his presidency—indeed, the height of his involvement came during the final weeks, with the presentation of the "Clinton Parameters." The administration, however, made only limited use of its impending end to leverage concessions. Moreover, it had neutralized one of the primary "sticks" in its arsenal, the threat to apportion blame for failure, with a promise to Arafat to refrain from doing so. Clinton partially violated this following Camp David, by indicating that Arafat bore primary responsibility, but this was done in a restrained manner, with a view to keeping the negotiations alive.[13]

Barak's primary negotiators, Foreign Minister Ben-Ami and his bureau chief, Gilad Sher, were highly critical of the US role, especially at the summit. For all of Clinton's boundless good will, unflagging efforts, and mastery of even the most arcane minutiae of the negotiations, Ben-Ami maintains that he was an ineffectual mediator, who was incapable of exerting the overwhelming pressure required, allowed Arafat to get away with his continual refusal to make decisions, and let the summit "run itself." Sher believes that the US "peace team" was simply worn out after years of intensive efforts and lacked the necessary diplomatic creativity and assertiveness. It did initiate structured negotiating processes at the summit on a few occasions, assigning "homework" to the sides and outlining positions, but repeatedly failed to follow through. He also maintains that Secretary of State Madeleine Albright was viewed by the sides, especially Arafat, as weak.[14] Justified or not, these views informed the sides' actions during the negotiations.

### Pathology 1: An Unplanned Process

If ever an issue required well thought-out policy planning, it was the negotiations with the Palestinians. An assessment prepared at the beginning of Barak's tenure found that there were six primary areas to be negotiated, requiring a whopping 450 discrete decisions.[15]

Unlike the other case studies in this book, Camp David II was, indeed, very much a planned process. Extensive, in-depth planning began within days of Barak's assumption of office, with the participation of virtually all governmental agencies and covering all possible dimensions of an agreement. Endless papers were prepared, options explored, and issues assigned for study. Brainstorming sessions were held with officials from the various agencies and outside experts, and the findings were presented to Barak for approval, or at his discretion, to the MCoD or full cabinet. It was a dynamic interagency process, run directly by the premier's bureau, in which requests for information, assessments, and recommendations flowed to and from the IDF, MoD, intelligence agencies, INSC, MFA, MoF, and more. A special Peace Administration was established to coordinate and integrate the process.[16]

Given Barak's willingness to make dramatic concessions, it was certainly hard, probably impossible, to fully map out all of Israel's bargaining positions in advance. Barak knew where he would start, but not where things would end, especially since many of his concessions would be a function of Arafat's positions, and Arafat was a difficult and mercurial partner at best.

Barak believed that a breakthrough would be reached not by means of careful policy planning and negotiations between senior officials, who would lack the authority to make the tough decisions, but only by creating a "pressure cooker" situation in which the two leaders would be put to the ultimate personal test. Consequently, Barak's efforts were designed from the beginning to create the "moment of decision" in which both he and Arafat would have to face the contradictions between their national myths and practical interests and make the ultimate concessions.[17]

Upon entering office Barak sketched out the overall contours of an agreement:

- Preservation of Israel's character as a Jewish and democratic state.
- A Palestinian state on the 1967 borders, with minor border corrections.
- 80% of the settlers (as opposed to settlements) to remain under Israeli sovereignty in settlement blocs.
- Israeli sovereignty over a united Jerusalem, including the Jewish holy sites.
- Resolution of the refugee problem through compensation and resettlement in the Arab countries and future Palestinian state. Israel would not recognize a "right of return" or responsibility for the creation of the problem but would contribute to international resettlement efforts.
- Demilitarization of the Palestinian state and other security arrangements. The Jordan Valley would remain under Israeli sovereignty for an extended period, as a security zone, but could be divided in the future.
- No territorial swaps.[18]

Barak subsequently deviated from these guidelines substantially at Camp David and thereafter, especially in regard to Jerusalem, territorial swaps, and the Jordan Valley. The demand that the agreement include an "end of conflict" clause was added later. A coherent overall end-state had, however, been formulated.

Following the agreement with the Palestinians in September 1999 on the timetable for the interim and final agreements, Ben-Ami wrote Barak that if he truly intended to meet the highly ambitious deadline he had set,[19] it was necessary to formulate Israel's positions before the negotiations began. Ben-Ami recommended that Israel adopt a "trade-off" approach between territory and sovereignty, with the extent of territory ceded to be a function of the Palestinians' willingness to accept limitations on their sovereignty and to respond to Israel's needs on security and settlements. Ben-Ami further recommended that Israel work with the United States to reach agreed "red lines" and that a contingency plan be formulated in case the negotiations failed.[20]

In October 1999 Barak consulted with various experts and public figures on the interim and final agreements and then convened a series of marathon meetings with ministers, senior officials, and academic experts. In November, in a meeting he convened in preparation for the interim agreement talks with Clinton and Arafat, the IDF legal adviser presented a list of twenty-five different issues that might be raised.[21]

In late 1999 Sher came to the conclusion that a final agreement could not be reached by the planned September 2000 deadline. Given the decision to withdraw from Lebanon by the summer, Israel's entire leadership, including the premier, would simply be too busy to give sufficient attention to the negotiations with the Palestinians. He thus submitted a policy paper to Barak proposing that the negotiations focus on a comparatively long-term (four-year) interim agreement, with a substantial Israeli withdrawal as an inducement for the Palestinians.[22]

In early 2000 Ben-Ami submitted a number of position papers to Barak and held in-depth discussions with him on the core issues, such as Jerusalem and the refugees, as well as Israel's negotiating strategy. In March Sher again grew concerned about the timetable and initiated a policy review regarding Barak's decision to push for a final agreement that year, questioning whether a postponement might not be preferable. On April 1 Barak was given a policy paper analyzing Israel's options, on the assumption that an interim agreement was concluded by the summer, a Palestinian state was established by year's end, and the final agreement was postponed until the summer of 2001.[23]

In May 2000 Barak, Sher, and Ben-Ami considered the possibility of dividing the West Bank into three areas: a Palestinian state, areas to remain under Israeli control, and areas on whose final status a decision would be postponed for five years. On May 21 Barak instructed that two papers be prepared: the first was to set out the issues that were likely to be raised in a summit, including areas of Israeli flexibility; the second was to deal with the practical issues of water, economics, regional cooperation, law enforcement, and more.[24]

On June 1 Sher submitted a "status paper" to Barak in which he returned to the time factor and again concluded that a permanent agreement could not be reached by September. On June 18 the IDF presented three options: a final agreement, a unilateral Palestinian declaration of independence, and an Israeli diplomatic initiative designed to induce the Palestinians to postpone the declaration. The Peace Administration and INSC prepared papers dealing with the consequences of a unilateral Palestinian declaration, including the creative possibility of a "coordinated unilateral declaration." The Peace Administration conducted a simulation exercise, which came to the discouraging conclusion that the worst-case scenario—of the summit ending in failure and violence—was the most likely, though it did not preclude the possibility that an interim agreement, but not a final one, could be achieved. Barak went over the various documents in painstaking detail.[25]

In preparation for Camp David, the IDF Planning Branch presented detailed options for a withdrawal from the West Bank, ranging from 70% and up, with an analysis of the security and political ramifications thereof. Barak instructed the INSC to prepare a policy paper on the Palestinian refugee issue. MI continued to assess, as it had for months, that Israel and the Palestinians were on a collision course. Arafat, in MI's view, viewed himself in historic terms, as the embodiment of the Palestinian national movement, and as such would refuse to make major concessions, such as acceptance of the 90% of the West Bank that Barak was willing to cede, would reject the Israeli demand for an "end of conflict," and would turn to violence if his demands were not met.[26]

At the request of the negotiating team, in some cases even Barak himself, policy support was also provided by extragovernmental sources. In October 1999 Barak requested that a number of external institutions prepare policy papers regarding a possible referendum on a final settlement. In April 2000 Barak received a think tank paper on the refugee issue, which set out the legal, moral, and practical issues. The Israeli team repeatedly consulted with a renowned British expert on international law, on the issues of the end of conflict, relationship between interim and final agreements, holy sites, Palestinian state, refugees, and more.[27]

All in all, the Barak team conducted an effective policy formulating process. Virtually all issues of relevance were studied in detail and numerous options were considered. A remarkable willingness to reassess deeply held assumptions and beliefs and to devise new and creative options characterized the process throughout. The overall objectives and game plan were clear from the outset, even if Barak made numerous and at times dramatic changes to Israel's positions in the hopes of reaching a breakthrough.

Jerusalem was initially the exception to this general rule. For political reasons elaborated in Pathology 2, the Israeli delegation arrived at Camp David having conducted extensive preparations on all issues except Jerusalem, which was perhaps the most complicated of all. During the summit, however, the delegation held a series of historic discussions on Jerusalem, including an in-depth, no-holds-barred brainstorming session on the 17th, which lasted six hours. Ben-Ami, with some hyperbole, called it "the most important meeting [ever held] in Israeli politics," describing the atmosphere as "stormy and exciting, accompanied by a sense of an "historic experience." Step by step, Barak and the others stripped away the layers of emotion, ideology, and religion surrounding Jerusalem, as well as security and functional issues, to reach a bare-bones definition of Israel's vital interests.[28]

Barak opened by stating that there was little room between Israel's starting positions on Jerusalem and its final ones and that the city's boundaries would have to be expanded to provide room for both an Israeli and Palestinian capital. Minister Amnon Lipkin-Shahak stressed that the very term "Jerusalem" had to be defined, since the refugee camps in east Jerusalem could hardly be equated with the Temple Mount, and that he was unwilling to "fight to the end" for recently built neighborhoods. In response to Sher's question regarding Israel's "red lines" in Jerusalem, Barak stated that ongoing Israeli sovereignty over Jerusalem was of the utmost importance and to this end that Israel had to retain control over security, law enforcement, construction, urban planning, and the holy places. It was not clear, he stated, that an agreement on Jerusalem was achievable.[29]

The full import of the discussion was best expressed by Barak:

> I have no idea how we will leave [the summit], but it is clear that we will face the world united if agreement is not reached because of the issue of sovereignty over our First and Second Temple. This is the center of our existence, the very anchor of the Zionist endeavor. . . . This is the moment of truth . . . a discussion that is tearing each of us apart. . . . The decision is very similar to the one taken on the Partition Plan and the establishment of the State of Israel. . . . We are thirteen people cut off from the real world, being asked to decide things which will have an impact on the fate of millions. . . . I do not see him [Rabin] or any other premier transferring sovereignty to the Palestinians over the First or Second Temple.[30]

Barak ended the meeting with directions for preparations he wanted done immediately—new information on Jerusalem, maps, an assessment of the dual-municipality concept, and of a possible separation between functional and religious autonomy on the Temple Mount—that is, much of the planning that should have been conducted well in advance. In practice, it was only later, following the summit, that extensive Israeli planning on Jerusalem was finally carried out and various options were weighed for dividing the city, including some highly creative ideas whose political and physical feasibility were questionable.[31]

Aside from Jerusalem, there were at least two major flaws in the process. Ben-Ami believes that the ongoing absence of clearly defined "red lines" encouraged Arafat to adopt maximalist positions and persist in his rejection of Israel's proposals, in the confidence that Barak would further compromise. For example, Barak started the talks with an offer to withdraw from 66% of the West Bank but had reached 87% by the time of Camp David, 91% at the summit itself, and ultimately 97% under the Clinton Parameters.[32] Sher believes that Barak, a political neophyte, failed to seek out vitally important political advice, unlike his active search for substantive policy support, with important ramifications for the negotiations. Ministers Peres and Ramon, for example, both sought to convince Barak that an attempt to reach a final agreement at Camp David, including Jerusalem, would guarantee failure and that this issue should be left for a later date.[33]

If the process was highly planned, the question remains whether it was sequential or otherwise. When Barak took office in July 1999 he was a breath of fresh air in the Middle Eastern scene, a human dynamo just waiting to set his transformational ideas in motion. Barak announced that he would seek to reach final peace agreements with both Syria and the Palestinians within fifteen months and that Israel would withdraw from Lebanon within one year, by agreement if possible, unilaterally if necessary. By the end of his first month in office he had already met twice each with Egyptian president Mubarak and Palestinian leader Arafat as well as with Clinton and the leaders of Russia, Britain, Jordan, and Morocco.[34]

Barak attached enormous importance to the meeting with Clinton, as a first opportunity to gain his trust and active support for his peace plan and, in effect, have Clinton adopt the plan as his own. Barak presented the details of the plan to Clinton, including the thorny issues of Jerusalem and the refugees. Postponing them, he maintained, difficult as they were, would only ensure failure. A final agreement would be based on an independent Palestinian state, with Jerusalem to remain under Israeli sovereignty and the refugees to be resettled in their countries of residence. Most settlers would be concentrated in a few blocs, under Israeli sovereignty, and the Jordan River would remain Israel's security border. Barak envisaged a two-stage process, an interim Framework Agreement on Permanent Status (FAPS) by February 2000, which would set out the principles for a final agreement, except on Jerusalem, and a Comprehensive Agreement on Permanent Status (CAPS), including Jerusalem, by October. Barak was already thinking at this time in terms of a trilateral summit with Clinton and Arafat, as a means of reaching a breakthrough.[35]

Barak explained that this extraordinarily ambitious timetable stemmed from a number of reasons: his electoral promise to withdraw from Lebanon within a year, Clinton's commitment to the Palestinians to seek a final agreement within that time, the American electoral cycle, and the need to maintain pressure on the sides to make the difficult concessions required. Moreover, Barak sought to achieve his objectives while Clinton, a known and friendly quantity, was still in office.[36]

The first of many crises with the Palestinians erupted following Barak's and Arafat's second meeting in late July 1999, when Barak expressed his wish to postpone an already long overdue Israeli withdrawal and subsume it in the final agreement. The crisis was averted in September, however, when Barak agreed to conduct the withdrawal by January 20, in exchange for Palestinian acceptance of his game plan—the interim agreement within six months and a final one within a year—instead of further step-by-step agreements. Formal talks on the interim agreement began on September 13. By this time Barak had already drafted a proposed framework agreement.[37]

In November Barak proposed that the Palestinians be given sovereignty over 66% of the West Bank and virtually all of Gaza. Barak, Clinton, and Arafat met and agreed to convene a trilateral summit in January or February to complete the interim agreement. By the end of November Barak had turned his attention to the Syrian track and put the Palestinians on hold, but in December agreement was reached to submit a first draft of an interim agreement to the United States by January 10, 2000, and conclude the agreement by February. The January 10 deadline passed without agreement, and the United States recommended that the interim agreement be discussed only orally at the trilateral summit and that an intensive series of meetings then be held to work out a written version by February 15, the initial target date. The summit was never held and instead Barak and Foreign Minister Levy met with Arafat on January 17.[38]

In February Israel's attention was focused on a severe escalation with Hezbollah. March was devoted primarily to the failed Geneva Summit with the Syrians, but Clinton, Barak, and Arafat met again and agreed that May would be the new target date for an interim agreement. Two months behind schedule, Israel finally completed the further withdrawal in the West Bank, which had been agreed upon the previous September. Israel's unilateral withdrawal from Lebanon was the primary focus of attention in April, but an Israeli-Palestinian backchannel was established in Stockholm and made substantial progress, with Israel now agreeing to relinquish 87% of the West Bank. In order to leave sufficient time to prepare for a trilateral summit, agreement was also reached on a further delay of the interim agreement, now set for late June.[39]

In June 2000 Clinton acceded to Barak's repeated request that he convene a summit. Clinton was not convinced that the timing was ripe or that sufficient progress had been achieved by other means, but Barak's determination to hold the summit at the earliest possible date, as well as the exigencies of the American electoral cycle, won out. Until the summit, the sides were to conduct intensive negotiations to try to narrow the gaps. A final agreement by September remained the goal.[40]

For Barak, the Camp David Summit was a make-or-break historic opportunity to end the Israeli-Palestinian conflict, and the Israeli team put forward far-reaching proposals in virtually all areas. Israel agreed to a Palestinian state in all of Gaza and 91% of the West Bank and to the return of tens of thousands of Palestinian refugees on a "humanitarian" basis, though not to a "right of return." Some 80% of Israeli settlers would remain in blocs under Israeli control. Jerusalem was the primary sticking point, but here, too, Barak initiated and accepted radically new positions. Arafat and the Palestinian delegation were almost entirely passive, pocketing the Israeli concessions and then demanding more. With only one exception, Arafat put forward no substantive proposals of his own.[41]

Following the summit, Clinton and mediator Dennis Ross clearly placed the onus for failure on Arafat. Although some would subsequently criticize Barak's role at the summit and Arafat did succeed in extracting further concessions over the following months, there is no doubt that Barak came to Camp David prepared for historic compromise. When it became evident that his overarching goal, a final agreement, could not be reached, Barak backpedaled and agreed to an interim agreement, which would leave Jerusalem and the end of conflict issues for the future, but the Palestinians rejected this, too.[42]

Between Camp David and the end of the Clinton presidency, the sides held fifty more meetings, culminating in the presentation of the Clinton Parameters on December 23, 2000. By this time Israel had agreed to transfer 97% of the West Bank to the Palestinians, with a partial land swap as compensation.[43]

Pathology 1, an unplanned process, was partially substantiated. Barak recognized from the beginning that the exigencies of the negotiating process would require concessions exceeding what he initially considered to be Israel's red lines. He was prepared for this and determined to reevaluate virtually every existing Israeli policy and pursue every avenue possible in order to reach a breakthrough. As such, the process was knowingly highly improvisational. He zigged and zagged between the Palestinian and Syrian tracks and his final positions were, indeed, very different from his original ones. The process, however, was highly planned, numerous options were explored, and even if Barak's positions changed over time, his objectives were clearly formulated. Barak had an overall game plan from the beginning, in terms of both the negotiating process and the substance, and this was largely a case of incremental, not sequential, decision making.

## Pathology 2: A Politicized Process

With Barak seeking a final agreement, including the highly divisive issues of Jerusalem, settlements, and refugees, politics could not but have been a major factor. In fact, Barak's fractious coalition began coming apart almost from the start and unraveled rapidly as the negotiations progressed. By Camp

David Barak was left with a minority coalition and as the momentum for early elections grew in the final months of the negotiations, in late 2000, he was forced to frantically try to outrun the political tide overtaking him.[44]

Barak's political strategy was predicated from the outset on his hope that he would be able to present the public with a one-time, take-it-or-leave-it package deal for peace. With agreement on Jerusalem, settlements, refugees, and security and the prospect of finally ending the conflict, Barak believed that he would be able to overcome political opposition. If the coalition fell, a likely outcome, new elections would constitute a referendum on the agreement; if it survived, a special referendum would be held.[45] The key, however, was to reach the one-time package.

Barak believed that the political costs of a final agreement would not be significantly greater than those incurred in a series of crisis-plagued partial agreements. Indeed, it might even be lower, for all of the issues would be resolved at once and the Palestinians would finally have to put an end to terrorism and violence.[46] Barak's understanding of the politics at play was best expressed by his instructions to Sher in May 2000, as they appear in the epigraph at the beginning of this chapter.

Barak's decision to "go slow" on the Palestinian track in late 1999 and early 2000 was an early example of the effects political considerations had on the negotiations. The accepted political wisdom in Israel had long held that the public could not absorb major concessions on two tracks simultaneously, and Barak, having promised to withdraw from Lebanon within one year, had little choice but to put the Palestinians on a partial "hold" while he focused on the negotiations with Syria and withdrawal from Lebanon.[47]

In May 2000 Barak spoke of transferring 77% of the West Bank to the Palestinians (up from 66%), with 13%–15% to remain under Israeli sovereignty and control over 8%–10% to be decided in the future. Although it was clear to Barak that this would not be acceptable to the Palestinians, he did not feel at this time that he could get out ahead of popular leaders such as Ministers Shimon Peres and Chaim Ramon. On May 15 bloody riots broke out in Israeli Arab towns, the very same day Barak was to have announced the transfer of three villages in east Jerusalem to Palestinian control. The violence added to Barak's coalition problems, further weakened him, and prevented the transfer. A few days later, the ongoing violence forced him to recall Israel's delegation from the Stockholm talks, in which considerable progress was being made.[48]

During the weeks prior to Camp David, Barak tried to reach out to respected right-wing leaders, such as Jerusalem mayor Ehud Olmert and former Likud minister Dan Meridor, to obtain their support for the concessions that would be required. He also attempted to reach out to settler leaders. By the time of the summit, however, Barak had been so weakened politically that it was no longer clear that he could have carried a referendum on an agreement, had it ended in success. His insistence on an "end of conflict," which Arafat rejected, was partly motivated by concern that the referendum's outcome would depend on this. During the summit, after weeks of parliamentary maneuvering, the coalition was forced to pull the bill providing for a referendum when it became clear that it lacked a majority.[49]

Barak's coalition was a hodgepodge of seven parties, from far left to hard right. Barak, however, chose to begin his premiership with as broad a coalition as possible, in the knowledge that it would unravel as the negotiations progressed. Coalition maintenance rapidly became a nightmare.

By late 1999, just months into Barak's term, the basic fault lines between the different coalition partners had emerged. The inevitable clash between the left-wing Meretz and orthodox Shas parties first emerged over the latter's parochial school system. In December the Knesset approved four opposition motions, over the coalition's objections. In February 2000 Shas joined a vote of no confidence, even though it was a coalition party, ostensibly over the Palestinian issue, but in reality over the same school issue.[50] The Shas-Meretz crisis continued in March, while the negotiations with Syria were under way in Geneva.[51]

In April and May, while Israel was preparing for the withdrawal from Lebanon, ongoing coalition friction further undermined Barak's authority and forced repeated delays in his promise to transfer three villages on the outskirts of Jerusalem to Palestinian control. In May Barak was forced to devote a large portion of his time to the now chronic Meretz-Shas conflict and to an attempt to convince Shas and the other religious parties to remain in the coalition and support the villages' transfer. Having given assurances to Clinton and Arafat that the transfer would be carried out, it became a test case of his leadership, but Barak was forced to postpone it once again. The cabinet finally approved the transfer later in May, but the National Religious Party (NRP) announced that it would leave the coalition if it was actually carried out. Palestinian violence on the intended day of the transfer led to a further delay and allowed the NRP to remain in the coalition.[52]

In May Foreign Minister Levy, frustrated by Barak's decision to appoint Ben-Ami as Israel's chief negotiator, sidelining Levy, decided to make his displeasure known and distanced himself from Barak on the negotiations. Having been Barak's closest political ally, Levy's actions were a further blow to the premier's standing.[53]

On June 7 the Knesset approved a preliminary motion to dissolve the coalition. Three coalition parties (Shas, the NRP, and Natan Sharansky's Russian party) voted in favor and a binding vote was scheduled for August, forcing Barak to announce that he would form a new coalition. Barak initially intended to fire the Shas ministers, then backtracked, but the latter threatened to resign of their own accord on the 13th. On the 20th the Shas ministers actually submitted their resignations but rescinded them on the 23rd, following the resignation of the Meretz ministers. On the 25th Sharansky threatened to resign.[54]

In mid-June, in the midst of the coalition crisis, Ben-Ami recommended that a number of confidence-building measures be taken toward the Palestinians, who were growing increasingly concerned about Israel's ability to go forward. Barak replied that "I would do it if I had a coalition."[55] Shas leader Ovadia Yosef spoke out against territorial concessions to the Palestinians, while Levy and Sharansky called for the adoption of clear "red lines" in the negotiations. On June 27 Barak convened an unusual meeting of MKs from all of the coalition parties, briefing them for the first time on the negotiations and asking for their support. Sharansky and the NRP announced that they would resign if the summit was held. Barak, in a most unusual, almost desperate act, asked US mediator Ross to meet with the members of the coalition parties.[56]

By this time the coalition was in a state of free fall, with Barak confiding to Ben-Ami that "going to the summit will signal the coalition's collapse." Levy, in both a fit of pique over his ongoing marginalization and sincere differences over the conduct of the negotiations, announced that he would not accompany Barak to Camp David. In the final days before the summit, the NRP, Sharansky's Russian party, and Shas (which subsequently reversed course once again) bolted from the coalition. Barak arrived at Camp David with a minority coalition and a governing mandate that was unclear at best. Coalition machinations continued even during the summit, with Barak forced to devote time to a motion to hold early elections.[57]

Barak's sensitivity to public opinion was acute throughout the process. During Camp David alone he conducted eight different polls to assess public reactions to possible concessions. Despite strong right-wing pressure, polls throughout the process demonstrated that 65% of the public were willing to make far-reaching concessions in exchange for peace, but ongoing Palestinian violence and terrorism greatly undermined support for the negotiations, especially following the uprising in September 2000, and Barak's popularity plunged.[58]

The negotiations' failure, rapid collapse of Barak's coalition, and announcement of early elections prevented public opinion from coalescing in the kind of massive, ongoing opposition one would have expected over such a deeply controversial issue, or as happened, for example, in the far lengthier disengagement process in 2005. Nevertheless, public opinion was deeply engaged throughout and contributed to Barak's downfall. To cite just one example, at the height of Camp David, 150,000 people demonstrated against the evolving deal.[59] The unraveling of his coalition was a function not just of coalition politics but of the hemorrhaging and ultimate collapse of his public support.

No other issue better illustrates the impact of public opinion than Jerusalem. Indeed, it was clear from the beginning that Jerusalem would be one of the most difficult issues, even a deal breaker, both substantively and politically. Barak, determined as he was to "crack" even this ultimate issue, first had to shore up his credentials with the right wing. Early on, at the beginning of his premiership, he thus ordered that measures be taken to strengthen Israel's control over Jerusalem.[60]

In early 2000 Barak discreetly floated a number of trial balloons regarding possible solutions to the Jerusalem issue, to test public reaction. He also made the tactical decision to postpone negotiations on Jerusalem until a summit was held, at which time it would be discussed as part of the overall package of trade-offs. Barak believed that the public would support major concessions on Jerusalem, such as the city's division, only if the entire agreement was contingent on this. Consideration was also given, on a number of occasions, to the possibility of concluding a final agreement on all issues other than Jerusalem.[61]

Jerusalem's political consequences, according to Ben-Ami, "terrified" Barak. On July 17, at the height of the summit, Barak told Clinton that "I can not allow myself to go further [on Jerusalem] morally or politically" and then explained to Ben-Ami that "there are things that are beyond the mandate I received from the voters."[62] Indeed, Barak was so concerned about Jerusalem's political impact that he instructed his negotiators—even the IDF Planning Branch, long a locus of policy planning on ultrasensitive issues—to refrain from any preparatory work on Jerusalem, even it when it became clear that it would be a primary focus at Camp David. Barak feared that a leak of the very fact that Jerusalem had been under study would cause such controversy that he would be unable to make the necessary concessions. A partial solution was found in the form of unofficial assistance from a Jerusalem think tank, but Barak ordered an immediate halt to all contacts with it when this became known. Not surprisingly, Barak also instructed his negotiators to refrain from any substantive negotiations on Jerusalem in the months before Camp David and in May, during the Stockholm talks, even banned any mention of Jerusalem in Israeli documents.[63]

Politicization had a mixed but ultimately decisive effect on the negotiations with the Palestinians. Throughout most of the process Barak conducted the negotiations as if no domestic constraints existed, despite raging partisan politics, a rapidly unraveling coalition, and strong public opinion. Although he was forced to engage in some political maneuvering, Barak was convinced that he would prevail if a final peace agreement was presented to the public and he made major concessions at Camp David and thereafter despite having lost his coalition majority and the impending elections. Conversely, some of the concessions he made in the last months were clearly affected by the electoral clock and it is questionable whether Barak would have been able to obtain approval had an agreement been reached. Most important, partisan politics and public opinion led to the early fall of his coalition, to his electoral loss, and to the talks' collapse. Politicization thus had a major impact on the process, and all three dimensions of Pathology 2 were substantiated at a high level

## Pathology 3: Semiorganized Anarchy

On the one hand, Barak was very much in control of the process. He pressed ahead with his own game plan unwaveringly, despite broad opposition, the loss of his coalition majority by the time of Camp David, and the specter of early elections thereafter. To a degree, his early fall from office stemmed not from Israeli coalition politics and public opinion but from Arafat's rejection of every proposal that Barak and Clinton made, dramatic though they were, which left the premier empty-handed. Barak, however, was irreversibly weakened by the political process, and his electoral loss, after just eighteen months in office, dashed hopes for a breakthrough to peace.

From the beginning, Barak's political strategy for gaining approval for what he knew would be a highly controversial peace agreement, reflected the weakness of his position. Instead of seeking to build a political consensus for the agreement, he sought to force the issue by holding either a special referendum or early elections, which would constitute a de facto referendum, with the public forced to choose between a highly unsavory package or no peace at all. The very fact that Barak had to risk his political career in the attempt to reach an agreement was a further indication of the weakness of his office. Premiers willing to go that far, in any country, are a rarity. The bottom line is that Barak cannot thus be said to have been in control of the process.

To keep the cabinet and even the MCoD from impinging on his freedom of maneuver and consequent ability to conduct the negotiations, Barak did his best to keep the issue away from them or to present matters in ways that largely precluded their ability to truly shape matters. With the cabinet wracked by partisan politics and the coalition coming apart from day one, Barak conducted most of the real decision making in various informal forums.

As the following examples illustrate, neither the cabinet nor the MCoD were truly the locus of decision making. In June Barak convened the cabinet in response to repeated complaints from ministers that they had been sidelined on the negotiations. In ostensibly acceding to their wishes, Barak spoke only in general terms, refusing to elaborate on Israel's positions, and most of the time was devoted to assessments by the defense establishment.

This time-honored method of ensuring that there would not be sufficient time for substantive policy discussion served to guarantee his ongoing freedom of maneuver.[64]

In September 1999 Barak informed the cabinet that the proposal he had made to the Palestinians—postponement of further limited withdrawals in exchange for setting a one-year deadline for a final agreement—would be presented for its approval if accepted by the Palestinians. No discussion took place regarding this or other options, and the cabinet's role was largely moot in any event, since it would be asked to consider the proposal only after the Palestinians had already accepted it.[65] In the days prior to Camp David, a historic turning point at which Barak intended to make dramatic proposals, he convened only one cabinet meeting. Little of the extensive planning process conducted prior to the summit, or earlier, ever reached the cabinet.

The fear of leaks was constant, both for reasons having to do with the conduct of the negotiations themselves and domestic politics. Barak was long known to harbor a fear of leaks bordering on paranoia and kept his true thoughts to a very small group of confidantes. In this case his fears were justified. An Israeli leak of the draft peace agreement with Syria almost derailed the negotiations. A Palestinian leak of the breakthroughs achieved in Stockholm in May 2000 led the Palestinians to retract important concessions and to the demise of this heretofore effective back channel. Sher prefaced submission of a paper to the Palestinians in Stockholm with the comment that it would be a "political death blow" for Barak and Ben-Ami if its contents became known publicly.[66]

Barak was especially afraid that the Palestinians would learn of Israeli fallback positions. At one point he instructed the Peace Administration to cease work on possible alternatives to a final agreement, out of fear that Arafat would refuse to make the concessions necessary to reach a final agreement if he learned that Israel was even considering other options. Barak refused to even read a think tank study that outlined alternatives to a final agreement and, remarkably, called the chairman personally to demand that he refrain from discussing this option with his Palestinian counterparts, out of fear that Arafat would use it as a pretext to avoid a final agreement.[67]

The IDF refrained from holding a pre-summit simulation of the negotiations out of fear of leaks. In the days prior to Camp David, Barak directed that an MI assessment of the Palestinians' anticipated positions be presented to the cabinet "with adjustments, because everything leaks there."[68]

The fear of leaks was especially severe regarding written documents. In June 2000 Clinton informed Barak that he would agree to convene a summit only if he had a document to work from, but Barak refused to put his positions in writing, stressing that neither side could do so, since a document might leak and paralyze them. In a conversation with Sher in mid-June Barak stated that "our positions, as known to the president, are much more advanced than what we can document in writing." He thus directed that "no working paper whatsoever [describing Israel's positions] should be submitted prior to the summit, to ensure that it does not come back to us like a boomerang." In June, in an attempt to encourage Israel to say something new but in a manner that would not require that it expose its positions, American negotiator Ross asked Ben-Ami and Sher what they believed the *Palestinians'* areas of flexibility to be. They submitted a detailed paper in response, which Ross viewed as an extraordinary indication of what Israel could accept in an endgame, but Sher informed him, after consulting with Barak, that the paper "did not exist."[69]

In terms of leaks, Barak was most concerned regarding Jerusalem. In June, prior to Camp David, Barak instructed his negotiators to avoid any documentation on Jerusalem, whether preparatory papers or summaries of meetings with the Palestinians. "Be careful during discussions of Jerusalem," he warned, "do not document positions. No drafts or written documents are permissible, just some notes and oral discussions."[70]

At Camp David the fear of leaks, especially of documentation of concessions, led to a significant hardening of Israel's positions on a number of occasions. During the summit, Barak refused to update Egyptian president Mubarak on the progress achieved and insisted that Clinton refrain from doing so as well. Consequently, the Egyptians were briefed only by the Palestinians and did not know of Israel's far-reaching concessions, a factor that presumably contributed to Egypt's refusal to pressure Arafat to compromise.[71]

Pathology 3 was substantiated to a high degree. Barak was not in control of the process and the cabinet was not the locus of decision making. Leaks were a major problem.

## Pathology 4: An Uninstitutionalized Process

From the time he took office until his government's final collapse, Barak was a man on a mission. A former CoS and highly decorated commando officer, Barak had enjoyed a meteoric political rise. As premier he was determined to transform Israel's strategic circumstances virtually overnight or, more precisely, within a period of twelve to eighteen months. Rarely had an Israeli premier entered office with as clear a strategic vision as Barak and in pursuit thereof he was willing to make dramatic concessions, going far beyond what any of his predecessors had ever contemplated. Indeed, Barak recognized from the beginning that the negotiating process would inexorably lead to concessions that exceeded even what he considered to be Israel's maximum. Barak raised his negotiating strategy—a few months of bilateral negotiations with the Palestinians, followed by a trilateral summit with Clinton—at his very first meeting with the president, just days after he took office.[72]

Barak was fond of comparing himself to Israel's founding father and first premier, Ben-Gurion, who made the historic decision to accept the 1947 UN Partition Plan, despite the agonizing concessions required, and who had led the battle for independence. The decisions he would have to face, Barak believed, would be no less fateful or painful. He would be the premier who would make the breakthrough to peace with Israel's most incorrigible enemies, the Palestinians and Syrians, and who would preside over the determination of Israel's final borders. To this end, he was prepared to fundamentally reassess and overturn virtually all previous Israeli strategic thinking and to risk his political career. It was a damned-be-all approach. He would either achieve peace and change the course of the Middle East or expose the Palestinians' and Syrians' fundamental refusal to come to terms with Israel.[73] At the end of what proved to be a brief and tempestuous tenure as premier, Barak ultimately failed to achieve two of his three objectives, peace with Syria and the Palestinians, and even the withdrawal from Lebanon, the third objective, had to be carried out unilaterally.

Barak was critical of the Oslo Agreement from the beginning. As CoS at the time, he had expressed concerns over the agreement's security ramifications. Subsequently, as a minister under Rabin, he abstained on the Oslo II Agreement, which provided for a series of Israeli withdrawals, out of concern that Israel was being forced to cede territory for no more than vague Palestinian promises. He also believed that the "step-by-step" approach embodied in Oslo was fundamentally flawed and weakened Israel's negotiating position. It forced Israel's governments to invest their political capital repeatedly, in exchange for interim agreements, rather than doing so all at once, for a final one. Moreover, Israel was forced to continually relinquish pieces of territory without achieving its overall objective, a final peace. Barak believed that a final agreement would require a "package deal" in which both sides would have to make major concessions, for example, the Palestinians on Jerusalem and the refugees and Israel on territory, borders, and settlements. The necessary Palestinian flexibility would not be forthcoming, however, if Israel no longer held sufficient territory as a bargaining chip.[74]

The negotiations with the Palestinians entailed truly wrenching concessions on the core issues of the Arab-Israeli conflict, and a deep sense of history weighed heavily on the Israeli decision makers, none more so than Barak. He repeatedly warned ministers that Israel, like the Titanic, was about to crash into an iceberg and that it had to change course before it was too late.[75] On May 9, 2000, Barak stated: "We are on the verge of some of the most difficult decisions this decade, if not the entire history of the state. We do not really know to what extent it will prove possible to reach a reasonable equilibrium between the two sides' primary needs. . . . It is very important that we be aware of the [need to] 'change diskettes' [which is Israeli slang for mind-sets]."[76]

Barak's sense of foreboding was particularly acute on the sixth day at Camp David, in a private message to Clinton:

> I do not intend to allow the State of Israel to fall apart psychologically or morally. The State of Israel is the realization of the Jewish people's dream for generation upon generation. . . . There is no way that that I will preside over the closing of this saga at Camp David. . . . It is my belief that it is now or never. . . . There is no power in the world that can force collective national suicide on us.[77]

For better or worse, the process was very much an idiosyncratic one, in which Barak the man played an important role. His long-standing tendency to work alone, as a one-man show, was manifest from the beginning. He formulated the overall strategy and negotiating approach and kept close control of Israel's negotiating positions; despite the extensive policy planning carried out, even his closest advisers were often ignorant of his true thinking. Arguably only someone as audacious—some might say reckless—as Barak would have dared to achieve what he set out to do and adopted the "go-for-broke" approach he took. He also bears the onus for failing to handle the domestic politics involved in a manner commensurate with the scale of his ambitions.

The posited idiosyncratic nature of the process was manifested to a high degree. Conversely, Barak's policy planning process was an effective one and was not marred by significant policy input-output disconnects, nor were there serious problems of policy coordination and integration. Pathology 4 was thus partially substantiated.

## Pathology 5: Primacy of the Defense Establishment

The defense establishment, first and foremost the IDF, was deeply involved in the negotiations with the Palestinians throughout the process. Most of the expertise and planning support for the negotiating process was provided by the IDF, and the IDF and defense establishment as a whole were the primary bureaucratic players. Barak, moreover, had ensured his control over both the negotiating process and defense establishment through a calculated decision to serve as both premier and defense minister.[78]

On the eve of the negotiations' final collapse in late 2000 and early 2001, however, some differences did emerge between Barak and the IDF. CoS Shaul Mofaz openly criticized Barak's headlong rush toward an agreement, including his acceptance of the Clinton Parameters, warning that they constituted an "existential threat" to Israel. In what was clearly an overdose of hyperbole, Ben-Ami described this admittedly unusual statement as "tantamount to a military coup d'état."[79] It certainly reflected growing IDF concern, shared by many at the time, over what appeared to be a "clearance sale" of long-held Israeli positions. As with the other sources of domestic opposition, however, Barak paid little heed and continued his pursuit of a breakthrough unabated. With this exception, the defense establishment was usually highly supportive of Barak's efforts.

The MFA's role in the process was limited. Barak shunted Foreign Minister Levy aside from the beginning, preferring to appoint Internal Security Minister Ben-Ami and his bureau chief and confidante, Sher, as chief negotiators. Ben-Ami was ultimately appointed foreign minister, but this was only in the final months of the negotiations and his influence was personal, rather than institutional. The INSC had just been established and played virtually no role, though the national security adviser himself was involved in some of the planning, on the basis of his personal relationship with Barak.

Pathology 5 was partly substantiated. The IDF and defense establishment as a whole were the primary sources of expertise and the primary bureaucratic players. Despite the centrality of the defense establishment, however, particularly strengthened in this case by Barak's dual role as premier and defense minister, the fact is that it was unable to gain cabinet support for its preferences. Barak went ahead anyway and in this sense his views prevailed, but in the end his fall reflected the primacy of partisan political considerations over defense ones. A fair judgment would thus seem to be that the positions of the defense minister and establishment prevailed at only a moderate level.

**Table 6 Manifestation of Pathologies in Camp David II**

| Category | Manifestation | Rating |
|---|---|---|
| *Unplanned Process* | Sequential Decision Making | Mod. |
| | Improvisation | Mod. |
| | Absence of Policy Planning, Objectives, and Options | Low |
| *Politicized Process* | Public Opinion | High |
| | Coalition Maintenance | High |
| | Politics Reign Supreme | High |
| *Semiorganized Anarchy* | Leaks | High |
| | Dysfunctional Cabinet | High |
| | Premier Not in Charge | High |
| *Uninstitutionalized Process* | Insufficient Coordination and Integration | Low |
| | Policy Disconnects | Low |
| | Idiosyncratic | High |
| *Primacy of Defense Establishment* | Positions Prevail | Mod. |
| | Primary Bureaucratic Player | High |
| | Primary Source of Expertise | High |

Mod. = Moderate

# CHAPTER EIGHT

# Disengaging from Gaza, 2005

> After years of trying to reach a negotiated settlement we came to the
> conclusion, during the summer of 2003, that there was no partner, that
> we were playing solitaire and if that was the case, that we had to deal
> the cards ourselves.
>
> —Dov Weisglass, Sharon bureau chief

> Disengagement was a missed opportunity of historic proportions. . . .
> One does not do something without looking two steps forward, but
> no one did.
>
> —Giora Eiland, national security adviser

In December 2003 Premier Sharon took both Israel and the world by surprise with the announcement of his plan for unilateral "disengagement"
(withdrawal) from Gaza. Sharon never fully explained this historic decision
and his motivations remain a matter of conjecture to this day. As one of the
driving forces behind the settlement movement, Sharon's announcement
was a radical departure for him personally and for the Likud Party, indeed,
from virtually all previous Israeli strategic thinking, which held that territory and settlements would be ceded only in exchange for peace.

## The Strategic Setting

The idea of withdrawing from Gaza, though not unilaterally, was part of a
broader trend in Israeli thinking that began in the early 1990s and sought to
bring about a separation between Israel and the Palestinians. In 1992 Likud
minister Roni Milo recommended to Premier Shamir that Israel withdraw
from Gaza and in 1993 Premier Rabin spoke of a withdrawal from both Gaza
and Jericho, as a first step toward implementation of the Oslo Agreement. In
March 1993, with terrorism on the rise, Rabin declared that the "diplomatic
objective of a (peace) agreement is to take Gaza out of Tel Aviv, through

agreement, not unilaterally" and in August 1994, following a particularly horrific bombing, he first spoke of "separation." In January 1995 the cabinet directed that options be developed for physical separation of the Israeli and Palestinian populations.[1]

Separation gained increasing support over time, as did unilateralism, particularly during Barak's premiership (1999–2001). During the 2001 elections Labor candidate Amram Mitzna ran on a platform explicitly calling for unilateral withdrawal from Gaza but was trounced by Sharon at least partly over this issue. In June 2002 MK Chaim Ramon, a former and subsequent Labor minister, called for unilateral determination of Israel's borders, on a demographic basis.[2]

The growing interest in separation from the Palestinians was mirrored in defense planning. An INSC policy review during the latter part of Barak's premiership raised the option of "[self-] initiated" separation, including unilateral determination of Israel's borders, withdrawal from isolated settlements and construction of a security fence. In October 2001, at the height of the Intifada, the IDF Planning Branch devised a plan for the establishment of a Palestinian state in Gaza and approximately half of the West Bank, with all of the settlements in the former and seven in the latter to be dismantled.[3] Nothing better exemplified the support for separation than the 2002 decision to build the West Bank security fence: initially designed to prevent terrorism, it rapidly became a means of separation as well.

When Sharon announced the disengagement plan in December 2003, the peace process was on the verge of collapse. The Palestinians had rejected Barak's dramatic proposals at Camp David and the even more far-reaching Clinton Parameters, and a massive wave of terrorism was under way (the Second Intifada). On-again, off-again talks had gone nowhere and Israel's international standing deteriorated severely. The previous year, the Arab League had announced a peace plan that was widely hailed by the international community, further adding to Israel's isolation.[4]

In June 2002 President Bush announced a "vision" for peace in the Middle East, which called for a cessation of settlements and establishment of an independent Palestine, along with an end to terrorism, reform of the PA, and replacement of the now widely discredited Yasser Arafat. In April 2003 Bush announced the "Roadmap," a detailed and phased plan for the practical implementation of the "vision." Israel initially reacted with deep concern, fearing that it would lead to considerable disagreement with its closest ally. International isolation was one thing, friction with the United States an entirely different matter.[5]

The Roadmap notwithstanding, Arafat continued to abet terrorism and successfully thwarted all efforts to make the reforms it mandated. Many in Israel came to believe that Arafat's true objective was not peace but Israel's ultimate destruction through massive terrorism, international isolation, and the force of demography. Premier Mahmud Abbas, on whom much of the international community pinned its hopes, resigned in frustration. By mid-2003 Israel came to the conclusion that it simply did not have a Palestinian partner for negotiations.[6]

The United States, some Arab states, and much of the international community largely shared Israel's negative view of Arafat, but not its willingness to leave the peace process in abeyance while it focused on defensive military measures. In September 2003 the United States made it clear to Israel that it would not tolerate an impasse, in November the Security Council officially endorsed the Roadmap, and the United States cut loans to Israel over settlement activity while calling on it to respond favorably to Syrian peace "feelers." Indeed, it was becoming increasingly apparent that in the absence of an Israeli initiative, international pressure might grow severe and even lead to Israel's long-standing nightmare, an imposed solution.[7]

Israel had to do something, but this does not explain the radical decision to withdraw from Gaza completely. There was no expectation at that time, international or just American, that Israel would take such a dramatic step. The prospects for peace and the security situation appeared so dismal that Israel would have gained widespread international acclaim had it taken comparatively minor measures.[8]

Two primary explanations have been offered for Sharon's dramatic decision. One holds that Sharon, like Begin nearly thirty years earlier, was really motivated by a desire to cut Israel's losses and further solidify its control over the West Bank. By going as far as he did, Sharon may have sought to deflect international pressure from the West Bank, viewing Gaza as a small price to pay. Sharon himself told Gaza settlers that "we are trying to save as much as possible of Judea and Samaria. It is at your expense, but I had to [do it]" and stated publicly that "in a unilateral process there will be no Palestinian state. This situation could continue for many years."[9] On another occasion he emphasized that the disengagement plan distinguished between "goals worth fighting for, because they are truly vital, like Jerusalem, the big settlement blocs, the security areas and preservation of Israel's character as a Jewish state, as opposed to objectives which we all clearly know will not be achieved and which most of the public is justifiably unwilling to sacrifice a great deal for."[10]

A more far-reaching explanation viewed disengagement as a means of precluding the possibility that a Palestinian state would ever be established. Though roundly denied by Sharon, his bureau chief, Weisglass, lent credence to this approach in a highly controversial interview: "The whole diplomatic process was frozen [by disengagement]. . . . When you freeze the process, you prevent the establishment of a Palestinian state and prevent discussion of the refugees, borders and Jerusalem. The whole package called a Palestinian state is off the agenda for an indefinite period. . . . [Disengagement] is a bottle of formaldehyde in which you put the President's formula [i.e., "vision"] for a very long period."[11] Sharon's desire to circumvent US pressure to pursue Syrian peace feelers may have further contributed to these considerations.[12]

A number of additional factors certainly contributed to Sharon's decision. Ongoing terrorism by the Palestinians, Hezbollah, and others, further compounded by general national fatigue with the ceaseless violence, weighed heavily on Israeli thinking at the time. The Intifada had led to the deaths of over one thousand Israelis, and thousands had been wounded. In December 2003, an average of fifteen terrorist attacks were attempted in the West Bank and Gaza each day. Even after Israel succeeded in putting a virtual end to suicide and other types of bombings, rocket fire from Gaza continued.[13]

After more than fifteen years of Palestinian violence, however, it had become increasingly clear that there was no purely military solution to the threat. Israel had succeeded in greatly reducing terrorism, but it could not erase Palestinian nationalism, and its hold on the Palestinian population was increasingly costly.[14] Fed up with the ongoing bloodshed and high cost of occupying Gaza, Israel sought a new solution to the security threat it posed.

Recognition of the limits of military action now merged with a growing awareness that demographic trends were irreversibly in the Palestinians' favor and that continued settlement would endanger Israel's character as a Jewish and democratic state. Indeed, by the late 1990s and early 2000s, the force of demography had become so extreme that many on the right, including Sharon, were forced to change decades-old ideological convictions. Sharon stressed on a number of occasions that disengagement "ensured" Israel's future as a Jewish and democratic state. Ehud Olmert, Dan Meridor, and Tzipi Livni, leading stalwarts of the Likud right, all underwent similar political transformations during this period.[15] By withdrawing from Gaza, Israel would be able to maintain a clear Jewish majority for decades, even if it retained the West Bank.

Disengagement also reflected changing Israeli perceptions of the strategic importance of territory:[16]

- Whereas territory had heretofore been viewed as a source of vital strategic depth, Palestinian violence brought the security threat directly to Israel's home front. In some ways, territory was becoming more of a liability than an asset.
- Settlements had long been viewed as an integral part of Israel's security policy, whose very existence determined its borders and contributed to its defense. This was clearly no longer the case.
- Previously, territory had been considered an essential bargaining chip. With the exception of the peace with Egypt, however, the "land for peace" formula, which lay at the heart of Middle Eastern diplomacy, had failed to produce the desired outcome.[17]

Finally, disengagement was predicated on the assumption that there was no one on the Palestinian side both desirous and capable of reaching a negotiated solution and thus that withdrawal would have to be unilateral. As one senior IDF officer intimately involved in disengagement put it, "if we had tried to withdraw from Gaza by agreement, we would still be there today. Negotiations with them [the Palestinians] were impossible."[18]

The United States played a vital role in the early stages of the disengagement process; indeed, it was US insistence in September 2003 that it would not tolerate an impasse that was the plan's proximate cause. The first in a series of intensive US-Israeli consultations took place in November, as the initially skeptical United States sought to shape what was still an only half-baked Israeli initiative as the condition for its support. As the proposal was fleshed out, however, and modified according to its demands, the United States came to see its advantages. Why, indeed, not let Sharon withdraw from Gaza and dismantle the settlements? The United States thus took it upon itself to "sell" disengagement to the Palestinians, Arabs, and international community.[19]

For Israel, US support was crucial, to garner not only international support but domestic as well. In an exchange of letters on April 14, 2004, Bush recognized two principles of vital importance for Israel: that the West Bank settlement blocs would remain a part of Israel in a final agreement and that the Palestinian refugee issue would have to be resolved within the future Palestinian state, without a "right of return" to Israel.[20] These assurances were key to Sharon's ability to muster the political support he needed for disengagement.

US support did not come cheaply. It insisted that disengagement be an integral part of the Roadmap, that is, a step toward the establishment of a Palestinian state, not an alternative to it. Moreover, to counter the Palestinian criticism that Israel was merely trying to unload an area it did not want anyway in exchange for further securing its control over the West Bank, the United States demanded that some settlements be dismantled there, too. In setting these and other conditions, the United States partly came to replace the Palestinians as Israel's missing negotiating partner.[21]

Egypt was Israel's other primary interlocutor, focusing on border security along the "Philadelphi Corridor," the narrow (tens of meters wide) strip along the Gaza-Egypt border, through which Hamas had smuggled arms and rockets for years. Israel sought an Egyptian commitment to take full responsibility for security along the corridor and insisted that it would withdraw from the corridor only at a later stage, if Egypt succeeded. Egypt, for its part, preferred a more limited role, agreeing to patrol the corridor but not to bear responsibility. A breakthrough was reached in March 2005 when Israel agreed to withdraw from the corridor concurrently with the rest of Gaza, in return for heightened Egyptian security measures. Numerous details remained to be worked out, however, and final agreement was reached only days before the actual withdrawal.[22]

## Pathology 1: An Unplanned Process

Disengagement was a classic case of adopting a policy first, asking why and planning second. It was a solo decision. No policy planning processes or cabinet meetings preceded Sharon's decision, Israel's objectives had not been spelled out, nor were different options weighed for achieving them. Consequently, Sharon spoke only in vague terms when he first announced the disengagement plan in December 2003. According to Sharon:

- Israel sought a negotiated two-state solution but would disengage from Gaza unilaterally if talks failed. The Palestinians would obtain much less through disengagement than negotiations.
- Settlements would be relocated to reduce the number of Israelis living among the Palestinian population to the extent possible, but Israel would strengthen its control over the areas it intended to retain in a final agreement.
- The settlements' new placement would be designed to establish an effective security line, pending a final agreement, and would thus not constitute Israel's permanent border. IDF forces would redeploy on new defensive lines.
- Disengagement would reduce terrorism while making it easier for Israeli forces to fulfill their missions, minimize friction with the Palestinians, and strengthen Israel's economy.[23]

In January 2004 Sharon presented the outlines of the disengagement proposal to National Security Adviser Eiland and tasked him with fleshing them out into a comprehensive plan. Impressed by Sharon's willingness to make far-reaching concessions, Eiland suggested that Israel would achieve more through a negotiated process than a unilateral one and asked for two weeks to formulate additional options. Sharon refused, stating that he was interested only in recommendations regarding the optimal ways of implementing disengagement. He would later claim that he had weighed four options, but there is no evidence that they were ever considered by anyone other than Sharon himself.[24]

Eiland asked Sharon how long he had for the planning process and was told four months:

I quickly found out, however, that Weisglass had already met with the Americans and committed to a major unilateral move in Gaza and the West Bank. The Americans were under the impression that we were talking about a withdrawal from 60–80% of the West Bank. . . . Sharon committed to withdrawing from eighteen settlements in Gaza and so our cards were mis-played. The horses had left the stable. The planning process I had begun shattered.[25]

The INSC began crash planning and Eiland presented Sharon with the first draft of a plan just a few weeks later on February 9, with a variety of options; regarding Gaza, they ranged from dismantlement of the three northern settlements alone, to a complete withdrawal; regarding the West Bank, from the status quo, to consolidation of all settlements in three primary blocs.[26] The options clearly went beyond Sharon's directive that Eiland address only the optimal means of implementing the decision to disengage from Gaza and brought into play some of the broader considerations Eiland wished to ad-dress. There is no indication, however, that this had any impact. Sharon was committed to a large withdrawal from Gaza, while his consideration of the West Bank options appears to have been limited to one factor, the minimum number of settlements Israel would have to dismantle in order to obtain the American quid pro quo (as described in the Bush letter of April 14).[27]

The planning process continued throughout 2004. It was one of the more detailed, carefully thought out, and integrative policy planning processes in Israel's history, and the INSC, with the participation of virtually every governmental agency, delved into all facets of the disengagement concept. It rapidly transpired that what had appeared, at first glance, to be a rela-tively straightforward concept, primarily diplomatic and military in na-ture, was far broader, with ramifications for almost all aspects of life in both Israel and Gaza. To illustrate, the settlers would have to be provided with new homes, which required the involvement of the Ministries of Housing and Infrastructure; with new jobs or businesses, which brought the Minis-tries of Labor and of Industry and Commerce into the picture; and with ongoing educational, health, and social services, which brought these min-istries into the process. Since many settlers would continue working as farmers, the Ministry of Agriculture was also involved. Similarly, the need to continue providing Gaza with water, gas, electricity, and telecommunica-tion services required the involvement of the relevant agencies. Needless to say, the IDF, MoD, MFA, Ministry of Domestic Security, and intelligence agencies also were all deeply involved.

Each day raised complex new issues that Sharon had not taken into ac-count when announcing the plan. Some involved fundamental questions, such as the extent of the withdrawal from Gaza and the West Bank; others were much more mundane, for example, the future of the planned Gaza airport. In the absence of clear direction from Sharon, the INSC and other agencies had an only limited understanding of his thinking and often found themselves groping in the dark.[28]

In May 2004, following the failure of a Likud Party referendum to ratify the disengagement plan, Sharon proposed an amended plan to the cabinet.

As ultimately adopted on June 6, it stated that the objective was an unspecified "improved security, diplomatic, economic and demographic reality" and that:

- The cabinet would decide whether and which settlements to dismantle in Gaza, in four groups, depending on the circumstances at the time. Four settlements would also be dismantled in the West Bank.
- No settlements would remain in Gaza in a final agreement, but Israel would retain some parts of the West Bank, including central settlement blocs, security zones, and areas where Israel had additional interests.
- The withdrawal would reduce friction with the Palestinians and nullify claims regarding Israel's ongoing responsibility for Gaza.
- Israel would maintain a military presence along the Philadelphi Corridor but would consider a future withdrawal depending on the security situation and Egyptian cooperation.
- As a rule, private homes and sensitive structures, such as synagogues, would be razed, whereas industrial, commercial, and agricultural ones would not.[29]

The disengagement process was largely about short-term gains, improvisation, and sequential decision making. In the fall of 2003 Sharon concluded that Israel had to do something to end the diplomatic impasse. Weisglass, the only person he consulted with, proposed that Israel withdraw from Gaza unilaterally. In so doing, Weisglass believed, Israel would assuage international opinion and preserve the Roadmap as the accepted basis for negotiations. Under the sequence set out by the Roadmap, a Palestinian state would be established only after the Palestinians had succeeded in ending terrorism and reforming the PA, that is, not for many years at the very least.[30]

When Sharon first presented the disengagement "plan" to the public in December 2003, a comprehensive strategy did not exist, indeed, was little more than a general concept, what NSA Eiland subsequently called an "amorphous term . . . [not a] developed idea, rather a desire for an idea." In January Sharon thus appointed Eiland to turn the idea into a fleshed-out strategy and coordinate the interagency process necessary for implementation.[31]

By this time Weisglass had already conducted a series of meetings with the United States, in which he conveyed the impression that Israel would withdraw from all of Gaza and most of the West Bank. The initial guidelines Sharon provided to Eiland, however, called for withdrawal not from the West Bank but Gaza, and even there only a partial withdrawal. The three northern Gaza settlements, which were territorially contiguous with Israel, would remain and the withdrawal would be to a new border, not the 1967 line.[32]

With his own thinking not yet fully elucidated, Sharon first spoke publicly of his intention to withdraw from all of Gaza and to dismantle four settlements in the West Bank only on February 3, 2004. He stressed that it would be unwise, from both a security and demographic perspective, to remain in Gaza and that the belief that Israel could bear long-term responsibility for the Palestinians was simply misguided. Even Eiland, who believed that the number of settlements to be dismantled in Gaza was still under review, was taken by surprise.[33]

Weisglass and Eiland met with Secretary of State Rice in late March 2004 and presented two options. One called for a complete withdrawal from Gaza, including the Philadelphi Corridor. The other added a withdrawal from four to six settlements in the West Bank to the first proposal, with the precise number to be a function of the American quid pro quo. Originally conceived as a purely unilateral move, disengagement had now become a means of obtaining "compensation" from the United States, which Sharon sought both for substantive diplomatic reasons and to promote support for the plan within the Likud Party and the Knesset. The two countries began a series of intensive consultations and reached agreement on the basic principles by mid-March.[34]

The future of the Philadelphi Corridor remained a crucial issue throughout the process. In a meeting with Sharon on March 17, 2004, the defense chiefs presciently warned that if Israel withdrew from Philadelphi, Hamas would turn Gaza into a huge arsenal and rockets would rain on Israel, forcing it to take repeated countermeasures in the future, including major incursions. Sharon decided to retain control of the Philadelphi Corridor until stability was assured but later changed his mind, and Israel withdrew from it along with the rest of Gaza, leading precisely to what the defense chiefs had foreseen.

The March 17 meeting produced agreement on the West Bank settlements issue. Four would be dismantled, not the broader option of seventeen to twenty that Sharon had been considering. Conversely, the issue of whether to fully withdraw from Gaza, the center of the entire plan, or retain the three northern settlements, was still unresolved. The future of the physical assets in the Gaza settlements (private homes, commercial and public buildings, infrastructure) first came up for consideration in March. The INSC proposed transferring them to the Palestinians for refugee resettlement and calculating their monetary value against future Palestinian demands for compensation for abandoned refugee property. Others favored razing them.[35]

By this time it had also become clear that Sharon would be hard-pressed to gain cabinet approval for disengagement, despite the American quid pro quo. To circumvent the cabinet, Sharon had initially intended to submit the plan to a national referendum, but it now turned out that this would require legislation, since provisions for referendums did not exist under Israeli law, and passage of the necessary legislation would be as difficult and protracted as that required for the plan itself. Sharon backtracked and decided to hold a Likud Party referendum instead. Much to his surprise, however, the party referendum rejected disengagement on May 2. Forced to zigzag once again, Sharon made a few changes to the plan and went back to square one, the cabinet, for its approval, now granted on June 6. Two primary changes were made: the settlements would be divided into four groups, with the cabinet required to approve the dismantlement of each group separately, and it was decided to raze the private homes and sensitive buildings in the settlements, such as synagogues.[36]

In a meeting with Sharon on May 23, the defense chiefs expressed bewilderment over the provision regarding the four groups, wondering whether the decision on disengagement would now be made in four stages, or whether one overall decision would be implemented in four stages. Deeply concerned by the heightened dangers of terrorism they foresaw in the protracted and uncertain first possibility, they greatly preferred the second. Eiland had first presented the idea to the defense chiefs a few days earlier, eliciting considerable criticism. "Eiland was asked to draft something from today to today [i.e., virtually immediately], no one saw the plan and we did not know what it meant," one participant commented.[37]

In November 2004, a year after announcing disengagement, Israel began seeking international recognition that it would constitute "an end to occupation" in Gaza. It rapidly transpired, however, that Israel's desire to retain control of the Philadelphi Corridor, border passages, and air and sea space would not enable such recognition. Last-minute efforts were made to devise various creative formulations, which would at least recognize a decrease in Israeli responsibility, but to no avail. Had Israel thought of this in advance and made disengagement contingent on it, it is quite likely that the international community, avid for any progress, would have been far more forthcoming and that a satisfactory formula could have been found. By acting without fully thinking through its actions, Israel forfeited an important international quid pro quo.[38]

Though ostensibly resolved by cabinet approval of the amended plan in June 2004, the future of the homes and other structures in Gaza remained very much on the agenda. In May 2005 Mofaz recommended that the cabinet overturn its previous decision to raze the homes, but Sharon was still in favor. In the end, the issue was resolved in June in an unexpected manner, when the Palestinians, who preferred to use the land to build high-rises, asked that the homes be razed.[39]

If disengagement began as an immediate response to pressing needs, rather than a long-term strategy, it ended that way as well. No decisions were made regarding the "day after," that is, the future of the peace process as it pertained to the West Bank.[40]

Pathology 1 was fully substantiated. Disengagement was, in essence, an improvisation designed to gain time and forestall international pressure while hopefully improving security. Although a desired endgame had been predetermined, the process was essentially sequential, with fundamental decisions regarding the nature of the policy made only as events unfolded.

If the exigencies of real-world decision making often require that policies be adopted before all of the details have been fully worked out, including at times even central components, the decision to disengage was made before any policy planning was conducted. Even the comprehensive process begun thereafter was limited to how to best implement a decision that had already been made. Israel's basic objectives were never considered by the premier or cabinet in a systematic fashion, and the absence of planning impaired its ability to negotiate effectively. By announcing in advance that it would fully withdraw, for example, Israel ceded most of its negotiating cards and was consequently unable to achieve a number of important goals, such as recognition of the "end of occupation."

## Pathology 2: A Politicized Process

The disengagement process was all about partisan politics and coalition maintenance. For eighteen months Sharon was forced to ride a perpetual political roller-coaster in order to gain approval for the plan and bring about its implementation. A master political manipulator, Sharon had to marshal all of his highly honed skills to manage the political circus he faced, in the cabinet, Likud Party, Knesset, and public at large. He prevailed in the end, but his coalition collapsed and he was forced to break away from Likud and form a new party.

Sharon's initial reaction to disengagement, when Weisglass first proposed it, was negative, out of fear of the political ramifications for the Likud. A week later, however, he requested that Weisglass raise the issue with Sharon's son Gilead, whom Weisglass referred to as Sharon's "control group." Gilead's sole concerns revolved around the potential ramifications for his father's political future; once he was satisfied on this account, he had no substantive objections. Shortly thereafter the plan was first presented to the "Ranch Forum,"* which was not initially enthusiastic but ultimately concluded that a diplomatic initiative was the most effective way of restoring Sharon's plummeting popularity. Sharon's sensitivity to the politics of the issue was so great that he personally called a journalist to deny a report about a withdrawal proposal that was supposedly under consideration at the time by the IDF Planning Branch.[41]

In anticipation of broad cabinet opposition, Sharon began exploring the possibility of holding a national referendum on disengagement within weeks of the initial announcement. It then turned out, as noted, that this was not feasible, but Sharon still faced an open rebellion within the Likud and a leadership challenge from Finance Minister Netanyahu. Never one to despair, he

---

* The Ranch Forum comprised Sharon's closest political advisers, who met at his ranch.

decided to hold a Likud Party referendum instead, in the hope that it would provide the plan with a similar degree of public legitimization.[42]

The positions of the Likud ministers were in a constant state of flux, as they jockeyed to stake out positions that would enable them to oppose disengagement in public and placate their constituents, while avoiding a clash and even a rift with Sharon. In February 2004 Netanyahu and four other Likud ministers issued a joint statement strongly opposing disengagement, but Sharon's announcement of the party referendum, along with President Bush's letter of April 14, temporarily stalled their efforts. Netanyahu changed course and announced that he would support disengagement, but only if the border crossings remained in Israel's hands and the security fence was completed first. Foreign Minister Shalom and Minister Livnat followed in his wake.[43]

On May 2, despite intensive lobbying by Sharon, the party referendum rejected the disengagement plan. Sharon was stunned but rallied rapidly, made the noted changes to the plan, and resubmitted it to the cabinet at the end of the month. Throughout May Sharon struggled to assemble a cabinet majority for the amended proposal. One of the weak links, Shalom, apparently tied his vote to an assurance from Sharon that he would remain foreign minister even if the coalition collapsed. Netanyahu adopted a passive approach, awaiting the coalition's fall and his presumed succession to the premiership.[44]

The amended proposal was first presented to the cabinet on May 28, 2004, but discussion was postponed due to ongoing opposition. On the 30th Sharon was again unable to achieve a majority. The raging seven-and-a-half-hour meeting turned into a tense personal confrontation with Netanyahu and other ministers. Sharon rejected all compromise proposals and threatened to call for early elections.[45]

Following the meeting, Sharon continued to lobby the recalcitrant ministers. Netanyahu positioned himself at the head of the opposition, declaring that he could not vote in favor of a proposal that had been rejected by the party referendum unless changes were made (precisely the reason had Sharon had formulated the amended proposal). The other Likud "rebels" battled on. Sharon fired two ministers from a right-wing coalition party after they announced that they would vote against the plan. One spent the weekend in hiding to avoid being served with the letter of dismissal.[46]

With Sharon applying the "political screws," the amended plan was finally approved by the cabinet on June 6, 2004. Netanyahu, who preferred to avoid a showdown and to focus on his preparations for the future succession, voted in favor.[47] The vote was a case of political theater. The ministers approved the concept of disengagement in principle but still had to vote on the actual withdrawal in four "groups." Both sides could claim victory— Sharon, that the plan had been approved; the "rebels," that they still had to approve each of the "groups" and that the process was, therefore, still reversible. The battle, however, had just begun.

The day after the vote, the Knesset held two "votes of no confidence."[†] Two of the six members of the National Religious Party and fifteen of forty Likud members defected. Sharon was able to survive the votes only with the support of the opposition, and the coalition now commanded a minority of just fifty-nine Knesset seats. In early July a further vote of no confidence ended in an embarrassing tie.[48]

With a minority coalition and the Shinui Party threatening to bolt as well, Sharon began coalition talks with Labor and two religious parties. His problems continued, however, as a majority of Likud MKs made their support for a coalition with Labor contingent on the inclusion of the religious parties. Shalom now took the lead in opposing Sharon, both in regard to disengagement itself and the attempts to form a new coalition. In mid-August the Likud convention overwhelmingly rejected a coalition with Labor.[49]

A particularly loud and tense exchange took place during the cabinet meeting of August 30, with a visibly agitated Sharon warning that he would not be tied down and would set a fixed timetable for withdrawal. In September 2004 Netanyahu demanded that a national referendum be held, maintaining that this was the only way to provide disengagement with the necessary public legitimacy. On October 11 the Knesset humiliated Sharon, rejecting the Premier's Political Statement, the largely ceremonial opening of the winter session.[50]

On October 25, 2004, the Knesset approved the disengagement plan. It was a historic occasion. The plan could have been approved solely by the cabinet, but Sharon reasoned that it would be easier to gain support for the settler compensation bill, which did require Knesset approval, if it had approved the plan itself. In the days before the vote, the "rebels" renewed their calls for a referendum, with the battle raging until just minutes before the vote. The following day, Netanyahu decided to contest the Likud leadership and renewed his demand for a referendum. On November 8 the Likud Knesset faction voted to hold a referendum, thereby providing Netanyahu with an excuse to retract his threatened resignation. The "rebels" now included over half of the Likud Knesset faction. The National Religious Party quit the coalition and Sharon renewed coalition talks with Labor. A national unity coalition was established on December 25.[51]

In February 2005, Shalom, with the support of longtime Sharon ally Knesset speaker Reuven Rivlin, announced a new campaign in favor of a referendum. In mid-February, following a seventeen-hour debate, the Knesset approved the compensation law, needed to actually carry out the disengagement plan. Sharon did not leave his seat for seven hours. In March, with great effort, Sharon managed to obtain Likud support for

---

[†] If a vote of no confidence is approved, the coalition falls and a new one must be formed or elections called.

the annual budget bill, but the "rebels" won the round by making their support contingent on his willingness to submit the referendum proposal to a vote in the Knesset. On March 28 the Knesset finally rejected the refer-endum once and for all. It was an important victory for Sharon, but the rift within Likud was severe.[52]

The battle raged on. In May 2005 Netanyahu charged that disengagement would lead to a significant increase in terrorism and in June announced that he would vote against the final decision to carry out the withdrawal. In July the "rebels" announced that they would submit a bill calling for a three-month postponement of the withdrawal, scheduled for August, but the post-ponement was voted down. On August 7 Netanyahu resigned as a minister.[53]

The withdrawal took place as scheduled in late August, but the damage to the Likud was irreparable. A few months later, Sharon and other Likud leaders broke off and formed the Kadima Party.

Politics affected not only the process but the options considered. In March 2004 Likud opposition led Sharon to jettison an option he was considering for the dismantlement of up to twenty settlements in the West Bank. The future of the private homes and public structures in Gaza also became em-broiled in politics. Right-wing opponents raised the specter of Palestinian terrorists publicly celebrating the transfer of homes to them and even vying for the size of the house gained, based on the number of Israelis they had killed. The specter of synagogues being publicly desecrated was similarly raised. The decision was thus made to raze them.[54]

The fall of 2002 to the winter of 2003 was a public opinion nightmare for Sharon. A group of reserve pilots, the esteemed vanguard of the IDF, an-nounced in September that they would refuse to fly in the West Bank and Gaza. The "Geneva Initiative," a joint Israeli-Palestinian peace plan calling for an almost complete Israeli withdrawal, was launched in October and received with great acclaim both in Israel and abroad. The "People's Voice" initiative, led by a former head of the ISA, was also launched at this time and it, too, gained widespread support in Israel. Sharon feared that these public campaigns would weaken him politically and possibly even end up replacing the Roadmap. At the end of October he was questioned by the police on corruption charges.[55]

Also at the end of October, in a rare case of sharp and public criticism from within the heart of the defense establishment, CoS Yaalon stated that "the government's policy is destructive" and that "the situation in the Terri-tories is on the verge of catastrophe." Further stinging criticism from the defense establishment came in mid-November, when four former heads of the ISA participated in an unprecedented joint interview, in which they warned that Sharon was leading the nation to its doom and urged him to negotiate with the Palestinians on the basis of either the Geneva or People's Voice initiatives. Sharon's popularity plummeted from its usual 55%–60% to a low of 34%.[56]

Some have argued that Sharon's announcement of the disengagement plan in December was designed, at least part in part, to deflect these domestic difficulties. Be that as it may, it set the stage for growing, ultimately massive, right-wing opposition. In late December thirteen soldiers from the IDF's most elite commando unit announced that they would refuse to take part in the withdrawal, as did thirty-four reserve officers in January. In mid-January, 120,000 people demonstrated against disengagement in Tel Aviv, and on Independence Day, in April 2004, masses flocked to the Gaza settlements as a sign of support.[57]

The Likud referendum on May 2 was one of the high points in public opposition. In a highly orchestrated campaign, settlers from Gaza and the West Bank made targeted appeals, in person, to most of the 190,000 registered party members. Their extraordinary political mobilization contributed to Sharon's defeat in the referendum. In July, 130,000 opponents of disengagement formed a human chain from Gaza to the Knesset. In October, 15,000 children from the settlements participated in a demonstration opposite the Knesset. In December a settler leader called on settlers to refuse to obey the disengagement law the Knesset had just passed, while others began speaking in inflammatory terms of an "expulsion" of Jews and called on their supporters to resist the law, even at the risk of prison. Numerous settlers started wearing Stars of David on their chests, an intentionally provocative allusion to the Holocaust.[58]

In January 2005, 150,000 people demonstrated against disengagement in Jerusalem. In February, settlers warned of a rift among the people and expressed their willingness to fight disengagement even at the cost of lives. The head of the ISA decided to go public, warning of threats against Sharon and other ministers. In April, 50,000 people demonstrated in the Gaza settlements. In May, demonstrators blocked dozens of intersections around the country and 45,000 marched in the Gaza settlements. In June, opponents distributed one million streamers.[59]

The public battle reached its height in the weeks preceding the withdrawal in August 2005. Gaza settlers accosted IDF soldiers and blocked roads throughout Israel. Rabbis issued injunctions prohibiting soldiers and police from participating in the withdrawal, urged supporters to move to the settlements to physically prevent it, and even called for Sharon's death. Sixty-three soldiers announced that they would refuse to participate in the withdrawal. Twenty thousand soldiers and police were deployed to prevent disengagement opponents from marching to Gaza, but some 20,000 managed to do so on three occasions. Seventy thousand people prayed at the Wailing Wall, including 110 soldiers who announced that they would refuse to obey orders. Another 150,000 people demonstrated in Tel Aviv.[60]

Although opponents of disengagement largely ruled the streets, opinion polls showed an ongoing majority in favor. In June 2004, 66% supported disengagement and 59% still did so in January 2005, even though 75%

believed that the settlers would use violence to prevent it. Just days before the withdrawal, 58% were still in favor, despite a 75% majority who believed that it would be a first step toward withdrawal from the West Bank, too.[61]

Pathology 2 was fully substantiated. Disengagement was characterized by extreme partisan politics, coalition machinations, and public involvement, all of which had a major impact on the length and nature of the process. Sharon bowled ahead against all opposition and, remarkably, the political battle had virtually no impact on the substance of the process. It did, however, cost him his coalition and even the future of his party, as Kadima broke off from Likud.

## Pathology 3: Semiorganized Anarchy

The raging eighteen-month political free-for-all was both a clear demonstration of the Israeli premier's statutory weakness and an affirmation of what a truly determined premier can achieve. The highly organized opposition of a large and deeply motivated minority of the public and ceaseless efforts of leading ministers would have defeated a lesser leader than Sharon.

In the end, however, Sharon prevailed. He was forced to backtrack, go over the heads of the cabinet, face down repeated leadership challenges, and cajole and coerce his party and cabinet. Through masterful political maneuvering Sharon was able to stay ahead of the process and ultimately achieved what he wanted. The price, however, was very heavy, arguably unacceptably so. Not only did his coalition fall, but Sharon was forced to break away from the Likud and form a new party. It is the rare political leader who has the tenacity and audacity to act as Sharon did, and the fact that he ultimately achieved his objectives hardly makes his example stand out as a model of a premier in charge.

The cabinet plenum was the locus of decision making, no special subcabinet forums were convened, and few MCoD meetings were held on the issue. Ostensibly, then, the cabinet was in charge, but the entire process was a bitter political brawl, with few substantive policy deliberations. In reality, the cabinet was sidelined from the beginning. Sharon made all of the major decisions on his own, with the assistance of two advisers, Weisglass and Eiland.

The cabinet learned of the disengagement plan at the same time as the public, when Sharon first announced it in December 2003. Since he had already decided on his preferred policy, the cabinet was never presented with options, and despite the months of raging debate and ongoing political crisis, the final decision was virtually identical to what Sharon wanted from the beginning. Sharon repeatedly sought to circumvent the cabinet, first through a national referendum and later a Likud one, a means of dubious political legitimacy. When the Likud referendum rejected the plan, an unabashed Sharon simply made a few minor changes and resubmitted the plan to the cabinet, this time successfully ramming it through.

Leaks were rampant throughout the disengagement process but had virtually no effect on the outcome. Once Sharon announced the plan, certainly by the time the concept had been worked out with the United States in March 2004, most of the planning and negotiations behind it were not particularly sensitive. Many details remained to be worked out, but for the most part the process was a political one, taking the form of raging cabinet debates, which were reported in the media in the minutest detail, and public activism, not sensitive behind-doors decision making. The one case where leaks were a factor was at the very beginning, prior to the plan's announcement, when Sharon first asked Weisglass to put the proposal in writing. Weisglass was so afraid of a leak, even from the Premier's Office, that he turned to a secretary from his former law firm and asked that she type it there over the weekend.[62]

Pathology 3, semiorganized anarchy, was partially substantiated. Sharon was ultimately able to achieve his objectives, but was only in partial control, forced to maneuver endlessly, to form a national unity government to temporarily preserve his coalition, and ultimately to leave it and establish a new party. A fair assessment would be that the posited pathology in this regard was moderately substantiated. The posited dysfunctional nature of the cabinet was fully substantiated; leaks were not.

## Pathology 4: An Uninstitutionalized Process

Ariel Sharon was a man of strong convictions. A lifelong hard-liner, he had been a primary driving force behind the settlement movement. Sharon liked to think in broad strategic terms but was, above all, a tactician who excelled at utilizing passing opportunities to achieve short-term gains.

During the 2001 elections, Sharon disdainfully denounced his Labor rival's call for a unilateral withdrawal from Gaza as dangerous naïveté. In March 2001 he stated that "to withdraw from Kfar Darom [a Gaza settlement] is tantamount to withdrawing from Kfar Saba [a large Tel Aviv suburb]." In April 2002 he famously declared that "the fate of Netzarim [another settlement] is the same as the fate of Negba and Tel Aviv. Withdrawing from Gaza will only encourage terrorism and increase the pressure on us."‡ During the fall of 2003, he continued to stress the importance of Israel's military presence in Gaza and rejected unilateral measures. Indeed, just weeks before announcing the disengagement plan, Sharon stated that "a unilateral move is a bad thing."[63]

‡ Negba, a kibbutz in the Negev, was renowned for its heroic stand in the War of Independence.

In point of fact, however, an evolution in Sharon's thinking had long been under way. In some ways, disengagement was an outgrowth of a concept he had advocated for years, of a long-term interim settlement, which was the most he believed the parties could agree on. During coalition talks in October 2000, Sharon had suggested that Likud and Labor adopt a common platform calling for an interim agreement, based on the establishment of a Palestinian state in the West Bank and Gaza and dismantlement of numerous settlements. Reports in March 2001, immediately after his election as premier, indicated that Sharon intended to withdraw from three settlements in Gaza. In June 2002 Sharon's office conducted an opinion poll regarding a unilateral withdrawal from Gaza, thereby indicating his early interest in this possibility. He repeatedly rejected his political advisers' advocacy of a full withdrawal from Gaza, not out of principle, but fear that this would be viewed as weakness.[64]

Demographic considerations clearly played a central role in Sharon's changing thinking. He also appears to have gained a deeper understanding of the changes that had taken place in the military nature of the conflict since the early 1970s when he, as the regional commander in Gaza, had successfully suppressed terrorism. In the early part of his premiership, Sharon was critical of the IDF for being insufficiently aggressive in the fight against terrorism, but as time passed he concluded that a broader approach was required. His view of the military importance of settlements also underwent a transformation, from a belief in their vital role in the early years, to an understanding of their limited relevance today.[65]

For these and other reasons, Sharon was forced to conclude that the dream of a Greater Land of Israel was no longer tenable. One of the earliest public indications of his changing thinking was a controversial statement before Likud Party members in May 2003, in which Sharon first used the word "occupation": "I think that the idea that it is possible to continue keeping three and a half million Palestinians under occupation—yes it is occupation, you may not like the word, but what is happening is occupation—is bad for Israel . . . [and] can not continue forever."[66]

Publicly, Sharon sought to downplay the changes in his approach. It was not that the settlements had been an error, he explained, but that the situation had changed, and if Israel did not take the initiative, the international community might impose a solution. Whereas a negotiated solution would inevitably lead to the rise of a Palestinian state, with critical ramifications for Israel, dramatic unilateral action would enable Israel to perpetuate the new situation for a lengthy period of time.[67]

Disengagement was very much a one-man show and case of idiosyncratic decision making. Some other leaders at the time, though probably none from the Likud, might have also considered unilateral withdrawal from Gaza an option, but it is doubtful whether anyone else could have surmounted the political obstacles Sharon faced. Long known as a "human bulldozer," Sharon's ability to run with the punches and master the political circus he faced was extraordinary, possibly unique.

The idiosyncratic nature of the process was also manifested by Sharon's unbending refusal to even consider negotiating with the Palestinians on disengagement. Disengagement had been predicated on Sharon's belief that Israel did not have a Palestinian partner for a negotiated solution and that it could thus only affect its future unilaterally. Sharon, however, even rebuffed suggestions that he try to negotiate with the Palestinians on those specific issues where agreement might be possible while retaining the right to act unilaterally if necessary.[68] Moreover, if Sharon's insistence on full unilateralism was arguably understandable while Arafat was alive, it is far harder to explain after his death in November 2004 and replacement by Abbas, who clearly represented a historic change. By negotiating with Abbas, Israel could have strengthened Abbas's domestic standing and improved his chances of actually becoming the effective interlocutor it sought.

Finally, the impact of the legal problems Sharon and his son Omri faced at the time cannot be completely discounted. Some believe that by taking a historic initiative he hoped both to make it harder for the prosecution to advocate that he be tried for such "petty" misdeeds and to facilitate his attempts to stonewall the legal proceedings against Omri, who was ultimately convicted.[69]

The disengagement DMP was characterized by an at least partial disconnect between the information provided to Sharon by the national security establishment and other political leaders and the decisions he adopted. Perhaps nothing better exemplified this than the defense chiefs' repeated warnings that disengagement would lead not to an improvement in security, Sharon's stated objective, but to the contrary.[70] Related to this, Sharon insisted on withdrawing from the Philadelphi Corridor, despite repeated warnings from the defense establishment that Israel would no longer be able to prevent the flow of weapons into Gaza and that it would turn into a base for rocket attacks against it, as indeed rapidly happened. Sharon's refusal to even consider the alternative policy options Eiland presented to him early in the process was a further example. The problem in each of these cases was not his rejection of the professional bureaucracy's positions, which is of course legitimate, but that these decisions either were made in the absence of rigorous analysis or reflected a failure to acknowledge the risks along with a conscious decision to accept them.

If the original decision to disengage was made in the absence of any interagency policy integration and coordination, the situation changed completely once Sharon tasked the INSC with fleshing out the concept. There were the usual bureaucratic battles: the MFA believed that it was not sufficiently involved, and the IDF, which was less than thrilled with the organizational lead bestowed on the INSC, was occasionally high-handed in its cooperation. The overall process from this stage on, however, was well coordinated and integrated. The problem was that this happened only after the major decisions had already been made, and the planning process was focused primarily, though not entirely, on implementation. A fair judgment would thus seem to be that the process as a whole was moderately coordinated and integrated.

Pathology 4 was partly substantiated. The posited idiosyncratic nature of the process was fully substantiated, the dimensions pertaining to the policy disconnect and problems of policy coordination and integration moderately so.

## Pathology 5: Primacy of the Defense Establishment

Sharon completely dominated the disengagement DMP. He made the major decisions on his own, and his consultations with the national security establishment, including the IDF and INSC, were limited primarily to the means of implementing decisions he had already made. They were nonetheless the primary sources of expertise and bureaucratic players. The MFA played virtually no role.

With the possible exception of Defense Minister Mofaz, none of the defense chiefs, including the CoS, even knew of the disengagement plan prior to its public announcement. The IDF chiefs, normally the most important part of the defense establishment, often of the entire government, were first officially apprised of the plan in a meeting with Sharon on February 17, 2004, two months after it had been publicly unveiled. Even then, they were still unsure of Sharon's true intentions and objectives, indeed, whether he really meant to carry out the withdrawal at all. CoS Yaalon, for example, became convinced that Sharon was serious only in March.[71]

Yaalon was dismayed when Mofaz first briefed him on the plan in January 2004 and informed Yaalon that he had already recommended that Israel fully withdraw from Gaza. Yaalon had been under the impression that Sharon intended to withdraw only from the three settlements in northern Gaza. He was especially troubled to learn of Weisglass's contacts with the United States, fearing that the bureau chief had made important security concessions without any input from the IDF. Yaalon's fears were born out in March when he learned the substance of Weisglass's (and later Eiland's) talks with the United States, including important military aspects of the withdrawal.[72]

During the February 17 meeting with Sharon, the defense chiefs expressed a number of reservations, focused primarily on the plan's unilateral nature, not the principle of withdrawal itself. They believed that a unilateral move would be perceived by the Palestinians as a sign of weakness, which would spur them to even greater terrorism, and were especially concerned about the security ramifications of a withdrawal from the Philadelphi Corridor.

Rather than strengthening Israel's security, the withdrawal, they presciently warned, would lead to its cities coming under fire and the IDF being forced to reenter Gaza. Regarding the West Bank, they recommended that Israel conduct only a limited withdrawal, not the large-scale withdrawal from seventeen to twenty settlements that Sharon had initially considered.[73]

Sharon, leery of the political ramifications if the defense chiefs' concerns became public, decided to address them, but did so in a typically Sharon type of way. He accepted their recommendation regarding the West Bank, though this was mostly for unrelated political reasons, and agreed that Israel would withdraw from Philadelphi only after stability had been assured. He also directed, however, that the planning necessary for a possible withdrawal be conducted, thereby laying the basis for this,[74] and in the end Israel did, indeed, withdraw from the corridor at the same time as the rest of Gaza, without any true expectation of stability. Rocket fire began within days.

Mofaz had been an outspoken opponent of unilateralism, warning during the 2002 elections that it would lead to the establishment of a terrorist entity right on Israel's border. Having only recently completed his tenure as CoS, however, Mofaz had no political base of his own and was entirely beholden to Sharon for his political career. With the change in Sharon's policy, Mofaz hastily revised his own position and enthusiastically supported a withdrawal from Gaza.[75]

In February 2005 Sharon and Mofaz took the virtually unprecedented step of refusing to extend CoS Yaalon's tenure to the traditional fourth year. Although Yaalon had expressed most of his reservations regarding disengagement in closed forums, he had spoken out against it and other issues in public on a number of occasions and he was considered by them to be something of a political liability. His replacement by Dan Halutz, known to have close ties with them, removed the only potential institutional opponent of consequence to disengagement and ensured its friction-free implementation, at least at the bureaucratic level.

Pathology 5, the centrality of the defense establishment, was substantiated at a moderate level. The IDF was uninformed of Sharon's intentions before he announced disengagement and during the early months thereafter, and the INSC had the primary planning lead. Nevertheless, the IDF certainly became the primary source of expertise and bureaucratic actor thereafter and throughout most of the process. A fair judgment would thus appear to be that these subdimensions of the posited pathology were manifested at a moderate level. Sharon attached importance to IDF positions and modified his positions somewhat but did not change them fundamentally. This part of the pathology was thus also manifested at a moderate level.

**Table 7  Manifestation of Pathologies in the Disengagement from Gaza**

| Category | Manifestation | Rating |
|---|---|---|
| *Unplanned Process* | Sequential Decision Making | High |
| | Improvisation | High |
| | Absence of Policy Planning, Objectives, and Options | High |
| *Politicized Process* | Public Opinion | High |
| | Coalition Maintenance | High |
| | Politics Reign Supreme | High |
| *Semiorganized Anarchy* | Leaks | Low |
| | Dysfunctional Cabinet | High |
| | Premier Not in Charge | Mod. |
| *Uninstitutionalized Process* | Insufficient Coordination and Integration | Mod. |
| | Policy Disconnects | Mod. |
| | Idiosyncratic | High |
| *Primacy of Defense Establishment* | Positions Prevail | Mod. |
| | Primary Bureaucratic Player | Mod. |
| | Primary Source of Expertise | Mod. |

Mod. = Moderate

# CHAPTER NINE

# Back Again

## The Second Lebanon War, 2006

> Since the goals of the war were never defined and because no one
> clarified what the army was and was not capable of doing, they began
> chasing an unattainable achievement. Instead of sticking to the IDF's
> operational plan, they started improvising. They improvised,
> improvised and then improvised again.
>
> —Former CoS Moshe ("Bogie") Yaalon

> What was missing [during the war] was a more effective mechanism
> for the preparation of systematic position papers, analyses and
> assessments of options. . . . There was no mechanism like this. . . . In
> practice, the only staff body that exists in the State of Israel today is
> the defense establishment.
>
> —Former premier Ehud Olmert

On July 12, 2006, two IDF soldiers were kidnapped and eight killed in a
Hezbollah attack along the Lebanese border. Within hours, the IDF was
striking targets in Lebanon, in what would turn out to be Israel's longest
war since the War of Independence.

There were three primary decision points during the war: the initial decision to respond massively to the Hezbollah attack on the 12th; the decision on
the 13th to strike the Dahia neighborhood in Beirut, home to Hezbollah's
headquarters and leadership; and the decision on August 9 to launch a major
ground operation, just prior to the Security Council's announcement of a
cease-fire resolution.

### The Strategic Setting

In May 2000, as seen in Chapter 6, Israel withdrew unilaterally from the
security zone it had controlled in southern Lebanon for eighteen years.

With no preconditions and UN confirmation that it had fully withdrawn from Lebanon, Israel maintained that no basis existed for further conflict and that it thus expected a quiet border. In support of this expectation, it enunciated a clear deterrent policy, stating that it would retaliate massively to any further Hezbollah attacks. It rapidly became clear, however, that Israel could not put this declaratory policy into practice. With the outbreak of the Palestinian uprising (Intifada) and massive terrorism in September 2000, Israel found itself diplomatically and militarily unable to wage two wars concurrently and forced to choose between conflicting strategic priorities. In these circumstances it chose to give priority to the Palestinian issue, at the expense of the retaliatory posture on the Lebanese front.[1]

In December 2000, Hezbollah killed three Israeli soldiers, in its first major challenge to the calm that had prevailed since the withdrawal. Israel refrained from responding, setting a pattern that largely continued throughout the ensuing six years and thus conveying the message to Hezbollah that Israel's declaratory deterrent policy was just that, declaratory. Over the years Hezbollah continued to conduct low-level border provocations designed to maintain pressure on Israel, cause it to bleed, and ultimately draw it into a major confrontation, at a timing of Hezbollah's choosing.

Hezbollah had become the primary political force within the Shiite community and a leading player in Lebanon generally. Fundamentally, however, it was viewed in Israel as a jihadi organization dedicated to Israel's destruction. Hezbollah claimed credit for Israel's withdrawal from Lebanon, portraying itself as the first Arab force that had succeeded in compelling Israel to withdraw from conquered territory. With Israel out of Lebanon, however, Hezbollah had a difficult time justifying ongoing operations against the "occupation," and its Arab, international, and, most important, Lebanese legitimacy for doing so waned. Syria's forced withdrawal from Lebanon in 2005, with the promise that it held out for reconstruction and reform of that war-torn country, further weakened Hezbollah's position.

The US "global war on terror," following 9/11, imposed additional constraints on Hezbollah's freedom of maneuver. Together with its Iranian and Syrian sponsors, Hezbollah now found itself subject to growing US, international, and even Arab pressure to moderate its behavior, fearing that it might be next on the US "hit list." UNSCR 425 and 1559, which called, inter alia, for the dismantlement and disarmament of all Lebanese militias and restoration of the central government's authority, further contributed to the pressure, threatening to weaken Hezbollah's influence in Lebanese politics.

Hezbollah was in a bind, hard-pressed to justify operations against Israel, unwilling to forgo its commitment to do so. Between 2000 and 2006 it thus struck a careful balance, launching repeated low-level border attacks to maintain its jihadi identity and keep pressure on Israel,* while refraining from attacks of a magnitude that would provoke a major conflagration and incur domestic Lebanese wrath. From Israel's perspective, Hezbollah appeared to be biding its time, awaiting circumstances more conducive to the desired escalation.[2]

Israel, too, was in a bind. The small number of incidents, though painful, did not justify a major response, particularly given the preoccupation with the Palestinian front, and Israel had little choice but to exercise restraint. It thus sought to perpetuate a tenuous balance of terror with Hezbollah, to maintain the relative calm for as long as possible and avoid providing it with a pretext for escalation. Conversely, no one in Israel believed that the calm would last for long. With Iran's and Syria's backing, Hezbollah would eventually find a pretext for renewing hostilities. Moreover, Hezbollah was using the passing time to build a truly massive rocket arsenal, with a range now reaching the outskirts of Tel Aviv and numbering over thirteen thousand rockets, compared with "just" seven thousand at the time of the withdrawal in May 2000.[3]

The rocket arsenal presented a severe threat that Israel would have to face sooner or later. Given the rockets' small and mobile nature, however, it was clear to the IDF that there was no easy means of eliminating them and that the entire north would come under extensive fire if and when it sought to do so. In the absence of a better alternative, the policy of restraint continued, pending an almost preordained clash. Indeed, MI's Annual Assessment in December 2005 presciently predicted that a clash was likely during the coming year, possibly in the summer. A month earlier, the IDF Planning Branch recommended that Israel use the next Hezbollah attack as a pretext for ending the policy of restraint and seek to effect a strategic change in the situation. Premier Sharon and his successor, Olmert, approved the recommendation, putting a conditional end to the policy of restraint.[4]

Events immediately prior to the Hezbollah attack of July 2006, which precipitated the war, further exacerbated Israel's security concerns. Following the withdrawal from Gaza the previous August, Hamas and other Palestinian organizations fired over a thousand rockets into Israel, and in late June two Israeli soldiers were killed and one abducted on the Gaza border. For the second time, it now appeared that even a complete Israeli withdrawal from Arab territory had led only to a deterioration in the security situation. Israel's deterrent image was in danger of crumbling.[5]

Adding to the difficulties, the Olmert government was seeking at the time to promote a new peace initiative calling for unilateral withdrawal from most of the West Bank (the "Consolidation Plan"). The perceived failure of the two previous withdrawals, however, threatened to undermine the strategic

---

* During the year before the war, at least three attempts were made to kidnap IDF soldiers, and Israeli towns and military outposts were shelled repeatedly.

rationale behind the new proposal; if Hezbollah and Hamas could continue firing on Israel with impunity even after it had withdrawn, the public would not support a further withdrawal. By demonstrating Israel's clear resolve to prevent further attacks after withdrawing from territory, the massive response to the Hezbollah attack was designed, at least in part, to "save" the Consolidation Plan and with it the prospects for progress with the Palestinians.[6]

On a broader level, Israel viewed Hezbollah as part of the intensifying conflict with Iran. An Iranian proxy, trained, armed, financed, and guided by Tehran, Hezbollah was the spearhead of its long-term effort to weaken and ultimately destroy Israel. Moreover, it had long been assumed in Israel that Iran had provided Hezbollah with the rocket arsenal not just to deter Israel from responding to Hezbollah attacks, but primarily as a means of threatening it with severe punishment, right from its border, in the event that either it or the United States decided to attack Iran's nuclear facilities. A strategic threat in its own right, Hezbollah was thus part of a far greater one, in this case potentially existential.[7]

From an international and regional perspective, the timing of the war in 2006 was propitious for Israel. With the United States pursuing a war on terrorism, in which Hezbollah and its Iranian and Syrian sponsors were primary targets, US support for an Israeli effort to significantly weaken Hezbollah could be counted on. Although the United States demanded that Israel refrain from actions that might undermine Lebanon's pro-Western premier, including attacks on its civil infrastructure—a demand that ultimately played a critical role in Israel's failure to achieve its war aims—Washington went to great lengths to facilitate a decisive Israeli victory. If "diplomatic time," that is, the window for operational success prior to international intervention to end the fighting, had constituted a basic constraint on Israeli policy in all previous conflicts, the United States now provided it with the cover needed to conduct operations largely free of such constraints. Only after weeks of inconclusive fighting, when it became clear that Israel would not achieve a decisive victory, indeed, when Israel itself sought a cease-fire, did the United States truly engage diplomatically.[8]

As always, calls for a cease-fire and anti-Israeli invective were prevalent in the UN and Arab world. European leaders repeatedly pressed Israel to limit the scale of the operation and only the United States opposed proposals in the Security Council for an immediate cease-fire. The EU even weighed the possibility of dispatching an international force to Lebanon to end the fighting. On the whole, however, European and other countries and the Security Council showed a rare understanding for Israel's actions. Indeed, a G-8 declaration on July 16 and the "Rome Conference" on July 26 endorsed most of Israel's demands.[9]

Only toward the end of the war, on August 9, did the international response truly become problematic for Israel, but here too in a limited way. Israel's decision to finally launch the long delayed ground operation may have been designed, in part, to dissuade the Security Council from adopting unwanted modifications to the draft of UNSCR 1701, which put an end to the fighting. Fundamentally, however, Israel viewed the resolution as an important achievement.

Popular fury in the Arab world was as vociferous as ever, but Egypt, Saudi Arabia, and Jordan, fearful of Iran's and Hezbollah's destructive regional role, reacted with notable reserve. Indeed, all three viewed the war as a means of weakening Iran and Hezbollah, and their response was muted. Unable to openly support Israel against fellow Arabs, they did publicly place the onus for the war's outbreak on Hezbollah and Iran, an unprecedented event.[10]

The radical actors were not in a position to significantly affect Israel's decisions. Fifteen years after the end of Soviet military assistance, Syria was a weak state with a badly outdated military, fearful that a confrontation with Israel might endanger the regime's very survival. More isolated than ever, Syria had been forced to withdraw from Lebanon in 2005 and now faced indictment by an international tribunal for its presumed role in the assassination of Lebanese prime minister Rafic Hariri.[†] Iraq was mired in a bloody internal quagmire, and the Palestinians were in a state of internecine chaos. Iran still lacked significant means of attacking Israel directly and was preoccupied with international pressure over its nuclear program and involvement in Iraq.

## Pathology 1: An Unplanned Process

The Hezbollah attack on July 12 was clearly an intentional provocation, designed to incite an escalation, though not of the magnitude that actually took place. If the timing of the attack was a surprise, Hezbollah's determination to abduct IDF soldiers was not. Indeed, just forty-eight hours before, the IDF had lowered an abduction alert declared on the Lebanese border and only a few weeks before that had conducted a simulation exercise of a scenario virtually identical to the one that actually unfolded on July 12.[11]

Both Premiers Sharon and Olmert had already concluded, months earlier, that the long-standing policy of restraint and containment had run its course and that Israel would have to respond forcefully to Hezbollah's next provocation. A major Israeli response was thus in the offing, but its nature and timing were Israel's to choose, especially since the IDF was clearly ill prepared. Nevertheless, Israel decided to respond that very day.[12]

The Winograd Commission, the investigative body established to investigate the war's failings, was bitterly critical of the DMP, especially the

---

[†] The tribunal ultimate came to the conclusion, some years later, that Hezbollah, not Syria, bore primary responsibility for the assassination.

formulation of objectives and options. In findings eerily reminiscent of the 1982 invasion of Lebanon, it found that the war's objectives were never deliberated in depth, were never fully elucidated, were unattainable to begin with, and were understood differently by various ministers and officials. Moreover, the absence of clearly defined objectives was found to have had a highly deleterious impact on Israel's ability to conduct wartime operations, achieve its goals, and adopt an appropriate exit strategy.[13]

Immediately after the attack on the morning of July 12, Olmert and Peretz agreed that Hezbollah had, for all practical purposes, declared war and that Israel would have to respond in an unprecedented manner. To this end, they instructed the IDF to prepare options to be presented to a cabinet meeting that evening. The Air Force was ordered into immediate action, bombing Hezbollah targets, in a significant counterattack that virtually ensured a further escalation.[14]

At 2:30 p.m. Peretz met with the defense chiefs. The IDF advocated an operation designed to deal Hezbollah a heavy blow, change the balance of deterrence, and lead to a diplomatic process that would provide for the release of the abducted soldiers and implementation of UNSCR 1559. Three options were presented:

- A massive air operation against Hezbollah targets and Lebanon's civil infrastructure, including electric, transportation, and petrol nodes. Hezbollah's rocket arsenal would *not* be attacked, due to the difficulty in finding the short- and medium-range rockets and out of fear of a massive rocket reprisal against Israel's north.
- An air attack solely on Hezbollah's rocket arsenal.
- A major ground operation.[15]

Halutz stressed that the rocket arsenal could not be destroyed from the air alone and recommended the first option. Mossad director Dagan maintained that the international community would not allow Israel to attack Lebanon's infrastructure, whose reconstruction it had financed, and to weaken its government. He thus favored an attack focused on the rocket arsenal, raising the possibility of delaying Israel's response for a few days in order to better prepare. MoD political-military director Gilad warned of the expected rocket attack against Israel's north and stressed that a major ground operation, not a limited air strike, would be required. Peretz preferred the second option, an attack on the rocket arsenal alone, but said he would present all three to Olmert.[16]

Olmert met with the above officials later that day in preparation for the evening's cabinet meeting. Halutz again proposed an air attack against Hezbollah targets and Lebanon's civil infrastructure. Dagan warned that an air attack alone would not be sufficient and advocated a major ground campaign. ISA head Yuval Diskin opposed an attack on the Lebanese infrastructure. The head of the IDF Operations Branch presented both those objectives that the IDF believed it could achieve through military force and those that it could not (e.g., return of the hostages and a decisive defeat of Hezbollah). The former included

- Strengthening Israeli deterrence.
- Inflicting a heavy blow to Hezbollah.
- Implementing UNSCR 1559, including dismantlement of Hezbollah.
- Creating conditions for the hostages' release.[17]

Olmert, deeply relieved to hear Halutz's view that a major ground operation would not be necessary, supported an air attack against Hezbollah targets but, contrary to Halutz's recommendation, decided that this would include the rocket arsenal from the outset. Given the US demand that Israel refrain from attacking Lebanon's civil infrastructure, Olmert decided to restrict targets of this nature solely to those transportation nodes that would impede Hezbollah's ability to spirit the abducted soldiers out of Lebanon (e.g., Beirut airport) and to roads and bridges that would facilitate deployment of Hezbollah forces in the south.[18]

Formally, the cabinet decision on July 12 merely authorized a "strong" air strike against Hezbollah, with the "Septet," the ministerial forum Olmert established for expedited and discreet wartime decision making, to determine specific targets. Most of the ministers believed that they had approved an operation limited both in timing and scope. Peretz believed that the international community would not permit the operation to last more than ten to fourteen days. Livni, in contrast, believed that the operation would end the first night, or at the latest the following afternoon. Ministers Dichter and Pinnes thought it would last a few days, whereas Herzog felt otherwise, stating that the atmosphere was clearly one of war, not just an operation. One minister admitted that he did not truly understand what he had voted for, while Minister Mofaz, formerly a defense minister and CoS, remarkably stated that "with the thinking stage still underway, I did not see anything wrong if the objectives were to be set only two to three days later" (i.e., after the operation had already been launched).[19]

The cabinet decision stated that Israel held the government of Lebanon responsible both for attacks from its territory and for the return of the abducted soldiers and demanded that it implement UNSCR 1559.[20] Olmert later claimed that the objectives, at this stage, were as follows:‡

- *Change* the strategic situation in southern Lebanon.
- Push Hezbollah *away* from the border and *deter* it from further attempts to abduct soldiers.
- *Strengthen* Israel's deterrent posture.

---

‡ Italics added here and below to emphasize the ambiguous and far-reaching terms used in defining objectives.

- Return the abducted soldiers.
- Engender a diplomatic process leading to *international intervention* and *full* implementation of UNSCR 1559.[21]

During the meeting, Livni asked Halutz if the hostages could be freed through military action and how he defined victory. Halutz responded in the negative, stating that the goal was to deter future kidnappings, not free the hostages, that there was no such thing as "victory" in a war of this nature, and that the objective was to promote effective international intervention. Livni then suggested that implementation of Resolution 1559 and restoration of Israeli deterrence be defined as the objectives.[22]

On July 13 the IDF submitted a document to the cabinet that set out the war's "strategic purpose":

- Inflicting a *severe* blow to Hezbollah.
- *Deepening* Israeli deterrence and *framing* bilateral relations with Lebanon.
- *Ending* terror from Lebanon.
- *Pressing* Lebanon and the international community to implement UNSCR 1559.
- *Pressing* Hezbollah to return the hostages.
- Keeping Syria out of the conflict, reducing possible linkages to the Palestinian front, and avoiding a major ground operation.[23]

During the Septet meeting on the 13th, which approved the attack on Dahia, Livni expressed her sense that the war's objectives were ill defined and that the IDF was "leading" the cabinet (i.e., "by the nose"), along with a sense of foreboding regarding the ultimate outcome. Just before the meeting Mofaz expressed private concerns to Olmert regarding the absence of clearly defined objectives.[24]

On July 17, in the Knesset, Olmert compounded the ambiguity regarding the war's objectives, adding an entirely new Palestinian dimension:

- Return of the abducted soldiers.
- An *end* to Hezbollah rocket attacks on Israel and the threat thereof.
- Implementation of UNSCR 1559, including disarmament of Hezbollah, extension of Lebanese sovereignty over southern Lebanon, and deployment of the Lebanese Army.
- *An end to Palestinian terror from the Territories and rocket attacks.*[25]

In a Ministry of Defense meeting on July 18, Peretz raised the question of the war's objectives, were it to last another five to six days.[26] In the MCoD the following day, he stated that the objectives were to "refrain from conquering Lebanon and from expanding [the war] to Syria . . . [while instead] promoting a new situation in Lebanon, release of the hostages, [as well as] breaking, eliminating and all sorts of definitions regarding Hezbollah." He was careful to stress that he "wished to avoid setting an overly high threshold for the war's objectives, because in the end we will find ourselves going in circles around a threshold that no one intended."[27] A statement of objectives stressing what Israel would *refrain* from doing and "all sorts of definitions" was certainly novel.

On July 19 the MCoD called for continued fighting against Hezbollah but made no mention of Olmert's Palestinian dimension of the previous day. The stated objectives were

- Return of the hostages.
- Ending Hezbollah rocket fire.
- Implementation of Resolution 1559, including disarmament of Hezbollah and deployment of the Lebanese Army in the south.[28]

On July 20 Olmert found it necessary to ask Halutz to clarify the objectives of the limited military action then under way. Peretz apparently harbored similar doubts, as he too asked a similar question during an MoD strategy session that day.[29]

On August 9, nearly a month after the war began, the MCoD approved the major ground operation, adding one partially new objective and one entirely new one:

- Return of the abducted soldiers.
- Immediate suspension of all hostile action against Israel from Lebanon, including rockets.
- Full implementation of Resolution 1559.
- *Deployment of an international force in southern Lebanon,* along with the Lebanese Army.
- *Preventing Hezbollah from rebuilding its operational capabilities,* especially the resupply of weapons from Syria and Iran.[30]

The ambiguous character of many of the objectives in these various iterations is striking. For example, it was never made clear what a "severe blow" to Hezbollah constituted, nor what was the nature of the desired "change in the situation in southern Lebanon." No mention was initially made of the kind of "international intervention" Israel sought, how far Hezbollah was to be "pushed away" from the border, or if Israel truly thought that Resolution 1559, including disarmament and dismantlement of Hezbollah, could be "fully" implemented. If Israel was truly serious about preventing Hezbollah rearmament, it should have insisted that UNSCR 1701, the ceasefire resolution that ended the war, expand UNIFIL's mandate to monitoring of the Lebanese-Syrian border. "Deepening" Israeli deterrence and "framing" bilateral relations with Lebanon were entirely amorphous terms.

If the definition of the war's objectives was faulty, the formulation of options was no better. On July 12 the cabinet was presented with just one option, the IDF's proposal, was given to believe that success was highly likely, and was pressured by the premier, openly impatient and pushing for a rapid decision, into a virtually immediate decision. The overarching strategic decision made by the cabinet during the war, to abandon the six-year-long policy of restraint, was adopted almost reflexively, with virtually no thought given to other options. The fact that additional options existed and had even been raised earlier that day in the premier and defense minister's meetings with the heads of the defense establishment was never brought to the cabinet's attention.[31]

The absence of an exit strategy was a particular reflection of the poorly defined options, especially since the entire wartime strategy was essentially diplomatic in nature, seeking international intervention as the means of effecting the desired change in southern Lebanon. On July 13 Livni instructed the MFA to draft a proposed exit strategy, presenting it to Olmert on the 16th, but he was not yet interested in a cease-fire and accepted it as a working basis for a diplomatic solution only on July 23. By that time, the INSC, IDF, and MoD had also recommended that an exit strategy be adopted. Olmert, however, was still focused on providing the IDF with the time needed to prevail and had not formulated criteria that would serve as a definition of success and the basis for ending the fighting. Had the proposals for an exit strategy been presented to the cabinet they might have had an important impact, in as much as they presaged most of the important elements ultimately adopted by UNSCR 1701, with Israel's approval, a month later, including deployment of both an international force and the Lebanese Army in the south.[32]

On July 13, following the highly successful overnight attack on Hezbollah's long-range rockets,§ the cabinet decided to expand the fighting to the Dahia neighborhood, even though this was bound to lead to a major escalation. No other options, including a possible end to the fighting at this point, were discussed, on the basis of the initial successes.[33]

Two weeks later, at the MCoD meeting on July 27, the IDF presented five options, ranging from an immediate cessation of hostilities to an operation extending north to the Awali River. The IDF's own preference apparently lay somewhere in the middle.[34] To experienced bureaucratic players, this must have been reminiscent of the old story about the options presented to US decision makers facing an international crisis: capitulation, nuclear war, and a third option, the one the bureaucracy really wanted.

During the MCoD meeting on August 9, Halutz insisted that the IDF proposal for a ground operation be approved as is, all or nothing. The operation was to take ninety-six hours to conquer the area up to the Litani River, followed by four to six weeks to clean out Hezbollah positions,

---

§ The short- and medium-range rockets, which comprised the vast majority of Hezbollah's arsenal, were mobile and almost impossible to find, and the IDF had stated from the beginning that these could not be eliminated from the air. Conversely, it correctly estimated that it could destroy the long-range ones, which were stationary.

prior to its handover to an international force or the Lebanese Army. Halutz was adamant that only an operation of this magnitude could achieve the objectives the MCoD had set, that there were no other options, and that the operation would have to begin that very night, since the forces could no longer be kept "taut like a spring." No other options were presented. The MCoD gave conditional approval, authorizing Olmert and Peretz to make the final determination. The day before, urgently seeking additional options, Olmert had met with Mofaz, who recommended an alternative plan. Olmert was enthusiastic and instructed that Mofaz's plan be presented to the MCoD on the 9th, but backed off in midsession in the face of Peretz and Halutz's adamant opposition.[35]

In seeking to explain the faulty wartime DMP, the Winograd Commission focused on the cabinet and IDF's ongoing inability, from the beginning of the war to the end, to choose between two fundamental options: a short and immediate response to deter Hezbollah from future abductions or a major operation to fundamentally change the situation. It found that both the civilian and military leaders understood the choice but that their desire to avoid a major ground operation created a basic reluctance to even engage in the necessary planning and to present the issue to the cabinet for a decision. A number of reasons explained the cabinet's reluctance: fear of casualties, concern that the economic costs of a reserve mobilization would create public pressure to launch the operation and get it over with, as indeed occurred, and what the Commission dubbed the IDF's almost "mystical" fear of the "Lebanese quagmire" and of attempts to occupy territory and then exchange it for political ends.[36]

Minister Eitan Kabel, a reservist who fought during the war, best summed up the absence of effective policy formulation, especially of well-formulated objectives and options:

> I naively thought that one goes to war only after each minister receives a "war file." . . . In every [military] mission I have gone on . . . the level of preparation was higher than that of the July 12th cabinet meeting. . . . No one in the cabinet stated the objectives and the timetable. . . . We were told "guys, we have to end the meeting quickly in order to approve [operational] orders." . . . The meeting should have lasted ten hours and the politico-military echelon should have been crucified . . . what do you want to achieve and how? When I heard months after the war that [Mossad director] Dagan and [MoD politico-military director] Gilad had recommended that we refrain from an immediate response, I wanted to break someone's head. These things were not presented to us. If they had been, the cabinet might not have unanimously supported the operation.[37]

Improvisation and sequential decision making characterized the entire process. Indeed, the Winograd Commission found the absence of a coherent overall strategic construct and the "rolling" nature of the DMP to be the primary sources of the war's failings.[38] In the Commission's words, "The stunning and dire conclusion is that the only significant decision made by the cabinet . . . was to support a military operation which would probably lead to rockets on the home front and whose outcome was unclear. [This was done] without knowledge of the planned operation's extent, practical objectives or purposes."[39]

On July 12 the cabinet approved a "strong" air strike against Hezbollah without elucidating what this constituted. In response to the CoS's insistence that an attack on Lebanon's civil infrastructure was an essential component of the IDF's war plan, it also approved limited attacks on "dual use" targets, such as roads, but not those of a purely civilian nature, such as power stations. Sequential decision making was built into the war plan itself. The "triumvirate" (premier, defense minister, and CoS) was aware from the outset that the operation might have to be expanded significantly but hoped that this would not prove necessary and chose not to raise the matter in the cabinet on July 12. In fact, the IDF war plan envisaged a suspension of hostilities on July 17 to assess the situation and decide whether and how to proceed. In practice, however, neither the suspension nor the situational assessment ever took place.[40]

For CoS Halutz the war's length and scope were flexible variables, which would be determined by Hezbollah's response to the IDF counterattack on July 12 and 13 and by cabinet willingness to approve further operations. He initially took into account the possibility that operations might end as early as the 13th, or within days if Hezbollah exercised restraint, but the military planning he presented to the cabinet on the 12th was based on an assumption of six to eight weeks of fighting, with a decision to be made at the end of the first week whether to launch a ground operation. On July 15 Halutz reportedly believed that the war would last fourteen to sixteen more days. The head of the Operations Branch initially believed that the war would last four to six days but that things went awry. By the 15th he believed that weeks would be required.[41]

On July 13, in response to a rocket attack on Haifa, Olmert consulted with Mofaz on the IDF proposal to bomb Hezbollah targets in Beirut's Dahia neighborhood. Mofaz was favorable and Olmert immediately issued the necessary instructions, only to rescind them when Mofaz pointed out that an escalatory decision of this sort required approval either by the MCoD or "Septet." The latter met the following day and granted approval. Also on the 13th, as noted, Foreign Minister Livni began drafting an exit strategy at her own initiative.[42]

On the 14th the Septet first discussed the possibility of broadening the operation into a full-scale war. Following the successful destruction of Hezbollah's long-range rockets and the bombing of Dahia, an atmosphere of euphoria had gripped some of the ministers. Peretz, for example, favored an attempt to completely destroy Hezbollah and kill its leader, Hassan Nasrallah. Others were more cautious and Olmert, Livni, and Domestic Security Minister Dichter were opposed to a further expansion of the fighting. Livni believed the blow to Hezbollah to be so severe that a dramatic change in southern Lebanon could now be achieved through diplomatic means.[43]

On the 14th senior IDF officers recommended to Halutz that an exit strategy be formulated. He agreed on the 19th, and a special team presented its findings to Olmert on the 22nd. It concluded that the IDF had exhausted its target list, that the benefits of military action had thus been fully realized, and recommended that Israel agree to end the fighting if an international force was deployed. On the 22nd the MoD also proposed an exit strategy. Halutz, however, pressed for seven to ten days to end the fighting on a more favorable basis.[44]

On July 23, at the end of the second week, the IDF still had less than a brigade in Lebanon. On August 1 it was still conducting battalion- and brigade-sized raids but then withdrawing, and its total force in Lebanon on August 5 was only ten thousand strong. Little could better express the cabinet's desire to avoid a significant ground operation.[45]

On July 27, with the fighting lagging and no end in sight, the MCoD faced a fundamental choice between expanding the war or agreeing to a cease-fire, without having achieved a reduction in rocket fire. Halutz, who had initially opposed a major ground operation, now recommended this, along with an attack on Lebanon's civil infrastructure and approval for another month of fighting. Pressed hard by the ministers, he was unable to explain what this proposal would achieve and how it would contribute to Israel's objectives. The MCoD approved the first significant mobilization of reserves, "just in case," an act that some ministers viewed as virtually guaranteeing their later use. Although deployment of an international force in Lebanon had been under consideration from the beginning, indeed, had been part of the IDF's prewar planning, the MCoD now discussed this option for the first time.[46]

Deputy CoS Moshe Kaplinsky best expressed the sequential nature of the DMP on July 28, saying "it is entirely clear to me that if we put the big plan on the table tomorrow, it will not be approved and then we will look bad. The right thing to do is to start with this thing [a smaller operation] and be ready for the big plan."[47]

Improvisation and sequential decision making continued to the end. On August 1 the IDF received MCoD approval to conquer a six-kilometer-wide security zone along the border, in effect to reestablish the security zone Israel had withdrawn from six years earlier. In the Septet on August 5 Halutz strongly pushed for a major ground operation. Olmert and Peretz remained opposed but had an increasingly difficult time withstanding IDF pressure.[48] Their ultimate acquiescence was a major focus of the postwar criticism.

On August 9, with a Security Council cease-fire resolution looming, the MCoD finally approved the ground operation, but even then only "in principle," with Olmert and Peretz authorized to decide when (and thus if) to actually launch it. Originally conceived in prewar planning as an immediate follow-on to the initial air attacks, the IDF plan now called for a ground operation up to the Litani River in order to "significantly diminish" Hezbollah rocket fire, which had continued unabated for a month, to destroy Hezbollah targets, and to kill as many of its fighters as possible. Reports of the operation's intended length vary from two to four weeks. The main period of combat was apparently planned to last five days; the cabinet, however, approved only three; and in reality the operation was ended after little over one.[49]

On August 10, still seeking an alternative to a major ground operation and apparently wary of Halutz's contention that the forces could no longer be held "taut," Olmert called the division commanders personally, only to be informed that they had no problem waiting, if necessary. The operation was put off by another day, but Olmert's doubts were still not fully assuaged. In a closed meeting he confided that "the army says it will take a month with two hundred dead. I say it will take two months and four hundred dead and in the end we will reach an agreement which is no better than the one we have now, maybe worse." Following the war, Olmert reportedly admitted that if he had known of the IDF's true capabilities, he would have never gone to war.[50]

For two days, despite repeated pressure from Peretz and the authority the MCoD had granted them to launch the operation, Olmert refrained from doing so. On August 11, however, with the Security Council cease-fire resolution imminent, he finally directed the IDF to act. Even then the decision was half-hearted, with the IDF instructed to be ready to stop at any time, with no more than six to eight hours' notice. Olmert later claimed that his decision was designed to thwart last-minute changes to the Security Council resolution, a view disputed by others. The IDF, in any event, failed to achieve its military objectives in the final thrust. Minister Ben-Eliezer, a former defense minister and general, would later state in regard to the strategic rationale behind the last-minute decision, "I have no idea. I have no idea. I think the move was superfluous."[51]

The "rolling" nature of the war led to severe criticism regarding the absence of clear objectives and of the continually changing timelines. Olmert shared the sense of frustration: "the army asked for another ten days and another ten days . . . the army always asked for more time."[52] On July 17 even the head of the IDF Planning Branch turned to the CoS in exasperation, demanding to know why he had asked the cabinet for more time: "How did you do nonsense like that? The army has to have clear objectives and timelines. The easiest thing for the politicians is to give us time, but you dug a hole that we will not be able to get out of."[53] When asked to explain how a limited operation ultimately became a war, Mofaz stated that "to my sorrow, it 'rolled' into a war." Another senior minister later said, "we approved an operation, not a war and then kept approving more and more operations. At no stage was there a complete picture."[54]

Pathology 1 was manifested to a high degree. Israel was aware of Hezbollah's intention to provoke an escalation and of its massive buildup and had decided well in advance that it would have to respond forcefully to the next provocation. Nevertheless, it did not formulate a coherent strategy with well-defined objectives and did not give serious consideration to alternative options. The leadership improvised throughout, making decisions on a sequential basis.

## Pathology 2: A Politicized DMP

The war in Lebanon was not politically divisive, and neither partisan politics nor coalition maintenance had a significant effect on the process. By rapidly taking decisive action and then further expanding the operation, Olmert defused opposition from the right. Given the events preceding the war, including the perceived failure of the unilateral withdrawals from Lebanon and Gaza and the recent abductions on both borders, the left supported the war, too. Indeed, with dovish Labor Party leader Peretz serving as defense minister, opposition from the left could have come only from the fringe.[55]

Disagreement within the cabinet was limited to begin with and was substantive in nature, not political, with ministers going out of their way to mute it. Livni never made an issue over the exit strategy issue. Mofaz remained silent throughout the war and, in effect, even voted against his own proposal for a ground operation when asked to back down by Olmert. Other ministers intentionally withheld criticism in order to maintain a united front.

The public was overwhelmingly supportive throughout the war, further strengthening the cabinet's resolve to act firmly. Even when criticism did emerge toward the end of the war, it was over the cabinet's willingness to end the fighting without having achieved Israel's goals, not about the war itself. Indeed, after a month of massive rocket fire, in which the residents of the north were largely confined to shelters and 300,000 people fled their homes, the public was more than willing to give the government additional time to prosecute the war—if only it would do so effectively. On July 21 a whopping 90% supported continuation until Hezbollah was pushed back from the border. On August 8, 71% supported expanding the fighting to the Litani River.[56]

The search for politically important imagery influenced decisions throughout the war, for example, in the insistence on the bloody fighting to take the town of Bint Jbail, the site of Hezbollah leader Nasrallah's humiliating depiction of Israeli society as a "cobweb." Although the cabinet failed to adopt a clear exit *strategy*, considerable attention was given to an "exit *photo*," that is, a decisive achievement that would allow it to "declare victory" and end the fighting, regardless of the overall outcome. On July 26, for example, Mofaz proposed that an effort be made to kill Nasrallah.[57]

If public opinion was basically a source of political strength for the wartime leadership, they nevertheless became increasingly concerned over the possibility that support might erode and even result in a backlash, especially as the war grew protracted and a sense of failure set in. Public opinion may also have been a factor behind what some considered the overly audacious commando operations staged during the final days of the fighting.[58] Former CoS Yaalon was particularly scathing, stating that these operations "did not have a politico-military objective, but a 'spinology' one. [They were] designed to provide the missing picture of victory. When it became clear that the air operation could not deliver the goods . . . a desperate search began for some move that would provide a sense of victory."[59]

On August 6, with public frustration growing over the ongoing rocket attacks and inconclusive fighting, Peres warned Olmert that "another week of Katyushas and ten more dead and you will no longer be premier." During the August 9th MCoD meeting Livni stressed that "if we don't approve the [ground] operation we will look like the enemies of the people." On the 11th, in response to a warning by Minister Ben-Eliezer, long known for his political acumen, that Peretz's political career would be over if the war ended as things then stood, Peretz asked for an urgent meeting with Olmert and pressed for the ground operation. Olmert approved the ground operation in the end at least partly out of fear that he would pay a heavy political price if he failed to order an operation that had been approved by the cabinet, with the support of the defense minister and IDF.[60]

The posited pathology, of a highly politicized DMP, was partially born out. Partisan politics and coalition maintenance were not issues in the 2006 war but public opinion very much was.

## Pathology 3: Semiorganized Anarchy

Given the broad cabinet support for the war, Olmert enjoyed rare control and freedom of maneuver throughout the process. Although it has been argued elsewhere in this book that Israel's premier is a statutorily weak leader, often at the mercy of the contending forces within his coalition, this was not true of the war in Lebanon. Indeed, Olmert was able to gain cabinet approval for almost every proposal he wanted, largely without challenge

The cabinet and its subforums, the MCoD and Septet, were not the true locus of decision making throughout most of the war. To their credit, they were not rubber stamps and did modify or reject a number of IDF proposals, including its repeated request to attack Lebanon's civil infrastructure. In practice, however, most of the real wartime decision making was conducted in the small and informal consultations Olmert held with the senior defense leadership; the approach agreed upon in these meetings was then brought to the MCoD, occasionally the cabinet plenum and Septet, for approval.[61] Only in the two meetings on the ground operation at the end of the war, on August 9 and 11, was the cabinet the true locus of decision making.

Throughout the war situational assessments and policy options were presented to the cabinet, MCoD, and Septet almost solely by the policy advocates, primarily the CoS. Few written background materials, in-depth reviews of the situation, or position papers were presented, and the meetings were devoted largely to assessments, leaving insufficient time for discussion of policy. In the absence of authoritative cabinet-level advisers and an honest broker (the INSC played virtually no role), a number of ministers found it necessary to consult with former and current officials they knew personally and with outside experts.[62]

The fear of leaks had a significant impact on the DMP from the start. On July 12, the very first day of the war, Olmert was already so concerned about potential leaks that he directed that details of the planned operation be withheld from the cabinet plenum and MCoD and ultimately decided to refrain even from a discussion of Israel's options. In need of a forum for expedited and discreet wartime decision making, to weigh and approve Israel's war plans and operations, he established the Septet, but it proved no better. Indeed, sensitive information leaked within hours of its very first meeting, held later that day, and Olmert largely ceased convening it (just two more meetings were held throughout the war). As a result, the real decision making was conducted in the premier's informal consultations, and Israel went to war without an effective policymaking forum, whether statutory (e.g., the cabinet or MCoD) or otherwise (e.g., the Septet).[63]

The fear of leaks continued to affect the process throughout the war. During the MCoD meeting on July 27, Vice Premier Peres stated that "I do not wish to raise ideas here, because I raised ideas once or twice and then found them in the paper in a distorted way the next day, which got me very angry. If a smaller group is convened I will say what I propose." Olmert again refused to discuss the details of military operations, averring that "we do not have to inform the whole world what we do and do not intend to do."[64] Meetings of the MCoD thus came to be seen as the equivalent of "informing the whole world."

Pathology 3, semiorganized anarchy, was partially substantiated. In contrast with the posited pathology, in this case the premier was almost fully in charge, but the cabinet and subcabinet forums were not the locus of decision making, bearing out their dysfunctional nature, and leaks had a major impact on the processes.

## Pathology 4: An Uninstitutionalized DMP

During the war a change took place in the roles and relative power of the members of the triumvirate (i.e., premier, defense minister, and CoS). The CoS fully deferred to his civilian masters, of course, but had inordinate influence over the process. Unlike most of their predecessors, Olmert and especially Peretz, serving in his first cabinet position, had little experience in defense affairs and were thus highly dependent on Halutz for information and advice. Halutz himself ultimately came to the conclusion that his greatest wartime mistake had been to underestimate how deeply Olmert and Peretz had been affected by their inexperience and consequent inability to fully comprehend the information provided to them. Moreover, in contrast with many former premiers, such as Rabin, Barak, and Sharon, who were defense experts in their own right and were usually deeply involved in all defense planning, even of an operational nature, Olmert took something of a "chairman of the board" approach, further adding to Halutz's influence. In effect, as noted, Olmert and Peretz largely abdicated the policy formulation function to Halutz and the IDF.[65]

Halutz, moreover, was a highly respected and popular figure, commonly assumed to be a future candidate for premier. With a self-confident aura and gift for oral presentations, he played a crucial role in convincing Olmert, Peretz, and the entire cabinet of the necessity of a major response on July 12 and of its subsequent expansion. Convinced of the IDF's ability to prevail decisively and clearly desirous of facilitating approval for the further prosecution of the war, Halutz appears, on more than one occasion, to have refrained from presenting the cabinet with a full picture of the situation and of the consequences of the various options. To cite just one example, he refused to respond substantively on July 12 when Peres pressed him to explain how he expected Hezbollah to respond to the IDF's recommended option and how the IDF would react to each possible Hezbollah response. It is especially hard to understand how he allowed the cabinet to believe that the war's objectives could be achieved from the air, when prewar IDF planning, which he fully shared, stated quite the opposite.[66]

The basic decision to go to war in 2006 was consensual, supported across the political spectrum, and in this sense was not a matter of idiosyncratic decision making. Conversely, the nature of the subsequent DMP was affected by the character of the three primary decision makers involved, Olmert, Peres, and Halutz, and the personal interaction between them, leading to a moderate manifestation of this dimension of the posited pathology.

During the years before the war, the national security establishment had devoted considerable strategic thought to the Lebanese front and to a future round with Hezbollah. The absolutely vital conclusions derived from this process, however, central to Israel's entire military strategy, were never conveyed to the cabinet,[67] with a significant impact on its conduct of the war. A pronounced disconnect thus existed between policy inputs and outputs. To illustrate, the cabinet never knew that

- Sharon and subsequently Olmert had already decided that the previous policy of containment and restraint had run its course and that a more aggressive approach would have to be adopted in the future.[68]
- The IDF had concluded that Hezbollah's rocket arsenal could not be eliminated from the air and that even a major ground operation would not suffice, since Hezbollah could simply move the rockets further north. To be fully effective, a ground operation would have required the conquest of all of Lebanon, house-to-house fighting to root out the rockets, and a long-term occupation to prevent resupply of Hezbollah. No one in Israel, however, even contemplated an operation of this magnitude.[69]
- A special review of Israel's strategic doctrine, completed just months earlier, had concluded that Israel did not have an effective military response to the rocket threat.[70]
- The IDF's prewar strategy was therefore essentially diplomatic in character, designed to cause a crisis that would lead to international intervention and to a (positive) "change" in the situation in southern Lebanon.[71]

Presented on July 12 with the sole option of the IDF's proposed response, the cabinet did not discuss the possible need for a major ground campaign; to the contrary, Halutz led it to believe that the war's objectives could be achieved from the air alone. None of the ministers inquired whether the IDF was properly trained and equipped to carry out the operation, and the IDF did not indicate otherwise. Although the cabinet was informed that even a limited operation would result in a massive Hezbollah rocket attack, virtually no consideration was given to the fact that the home front was woefully unprepared, a glaring failure that would be the focus of much postwar criticism.[72]

A further striking manifestation of the policy disconnect occurred during the crucial July 12 meeting, when the cabinet rejected the IDF's request for approval to attack Lebanon's civil infrastructure. Neither the ministers nor the IDF itself raised the obvious question, whether Israel's objectives could still be met without an attack on what the IDF defined as a central component of its entire military strategy. Similarly, the cabinet decided to attack Hezbollah's rocket arsenal from the outset, rather than follow the IDF's recommendation that this be done only at a later stage, if and when a ground operation was approved. Little consideration was given to the possible ways that the operation might evolve in practice, an exit strategy was not formulated, and no timeline was set, despite the fact that "diplomatic time" had been a primary factor in all of Israel's wars. If policy formulation is all about linking objectives with means, Israel went to war with potentially fatal disconnects from day one.[73]

At some point during the early days of the war, both the IDF and the political leadership, driven by a desire to achieve a decisive outcome and buoyed by the initial successes, appear to have become enamored of the purely military options and to have simply lost sight of the fundamentally diplomatic nature of Israel's strategy. An analysis by MI on July 14, which questioned the war plan's ability to meet its stated goals, received little attention. Livni's exit strategy, presented to Olmert on July 16, was not given serious consideration until a later stage, when the IDF had proved unable to achieve the stated objectives. Even then, the diplomatic option was adopted reluctantly, for lack of a better alternative, rather than as the heart of the original plan.[74]

Mobilization of reserves was first raised on July 27. Whereas the reserves had previously been the backbone of the IDF, defense cuts in the years before the war had gutted the reserves' training, equipment, and weapons, and the IDF had estimated that four to fourteen days would be required to retrain and resupply them, in the event of a major confrontation.[75] Olmert and Peretz must have known of this; Halutz, who now estimated that a week would be required, certainly did, as did Mofaz. This vital information was never presented to the cabinet.

Perhaps the most egregious example of the policy disconnect was the MCoD's decision on August 9 to approve the major ground operation and a further month of fighting, even though the Security Council cease-fire resolution was expected at any moment. When finally launched, after weeks of dallying, the operation had to be ceased after just over a day, long before its objectives could have been achieved.

Policy coordination and integration were flawed throughout much of the war. Initially good between Olmert and Peretz, the process deteriorated as events turned sour. The nadir came on July 30 following an abortive air strike in which numerous civilians were killed. To assuage international opinion, Olmert reached agreement with the United States on a temporary suspension of air strikes, but Peretz, wary of Olmert's propensity for making decisions without him and of being blamed for having failed to stand up for the IDF, refused to transmit the order. It was an unprecedented event in Israeli history and Olmert was livid. The standoff was resolved a few hours later, when Olmert's military secretary conveyed the order to the IDF.[76]

The situation with respect to Livni was even worse. An orderly process of consultation between Olmert, Peretz, and Livni did not take place at any time during the war, and the MoD and MFA operated independently of each other, as if the war had no diplomatic dimensions. Despite the clearly diplomatic nature of many of the issues discussed and the war plan's fundamentally diplomatic nature, Livni was not invited to most of Olmert's consultations, in which Peretz, Halutz, and a variety of defense officials regularly participated. Indeed, Livni was so isolated that she found it necessary to request, as early as July 14, that she be informed in advance of the issues to be raised in meetings of the cabinet and Septet and that she be allowed to meet separately with IDF officers in order to prepare for them. The MFA as a whole was even less privy to the DMP. The Winograd Commission, which praised the MFA for its early proposal for an exit strategy, nevertheless stressed that it, too, did not sufficiently integrate the diplomatic and military aspects of the issue.[77]

Only on July 27, two weeks after the war had begun, was a senior interagency coordinating group finally established, headed by Olmert's bureau chief. A partial indication of its influence may be reflected by the fact that one MCoD member did not even know of its existence.[78]

The home front was perhaps the most extreme example of failed interministerial policy coordination and integration. Hezbollah fired 4,000 rockets at 160 Israeli cities, towns, and villages, damaging 6,000 homes. Three hundred thousand residents fled to the south, a million sought refuge in shelters, and normal life ceased in the north, with nongovernmental organizations and concerned individuals providing the social services, even food, that governmental agencies failed to supply. Formally, responsibility was divided between the IDF's Home Front Command and the Ministries of Defense, Internal Security, and the Interior, but with no single body clearly in charge, no one was truly responsible and chaos prevailed during the early weeks.[79]

The posited pathology, of an uninstitutionalized DMP, was partially substantiated. Idiosyncratic decision making was substantiated at a moderate level. Conversely, a severe disconnect existed between policy inputs and outputs, and the level of interministerial coordination and policy integration was grossly deficient, thereby substantiating these subdimensions at a high level.

## Pathology 5: Primacy of the Defense Establishment

The IDF's primacy was clear throughout the war. Not only was it the only agency that prepared military options; it also played a central role in formulating diplomatic ones and was virtually the only agency that sought to define the war's objectives. Indeed, the political leadership nearly abdicated responsibility for the formulation of objectives—*the* classic function of a political leadership—to the IDF.[80] Olmert and Peretz were not passive rubber stamps, nor was the cabinet, but it was the IDF, with very few exceptions, that formulated the objectives and options, and almost everything it proposed was accepted, even when against the civilian leadership's better judgment.

On August 8, still hoping to avoid the need for a ground operation and in search of additional options, Olmert met with Mofaz and presented the IDF's proposal for a ground operation to him. Mofaz was adamantly opposed and proposed an alternative plan in which Olmert took great interest.[81] Remarkably, however, Halutz was unwilling to even raise Mofaz's proposal for consideration by the General Staff and Peretz was equally adamant regarding the cabinet, stating:

> I was totally opposed to a member of the MCoD (i.e. Mofaz) presenting it with operational proposals. . . . If a norm of this sort is established, it will be catastrophic. . . . Every party will draft reserve generals to be their party advisers, to prepare alternative plans. We will find ourselves in a situation in which we start making [political] deals about who adopts whose plan. . . . The IDF presents the plans and the MCoD can say "please go back home and bring us other plans."[82]

At Olmert's insistence, Mofaz's proposal nonetheless was presented to the MCoD on August 9, together with the IDF plan. During the meeting, however, Olmert grew concerned that Halutz would resign if Mofaz's proposal was brought to a vote and that Peretz, too, would have a hard time living with this. Concerned about the public reaction to a rift on such a vital wartime decision, Olmert reversed course and killed Mofaz's proposal. In mid-meeting notes to Minister Eitan, head of a coalition party, Olmert warned that "if you support the Mofaz plan there will be a rupture with Peretz," and to Livni he wrote that "it is impossible *not* to accept the army's position, because it means risking a confrontation with them and they do not have another plan." He further instructed his bureau chief to try to dissuade Mofaz from causing a confrontation. Moments before the vote, Olmert requested MCoD approval for the IDF's proposal, saying "there is a defense minister, there is a CoS, they are our advisers and we rely on them to present us with military recommendations." Mofaz's proposal was not brought to a vote and the MCoD approved the IDF plan. Mofaz himself voted for the IDF plan.[83]

At no time did Olmert and Peretz fail to fully support the IDF, repeatedly granting it more time and resources, as preceding levels of action failed to produce the promised results. Although they did not approve every request, it is hard to think of many cases in which the political leadership provided the IDF with such freedom of action and support. Olmert and Peretz's greatest mistake may have been that they were too supportive, approving virtually everything the IDF sought and letting it decide when, how, and above all *what* should be done, their own foremost responsibility.

The weakness of the other planning bodies further contributed to IDF primacy. Only the IDF submitted options for Israeli policy on July 12 and 13 or before the August 9 decision to launch the ground operation. The INSC submitted its first policy paper on July 16 and another on July 20,[84] but its role was negligible. The MoD Politico-Military Division may have had some influence within the ministry, but not beyond. The MFA's exit strategy was never presented to the cabinet, though it may have had an impact on Olmert's thinking.

The heads of the ISA and Mossad participated in all important meetings and often challenged the IDF, but this did not usually result in serious consideration or force the IDF to further justify its positions. In any event, the ISA and Mossad are primarily operational bodies, with limited policy planning capabilities. Even within the IDF, policy planning was conducted primarily by operationally oriented commands, such as the Operations Branch and IAF, as well as MI. The Planning Branch, responsible for precisely this function, heretofore the primary planning entity in Israel, was sidelined, with little impact on the policy process.[85] The absence of clearly defined war objectives and of an exit strategy may partially reflect this bureaucratic reality.

The posited primacy of the defense establishment was fully born out. The IDF was the primary source of information and policy advice, by far the most influential bureaucratic player, and with rare exception, both its positions and those of the defense minister prevailed.

**Table 8  Manifestation of Pathologies in the 2006 Lebanon War**

| Category | Manifestation | Rating |
|---|---|---|
| *Unplanned Process* | Absence of Policy Planning, Objectives, and Options | High |
| | Improvisation | High |
| | Sequential Decision Making | High |
| *Politicized Process* | Politics Reign Supreme | Low |
| | Coalition Maintenance | Low |
| | Public Opinion | High |
| *Semiorganized Anarchy* | Premier Not in Charge | Low |
| | Dysfunctional Cabinet | High |
| | Leaks | High |
| *Uninstitutionalized Process* | Idiosyncratic | Mod. |
| | Policy Disconnects | High |
| | Insufficient Coordination and Integration | High |
| *Primacy of Defense Establishment* | Primary Source of Expertise | High |
| | Primary Bureaucratic Player | High |
| | Positions Prevail | High |

Mod. = Moderate

# III. FINAL THOUGHTS

*If a minister in any other country was to tell the cabinet that "only a miracle can save us," this would be a sign of impending doom. In Israel, on the other hand, this is merely a statement of policy. The miracle will have to happen—and invariably does.*

—Ephraim Kishon, Israeli satirist

*Empires like Britain were established almost without thought and then collapsed in an orderly decision-making process.*

—Shlomo Ben Ami, former foreign minister

# Conclusions and Recommendations

In a few years people will not be able to understand how it was possible [to function] without what we are now creating [the INSC]. The country needs a governmental organ which has neither sectoral nor other interests and which can view things from a national and integrative perspective.

—Uzi Dayan, former national security adviser

The role of a staff body is to think coldly in [our] hot hallways. Most of the subjects we deal with are burning hot, ideologically and emotionally, and in a situation such as this it is hard to make cold analyses. . . . If we had an orderly staff body it might reduce the number of mistakes by about 10% and that is a huge amount.

—Professor Yehezkel Dror, prominent Israeli political scientist

Having looked at each of the seven case studies in detail separately, it is now time to take a broader, comparative look, to tie things together, draw the appropriate conclusions, and make recommendations. This chapter presents a comparative summary of the findings in the seven case studies, along with a discussion of the discrepancies between the posited and actual outcomes, and reviews the book's key findings. It also reviews past attempts to reform the process, with particular emphasis on the INSC and the reasons it has yet to live up to its intended role, and argues that Israel can no longer afford its decision-making ills and continue business as usual. The chapter concludes with recommendations for further reforms needed on both the institutional and electoral levels in order for the process to improve.

## The Case Studies in Comparative Perspective

Table 9 presents a comparative summary of the findings in each of the case studies.

**Table 9 Summary of the Findings in the Seven Case Studies**

| Pathology | Subdimensions of Pathologies | Camp David 1978 | Lavi | Lebanon 1982 | Lebanon Withdrawal 2000 | Camp David 2000 | Gaza Disengagement 2005 | Lebanon 2006 |
|---|---|---|---|---|---|---|---|---|
| | | | | | | *Intensity of Manifestation in Case Studies* | | |
| Unplanned Process | Deficient policy planning processes; formulation of objectives, options | High | High | High | Moderate | Low | High | High |
| | Improvisation | Moderate | High | High | Moderate | Moderate | High | High |
| | Sequential decision making | Low | High | High | Moderate | Moderate | High | High |
| Politicized Process | Politics reign supreme | Moderate | High | Moderate | Low | High | High | Low |
| | Coalition maintenance above all | Moderate | Low | High | Low | High | High | Low |
| | Public opinion | Moderate | High | High | High | High | High | High |
| Semiorganized Anarchy | Premier not in charge | Low | ID | Moderate | Low | High | Moderate | Low |
| | Dysfunctional cabinet/MCoD | High | High | High | Moderate | High | High | High |
| | Leaks | ID | Low | ID | Low | High | Low | High |
| Uninstitutionalized Process | Idiosyncratic decision making | High | High | High | Low | High | High | Moderate |
| | Policy disconnect; inputs, formulation, implementation | ID | High | High | Moderate | Low | Moderate | High |
| | Insufficient policy coordination and integration | High | High | High | ID | Low | Moderate | High |
| Primacy of Defense Establishment | IDF/defense establishment: source of expertise, "closed circle" | High | Moderate | High | High | High | Moderate | High |
| | IDF/defense establishment: primary bureaucratic players | High | Moderate | High | High | High | Moderate | High |
| | Defense minister/IDF positions prevail | Low | Moderate | Moderate | Moderate | Moderate | Moderate | High |

ID = Insufficient data

As is apparent from the table, all five pathologies were substantiated at a moderate to high level, as were fourteen of the fifteen subdimensions (leaks being the exception). None were substantiated completely, along all fifteen subdimensions and in all seven cases, nor would one expect them to be. Some variance is par for the course. The question is whether the exceptions indicate a fallacy of the posited pathology, a need for modification or further refinement, or the exigencies of a specific case.

Given the qualitative nature of both the independent variables and resulting pathologies, a precise ranking of the latter's relative importance is not feasible, but a few points are worthy of note. The unplanned nature of the process (Pathology 1) and the primacy of the IDF and defense establishment (Pathology 5) were the two most strongly substantiated pathologies, whereas the politicized and uninstitutionalized nature of the process (Pathologies 2 and 4) were somewhat less so. Semiorganized anarchy (Pathology 3) was manifested at a lower level than expected, but this was the outcome of the unexpected results achieved regarding the leaks subdimension. Conversely, the subdimension of cabinet dysfunctionality was one of the two most strongly manifested of all fifteen (along with public opinion, from Pathology 2). Among the other subdimensions, the deficiency of policy planning, idiosyncratic nature of the process, and the IDF and defense establishment's roles as the primary sources of expertise and bureaucratic players were also strongly manifested. The impact of the IDF on actual policies adopted, however, was only moderate.

A breakdown by case study shows that the posited pathologies were manifested at the highest level in the cases of Lebanon in 1982 and the Gaza disengagement, followed by Lebanon in 2006. Interestingly, the overall manifestation of the pathologies was the weakest in the withdrawal from Lebanon, not Camp David II, the one case of a well-planned DMP. However, no discernible pattern was present.

PATHOLOGY 1: AN UNPLANNED PROCESS

The posited deficiency or absence of policy planning processes by the premier and cabinet-level forums, including faulty formulation of objectives and options, was substantiated at a high level in five cases and at a moderate level in one, thus substantiating this subdimension at a high level. The sole exception to this rule was Camp David II, in which the process was highly planned. In all of the cases, the cabinet and MCoD were presented by the policy advocates with only one option, which they could approve or reject. Ambiguity was the various prime ministers' preferred modus operandi.

All of the cases necessitated fundamental reevaluations of basic aspects of Israeli national security thinking, often involving broad changes in long and deeply held ideological beliefs. In all of the cases Israel's decision makers dealt with the gravity and complexity of the issues through considerable improvisation (four highly improvisational cases, three moderately). The process was also characterized by sequential decision making, though less so (highly sequential in four cases and moderately so in one). The two cases in which sequential decision making was not manifested, Camp David I and II, were both essentially diplomatic in nature and were characterized by incremental, not sequential, processes. It is unclear whether any conclusions can be drawn from these exceptions, especially since Camp David II was an outlier generally, the one highly planned DMP of the seven studied. In effect, the low manifestation of sequentialism in Camp David I is the only unexpected finding here.

## PATHOLOGY 2: A POLITICIZED PROCESS

Public opinion, as noted, was manifested at a very high level (six high, one moderate), indeed, was one of the two strongest subdimensions of all. Politics reign supreme (partisan politics) was moderately to highly substantiated, with three high and two moderate manifestations. Coalition maintenance was moderately substantiated, with three high, one moderate, and three low manifestations.

It is possible that the nature of the cases in which these two subdimensions were substantiated either moderately or not at all had an effect on the outcome. The three instances in which partisan politics were manifested at low and moderate levels were the three Lebanon case studies, all of which were essentially military in nature, two of them involving decisions to actually go to war. The three low manifestations of coalition maintenance also occurred in essentially military decisions, two of which were Lebanon cases and the third the Lavi. Conversely, Gaza disengagement and the two Camp David cases, especially Camp David II, more diplomatic in nature, were the focus of strong partisan and cabinet politics. The Lavi, like the other military cases, was consensual throughout most of the DMP but became a matter of intense partisan politics at the end.

These findings suggest the need for a partial modification of the high degree of politicization held to be characteristic of Israeli decision making. Unsurprisingly, it does not apply, or applies less, to decisions that are largely military and operational in character, involving matters of life and death, which impose somewhat greater discipline on the cabinet and in which there is a common tendency to "rally around the flag" in times of danger. Given the broad public consensus characteristic of these cases, those partisan disagreements that might have manifested themselves in the cabinet were minimal to begin with and were further muted by the need to preserve unity in the face of a military confrontation.

Second, even when facing highly controversial decisions, leaders went ahead with their preferred policies regardless and were often successful in finding ways of circumventing the political obstacles. Begin in Camp David and Lebanon in 1982, Sharon in the Gaza disengagement, and Rabin and Peres in the Lavi successfully achieved the outcomes they sought, and Barak's failure in Camp David II was at least as much the result of Arafat's intransigence as it was of Israeli politics. This finding might be thought to indicate that the *substantive* impact of politicization on Israeli decision making is less than presumed, even if the *character* of the process itself is highly politicized. Conversely, leaders such as Barak in Camp David and Sharon in the Gaza disengagement lost their coalitions and positions due to political turmoil, and the greatest substantive impact of politicization may be on those issues that are *not* brought up for cabinet discussion at all. Though interesting and worthy of further consideration, this conclusion does not seem to truly stand up to scrutiny.

PATHOLOGY 3: SEMIORGANIZED ANARCHY

The premier was posited to be only partially in control of the process: a strong leader in some cases, where he was in firm control of his party and coalition; weak in others. This was borne out. The premier was in charge in three cases (Camp David I, Lebanon withdrawal, and war in 2006) and was moderately so or not in charge in three others (Camp David II, Lebanon1982, and Gaza disengagement), with one case of insufficient information. Not surprisingly, the premier's control was closely correlated with the degree of politicization: greater control in those cases in which politicization was less intense, less so when politicization was high. Even when premiers were in charge, this entailed enormous, even heroic, efforts on their part, including a willingness to risk their political futures, such as in Camp David II and the Gaza disengagement. Moreover, in all of the cases it was the premier's political power and acumen, his ability to wheel and deal, maneuver and manipulate, rather than formal prerogatives, that enabled success.

The posited dysfunctional nature of the cabinet and consequent absence of an effective cabinet-level policymaking forum was highly substantiated (six highs, one moderate). Indeed, the cabinet was not the true locus of decision making in any of the case studies.

The findings regarding leaks were the only ones among the fifteen subdimensions that did not support the posited pathology. Leaks were found to have a high impact in only two cases and a low impact in three, with two cases of insufficient data. These findings, which run contrary to all accepted wisdom regarding Israeli decision making, appear to reflect the limitations of the data available rather than a repudiation thereof. No other explanation is apparent.

Israel is a chaotic democracy with a frenetic political style, and most leaks are about the politics of the issues, who has taken what position, rather than hard information regarding Israeli capabilities and intentions. This, too, can be harmful. In late 2011, for example, considerable controversy erupted over reports of different Israeli leaders' positions regarding a possible attack on Iran's nuclear program, the greatest strategic threat facing the country, and during the 2006 Lebanon war some sensitive operational details did leak. It is unclear, however, what concrete conclusions Iran could derive from the reported controversy; one could make the argument that in some ways it served Israel's deterrent interests, and leaks regarding hard operational capabilities and intentions are the minority.

The findings suggest the possibility, subject to the above noted limitations regarding the information available, that the primary impact of leaks may be on the process, how premiers handle issues in the cabinet and with their advisers, rather than on the substance of the decisions made. This in itself is a very important factor, however, and to the extent that it is true, it substantiates the posited pathology: leaks were held to deeply affect the process.

## PATHOLOGY 4: AN UNINSTITUTIONALIZED PROCESS

Of the seven cases, five entailed highly idiosyncratic decision making, one did so moderately (Lebanon 2006), and only the withdrawal from Lebanon did not. The highly idiosyncratic nature of the DMP was thus largely substantiated.

Both the posited disconnect between policy inputs and outputs and problems of policy coordination and integration were substantiated at a moderate to high level. The policy disconnect was manifested at a high level in three cases (Lavi, Lebanon 1982, and Lebanon 2006), moderate in two (Lebanon withdrawal and Gaza disengagement), and low in one (Camp David II), with one case of insufficient data (Camp David I). Insufficient coordination and integration were manifested at a slightly greater level, with four high cases and one moderate, one that was not substantiated, and one case of insufficient data.

## PATHOLOGY 5: PRIMACY OF THE DEFENSE ESTABLISHMENT

The first two subdimensions, the IDF and defense establishment as the primary sources of expertise and bureaucratic players, were strongly substantiated, with five high manifestations and two moderate ones each. Conversely, the defense minister and IDF's positions prevailed only at a moderate level. This is as it should be. The IDF and defense establishment as a whole are rightly very important players in the Israeli DMP, and defense considerations should have a major impact. They are not, however, omnipotent, and the findings demonstrate the encouraging conclusion that the premier and cabinet often make decisions contrary to the defense establishment's preferences.

## Key Findings

The five posited pathologies were thus largely substantiated in the case studies. Going beyond the specific results obtained, which are of course subject to the vagaries of the specific cases and limitations of the information available, the following are the key findings derived from this study of Israeli decision-making processes.

First, Israel's DMP takes place within the context of a uniquely demanding external environment, is focused overwhelmingly on the short term, and is often improvisational and sequential in character. Typically held to be primarily reactive in character, Israel has made numerous attempts in recent decades to shape its environment, thereby adding a new element of proactivity.

Premiers manifest a clear tendency to avoid systematic policy planning, especially in the cabinet but even in the MCoD and informal decision-making forums. Consequently, policy objectives, priorities, and options are typically not well elucidated, with a highly deleterious impact on Israel's ability to achieve its goals. An in-depth discussion of this crucial finding appears below.

Israel does not have an effective statutory forum for national security decision making. The cabinet and MCoD are typically dysfunctional and consequently most real decision making is conducted by the premier in informal ministerial forums and in consultations with the defense minister, CoS, and other senior defense officials, at times the foreign minister. As seen below, passage of the INSC Law has led to a moderate improvement in the MCoD's decision-making processes but has not had a significant effect on the cabinet plenum and informal forums. The latter, in which the true decision making is actually carried out, are not supported, or only partially supported, by systematic policy planning processes.

By the time an issue reaches the MCoD and cabinet, the premier and relevant minister(s) have typically settled on a preferred course of action and present just one option that can be approved or rejected. Although the creation of the INSC has partially alleviated this, at least in the preparatory process prior to MCoD meetings, insufficient consideration of options remains a basic problem.

The DMP is surrounded by intense politicization, though the above analysis of the case studies indicates that actual policy outcomes, at least those involving decisions to use military force, may be somewhat less affected by this than might otherwise be thought. "What will fly," that is, the minimum consensus needed to obtain cabinet approval, not what is truly needed, is a primary determinant of cabinet decisions. Public opinion has a very strong impact on policy, as it should in a democracy, but given the complexity and importance of many of the issues Israel faces, and the short decision-making times usually available, this can also have a deleterious impact.

Israel's premiers are statutorily weak and their actual power is unduly contingent on their political skills and coalition exigencies. Premiers who are in firm control of their parties and coalitions can be powerful leaders, able to chart new directions, but even they are often forced to invest inordinate political efforts and to take unacceptable political risks, such as an end to their political futures, to achieve their objectives. Other premiers have been at least partial hostages of their coalitions, limited in their ability to lead.

The defense establishment, especially the IDF, is the most influential bureaucratic player, with by far the most highly developed policymaking capabilities. Though far from omnipotent—premiers act at times without its knowledge and even over its opposition—no other power center can compete with the IDF's influence and that of the defense establishment generally. The defense establishment's capabilities are a vital asset; it is the weakness of the civilian agencies, first and foremost the INSC and MFA, that is the problem.

Interagency integration of policy and coordination of action is deficient, both for reasons endemic to governments everywhere and as exacerbated by the nature of Israel's coalition system. Given the methodological limitations inherent in an attempt to rank "bureaucratic warfare" in different countries, the present research has not sought to do so and no definitive conclusions can be drawn. Nevertheless, bureaucratic warfare (in the sense of rivalry between the national security organs, as opposed to their ministerial heads), does not appear to be worse in Israel than in other countries—indeed, the severity of the threat may produce somewhat greater discipline.

Israeli decision making is highly idiosyncratic. Though this is probably true of most countries—certainly no student of US decision making would be surprised by a similar assertion—an at least somewhat more planned and institutionalized process in other governments may partially serve to stem individual whim.

Despite its numerous ills, the Israeli DMP does have a number of strengths and succeeds in turning some of its long-term pathologies into short-term advantages. The strengths include, inter alia, the ability to make rapid and flexible responses, the effective nature of planning processes within the defense establishment, the generally pragmatic character of decision making even at the political level, and the quality and motivation of the people involved.

Why, as per the second finding above, do Israel's premiers largely refrain from systematic policy planning? The INSC has existed since 1999 and so the problem is clearly no longer one of organizational capacity, if it ever was, but of a conscious decision to refrain from systematic planning. This conclusion leads to what may be the most controversial finding in this book, that in Israel's system of coalition-cabinet government, systematic policy planning—that is, formulation and consideration of alternative policy objectives, priorities, and options—is often inimical, at times diametrically opposed, to the premier's political needs. The following explains why.

First, policy planning requires a willingness to share one's thinking with others and to bring them into the process, but for an Israeli premier, living in a coalition cauldron, constantly afraid of leaks, the risks are too great. By articulating objectives, priorities, and options the premier risks a rift with coalition partners, even his own party, and a consequent threat to coalition stability. An objective or option raised for no more than initial consideration, let alone a conceptually developed policy initiative, is likely to become embroiled in Israel's raging political debates, thereby eliminating any realistic prospect of substantive analysis of the pros and cons. Indeed, the moment the premier's thinking becomes known to the cabinet, to individual ministers who oppose his policy, and certainly to the media, he risks losing control over the process. Even policy planning in the defense establishment and small informal forums may become known and pose unacceptable political costs. Premiers' fears of leaks and politicization of an issue, with a consequent loss of freedom of maneuver, are so great that they typically outweigh their calculus of the potential benefits to be derived from systematic policy planning.

Second, by elucidating objectives, priorities, and options, policy planning forces premiers to confront issues and choices that they may not wish to deal with, politically and/or substantively. Advisory bodies, such as the INSC, may recommend options the premier opposes or does not believe are politically "ripe," and if this becomes known his options may be circumscribed significantly. Ambiguity can be constructive and rather than augmenting a premier's range of options, systematic policy planning may greatly curtail it and even threaten his political career.[1]

Perhaps nothing better exemplifies this point than Sharon's 2001 decision to quash the INSC's National Security Assessment, which recommended that Israel act proactively to determine its final borders.[2] Just one year later, paradoxically, Sharon went far beyond what the INSC had recommended and decided to withdraw unilaterally from Gaza, but he did so by ramming the decision through the cabinet, without an orderly discussion of objectives and options. Had a discussion of this nature taken place, it would have required a politically divisive choice between differing visions of the future and would, in all likelihood, have derailed the process. Political commentator Nachum Barnea describes Sharon's decision to quash the assessment as follows: "If he ignored it he risked being asked difficult questions by a commission of inquiry; if he read it he could be asked why he had not acted accordingly. It is thus no wonder that he objected to the enactment of the 'INSC Law'—where there is law there is the High Court of Justice [judicial relief]."[3] It is no wonder that, with one exception, no further National Security Assessments have been conducted since, even though the 2008 INSC Law specifically mandates this.

The annual budgetary process is a further case in point. Rather than being a useful tool for articulation of national objectives, priorities, and consequent options, the highly politicized budgetary process is typically used to obfuscate defense needs, in relation to domestic ones, in the attempt to obtain cabinet approval for the budget, *some* budget, without leaving any coalition party so disaffected that it cannot live with it.[4]

Third, for a politically polarized nation, facing fundamental questions regarding its future character and functioning in an extraordinarily volatile environment, improvisation and sequential decision-making have two great virtues: they enable action without the need for clear articulation and prioritization of objectives and options, the very heart of the policy planning process, and facilitate flexible decision making in times of change and crisis.

Fourth, the failure to set clear objectives and priorities suits the premier and cabinet's political needs. In the absence of clear criteria for success, they are largely absolved of responsibility for failing to meet them, a clear benefit for leaders operating in a highly charged and frenetic political environment.

Fifth, the perpetual competition for political survival and the fear of leaks lead premiers and ministers to "keep their cards close to their chests" and to refrain from revealing their true positions. They thus prefer to focus discussion on the means of implementing preferred approaches, rather than objectives and options, again the essence of policy planning—that is, to discuss the how, not the what.[5]

Finally, due to the politicized nature of both the cabinet and MCoD, most premiers consider them to be forums not for true policy deliberation but for partisan political discourse. Indeed, under the Israeli system, the composition of the cabinet and MCoD is forced on the premier, not chosen by him. To the extent possible, premiers thus typically seek to keep important issues from them until they have adopted a preferred option, or events have precluded alternative options, and then to simply tough it out in the face of what is essentially just raucous partisan debate, rather than policy deliberation.[6] The last thing premiers usually want is a substantive cabinet discussion of objectives and options.

## Past Attempts at Reform

A number of reforms have been proposed over the years to address Israel's decision-making ills, many of which have either not been implemented or have not achieved the desired outcomes. Much of the impetus for these reforms came from major decision-making failures, chief among them the 1973 Yom Kippur War and 2006 Lebanon war. The basic need for reform, however, has been recognized since Israel's early years—indeed, many of the pathologies prevalent in Israeli decision making were apparent from the beginning. The following are some of the highlights of the past proposals for reform.

As early as 1963, just fifteen years after independence, Premier Ben-Gurion appointed a special commission to assess the national security DMP, which concluded that "it is essential for the premier to be in the possession of balanced assessments of political, defense and other matters, based on differing viewpoints and not originating from a single channel." To this end, the committee also recommended strengthening the MFA's Research Department and the appointment of an adviser to the premier on intelligence affairs. Its recommendations were not implemented. Levi Eshkol, Ben-Gurion's successor, sought to institute a number of reforms designed to promote greater institutionalization of the process and more systematic strategic thinking, including the establishment of an American-style NSC. The success of the 1967 war dissipated the momentum for reform, however, and nothing came of his efforts.[7]

The national trauma following the Yom Kippur War presaged the first period in which significant reform actually took place. In order to end MI's de facto monopoly on intelligence analysis and to promote greater analytical pluralism, a new research arm was established in the Mossad and the MFA's Research Division was expanded.[8] Israel's first significant strategic planning capabilities were established in 1974, with the creation of the IDF Planning Branch, and a few years later the MFA's Planning Division was also established.

"The story of policy planning in Israel," according to one informed observer, "*is* the story of the development of the Planning Branch."[9] As a military organ it could never become a full-fledged substitute for an NSC, but by the 1980s it had come to play a vital role in institutionalizing an orderly strategic planning process at the General Staff level and in providing policy support for the defense minister and premier as well. Through its increasingly highly developed ability to churn out quality policy papers, including areas exceeding its core competence in purely military and politico-military affairs, the Planning Branch ultimately evolved into the foremost strategic policy planning entity in Israel.

In 1974 one of the most sweeping proposals for reform ever made in Israel was submitted to the cabinet (the "Yaacobi-Yariv Plan"). The proposal called, inter alia, for the establishment of an NSC; a legal requirement that ministers present options to the cabinet, rather than just one preferred policy, and submit written reports on their ministries' policies and plans; and for a reduction in the size of cabinet committees. The cabinet approved all of the recommendations, with the exception of the establishment of the NSC, but these were never implemented in practice.[10]

In 1990 the cabinet adopted the recommendations of the blue-ribbon Koversky Commission but once again did not implement them. The Commission found that the cabinet DMP was characterized by a lack of systematic analysis and options, overdependence on the recommendations of policy advocates, deeply flawed information, a tenuous relationship between decisions and the actual resources allocated, and that many decisions were not in fact carried out. It again recommended that a policy support staff be established to serve the cabinet.[11]

Following the cabinet's failure to act on the Koversky Report, the Knesset, in a rare move, took the initiative. Acting at the instigation of MK Benny Begin (son of the former premier), the FADAC quickly and almost furtively recommended to the Knesset plenum that an NSC be established. Little debate took place and the necessary legislation was passed in January 1991, with little press or public attention. The entire reform actually consisted of an amendment only a few lines long. Passage of the amendment notwithstanding, the silence that surrounded its adoption continued. In carrying out the letter of the law, Premier Shamir appointed a staff of three full-time officials and a few outside advisers but showed little interest in its work, and by the end of his tenure it had basically "faded away." In 1992 Rabin appointed a small staff, but it, too, dissolved rapidly.[12] In subsequent years the amendment was not even renewed.

In 1996 Premier Netanyahu decided to establish a full-fledged NSC, but Defense Minister Mordechai was opposed and blocked action. A diplomatic fiasco in 1997, caused by a botched Mossad operation in Jordan, led to the establishment of yet another investigative commission (the Ciechanover Commission) and once again the establishment of an NSC was one of the primary recommendations. With the Commission's backing, Netanyahu decided to force the issue and the decision to establish the INSC was adopted by the cabinet (not the Knesset) in January 1999.[13] As with the American NSC on which it was modeled, the INSC's establishment reflected both domestic politics and external factors. Mordechai's resignation and Netanyahu's desire to implement a major reform in governance, just prior to the elections that summer, paved the way for the decision, while the increasingly untenable gap between Israel's complex external environment and the existing system's ability to cope with it, made the need for the INSC even more essential.

Under the cabinet decision, the INSC was to provide the premier with new decision-making capabilities, coordinate between all of the governmental bodies dealing with national security, and serve as a counterweight to the predominance of the defense establishment. The decision thus stated, inter alia, that the INSC would constitute an advisory forum for the premier and cabinet; direct staff work to increase coordination and integration between the national security agencies; prepare meetings of the cabinet, MCoD, and premier; make recommendations; and follow up on implementation.[14] The wording of the decision reflected the obstacles it sought to circumvent. It was made clear that the INSC was to focus on policy coordination and integration and on strategic thinking, but since no agreed definition of "national security" could be reached, its spheres of responsibility were not specified. To minimize bureaucratic opposition, the decision explicitly stated that the INSC would not supplant the existing agencies nor detract from their authority.

During most of its first decade the INSC was marginalized by the premiers in office, and with rare exception, the Gaza disengagement most prominently, they manifested little interest in its work and assigned it few tasks of importance. Between November 2003 and August 2005, for example, Premier Sharon convened thirty-six meetings on national security affairs (not including the cabinet and MCoD); of these, the INSC was not even invited to 47%. Similarly, the INSC participated in just three of the premier's twenty-six national security meetings held between December 2005 and January 2006 and was usually not even invited to preparatory meetings prior to MCoD and cabinet sessions.[15]

Much as in the case of the Agranat Commission of Inquiry following the Yom Kippur War, the failures of the 2006 Lebanon war and ensuing national trauma gave rise to a further major round of demands for reform of the DMP, both from the general public and the defense establishment itself. In response, the Winograd Commission was established to investigate the reasons for the war's failings generally and specifically of the DMP.

One of the Commission's most important recommendations, arguably the most important, was that the INSC's roles and authority be established by statute. The INSC Law was duly adopted in July 2008 and for the first time it now gained formal statutory status, under the new and more appropriate name of the National Security Staff. The new law incorporated all of the Winograd Commission's recommendations (see Appendix 2), with the exception of the establishment of an internal INSC intelligence team.

Under the new law, the INSC was to be subordinate to the premier and to focus primarily on policy support for him but also serve the cabinet. Its responsibilities were to include preparation and coordination of all prime-ministerial and cabinet forums in the area of national security, recommendation of topics and participants for all ministerial committees, follow-up on policy implementation, and presentation of policy options and recommendations to the premier and, at his discretion, the cabinet. Moreover, the law specifically stipulated that the INSC would be responsible for four areas that had proven particularly controversial in the past: submission of annual and multiyear politico-military assessments, preparation of staff work and options on the defense and foreign affairs budgets, analyses and recommendations regarding Israel's security strategy, and presentation of findings and options regarding major defense projects. The NSA was made a permanent participant in meetings of the cabinet, MCoD, and other cabinet forums.[16]

After a decade of bureaucratic irrelevance, change was immediate, if ultimately limited. Olmert began the process, which has continued during Netanyahu's second term, starting in early 2009. Having founded the INSC a decade earlier, but having been forced out of office before it had a chance to get under way, Netanyahu initially sought to give it a big boost, but in practice not that much has changed. Though considerably more influential than in the past, the INSC remains far from being the central player the law intended it to be.

THE INSC: AN APPRAISAL

The INSC survived its first decade, in itself no mean achievement, since its very existence was in doubt throughout much of this period.[17] With the passage of the INSC Law, however, it has now become a permanent fixture, gained a role of some consequence, and may have growing influence in the future. An appraisal of the INSC's role as of June 2012 requires separate consideration of its impact on the MCoD and cabinet plenum, Netanyahu's "Octet" (the latest incarnation of the various informal advisory forums most premiers have convened over the years), the interagency processes, and the premier himself.

*Effect on the MCoD and cabinet plenum.* In the early period following the passage of the INSC Law, two important changes were instituted in the work of the MCoD. For the first time in Israel's history, formal protocols were adopted for the preparation and conduct of MCoD meetings, both in peacetime and during crises, and an annual schedule of biweekly MCoD meetings was drawn up, instead of the former practice of ad hoc scheduling. The annual schedule was to be updated on a quarterly basis, and some meetings, on issues such as the defense budget or annual intelligence assessment, were to be scheduled a year in advance. Needless to say, last-minute changes are frequently made to the agenda, but today it is usually known in advance. In practice, the MCoD has only met once a month on average.

The INSC does now prepare MCoD meetings, procedurally and substantively, determining the agenda, participants (officials, not ministers), and order of presentations. Under the peacetime protocol the INSC is now supposed to circulate a draft agenda two weeks ahead of each MCoD meeting and to chair two preparatory interagency meetings, a general one ten days in advance and a more detailed one a few days later. The preparatory meetings are designed for purposes of situational assessment and to work out the final agenda, to gain an understanding of the various agencies' positions, a procedure that requires that they hold preparatory meetings of their own, and to formulate policy options and recommendations.

Although a significant improvement, the new situation leaves much to be desired. Agency participation in the preparatory meetings is not always at the appropriate hierarchical level. Background and position papers are not always circulated in advance and the various agencies tend to state the positions they intend to present in the MCoD only in general terms, either because these are still being formulated or, at times, because they wish to keep matters to themselves. The IDF and MoD, in particular, have been reluctant to cooperate with the preparatory processes and to present their proposed options. The protocol and preparatory process have become more of a guideline than a binding rule and are not always observed in practice.

Nevertheless, by the time issues reach the MCoD, participants (ministers and officials alike) now have a better understanding of them, of the policy options, and of the different agencies' positions. In some cases, the improved preparations do facilitate more substantive policy discussions, but the MCoD's unwieldy size continues to undermine its efficacy and leaks remain a significant problem. Some attempts have been made to close the severe gaps in expertise among MCoD members, primarily between those who are members of the Octet and those who are not, by holding special in-depth briefings, but this remains a serious problem.

Perhaps most important, the presentation of policy options has only partly improved. The INSC does often present options today, but not always. NSAs have concluded that a strict interpretation of the new law, whereby the INSC would always be responsible to present options and recommendations, in addition to this being done by the respective ministers, is untenable and sometimes do so only if the INSC favors an option that is different from that of the policy advocates. In so doing, the INSC has partly come to be viewed as a further policy advocate, another player, rather than the supraplayer whose role is to ensure that the premier and cabinet are presented with all relevant options. When the INSC does present options, this is usually in the highly abridged form of oral or PowerPoint presentations, at times in brief policy papers, rather than in-depth comprehensive ones. There are, of course, important exceptions. Prior to the Palestinian bid for UN recognition in September 2011, for example, the INSC submitted a formal policy paper that set out six different options.

Typically, the various agencies present their positions and then the INSC presents a summary of the options, with a policy recommendation. As the last to usually speak, the INSC enjoys a unique advantage, but this is often counterbalanced by the primacy of the other players, especially the defense minister and CoS, and the NSA must exercise sensitivity in addressing the advantages and disadvantages of the options they have recommended. If the INSC has gained the lead in preparation of MCoD meetings, the latter continue to be the dominant players in the meetings themselves. The bottom line is that the policymaking process in the MCoD has improved as a result of the INSC Law but has not changed fundamentally, and it remains an overly large and highly politicized forum.

For all practical purposes, the cabinet plenum has not been affected by the INSC and remains a highly politicized and dysfunctional forum. The INSC is represented in all cabinet meetings but participates little in what is still an unreformed process. Under Netanyahu, as under most but not all of his predecessors, the MCoD, not the cabinet plenum, is the locus of most formal national security decision making.

*Effect on the informal forums.* Netanyahu's Octet has been widely hailed for its in-depth and discreet discussions of major policy issues and has certainly proven to be more long-lasting and effective than many of the informal forums that preceded it. Whereas the MCoD under Netanyahu often meets only on a monthly basis, the Octet typically meets more than once a week. It is, however, a purely advisory body, lacking in statutory status, and is thus not a forum for actual decision making. Its significant influence stems from its impact on the premier's thinking and as a preparatory mechanism for MCoD meetings, in which the formal decisions are made. Efforts to date to institutionalize an INSC-led process in the Octet have met little success. Many of the subjects raised are of a military nature, and the premier's military secretary formally retains responsibility for preparing its meetings, without INSC involvement, but, lacking in any policymaking capabilities, does not in fact do so.

*Effect on the interagency process.* The passage of the new legislation has strengthened the INSC's stature vis-à-vis the other agencies, but only partially. Most agencies cooperate to a greater extent than in the past, but Defense Minister Barak remains opposed to the very need for the INSC and largely ignores it, with consequent ramifications for the degree of cooperation manifested by the IDF and MoD.

In reality, the INSC, as a body, is still precluded from much of the defense area, a critical weakness, and the premier's military secretary still enjoys virtually the same predominant position he has long had in this area, leaving the turf battles in the PMB unresolved. The IDF and defense establishment remain the preeminent players in the cabinet and MCoD, Octet, and the premier's informal consultations, and for reasons having to do both with a lack of sufficient personnel and defense establishment opposition, the INSC has yet to seriously engage in three of the special areas stipulated by the INSC Law: the defense budget, major weapons systems programs, and follow-up on policy implementation. One surprising example of the absence of INSC involvement in an issue that clearly had both defense and foreign policy ramifications, was the Turkish-led flotilla that sought to break the naval blockade on Gaza in 2010.

In recent years the INSC submitted an Annual National Security Assessment only in 2009 despite the statutory obligation to do so, and rarely submits in-depth policy reviews. Its primary means of influencing prime-ministerial thinking is thus through oral briefings and participation in the various forums. The INSC does chair various interagency consultative forums, for example, on relations with countries of particular importance to Israel, but with rare exception does not chair statutory interagency decision-making committees, such as the "deputy principals forum" headed by the American NSC, a serious lacuna that reflects its ongoing battle for stature.

*Effect on the premier.* If proximity is a sign of influence, the NSA now sits in the office adjacent to the premier, not in "exile" in a Tel Aviv suburb, as in the early years, or in splendid isolation a few floors away, as in the later ones. More important, the NSA now has both regularly scheduled meetings with the premier and special ones, as needed, and participates in all of the premier's foreign policy-related meetings with Israeli and foreign officials. He does not, however, participate in all of the premier's defense meetings, such as the weekly ones with the heads of the intelligence services, and many defense issues are still discussed and decided on without the NSA's participation or even knowledge, especially in the private consultations between the premier and defense minister.

The premier appears to be somewhat better prepared today for the various cabinet-level meetings and certainly for meetings with Israeli and foreign officials. Talking points and summations are prepared for him by the INSC in advance of the meetings, and at times preparatory meetings take place with the premier on the options available, all of which enhance his ability to manage meetings of the MCoD and Octet. Preparatory processes such as these took place in the past, of course, but are now done on a more structured basis and by a dedicated prime-ministerial staff. The INSC now also operates a round-the-clock situation room geared to providing intelligence updates tailored to the needs of the premier and cabinet.

Despite the significant improvement achieved, there is rare unanimity among officials and observers alike, further reinforced by the findings of the state comptroller,[18] that the INSC has yet to live up to its intended role or to substantially change the process. The reasons for this can be grouped into four primary areas.

*Statutory status.* Originally established by a cabinet decision, the INSC lacked a statutory basis until 2008. In the absence of defined areas of operational responsibility, enjoyed by all other agencies, the need for the INSC was not unequivocal and its very existence was in question. Some four years after the passage of the INSC Law, there is little doubt that it has strengthened the INSC but, as indicated by the above appraisal, only partially, and the jury is still out in terms of its long-term effect. Statute may force premiers to go through the motions and uphold the letter of the law, but they cannot be forced to do so in spirit.

*Prime-ministerial interest.* The INSC is designed primarily to serve the premier, but for the reasons elaborated above, including the tension between premiers' political needs and policy planning, the premiers in office during the INSC's early years were not interested in using it to institutionalize systematic planning processes. Indeed, they seemed averse to this, preferring to focus on their own preconceived notions and policy preferences. A bureau chief, like Sharon's Weissglass or Olmert's Yoram Turbovich, was sufficient for their purposes and the INSC was not needed. Relegated, for the most part, to secondary issues, the INSC became irrelevant to the needs of the premier and his senior advisers, who were almost entirely consumed by pressing daily affairs, and it atrophied in the absence of demand.[19]

It is still too early to assess whether the greater importance attached to the INSC in recent years, under Olmert and Netanyahu, is an indication of future trends or a short-lived reaction to the failures of the 2006 war and enactment of the new legislation. Although future premiers will presumably obey the letter of the law and appoint an NSA, the INSC's actual influence will be a function of the role accorded it by the specific premier in office and the existing political constellation at the time.

*Bureaucratic politics.* The INSC was the focus of intense bureaucratic warfare from the start and remains so today. The other senior officials in the PMB (the chief of bureau, military secretary, and foreign affairs adviser), who had long born responsibility for foreign and defense policy, fought hard to preserve their prerogatives, and the INSC Law, which did not address the PMB's internal composition, did not rectify the problem. The role of the premier's foreign affairs adviser has been downgraded but not eliminated, and the premier's military secretary retains his former stature, remaining the NSA's primary rival for influence. The IDF is likely to strenuously resist any change in the military secretary's role, and it is unclear whether future bureau chiefs will be restricted to their intended political and administrative roles or once again become the de facto NSA.

The various ministries and agencies similarly feared a loss of influence to the INSC and continue to fight aggressively to preserve their bureaucratic turf. The MFA was the most threatened from the outset and has conducted ongoing bureaucratic warfare against the INSC, to preserve its own shrinking share of the organizational pie. The far more powerful MoD and IDF, which had long opposed the establishment of an INSC, out of fear of a diminution of their unique stature, have responded by simply shutting it out, at times even withholding information and refusing to participate in meetings. This has improved somewhat, due to the need to observe the letter of the law, but not fundamentally.[20]

Bureaucratic players everywhere have a keen sense of the rising and waning fortunes of fellow players and adjust their behavior accordingly. In the absence of firm prime-ministerial support, the ongoing bureaucratic strife severely weakened the INSC, while its dependence on others for both its stature (the role accorded it by the premier) and vital inputs (information and participation from the IDF, MFA, and others) turned it into what the State Comptroller called a "structural cripple."[21] The premiers in office throughout the first decade, constantly embroiled in party and coalition politics, fighting to maintain their own positions, were loath to alienate the defense and foreign ministers and largely left the INSC to fend for itself. Even Netanyahu has refrained from resolving the ongoing tension between the roles of the NSA and military secretary and from intervening with the defense establishment to ensure fuller cooperation with the INSC, presumably to avoid friction with Barak and the IDF. To the extent that supporting the INSC entails political and bureaucratic strife, premiers will be reluctant to do so.

*An unnatural skin graft.* The INSC's limited influence to date is a function, above all, of the basic decision-making pathologies set forth in Chapter 2. To an extent, however, the attempt to establish an NSC-type entity in a parliamentary system is somewhat unnatural to begin with, akin to a body responding to a skin graft. It is not by chance that only a handful of countries have an NSC in the US sense (i.e., a senior advisory body to the president, responsible for coordinating and integrating the policymaking process and even directing the work of the different agencies at his behest), though organs bearing this name, with entirely different roles, are not uncommon. Of the few that do exist, most are in presidential systems, such as Russia and South Korea, with India and, interestingly, as of 2010 Britain, the prominent exceptions. Indeed, the very essence of an NSC, as a body sitting atop the policy process, at least partially conflicts with the nature of the parliamentary system, in which the premier is just "first among equals." Making this institutional arrangement work in any parliamentary system is thus a tall order, certainly in Israel's coalition system.

Some perspective is also warranted. In the far more propitious circumstances of a centralized presidential system, it took nearly twenty years before the US NSC achieved the position of prominence it has enjoyed ever since. Even so, its influence has fluctuated over the years in accordance with the preferences and leadership styles of the different presidents and NSAs. Indeed, during its first fifteen years, the US NSC was charged only with presenting the various agencies' positions to the president and coordinating between them, without an advisory role of its own.[22] It is thus hardly surprising that the INSC has yet to achieve its intended role. It is a process and if it succeeds in gaining even somewhat similar influence in thirty years this will be a remarkable feat. In practice, this is unlikely to ever happen in Israel's PR system, even if it remains a model to be emulated and a goal to strive for.

## Failings Tolerable No Longer

The myriad decision-making pathologies described in this book notwithstanding, Israel has in many ways been a historic success story. Its very survival is a triumph, but no less important, Israel has in many ways been a model of successful political, economic, and social development. This has certainly been the case in defense affairs, in which Israel has developed clearly disproportionate capabilities.

Israel must, therefore, be doing something right. The question is how a fundamentally flawed process has produced overall national success, even if many believe that the nation has been increasingly adrift in recent decades.

Part of the answer is that Israel has often succeeded despite its DMP, not because of it.[23] During times of great challenge and crisis, people are often able to discover new capabilities and sources of strength within themselves and to surmount the seemingly insurmountable. Facing historic, even existential, challenges, Israel had no choice but to rise to the occasion despite the decision-making ills of its governmental system. Fundamental Arab weaknesses and failings, not just Israel's abilities, also contributed to this.

A further explanation, as set out at the end of Chapter 2, has been the system's ability to cope with its own failings and at times even turn them into short-term, tactical advantages. In an extraordinarily volatile environment, Israel's predilection for improvisation, for example, a fundamental pathology in the long term, has been a short-term godsend, especially in the early decades. Moreover, the dramatic successes achieved during those years overshadowed the failures that did take place and the reality that most of Israel's decision-making pathologies have existed since independence, though some, such as the dysfunctionality of the cabinet, appear to have grown worse over time.

In recent decades, in any event, the system's ills appear to have finally caught up with it, and Israel has repeatedly failed to achieve its policy objectives, often even to formulate clear objectives, even when it has had the initiative. The old explanation, that Israel's extraordinarily demanding external environment forces it into an essentially reactive mode, precluding any substantive ability to set objectives and shape the environment, has certainly grown less valid, as demonstrated by Israel's comparatively proactive behavior in the seven case studies. At a minimum, Israel's environment poses greater opportunities today for proactive attempts to shape the nation's future course than in the past.

There have, of course, been some successful decisions of strategic importance in recent decades, both in terms of process and outcome. Positive outcomes, however, are not always a function of effective processes, as amply demonstrated by the two Camp David cases, and successful outcomes often divert attention from failures of process. In any event, the gap between Israel's needs and the system's ability to deliver has widened significantly, the number of failures has become untenable, and the cost has simply become too high. The fact that the pathologies identified in this book are manifested to varying degrees in all countries is of little comfort. As indicated by the following long, yet still partial list, Israel can simply no longer afford to continue business as usual.

First, Israel aspires to be an international scientific, high-tech, and cultural center and to serve as a spiritual center for the Jewish people around the world. As such it seeks to provide a safe and comfortable Western lifestyle, to promote immigration and prevent emigration. A situation of chronic strategic crisis is, however, inimical to Israel's ability to realize these fundamental national goals. As the existential threat has ebbed and the national focus has partly shifted inward, toward socioeconomic issues typical of a more "normal" society, public tolerance of the defense burden and the demands it places on other national goals has waned, at least somewhat.

The repeated failures of recent decades have undermined Israel's deterrence and shaken its self-confidence. Israel has not unequivocally won a major military engagement since 1967, including the 1969–1971 War of Attrition, Yom Kippur War, and 1982 and 2006 operations in Lebanon, as well as repeated lower-level clashes with Hezbollah and Hamas. Israel's deterrent strategy was predicated in the past on demonstrating to the Arab countries that they would lose every confrontation and should therefore refrain from aggression entirely or at least downgrade their ambitions accordingly. One or two inconclusive outcomes may arguably be acceptable; a long series becomes a dangerous pattern. Events of recent decades have been a source of mixed but certainly more encouraging signals for hostile Arab elements.

As the monolithic wall of Arab hostility has cracked in recent decades and Israel's ability to shape its external environment has increased, Israel has become increasingly proactive and has undertaken a number of initiatives, but has repeatedly failed to achieve the objectives it set for itself. Part of this continues to be for reasons beyond Israel's control—its external environment is still highly uncertain and difficult to mold—but part clearly stems from the ills of its own decision making.

Israel faces a variety of unusually difficult threats today, in some cases of unprecedented complexity. Hamas and especially Hezbollah constitute a new form of asymmetric warfare, in which the nonstate player no longer has to seek state sanctuary but largely *is* the state, acts from its territory with impunity, and has military capabilities that, at least in some areas, exceed those of any conventional military, as is the case, for example, with Hezbollah's rocket arsenal. Iran poses a threat that even a global superpower, the United States, is hesitant to confront. The Arab Spring holds out prospects for positive long-term change but also potentially dire dangers, such as an end to peace with Egypt and even Jordan.

As issues have become more complex and the cost of error has grown, Israel's ability to improvise and make decisions sequentially has decreased. Development of modern weapons systems typically takes a decade or two and the costs can be in the billions. Responses to new strategic threats, such as those posed by Iran, take decades to develop and cannot be improvised. The comparatively "easy" parts of the peace process, the agreements with Egypt and Jordan, have long been resolved, leaving the truly complex and dangerous core issues, with the Palestinians and Syria, to be addressed.

In an integrated global environment, Israel's national security interests are now affected by developments spanning the world, including far-off places such as North Korea, and it must take into account a far more complex web of considerations than in the past. Now that it is no longer a minor regional actor or "diplomatic island," Israel's actions have potentially global consequences, as, for example, if it had responded to Iraqi missile attacks during the two Gulf wars, or should it decide to attack the Iranian nuclear program. Its policies on the peace process are deemed by world powers to significantly affect their interests, and even its responses to limited local events have international repercussions. As a result, Israel's margin for error has decreased substantially and an already frenetic environment is likely to continue becoming even more so.

Although Israel suffered from a major quantitative disparity during the early decades of the conflict, it enjoyed a clear qualitative advantage, militarily, technologically, and in terms of societal mobilization. In recent decades the trends have begun to change, Arab societies and militaries have advanced rapidly and are likely to continue doing so, and the gap is closing. Moreover, the rise of asymmetric warfare undercuts Israel's qualitative advantage.

The rise of asymmetric actors and changing international norms have further complicated Israel's already limited ability to foresee the outcomes of its actions, both military and diplomatic, that is, to assess cause and effect and to link policies with their consequences. Israel's external environment has always been highly uncertain and difficult to predict; now it is more so.

Finally, it must be stressed that systematic policy planning is particularly important precisely in such uncertain circumstances. In a stable environment, events are relatively predictable and the need for planning is both less acute and easier to carry out. In an unstable environment, systematic planning is harder but far more important; in its absence, policy risks deteriorating into a series of ad hoc responses, without overall direction and purpose.

## Future Reforms

What can be done to improve the process? If we are to effect a change, the three root causes of Israel's decision-making pathologies must be addressed: its extraordinarily difficult external environment, the PR political system, and the weakness of the civilian national security organs.

Israel's ability to shape its environment has certainly grown over the decades, and many believe that it should be more proactive and forthcoming, primarily on the Palestinian issue. Indeed, a peace agreement with the Palestinians would have positive ramifications for Israel's strategic posture going far beyond the great importance of the agreement itself and would significantly increase Israel's ability to shape its environment, much as happened after the 1993 Oslo Agreement. Progress toward peace, however, is contingent both on political developments that are highly controversial in Israel and on the positions of the other side. Comprehensive peace unfortunately does not seem to be in the cards for many years to come, and Israel's environment will remain highly complex and demanding even after peace with the Palestinians and Syria. Although a less hostile environment would reduce the demands on the Israeli DMP, the solution to its ills does not lie here, at least for the medium to long term.

Reform of the PR system remains essential, indeed, the only way to fundamentally redress the pathologies of Israel's national security DMP, or for that matter, in domestic affairs as well. In the absence of electoral reform, the politicization, dysfunctionality of the cabinet, and other pathologies attendant to the PR system will continue to undermine whatever improvements can be hoped for either through changes in Israel's external environment or by "fixes" to institutions and processes. Countries the world over, however, are loath to make changes to their electoral systems—witness the ongoing existence of the American electoral college—and Israel is no exception. Israel did briefly adopt a new system in the late 1990s, under which the premier was elected separately by popular vote, while the Knesset continued to be elected on the basis of the existing PR system, but it reverted to the old one after two elections, when the new system's failings were deemed to be even greater. This painful experience makes the prospects of further electoral reform that much more remote. Vital though it is, electoral reform is not likely for the long term.

The primary hope for change in the foreseeable future is thus, by default, in the third root cause, the weakness of the civilian national security organs. After nearly four decades of institutional reform, however, all of the necessary organs of government now exist and Israel has a structurally mature national security establishment. The IDF Planning Branch has become a central player, and the MoD's Politico-Military Planning Branch, Mossad's research arm, the MFA's Policy Planning Division, and potentially most important of all, the INSC, have all been established. The need and latitude for "institutional fixes" is thus limited at this point, and the primary focus has to be on strengthening these existing organs' capabilities and on improving the process.

We turn first to a number of recommendations for improvement in this area, before exploring some directions for more fundamental change, should electoral reform become feasible at some later date. Whichever changes are adopted, it is essential that they be done without detracting from the capabilities of the IDF and intelligence agencies, whose policymaking strengths are a national asset.

## INSC AND CABINET

All prime-ministerial advisers dealing with foreign and defense affairs must be subordinated to the NSA, so that there is one focal point in the premier's office bearing overall responsibility for these matters. This recommendation would resolve the current anomaly whereby the INSC has become responsible for policy support for the premier's foreign policy work and meetings of the MCoD, while the military secretary remains responsible for his defense affairs and for the work of the Octet. Since the military secretary has no policy planning capabilities of his own, indeed, virtually no staff at all, the current situation in effect ensures that the IDF, not the INSC, remains the premier and cabinet's sole source of policy planning in defense affairs. To address this issue would mean subordinating the military secretary and foreign affairs adviser to the INSC, possibly as deputy NSAs, while the premier's bureau chief would cease virtually all involvement in national security affairs, coordinating any residual areas of responsibility with the INSC (e.g., his role as liaison to counterparts abroad, such as the White House chief of staff, who at times engage in relevant matters).

The INSC must participate in and be responsible for staffing *all* of the premier's formal and informal national security-related meetings, both in foreign and defense affairs, as mandated by the INSC Law. One comparatively easy change in this direction, of importance both in itself and as an indication of changing mind-sets, would be for the NSA to join and ultimately replace the military secretary as the only other participant in the premier's weekly meetings with the heads of the intelligence services (and his less frequent and ad hoc meetings with the CoS). Pending subordination of the military secretary to the INSC and development of the necessary organizational capabilities, which it does not currently possess, the INSC must at least be fully involved in the preparatory process for the Octet, as part of its overall integrative function, and must in the future bear responsibility for policy support for its successor forums.

Some of the premier's closed consultations with the defense and/or foreign ministers are overwhelmingly political in nature, and they are likely to wish to preserve discretion, meeting without the presence of senior officials. The NSA's role as a political appointee, unlike the military secretary, should partially ameliorate this problem and enable his participation in at least many, if not all, of the meetings of this sort. Given the virtues of occasional informal, unstructured discussions between the premier and the defense or foreign ministers, the INSC should at least be in a position to follow up on them, if not to prepare them.

The MFA, MoD, intelligence agencies, and especially the IDF will have to learn over time to live by the rules of a new game, in which they no longer call the shots alone, even in their respective areas of responsibility, and work under the guidance of the INSC. Under the existing electoral system, the foreign and defense ministers cannot be expected to take direction from an appointed official; even in the United States there is built-in tension between the NSA and the secretaries of state and defense. The ministries and agencies, however, can and must be subordinated to an INSC-led process and required to participate fully, at the appropriate levels, especially in the formulation of objectives and options. Part of the solution lies in reaching a common appreciation, realistically feasible only over time, that the INSC's integrative and coordinating role is to the benefit of all, rather than an imposition that comes at the expense of other players' prerogatives. More concretely, it is imperative that the INSC use its statutory authority to establish senior interagency policy planning and coordinating committees, akin to the US NSC's "deputy principals forum" (in Israel this would include the directors-general and heads of all of the national security ministries and agencies) and other interagency committees dealing with issues of major importance, for example, the interagency committee on the Iranian nuclear program currently chaired by the Mossad. The premier's firm backing is essential if this is to happen.

The INSC must fulfill the special responsibilities assigned to it by the INSC Law, which it has yet to undertake in practice, including annual and multiyear national security assessments, policy planning regarding the defense budget and major defense projects, and follow-up on policy implementation. These responsibilities were specially enumerated precisely because of their importance and the anticipated bureaucratic sensitivity, and every day that passes without the INSC fulfilling them, whether due to its limited resources or bureaucratic opposition, makes it that much harder to carry them out in the future. To be realistic, this is unlikely to happen regarding the defense budgets and projects while Defense Minister Barak is in office, and his successors will undoubtedly object strenuously as well. In the end, it will be up to the premier, as will be the case in regard to the annual and multiyear national security assessments and follow-up on implementation. The failure to fulfill these tasks, as with other aspects of national security planning, meets the premier's political needs, but the law is now on the INSC's side.

Formulation of clearly defined and actionable policy objectives, priorities, and options, with well-elucidated end-states, remains absolutely essential, arguably the most important reform at the process level. In practice, premiers are likely to remain averse to systematic policy planning processes, for the reasons mentioned earlier in this chapter, and pending electoral reform, further substantive change will probably not prove feasible in the cabinet plenum and only partially so in the MCoD. Although it is essential that the attempt be made to build on the progress already achieved in the MCoD and further institutionalize systematic policy planning to the extent possible, it is in the specially constituted subcabinet forums, such as Netanyahu's Octet and its future successors, the small informal meetings with the defense and foreign ministers and senior officials, and the premier's own preparations, that the greatest room for improvement may lie. In recognizing that these forums are the true loci of decision making in Israel, the need to strengthen and institutionalize their policymaking capabilities comes into particular relief, and it is here that the INSC may ultimately have its greatest impact. No statutory changes are required and other ministers and officials would be hard-pressed to object to the premier having the forums he chairs better prepared. What is needed is prime-ministerial determination to do so.

A recommendation to formulate clear objectives and options is, of course, easy to make, but far harder to implement in practice. Witness the failure of successive US administrations to do so or to even observe the eminently sensible guidelines of the "Powell Doctrine," which stated, inter alia, that the United States should always formulate clear objectives and a coherent exit strategy before applying military force.[24] In the real world there will always be countervailing political interests and pressures that can derail the most effective processes. What is needed is a change in mind-set and culture, over time, no less than in formal processes, with the objective of "getting it right" more of the time, not an unrealistic hope to do so all of the time.

A good starting point would be with the work of the premier himself, who already now enjoys better policy support than in the past, and on those issues that are of great importance but not politically divisive, for example, the Iranian nuclear program or Hezbollah's rocket arsenal. Institutionalizing systematic planning processes on issues such as these in the informal forums, including the Octet and the premier's small consultations, would be of great benefit in its own right, and cumulative positive experiences might have an at least partially positive spillover effect on other more controversial issues.

In recent years the INSC has become deeply engaged in short-term, day-to-day servicing of the premier's affairs, at the expense of more basic and in-depth strategic planning. On the positive side, an advisory body that is not engaged in daily affairs risks the danger of becoming irrelevant, as happened to the INSC in the past. Conversely, a careful balance must be managed to ensure that the INSC does not simply become another one of the many agencies in Israel dealing with pressing immediate issues, while it retains its unique role as an in-depth strategic planning entity.

Only a serious INSC-led process can counteract the tendency to improvisation and sequential decision making prevalent in the Israeli DMP.

All of the NSAs appointed to date have been senior defense officials and, with one possible exception, have brought the defense establishment's deeply imbued tradition of nonpartisanship and professional impartiality to this position. A vital norm for defense officials in a democracy, it is not entirely appropriate to the unique nature of the NSA's role. As a prime-ministerial adviser, unlike agency heads, the NSA must be keenly attuned to the politics of the issues and to the premier's political needs; otherwise he or she risks losing influence and even relevance. At the same time, NSAs must preserve their professional integrity, in their relationships both with the premier and with the national security establishment. It is a fine balance, but one that is crucial to the NSA's success.

The current size of the INSC staff is clearly insufficient if it is to fully assume the expanded role envisaged for it by the INSC Law, indeed, even for its current responsibilities. It must also be constituted to serve the needs of all members of the MCoD and informal forums, not just the premier, though it would clearly remain a prime-ministerial organ and serve the other players at his discretion.

MFA

The Winograd Commission and Shahak Committee emphasized the need to significantly strengthen the MFA's role in the DMP and its organizational capabilities to do so,* but their recommendations did not go nearly far enough; a special commission should be established to this end, to propose a comprehensive reform. The MFA has already begun this process on its own in recent years, instituting important reforms both at the structural level and in terms of its organizational procedures.†

Arguably, nothing has hurt the MFA's standing more than the practice, common in recent decades, of appointing foreign ministers primarily for reasons of coalition politics, rather than qualifications and personal stature,

---

* The Shahak Committee was charged with recommending practical measures to implement the Winograd Commission's findings.

† Under an important organizational reform instituted by the MFA in recent years, it now has an effective "executive": a top management team composed of the director-general, four vice directors-general (political affairs, multilateral affairs, public diplomacy, and administration), to which all of the regional and functional divisions report; the heads of the Policy Planning and Research divisions; and the ministry's legal adviser. In the past, the MFA had only one vice director-general, and the "executive," which then included all of the deputy-directors, was double its current size, making it an ineffective forum for purposes of policy planning and decision making. In recent years the MFA has also adopted annual work plans setting out organizational goals and priorities. As of 2011 the work plan is also updated on a quarterly basis.

and no change of consequence in its organizational fortunes will be feasible unless this ceases. The foreign minister must once again come to be seen, like the defense minister, as above the political fray and as an appointment based, first and foremost, on substance. Only then, for example, will premiers cease making the artificial distinction between their "defense" and "foreign" affairs meetings, largely as a means of excluding the foreign minister. Needless to say, virtually all prime-ministerial decision making on defense affairs entails important foreign policy considerations and the foreign minister must be fully integrated in the process.

Related to this, the politicization of the appointment and promotion process in the MFA must also end. It currently stems from three factors: a political compromise whereby the foreign minister and premier are allowed to make eleven political appointments to ambassadorships of their choosing; the involvement of the minister in the appointment and promotion process for ministry personnel generally, rather than a strictly professional process; and finally the entirely anachronistic and destructive role of the ministry's "workers' committee," a throwback to Israel's early socialist days, in which crony bureaucratic politics—who knows and is close to whom—plays a decisive role.

The MFA has long suffered from an organizational culture that viewed its role as that of a largely passive participant in the DMP, primarily a mouthpiece for policies formulated by others, rather than as an operational agency with a targeted "can-do" approach and clearly defined objectives and missions. Instead of just being a mouthpiece and focusing on the management of day-to-day foreign relations, the MFA must become deeply involved in the formulation of policy itself, both of a purely diplomatic and a broader politico-military, or national security, nature. To give just one vital example, the MFA should be involved in virtually every decision to use military force, in contrast with the current situation in which this is considered a "defense matter" and is decided on solely by the premier and defense minister, in cases of limited action, or brought to the cabinet or MCoD for approval in cases of more significant operations, without MFA involvement.

One way of addressing these politically and substantively difficult issues would be by passage of a "Foreign Ministry Law" akin to the existing INSC, IDF, and ISA laws that set forth the statutory basis and responsibilities of these organizations. Among other issues, the proposed law would provide for the following:

- A statutory requirement that the premier and defense minister consult with the foreign minister prior to approval of military action and on politico-military strategy (i.e., policy issues that are not of a purely military character, such as the defense budget, weapons, and force structure). To this end, the foreign minister or MFA director-general must be a permanent participant in all of the premier's policy-oriented and operational meetings with the defense minister and CoS. A limited waiver from this requirement would be granted primarily for purposes of immediate preventative actions (e.g., interdiction of terrorist or rocket attacks) and responses (e.g., striking a target after an attack, before it disappears), as is currently the case regarding the need for cabinet and MCoD approval.

- Making the director-general of the MFA a "state appointee," much like the CoS or heads of the intelligence services, whose tenures are for a fixed period, rather than being the sole prerogative of the foreign minister. This would provide for far longer terms in office and a greater ability to conduct policy planning, instead of the current situation whereby the director-general is replaced almost every time a new minister comes into office.
- The conditions for personnel appointments and promotions within the ministry, in order to eliminate the involvement of the "workers' committee" and minister in the process and do away with, or at least significantly curtail, the current eleven politically appointed ambassadorships (though a handful of key positions, such as the ambassadors to the United States and UN, might still remain political appointments, given their particularly sensitive nature).

If not by statute, it is essential that these changes be made by other means.

To further strengthen the MFA's input into the national DMP and promote greater policy integration, the MFA director-general should become a permanent participant in relevant meetings of the IDF General Staff and all other appropriate senior IDF and MoD decision-making forums, including operational ones. Similarly, a senior IDF officer should be a permanent participant in the MFA's top decision-making forums, including the "executive" (*hanhala*), its top management team, playing a role somewhat akin to that of the premier's military secretary and adding a vital politico-military perspective to the MFA's at times "ethereal" diplomatic thinking.

Within the MFA, it is particularly important that the Policy Planning and Research divisions be strengthened, in terms of professional expertise and organizational clout, and that their work be better integrated into that of the regional and functional divisions. To this end, a new vice director-general position should be created, responsible for both divisions. Further measures should also be adopted to increase the attractiveness of service in the two divisions, which were commonly viewed in the past as something of an organizational backwater, to make it a sought after way station for officials destined for rapid promotion.

Finally, the MFA must be strengthened in terms of personnel size, administrative autonomy, and budgets. One possibility would be to use the new MFA Law, as proposed, to designate the MFA as part of the "defense establishment," in contrast to its current status as part of the regular civil service. The defense establishment enjoys a far higher wage scale, easier allocation of personnel slots, generally heightened administrative autonomy, and far larger budgets. Although a change such as this might be possible through bureaucratic fiat or as ostensibly simple change in administrative designation, it is likely to lead to similar demands for special status by other ministries as well and thus to encounter considerable opposition. Whether by statute or otherwise, the problems faced by the MFA in these areas must be resolved. Comparatively minute sums by the standards of the defense establishment would have a dramatic effect on the MFA.

## MOD

A further area of possible reform is in the relationship between the IDF and MoD designed to subordinate the IDF to greater civilian oversight. As constituted ever since Israel was established (see Chapter 1), both the IDF and the MoD report separately to the defense minister, and the IDF is actually the dominant player, with the MoD neither designed nor staffed to conduct ministerial oversight over policy and budgets. The defense establishment as a whole also enjoys unique budgetary autonomy from the MoF. For all of the desirability of greater civilian control in a democracy, the existing system has generally worked effectively and change in this area must be approached with caution.

One possibility is to further strengthen the MoD's strategic planning capabilities, including the broad spectrum of politico-military and diplomatic issues currently dealt with by the IDF Planning Branch. This could be achieved either by means of an expansion of the MoD Politico-Military Division, thereby creating a costly parallel structure, or by transferring responsibility for this, and the necessary personnel slots, from the Planning Branch. This issue has dogged the MoD-IDF relationship ever since the Planning Branch was established in the 1970s, and at times it has even been made a joint IDF-MoD organ. The establishment of the MoD Politico-Military Division in the early 2000s was supposed to have resolved the issue, but as with other compromise arrangements never fully did. A final resolution of this ongoing conundrum is important, though not essential.

Finally, on the process level, although the posited impact of leaks was not substantiated in the cases studied in this book, the fear of leaks has an important effect on decision makers' expectations and the process as whole. In a reformed process, the premier would have to ensure secrecy, inter alia, by taking preventative measures, punishing offenders, and, first and foremost, observing the new norms himself. Leaks are endemic to all democracies and will remain so in Israel; the norms, however, were far more restrictive in the past and can become so again. Unlike most other recommendations herein, this one can be implemented largely by prime-ministerial determination to do so. As demonstrated by the relative secrecy of the current Octet's meetings, leaks are not a force majeure.

ELECTORAL REFORM

A truly substantive change in Israel's DMP would require more than just limited "fixes" to the existing process; it necessitates fundamental electoral reform. Proposals for reform of Israel's PR system are almost as old as the state, beginning with Ben-Gurion in the 1950s, and have ranged from limited changes that do not fundamentally alter the system, such as raising the electoral threshold to reduce political fragmentation, to dramatic changes, such as adoption of a presidential system. The various proposals have been presented in detail elsewhere and an in-depth treatment thereof goes beyond the scope of this book. It is nevertheless worth briefly mentioning some of the primary reforms proposed, which have revolved around three primary themes, of which the latter two are directly germane to the decision-making pathologies described herein.[25]

The first theme has focused on increasing Knesset accountability, with most proposals calling for the adoption of a two-tiered electoral system, under which either half or two-thirds of the Knesset's 120 members would be elected in single-seat constituencies and the remainder through the existing PR system. A balance between regional and national representation and a coherent party system would thereby be preserved. Some have advocated 120 single-seat constituencies, but this approach has not gained broad support, largely due to the belief that Israel's small size precludes the need for such deep regional representation and out of a desire to maintain party coherence. Alternative approaches have recommended seventeen constituencies, with the number of representatives in each to be based on the relative size of its population, or thirty constituencies with three members each and thirty elected by the PR system.

A second primary theme has focused on means of strengthening the premier's statutory authority and of determining, immediately after elections, whom the premier would be. Proponents of this latter objective sought to streamline coalition negotiations and end the current situation whereby weeks of political machinations are invariably required before a new coalition is formed and the identity of the new premier is confirmed. A more radical approach to these ends, which has received ongoing, if limited, support, is adoption of a presidential system. A middle-of-the-road approach was the now defunct reform in the late 1990s, whereby the premier was elected directly by popular vote and the Knesset through the existing PR system. An alternative approach, which has gained some traction, calls for the head of the largest party to automatically become premier. Given the fragmentation of Israeli politics in recent decades, however, this had led to concern that the head of a relatively small party would become premier, even though he or she did not truly command the support necessary for a stable coalition. A variant on this approach thus proposed that the premier's appointment be made contingent on his faction numbering at least thirty-five MKs, a rather small number in itself.

An entirely different approach to strengthening the premier's position and promoting coalition stability is the concept of a "constructive vote of no confidence." At present, a simple "vote of no confidence" which leads to the coalition's fall and requires either that a new one be formed or that elections be held, can be approved by a simple majority. Under the "constructive" approach, the bar for approval would be much higher: a majority of the Knesset—ranging from a simple one under some proposals to a nearly unattainable majority of seventy or even eighty MKs in others—would have to vote not only to dissolve the existing coalition but also in favor of an alternative one. Regardless of the specific majority adopted, the prospects of a vote passing would be greatly reduced and coalition stability increased commensurately. This would not, however, address the fundamental problem of the plethora of political parties represented in the Knesset and consequent need for multiple partners to form a coalition.

Over the years the premier's statutory authority to appoint and fire ministers has been broadened, as a means of strengthening his control over the cabinet, and some advocate a further expansion of his prerogatives. With only a handful of exceptions, however, premiers have not exercised their existing authority to appoint ministers who are not MKs, and they have similarly refrained from firing ministers, even in the most egregious circumstances, out of fear of the coalition consequences. Subject to a more fundamental reform of the system or additional measures to promote coalition stability, such as the "constructive vote of no confidence," this does not appear a promising direction for further change.

A third focus of reform has been directed at heightened cabinet efficiency. Some have called for a statutory limitation on the size of the cabinet and MCoD, a change that all recognize to be essential but that has been blocked by the parties' vested interest in keeping the maximum number of ministerial positions available to them. Indeed, in recent years the problem has been the establishment of new "make-believe" ministries, designed simply to add new ministerial positions, and the appointment of ministers without portfolio. Others have recommended that ministers, except the premier and vice premier, be required to resign from the Knesset, thereby enabling them to devote themselves more fully to their ministries, with the proviso that they would regain their seats upon leaving the cabinet.

Regardless of which of these and other reforms, if any, is ultimately adopted, it is essential both for purposes of governability and decision-making efficiency that they address two primary issues. First, the formal authority of the premier must be strengthened in order to make the cabinet more accountable to him and so that he can usually be expected to serve a full four-year term. The current situation, whereby the defense and foreign ministers are typically the premier's leading rivals and coalitions usually serve no longer than two to three years, must change. An expectation of a likely full four-year term would greatly reduce the pressure on premiers and ministers to focus so overwhelmingly on immediate political considerations and short-term achievements and would enable a more policy-based and planned, as opposed to politics-based, process.

Second, the cabinet must be restructured in a manner designed to make it a far less politicized and far more effective decision-making body. Efforts should focus primarily on the MCoD, which, to be effective, must be greatly cut in size and restricted to the relevant ministers. Ideally, it would consist of the premier, defense and foreign ministers, vice or deputy premiers, thereby finally lending some substance to these otherwise honorific titles, and, on an as-needed basis, the ministers of domestic security and finance. The total number of permanent participants would not exceed five to seven and no nonvoting members would be allowed. Senior officials would participate as necessary.

In concluding, a few notes of caution are in order. There is no such thing as a "correct" electoral system or national security DMP, certainly not a one-size-fits-all model, and the arrangements adopted by each country must reflect its unique circumstances and character. Moreover, all electoral systems and DMPs generate pathologies of their own and by reforming one system we are virtually assured to cause new ones. We can and must strive for improvement, but there are no guarantees of success and there are no panaceas. Even the best process would be hard-pressed to effectively address the demands of Israel's complex external environment.

"The Lord is my shepherd," says the Book of Psalms and fortunate this is, for the DMP in Israel is deeply flawed. Nearly sixty-five years after independence, the same basic political processes, which so successfully gave rise to the nation in its formative years, are still largely intact. Although the national security establishment's size and sophistication have changed beyond recognition, the decision-making processes at the prime-ministerial and cabinet level remain largely unchanged and increasingly incapable of addressing the demands placed on them. The Israeli DMP is probably less planned while also more chaotic and politicized than in other countries, but it also has its own strengths. What makes its failings different and unacceptable is that some are manifested to an inordinate degree and that the challenges Israel's external environment poses are such that it simply cannot afford them. Although reform is widely recognized as essential, the dysfunctions of the PR system, which account for much of the system's failings, are also the biggest impediments to change.

# The INSC Law, 2008

1. The cabinet and premier will have a National Security Staff, operated and directed by the premier.
2. The National Security Staff's roles will be the following:
   a. Coordination of national security staff work for the cabinet, MCoD, and any other ministerial forum.
   b. Recommending to the premier topics for meetings of the MCoD and other ministerial committees, as well as the participants and their hierarchical level.
   c. Preparation of cabinet and subcabinet meetings and—in addition to this being done by the respective ministries—presentation of policy options, their ramifications, and detailed recommendations.
   d. Responsibility on behalf of the premier for interagency national security staff work, presentation of options, their ramifications, and policy recommendations to the premier and, at his discretion, to the cabinet.
   e. Follow-up on implementation of decisions by the cabinet and its subcommittees and apprising the premier of this.
   f. Operation of a new National Center for Crisis Management.
   g. The law further enumerated four specific areas of responsibility:
      • Submission of annual and multiyear politico-military assessments to the MCoD and preparation of situational assessments on related matters. Similar assessments are to be presented to the premier by the various agencies at least once a year and to be discussed by the MCoD.
      • Preparation of staff work for the premier on the defense, foreign affairs, and other national security-related budgets, including options based on a broad perspective of national priorities.
      • Analysis of the national security strategy and recommended changes.

National Security Staff Law, enacted by the Knesset on July 29, 2008, as published in *Reshumot*, Jerusalem, August 7, 2008.

- Examination of defense projects with important politico-military ramifications and presentation of findings to the premier, MCoD, or any other forum the premier wishes, including options based on a broad assessment of national priorities.
3. The NSA is authorized to require the participation of representatives of the different agencies and ministries in meetings, at the level the NSA determines.
4. All information regarding foreign and defense affairs sent to the premier by the various agencies will be sent to the NSA as well.
5. The NSA will be a permanent participant in meetings of the cabinet, MCoD, and other cabinet forums. The NSA will also be a permanent member of the Committee of (Intelligence) Service Heads.
6. The premier will establish procedures regarding the INSC's operation within the PMB, including the mutual relations between the NSA and other senior officials.

# Recommendations of the Winograd Commission and the Shahak Committee

*Recommendation:* The INSC must be restructured in order to enable a fundamental change in its status. To this end:

1. The roles of the INSC must be defined clearly and include, inter alia, preparation of long-term, integrative staff work on politico-military affairs, and the presentation to the premier and cabinet committees of positions on all relevant issues under consideration by them. To this, the Shahak Committee added:
   a. The importance of the INSC presenting decision makers with options, an analysis of their ramifications, and a recommendation.
   b. The need to clearly define the INSC's relationship with the other officials in the PMB and with the various national security agencies.
   c. The INSC should be the premier and cabinet's *only* national security staff. The NSA should be directly subordinate to the premier and should serve as the premier's senior national security adviser.
   d. The name of the INSC should be changed to the Israel National Security *Staff*, which is more appropriate to its role.
2. The INSC should be charged with preparation and coordination of meetings of the MCoD. Materials and recommendations for the MCoD will be prepared both by the various national security bodies and the INSC.
3. The INSC should be charged with preparing cabinet discussions on the defense budget, including a comparison of defense and other needs.
4. The INSC staff should be strengthened radically, both qualitatively and quantitatively, through development of a multidisciplinary and highly experienced team and use of outside expertise.

State of Israel, *Winograd Commission: Interim Report*, 2007b, pp. 296–301; and State of Israel, *Recommendations of the Steering Committee for the Implementation of the Interim Report of the Winograd Commission* 2007a.

5. The NSA must be a personal appointee of the premier's, with the approval of the cabinet and Knesset Foreign and Defense Affairs Committee. A senior deputy to the NSA shall be appointed by the premier, with the approval of the cabinet, in order to ensure continuity over time. The senior deputy will serve for a period of six years, with a possible four-year extension. The Shahak Committee took exception to the role accorded the Knesset committee, which it found to be a violation of the separation of powers.

6. A National Assessment Team shall be established within the INSC, in order to integrate the intelligence information and assessments of the different intelligence agencies and provide both periodic and special National Security Assessments. Though part of the INSC, the National Assessment Team will enjoy full professional independence. Upon its establishment, the intelligence unit subordinate to the premier's military secretary will be abolished.

   a. The Shahak Committee supported the need for a small intelligence unit within the INSC to present the daily intelligence briefing to the premier and for its own internal needs, but recommended that the issue of a National Assessment Team be studied further in terms of its structure, personnel, and relations with the intelligence agencies.

7. Legislation should be enacted to establish the INSC's roles and authority, as well as the means of appointing its senior officials (as was done in July 2008, with the passage of the INSC Law).

8. To the general description of the INSC's duties above, the Shahak Committee added the following specifics:

   a. Coordination of national security staff work for the premier and formulation of assessments and policy recommendations for him.

   b. Recommendation to the premier of the MCoD agenda, preparation of its meetings, and follow-up on implementation of decisions.

   c. Coordination of national security staff work for the cabinet and cabinet committees, preparation of their meetings, and follow-up on implementation of decisions.

   d. Briefing the premier daily regarding the intelligence and defense picture, including its ramifications and the meetings required as a result.

   e. Coordination of a senior forum composed of the directors-general and deputy heads of the different ministries and agencies.

   f. Chairing interministerial and interagency forums, established by the premier.

   g. Maintaining reciprocal relationships with counterparts abroad.

   h. Involvement in preparation of the premier's visits abroad and in his diplomatic activities.

   i. The Committee singled out the following duties for particular attention:

- Preparation of annual and multiyear national security assessments for the premier and MCoD.
- Preparation of staff work for the premier and cabinet prior to discussion of the defense budget and the budgets of the security agencies subordinate to the PMO.
- Coordination of staff work for the premier in the area of counterterrorism.

j. In order to enable the INSC to perform its responsibilities, the NSA should participate in the following forums:
  - The Committee of the Heads of the (intelligence) Services (VARASH).
  - The premier's meetings with foreign representatives and diplomats.
  - Cabinet, MCoD, or other ministerial committees dealing with national security issues.

9. The Shahak Committee stressed that one of the reasons for the INSC's lack of influence was the ambiguity regarding its relations with the other officials in the PMB. While emphasizing the premier's prerogative to work with advisers as he or she sees fit, the Committee recommended the following procedures in regard to each of the primary functionaries in the PMB:

a. *Cabinet secretary.* The NSA and cabinet secretary must coordinate the preparation of cabinet and cabinet-committee meetings, circulation of materials to the ministers, and follow-up on implementation of decisions.

b. *Chief of staff/bureau chief.* Although the nature of this position is at the premier's discretion, the NSA should be directly subordinate to the premier.

c. *Military secretary.* The Committee sidestepped this issue, apparently seeking to avoid confrontation with the IDF, and merely recommended that the military secretary coordinate with the NSA. The Committee found that the role of the military secretary has grown over the years, beyond his basic role as the premier's liaison with the defense establishment, and that some had even come to see him as the premier's adviser on defense affairs. It stressed, however, that he does not in fact bear responsibility for politico-military staff work in the PMB and does not have the organizational capacity to do so. The Committee thus concluded that if the military secretary's responsibilities were limited to his intended functions, there was no need for him to bear the rank of general.*

d. *Foreign policy adviser.* Here, too, the Committee sought to avoid conflict, this time with the Foreign Ministry, though it took a clearer stand than in the case of the military secretary. The Committee stressed that

---

* Shahak Committee.

there was considerable overlap between the roles of the foreign affairs adviser and the NSA and determined that most should be carried out by the latter. It stated that if the premier wished to appoint a foreign affairs adviser, the latter's role should be of a more technical nature, such as coordination of prime-ministerial visits abroad, meetings with foreign officials, and preparation of speeches. In any event, the foreign affairs adviser should coordinate closely with the NSA.

*Recommendation:* Urgent establishment of a National Emergency Management Center, within the PMO, for both defense and civil crises, with a situation room connected to all existing crisis management centers, such as those in the IDF and Foreign Ministry. The Shahak Committee further added that the Center should:

1. Be established within the INSC and staffed by it, with representatives from the various agencies to expand it in times of crisis.
2. Provide an integrative and dynamic picture to the premier, cabinet, and MCoD and serve as a means of conveying reports and updates between the premier and various government agencies.
3. Not be a command body or a means of communicating directions to the defense forces and other agencies and not come between them, the premier, and ministers.
4. Produce, in noncrisis times, an integrative daily report covering the primary developments in Israel and the world, including defense issues, diplomacy, domestic issues, the media picture, expected developments and their ramifications, and issues of importance for further consideration.

*Recommendation:* Procedures should be adopted for the presentation of issues and recommendations to the cabinet and its subcommittees, particularly for the premier, minister of defense, and foreign minister. When cabinet decisions are based on the recommendations of one body, such as the IDF, a "second opinion" must be presented by another. The Shahak Committee further recommended that:

1. A differentiation should be made between three different types of cabinet-level meetings: strategy and policy meetings, designed to formulate long-term objectives, strategies, and policies; noncrisis meetings, designed to adopt specific decisions, on the basis of the different options proposed for achieving the above strategy and policy; and urgent situations requiring operational decisions, where time does not permit an integrative preparatory process.
2. The following procedures should be adopted for cabinet-level meetings on politico-military issues:

a. The NSA should open the meeting and present the issues to be discussed, the framework for discussion, and primary options. Each of the agencies should then present their viewpoints and recommendations, followed again by the NSA, who would provide an integrative perspective and identify dilemmas and primary issues to be resolved. The NSA would be responsible for preparing the meeting.

b. Aides, spokespersons, and advisers should not be permitted to participate in cabinet-level meetings. The most senior officials (e.g., chief of staff and directors-general of government ministries) would be permitted to participate during the presentation stage alone, during which the relevant minister would also be able to add additional officials as required. Only the premier may authorize additional participants.

*Recommendation:* The Foreign Ministry must be fully integrated in those defense issues that have diplomatic dimensions, including meetings of the premier, especially when military objectives are to be achieved through diplomatic means. Procedures should be adopted for the Foreign Ministry to hold consultations on matters of national security, with the participation of the PMO and defense establishment. To this the Shahak Committee added:

1. The foreign minister and director-general of the Foreign Ministry should hold periodic meetings on diplomatic aspects of national security issues, with the participation of senior representatives from the PMO and defense establishment.
2. The director-general of the Foreign Ministry should be a permanent participant in the minister of defense's weekly assessment meeting.
3. The Foreign Ministry should participate in preparatory interagency meetings for cabinet and subcabinet discussions of national security issues, especially those chaired by the premier or NSA.
4. The Foreign Ministry should participate in those interagency defense forums headed by the premier that include diplomatic considerations, including military operations (except for covert operations).
5. A plan should be developed by the Foreign Ministry for the strengthening of its Center for Political Research and Policy Planning Branch.

*Recommendation:* The number of nonministerial participants in classified meetings should be reduced significantly, and clear legal sanctions should be adopted and enforced against leakers. The Shahak Committee found the existing legislation and regulations sufficient and made only a few recommendations, focusing on increased awareness of the severity of the problem.

# List of Interviews

The following persons were interviewed for this book and earlier research. I am indebted to all for their willingness to help and the time they devoted.

Major General Yaacov Amidror (ret.), National Security Adviser, 8/24/11

Brigadier General (ret.) Dani Arditi, former National Security Adviser, 7/21/09

Professor Moshe Arens, former Minister of Defense, 6/21/06

Dr. Yossi Beilin, former Minister of Finance, Deputy Foreign Minister, 8/12/06

Dr. Eliahu Ben-Elissar, former Director-General of the Prime Minister's Office, Likud MK, and Chairman of the Knesset Foreign and Defense Affairs Committee, 6/10/91

Major General Uzi Dayan (ret.), former Deputy Chief of Staff and National Security Adviser, 5/23/06

Brigadier General (ret.) Udi Dekel, former Head of IDF Strategic Planning Division, Head of the Peace Administration, 6/24/07

Roy Dick-Keidar, former INSC Legal Adviser, 8/11/11

Mordechai Gur, former Labor Party Minister of Health, Chief of Staff, 6/30/91

Dani Halperin, former Economic Attaché, Israeli Embassy to the United States, 11/6/90

Isaac Herzog, Minister of Welfare, 1/10/10

Mike Herzog, Chief of Staff to Defense Minister Barak, 5/31/07

General David Ivri, former Director-General of the Defense Ministry, Commander of the Israel Air Force, and Chairman of the Board of Israel Aircraft Industries, 5/27/91 and 6/4/06

Dr. Eran Lerman, Deputy National Security Adviser, 8/30/11

Dr. Eli Levite, former Deputy Director-General of the Israel Atomic Energy Commission and former Deputy National Security Adviser, 6/4/06

Major General (ret.) Amnon Lipkin-Shahak, former Chief of Staff, cabinet minister, 6/15/06

Dan Meridor, Deputy Premier and Minister of Intelligence, former Minister of Justice, 5/30/06 and 9/1/11

Major General (ret.) Menahem Meron, former Director General of the Defense Ministry, 11/22/90

Ilan Mizrahi, former National Security Adviser and Deputy Head of Mossad, 1/11/09

Dr. Aryeh Naor, former Cabinet Secretary, 12/2/89

Dr. Nimrod Novick, former Foreign Affairs Adviser to the premier, 6/25/91 and 1/26/06

Ehud Olmert, former Premier, Minister of Health, and Minister of Trade and Commerce 7/8/91

Gideon Patt, former Minister of Tourism and of Trade and Industry, 5/91

Shimon Peres, former Premier, Defense Minister, Foreign Minister, Director General of the Defense Ministry, and Chairman of the Labor Party, 7/4/91

Ron Prosor, Ambassador to the UN, former Director-General of the MFA, 7/15/06

Yitzhak Rabin, former Premier, Defense Minister, Chief of Staff, and Chairman of the Labor Party, 6/11/91

Yehoshua Saguy, former Head of Military Intelligence and MK, 4/25/91

Moshe Shahal, former Minister of Energy and Infrastructure, 3/21/91

Silvan Shalom, Deputy Premier, Foreign and Finance Minister, 6/13/06

Major General (ret.) Gideon Sheffer, former Deputy Commander of IAF, Deputy National Security Adviser, Acting National Security Adviser, 6/21/06

Gilead Sher, Bureau Chief and Chief Negotiator with the Palestinians, 12/23/09

Sima Shine, former Deputy National Security Adviser, Head of the Middle Eastern Affairs Department in the Ministry of Strategic Affairs, 7/21/99

Dr. Ephraim Sneh, former Minister of Health and Transportation, Deputy Minister of Defense, Brigadier General, 12/4/09

Doron Suslik, Director of Communications, Israel Aircraft Industries, 10/1/90

Gad Yaacobi, former Minister of Economics and Planning, Transportation, and Communications 3/24/91

Major General (ret.) Moshe (Bogie) Yaalon, Deputy Premier and Minister of Strategic Affairs, former Chief of Staff, 7/20/06 and 11/1/11

Major General (ret.) Aharon Yariv, former Director of the Jaffee Center for Strategic Studies, minister, and Head of Military Intelligence, 8/2/89

# Notes

## Introduction

1. Horowitz and Lissak 1984, p. 3.

## 1. Constraints and Players

1. Ben-Meir 1995, p. xi; Merom 1999, pp. 413–415; Dror 2011, pp. 6, 16, 35.
2. Dror 1992, p. 82; Dror 1978, p. 158; Maoz 2006, pp. 8, 545.
3. Sima Kadmon, *Yediot Aharonot*, Weekend Magazine, 11/18/06.
4. George 1969 and 1980, p. 45; Stein and Tanter 1976, p. 100.
5. Uzi Dayan interview, 5/23/06; Udi Dekel, lecture, Tel Aviv University, 6/15/06; Dror 1992, p. 82; Dror 2006, p. 55; Dror 1989a, p. 69.
6. Dror 2006, p. 47; Dror 1992; Dror 2011, p. 31.
7. Horowitz and Lissak 1984, p. 5; Dror 1978, pp. 159, 162–163; Peri 2006, p. 49; Heller 2000, p. 10; Maoz 2006, p. 557.
8. Heller 2000, pp. 10, 12, Uzi Dayan interview, 5/23/06; Dror 2011, p. 4.
9. Arian 2005, p. 264; Ben-Meir 1995, p. 59.
10. Ben-Meir 1995, p. 46; Yaari 2004, p. 32.
11. Ben-Meir 1995, pp. 46–47; State of Israel, Prime Minister's Office, "Brodet Committee," 2007, p. 73.
12. Peretz and Doron 1997, p. 188; Dan Meridor interview, 5/30/06.
13. Ben-Meir 1995, p. 38.
14. Arian 2005, p. 266; Peretz and Doron 1997, p. 188; Gideon Sheffer interview, 6/21/06.
15. Arian 2005, p. 266.
16. Gideon Sheffer interview, 6/21/06; Uzi Dayan interview, 5/23/06.
17. State Comptroller, *Annual Report #52*, 2002a, p. 7.
18. Nahum Barnea, *Yedioth Aharonot*, 7/27/03.
19. Yoram Turbovich, testimony before the Winograd Commission, 12/27/06, pp. 16–18, 32.
20. Ben Caspit, "Get Me Galant," *Maariv*, 5/15/06 (NRG [Internet version]). Former CoS Yaalon also stresses the importance of the military secretary's role, in Erez 2006, p. 17.

21. Giora Eiland article in Brom and Elran 2007; Giora Eiland, lecture, Jaffee Center, 10/31/06.

22. Ben-Meir 1995, p. 32.

23. Ben-Meir 1995, p. 50; Maoz 2006, pp. 528–530.

24. Peri 2006, pp. 47, 57, 156; Ben-Meir 1995, pp. 88, 90, 94, 157–159; Yaari 2004, p. 41; State Comptroller, *Report on the National Security Council*, 2006, p. 44; Ofer Shelah, *Yediot Aharonoth*, Weekend Supplement, 1/2/04, p. 9; Amnon Shahak interview, 6/15/06; Mike Herzog interview, 5/31/07; Udi Dekel interview, June 24, 2007; Amir Oren, *Haaretz*, 12/14/01; Shaul Mofaz, Testimony before the Winograd Commission, 12/6/06, p. 10.

25. Yaari 2004, pp. 41–42; Gideon Sheffer interview, 6/21/06; Peri 2006, pp. 47, 156, Ben-Meir 1995, pp. 88, 90.

26. State Comptroller, *Annual Report #51*, 2001a, p. 83; Udi Dekel, lecture, Tel Aviv University, 6/15/06; Amos Harel, *Haaretz*, 11/1/07; Avi Issascharoff, *Haaretz*, 7/22/08; Moshe Yaalon interview, 7/20/06

27. State Comptroller, *Annual Report #52*, 2001, p. 73; Dan Meridor interview, 5/30/06; Silvan Shalom interview, 6/13/06; Yehezkel Dror, *Haaretz*, 9/30/02; Ben-Meir 1995, p. 123.

28. Ben-Meir 1995, p. 98.

29. Maoz 2006, pp. 503–504, 511–512 ; Peri 2006, pp. 48–50; Ben-Meir 1995, p. 95.

30. Peri 2006, p. 49; Ben-Meir 1995, p. 87.

31. Aluf Benn, *Haaretz*, 9/4/03; Maoz 2006, pp. 504, 511–512; State Comptroller, *Annual Report #46*, 1995, p. 1.

32. Maoz 2006, p. 504.

33. For a full description of the role of the committee, see Gilon 2000, pp. 376–377. See also Maoz 2006, p. 503; Caspit, "Get Me Galant"; State Comptroller, *Report on the National Security Council*, 2006, p. 41.

34. State Comptroller, *Annual Report #46*, 1995, pp. 1–2; Yossi Melman, *Haaretz*, 11/11/00; Maoz 2006, p. 512.

35. State Comptroller, *Annual Report #46*, 1995, p. 3; Ben Caspit, *Maariv*, 8/26/02 (NRG); Silvan Shalom interview, 6/1306.

36. Amir Oren, *Haaretz*, 12/14/01.

37. Official website, Premier's Office, www.pmo.gov.il/PMOEng/PM+Office/Bodies /depenergy.htm; U.S., Israeli Officials Confer over Iranian Nuclear Program, *Nucleonics Week*, 4/22/04; Janine Zacharia, "US Arms Expert Here over Iranian Nuke Threat," *Jerusalem Post*, 6/8/03; Federal News Service, 5/24/07; U.S.-Israel Strategic Dialogue, Office of the Spokesman, U.S. State Department, 6/7/07.

## 2. The Decision-Making Process

1. Dean Acheson's term, quoted in Jackson 1965.

2. Shlaim and Yaniv 1980, p. 242; Bilski 1980, p. 115; Peri 2006, p. 49; Dror 1992, 2006, and 2011, p. 5; Dan Meridor interview, 5/30/06; Shachar Ilan, *Haaretz*, 10/9/06. Moshe Yaalon agrees with the short-term focus (interview, 7/20/06); Yaari 2004, p. 31.

3. Peri 2005, p. 331.

4. Dan Meridor interview, 5/30/06, and conference at INSS, Tel Aviv, 10/17/07.

5. State Comptroller *Report on the National Security Council*, 2006, p. 26.

6. Brigadier General (ret.) Udi Dekel, lecture at Tel Aviv University, 6/15/06; Senior Officer interview, 6/24/08; General Shlomo Yanai, quoted in Peri 2006, p. 60.

7. Moshe Yaalon interview, 11/1/11; Peri 2006, p. 59; Drucker and Shelah 2005, p. 28; Senior Officer interview, 6/24/08.

8. State Comptroller, *Report on the National Security Council*, 2006, pp. 33, 34; BESA, *National Security Decision-Making in Israel*, p. 45; Weizman 1981, pp. 29, 36; Mordechai Gur interview, 6/30/91; Gur interview in Davar, 3/4/83; Ben-Elissar interview, 6/10/91; Ben-Meir 1986, p. 78; Moshe Yaalon interview, 6/20/06; Yair Hirshfeld, in Michael 2007, p. 531; Shelah 2003, p. 65; Akiva Eldar, *Haaretz*, 1/22/09; Aluf Benn, *Haaretz*, 1/23/09, pp. B4–5.

9. Bar-Zohar 2007, p. 402; Dayan 1981 p. 93; Aryeh Naor interview, 12/2/89; Haber 1979, p. 177.

10. Author's personal knowledge.

11. Senior Officer interview, 6/24/08; Giora Eiland, quoted in State Comptroller *Report on the National Security Council*, 2006; Aluf Benn, *Haaretz* 6/26/03.

12. Gideon Sheffer interview, 6/21/06; author's personal observation.

13. Moshe Yaalon interview, 7/20/06.

14. David Ivri interview, 5/27/91.

15. State Comptroller, *Annual Report #53*, 2002b, p. 8; Yossi Beilin interview, 8/12/06; Yehuda Ben-Meir, *Haaretz*, 8/7/87.

16. Silvan Shalom interview, 6/13/06.

17. Amnon Lipkin-Shahak interview, 6/15/06; Moshe Arens interview, 6/21/06; State Comptroller, *Report on the National Security Council*, 2006, pp. 28–30, 40; State Comptroller, *Annual Report #53*, 2002b, pp. 17–18; Yaari 2004, pp. 32, 34; Dan Meridor, conference at INSS, 10/17/07; Gideon Sheffer interview, 6/21/06; Yossi Beilin interview, 7/12/06; Ofir Pinnes-Paz, Testimony before the Winograd Commission, 1/7/07, p. 44; Chaim Ramon, Testimony before the Winograd Commission, 1/10/07, pp. 12, 28; Benny Begin, quoted in Aviva Lurie, *Haaretz*, Weekend Magazine, 6/27/97, p. 18.

18. Amnon Lipkin-Shahak interview, 6/15/06; Ben Caspit, "Get Me Galant," *Maariv*, 5/15/06 (NRG).

19. Moshe Yaalon interview, 7/20/06; *Haaretz*, Weekend Magazine, interview with Ari Shavit, 9/14/06.

20. Byman 2011. p. 5; Peri 2006, p. 151; Amos Harel, *Haaretz*, 7/14/09, p. A1; Anshil Peffer, *Haaretz*, 6/23/11, p. 3.

21. Giora Eiland, *Haaretz*, 6/12/06; Dror 1978, pp. 175–176, Dror 1989, p. 56; Dror 1992, pp. 179–180; and Dror 2006, p. 4.

22. Oren 2003, pp. 311–312; Segev 2005, pp. 344–345, 349, 351, 360–361, 363, 369, 387, 390–391, 393–394.

23. Oren 2003, pp. 311–312; Gazit 2003, p. 5; Kober, in Bar-Joseph 2001, p. 181.

24. Dan Meridor interview, 5/30/06; Gazit 2003, pp. 241–248.

25. Amos Harel and Avi Issacharoff, *Haaretz*, 1/9/09, p. B1; 1/14/09, p. A1; and 1/1609, p. B1; Aluf Benn, *Haaretz*, 1/1/09, p. B1; 1/16/09, p. B2; and 1/23/09, pp. B4–5; Akiva Eldar, *Haaretz*, 1/22/09.

26. Amram Mitzna, in Erez 2006, p. 57; Dan Meridor interview, 5/30/06; Ben-Meir 1986, p. 71; Dror 1992, pp. 57, 126, 178.

27. Byman 2011, pp. 5–6, 133.

28. Allison 1971; Hilsman 1959.

29. Silvan Shalom interview, 6/13/06.

30. David Ivri interview, 6/4/06; Amram Mitzna, in Erez 2003, p. 57, Dror 2006, p. 3; Nimrod Novik, lecture, Tel Aviv University, 6/26/06.

31. Udi Dekel, lecture, Tel Aviv University, 12/31/08; Akiva Eldar, *Haaretz*, 3/30/09.

32. Eiland 2007.

33. Nehemia Strassler, *Haaretz*, 9/6/09; 10/2/09, p. A23; and 7/18/10; Moti Basuk, *Haaretz*, 7/18/10.

34. Dror 2011, pp. 4, 14.

35. Dror 1992, 2006, 2011, p. 4; Cohen 1994, pp. 28–30.

36. Yaari 2004, p. 32.

37. Giora Eiland, in Brom and Elran 2007; Giora Eiland, Lecture, Jaffee Center, Tel Aviv University, 10/31/06; Harel and Issacharoff 2008, p. 394; Dani Arditi interview, 7/21/09.

38. Moshe Arens interview, 6/21/06; Gideon Sheffer interview, 1/21/06; David Ivri interview, 6/4/06; Barak Ravid, *Haaretz*, 8/18/11, p. A1.

39. Ben-Ami 2006, p. 290.

40. Shlaim and Yaniv 1980, p. 250; Dror 1978, pp. 32, 34, 84; Dror 1989, p. 57; Eli Levite interview, 6/4/06.

41. Silvan Shalom interview, 6/13/06; Eiland, in Brom and Elran 2007.

42. Bar-Zohar 2007, pp. 441, 443, 447, 449.

43. Silvan Shalom interview, 6/13/06; Makovsky 1996, pp. 25–26, 35, 118; Bar-Zohar 2007, pp. 425–426; Aluf Benn, *Haaretz*, 6/22/94, p. B2.

44. Bar-Zohar 2007, pp. 408, 410; Shamir 1994, pp. 167–169; Klieman 1990, pp. 134, 138.

45. Aluf Ben, *Haaretz*, 12/21/99.

46. Bar-Zohar 2007, p. 425; Aluf Benn, *Haaretz*, 10/15/07 and 7/29/09, p. B1.

47. Uzi Benziman, *Haaretz*, 12/19/07; Amos Harel and Avi Issacharoff, *Haaretz*, 1/9/09, p. B1; 1/1409, p. A1; and 1/16/09, p. B1; Aluf Benn, *Haaretz*, 10/7/07; 10/15/07; 1/9/0909, p. B1; 1/16/09, p. B2; 1/22/09; and 1/23/09, pp. B4–5; Akiva Eldar, *Haaretz*, 1/22/09.

48. Eli Levite interview, 6/4/06; Amram Mitzna, in Erez 2006, p. 57; Ari Shavit, *Haaretz*, 11/3/11, p. B1; Barak Ravid and Ophir Bar-Zohar, *Haaretz*, 11/3/11, p. B3.

49. Ross 2004, p. 589; Uzi Benziman, *Haaretz*, 3/31/00; Drucker 2002, pp. 71–72, 93; Amos Harel and Avi Issacharoff, *Haaretz*, 1/16/09, p. B1.

50. Ben-Meir 1995, p. xviii.

51. Giora Eiland, quoted in State Comptroller, *Report on the National Security Council*, 2006; Eiland, in Brom and Elran 2007; Peri 2006, p. 59.

52. Gideon Sheffer interview, 6/21/06; Dan Meridor interview, 5/30/06; Aluf Benn, Amos Harel, and Avi Issacharoff, *Haaretz*, 1/14/09, p. A1.

53. Aviva Lurie, *Haaretz*, Weekend Magazine, 6/27/97, p. 17; Yoel Markus, *Haaretz*, 11/2/007.

54. Dan Meridor interview, 5/30/06; Amnon Lipkin-Shahak interview, 6/15/06; Isaac Herzog interview, 1/10/10.

55. Tzachi Hanegbi, Testimony before the Winograd Commission, 1/21/07, pp. 28–29; Akiva Eldar, *Haaretz*, 6/1/00.

56. Dan Meridor interview, 5/30/06.

57. Yossi Beilin interview, 8/12/06.

58. Uzi Dayan interview, 5/23/06; Ben Caspit, *Maariv*, 5/15/06.

59. Silvan Shalom interview, 6/13/06.

60. Ben-Meir 1995, pp. xii–xiii; Makovsky 1996, pp. 76–78, 105; Amnon Lipkin-Shahak interview, 6/15/06; Aluf Benn, *Haaretz*, 6/22/94, p. B2; Dov Weisglass, Testimony before the Winograd Commission, 1/11/07, p. 26; Moshe Yaalon interview, 7/20/06; Caspit, "Get Me Galant"; Drucker and Shelah, 2005, p. 238.

61. Dan Meridor interview, 5/30/06; Silvan Shalom interview, 6/13/06; State Comptroller, *Report on the National Security Council*, 2006, p. 40; Caspit, "Get Me Galant"; Uzi Dayan interview, 5/23/06; Aluf Benn, *Haaretz*, 11/23/06; Ari Shavit, *Haaretz*, 8/13/09, p. B1.

62. Dan Meridor interview, 5/30/06; Silvan Shalom interview, 6/13/06; State Comptroller, *Report on the National Security Council*, 2006, p. 40, Caspit, "Get Me Galant"; Uzi Dayan interview, 5/23/06; Aluf Benn, *Haaretz*, 11/23/06; Ari Shavit, *Haaretz*, 8/13/09, p. B1; Peri 2006, p. 59; Peri 2005, p. 330; Dror 1978, p. 34; Drucker 2002, p. 59.

63. Yaari 2006, p. 11.

64. Ibid., pp. 7–19, 13.

65. Giora Eiland, *Haaretz*, 6/12/06; Dan Meridor interview, 5/30/06; Ofir Pinnes-Paz, Testimony before the Winograd Commission, 1/7/07, p. 33.

66. Drucker and Shelah 2005, p. 237.

67. Gad Yaacobi interview, 3/24/91; Eban 1977, p. 596; Dror 1992, pp. 177, 179; Shlaim and Tanter 1978, pp. 513–515. Gideon Sheffer and Moshe Yaalon confirm the failure to read documents in advance (interviews, 6/21/06 and 7/20/06, respectively).

68. Gideon Sheffer interview, 6/2106; Moshe Yaalon interview, 7/20/06; Yaari 2004 p. 34.

69. State Comptroller, *Annual Report* #53, 2002b, p. 17.

70. Ibid., p. 20; Moshe Yaalon interview, 7/20/06.

71. Yaniv 1987, p. 111; Schulze 1998a, pp. 215–237; Shimon Peres, Testimony before the Winograd Commission, 11/7/06, pp. 4, 7; Ofir Pinnes-Paz, Testimony before the Winograd Commission, 1/7/07, p. 2; Eli Yishai, Testimony before the Winograd Commission, 11/8/06, p. 4.

72. Eli Levite interview, 6/4/06; personal communication.

73. Tzachi Hanegbi, Testimony before the Winograd Commission, 1/21/07; Yitzhak Mordechai, Testimony before the Winograd Commission, 1/2/07; Indyk 2009, p. 81.

74. Yossi Verter, *Haaretz*, 8/24/07.

75. Nimrod Novik interview, 1/26/06.

76. Moshe Yaalon interview, 7/20/06; Eli Levite interview, 6/4/06; Dani Yatom, in Ministry of Defense 2004, p. 135; Eiland, in Brom and Elran 2007.

77. Uzi Dayan interview, 5/23/06; Amnon Lipkin-Shahak interview, 6/15/06; Peri 2006 pp. 60, 64; Dani Yatom, in Ministry of Defense, 2004, p. 135; Zeev Schiff, *Haaretz*, 6/16/95; Alu Benn, *Haaretz*, 1/14/97, p. B2.

78. Dov Weisglass, Testimony before the Winograd Commission, 1/11/07, pp. 9–10.

79. Ibid., pp. 5, 6.

80. Gilead Sher interview, 12/23/09; Sima Kadmon, *Yediot Aharonoth*, Weekend Magazine, 8/6/99, p. 4; Aluf Ben, *Haaretz*, 1/23/06; Amnon Lipkin-Shahak interview, 6/15/06; Moshe Yaalon interview, 7/20/06; Drucker and Shelah 2005, pp. 21, 23, 28, 40, 238.

81. Ari Shavit, *Haaretz*, 11/3/11, p. B1; Barak Ravid and Ophir Bar-Zohar, *Haaretz*, 11/3/11, p. B3.

82. Ben-Meir 1986, p. 68; Yossi Beilin interview, 8/12/06; Dror 2011, p. 150.

83. Kleiman, in Coffman-Wittes 2005, p. 111; Jones 2002, pp. 126–127; Makovsky 1996, p. 104.

84. Hoxie 1982, p. 108.

85. Uzi Benziman, *Haaretz*, 7/23/99, p. B3; Aluf Benn, *Haaretz*, 6/22/94, p. B2; 7/13/99, p. 3.

86. Moshe Arens interview, 6/21/06; Reuven Podhazur, *Haaretz*, 4/17/06; Yaari 2006.

87. Weizman 1981, p.118.

88. See, for example, Makovsky 1996, p. 104.

89. See Peretz and Doron 1997, pp. 208–209; Dror 2011, p. 151.

90. State of Israel, *Winograd Commission: Final Report*, 2008, p. 397; Makovsky 1996, p. 105.

91. Quoted by Brownstein 1977, p. 267.

92. Aluf Benn, *Haaretz*, 6/22/94, p. B2; 6/7/07.

93. Kleiman, in Coffman-Wittes 2005, p. 111.

94. Barak Ravid, *Haaretz*, 11/15/11, p. A4.

95. State Comptroller, *Annual Report #56a*, 2005; Giora Eiland, quoted in State Comptroller, *Report on the National Security Council*, 2006; State of Israel, Prime Minister's Office, *Committee to Examine the Defense Budget* ["Brodet Committee"], 5/17/07, p. 24; State Comptroller, *Annual Report #53* 2002b.

96. Barak Ravid, *Haaretz*, 9/1/07; Uzi Dayan, conference, Jerusalem Institute for Israel Affairs, 12/25/06.

97. Ariella Ringle Hoffman, *Yediot Aharonoth*, Weekend Supplement, 12/7/07, p. 9.

98. Klieman 1990, p. 131; personal communication; Gideon Sheffer interview, 6/21/06; David Ivri interview, 6/4/06.

99. Ariella Hoffman Ringle, *Yediot Aharonoth*, Weekend Supplement, 12/7/07, p. 7.

100. David Ivri interview, 6/4/06; Gideon Sheffer interview, 6/21/06; Moshe Yaalon interview, 7/20/06.

101. Personal communication.

102. Silvan Shalom interview, 6/13/06.

103. Dov Weisglass, Testimony before the Winograd Commission, 1/11/07, p. 25.

104. Amos Yadlin and Dani Yatom, in Ministry of Defense, 2004, pp. 16, 130–131, respectively; Eli Levite interview, 6/4/06.

105. Peri 2006, pp. 36, 213; Maoz 2006, pp. 522–523.

106. Dan Meridor interview, 5/30/06; Silvan Shalom interview, 6/13/06; Peri 2006, p. 51; Michael 2007, p. 533; Yoram Turbovich, Testimony before the Winograd Commission, 12/27/06, p. 3; Shai Feldman, in Erez 2006, p. 14; Yaari 2004, p. 34; Maoz 2006, pp. 501, 527.

107. Peri 2006, p. 57.

108. State Comptroller, *Report on the National Security Council*, 2006; Reuven Podhazur, *Haaretz*, 3/25/90 and 6/10/05; Horowitz and Lissak 1984, p. 17; 1989, p. 208; Peri 2006, pp. 13, 30–31; Drucker and Shelah 2005, p. 239; Silvan Shalom interview, 6/13/06; Perlmutter, in Art 1985, pp. 131, 133.

109. Moshe Yaalon interview, 7/20/06.

110. Amos Malka, Testimony before the Winograd Commission, 11/2/06, p. 20.

111. Quoted in Peri 2006, p. 69. For a virtually identical explanation, see Shelah 2003, p. 70; Ilan Mizrahi interview, 1/11/09.

112. Shai Feldman, in Erez 2006, p. 14; Peri 2006; Shelah 2003, p. 69; Sher 2001, p. 195.

113. Maoz 2006, p. 511; Shai Feldman, in Erez 2006, p. 14; Horowitz and Lissak 1984, p. 18; Ben-Meir 1986, p. 87; Ofer and Kober 1987, pp. 126–126.

114. Dan Meridor interview, 5/30/06; Silvan Shalom interview, 6/13/06; Maoz 2006, p. 501.

115. Shai Feldman, in Erez 2006, p. 14; Maoz 2006, p. 540, Horowitz and Lissak 1984, p. 18 and 1989, p. 209.

116. Horowitz and Lissak 1984, p. 19; 1989, p. 209; Dan Meridor interview, 5/30/06.

117. Maoz 2006, p. 556.

118. Ilan Mizrahi interview, 1/11/09; Sela 2007, p. 54; Michael 2007, p. 533.

119. Drucker and Shelah 2005, p. 179; quoted in Peri 2006, pp. 128, 160.

120. Erez 2006, p. 24; Dan Meridor interview, 5/30/06; Peri 2005, 2006, pp. 3, 75–76; Ben-Meir 1995, pp. xii, 145.

121. Ben-Meir 1995, pp. xiv, 106; Peri 2006, pp. 64, 95, 97, 113, 138; Harel and Issacharoff 2004, pp. 46, 85, 92; Drucker and Shelah 2005, pp. 34, 67; Amos Harel, *Haaretz*, 9/16/99, p. A1; Aluf Benn, *Haaretz*, 1/8/04 and 12/28/06; Ethan Bronner, *New York Times*, 1/3/11; Yonatan Lis, Moti Basuk, and Anshel Peffer, *Haaretz*, 10/20/11, p. A2.

122. Martin Indyk, quoted by Peri 2006, p. 69.

123. Peri 2005, p. 335; Harel and Issacharoff 2004, p. 92; Drucker 2002, pp. 331–333; Sher 2001, p. 195; Ben-Ami 2006, p. 282; Peri 2006, pp. 116–117; Ben-Meir, in Erez 2006, p. 17; Byman 2011, p. 126.

124. Maoz 2006, p. 524; Barak and Sheffer 2006, pp. 235–261; Horowitz and Lissak 1989, p. 211; Peri 2006, pp. 60, 159; Makovsky 1996, p. 118.

125. Peri 2006, pp. ix–x, 73; Maoz 2006, pp. 501, 521–523. Figures updated by author.

126. Maoz 2006, p. 525; Peri 2006, pp. 117–118; Barak and Sheffer 2006, pp. 235–261.

127. Nehemia Strassler, *Haaretz*, 12/21/06 and 10/2/09, p. A23.

128. "Brodet Committee," pp. 13, 25; *Haaretz*, 7/9/07; Nehemia Strassler, *Haaretz*, 12/21/06.

129. Barak and Sheffer 2006, pp. 235–261.

130. Natasha Mozgavya, *Haaretz*, 10/25/11.

131. Peri 2006, p. 155.

132. Gideon Sheffer interview, 6/21/06; Ben-Ami 2006, p. 282.

133. Ben-Meir 1996, p. 160; Maoz 2006, pp. 501, 527–528.

134. Yaari 2004, pp. 41–42; Rapoport 2007, p. 52.

135. Shai Feldman, in Erez 2006, p. 15; Moshe Yaalon, in Erez 2006, p. 17; Kleiman, in Coffman-Wittes, pp. 89, 138; Chaim Ramon, Testimony before the Winograd Commission, 1/10/07, p. 16; Tzipi Livni, Testimony before the Winograd Commission, 1/23/07, p. 37; Maoz 2006, p. 556; Jones 2002, p. 128.

136. Aluf Benn, *Haaretz*, 9/4/03; Gideon Sheffer interview, 6/21/06; Silvan Shalom interview, 6/13/06.

137. Former MFA director-general, personal communication.

138. Ben-Meir 1996, pp. xii–xiii; Klieman 1990, p. 149; Gidi Weitz and Naama Lansky, *Haaretz*, 10/25/07.

139. David Ivri interview, 6/4/06; Former MFA director-general, personal communication; Gideon Sheffer interview, 6/21/06.

140. Klieman 1990, pp. 143–147; Former MFA director-general, personal communication.

141. The MFA's failure to complete a policy review on Russia, in 2005–2006, which was subsequently assigned to the INSC, and to fulfill its diplomatic and economic roles in the Gaza Disengagement process are but some examples. Former Foreign Minister Shalom stresses the problem of leaks he faced from within the ministry, including on sensitive issues such as secret talks with Syria, Libya, and Chad. Silvan Shalom, interview, 6/13/06. See also Aluf Ben, *Haaretz*, 12/19/02; David Ivri interview, 6/4/06.

142. Author's own observations; Barak Ravid, *Haaretz*, 10/23/09, p. A3.
143. State Comptroller, *Annual Report #53*, 2002b, p. 64; Silvan Shalom interview, 6/13/06.
144. Former MFA director-general, personal communication; Aluf Benn, *Haaretz*, 10/5/06.
145. Author's own observations.
146. Uzi Dayan interview, 5/23/06.
147. Ibid.; interview with senior defense official, 6/4/06.
148. Personal communication, 1987.
149. Uzi Dayan interview, 5/23/06.
150. Peri 2006, p. 23; Dror 2011, p. 15.
151. Interview with senior defense official, 12/12/05 and 6/4/06.
152. Gideon Sheffer interview, 6/21/06; Uzi Dayan interview, 5/23/06; interview with senior defense official, 6/4/06; Moshe Arens interview, 6/21/06; interview with former senior cabinet minister, 5/30/05; Dror 1992, pp. 64, 168–169; 2011, p. 147.
153. Amnon Lipkin-Shahak interview, 6/15/06.

## 3. Camp David I

1. Markus 1979, p. 44; Weizman 1981, p. 23; Haber 1978, p. 49.
2. Markus 1979, p. 44; Weizman 1981, p. 23; Haber 1978, p. 49.
3. Markus 1979, p. 44; Weizman 1981, p. 23; Haber 1978, p. 49.
4. Haber 1978 (Shnat hayonah), p. 43; Quandt 1986a, p. 96; Stein, in Marantz and Stein 1985, p. 233; Aronson 1978, pp. 334, 338.
5. *Haaretz*, 10/2/77, p. 1; Simes 1979, p. 44; Yoel Markus, *Haaretz*, 9/4/77, p. 1; 9/9/77, p. 1; and 10/7/77, p. 13.
6. Quandt 2005, p. 190; *Haaretz*, 10/6/77, p. 1; 10/13/77, p. 1; and 10/16/77, p. 1; Quandt 1986a, p. 131.
7. Quandt 1986a, p. 131; 2005, 189, Ben-Ami 2006, p. 206.
8. Bar-Siman-Tov 1994, p. 55.
9. Quandt 1986a, p. 155; 2005, p. 192; Haber 1978, p. 177; Friedlander 1983, p. 115; Markus 1979, pp. 48–49; Sharon 1989, p. 402.
10. Perlmutter 1987, p. 375; Quandt 1986a, p. 206; *Haaretz*, 2/10/78; Dayan 1981, p. 115.
11. Quandt 2005, pp. 195–196; Perlmutter 1987, p. 375; A. Tamir 1988, p. 45; *Haaretz*, 2/10/78; Dayan 1981, p. 115.
12. Uzi Benziman, *Haaretz*, 3/26/79, p. 14; *Maariv*, 3/23/78, pp. 1–2; Harish, in *Maariv*, 3/24/78, p. 14; *Haaretz*, 3/6/78, p. 1.
13. Uzi Benziman, *Haaretz*, 6/19/78, p. 1; 6/23/78, p. 14; 7/24/78, p.1; and 7/28/78, p. 18.
14. Weizman interview in *Maariv*, Weekend Magazine, 12/13/91, p. 7; Ben-Elissar interview, 6/10/91; Markus 1979, p. 174; Benziman 1981, p. 200.
15. Weizman 1981, p. 341; Haber 1978, pp. 300, 305; Carter 1985, p. 43.
16. Quandt 1986a, p. 234; Markus 1979, p. 174; Benziman 1981, p. 200; Uzi Benziman, *Haaretz*, 11/1/91; Foreign Broadcasting Information Service, Middle East, 5929/A/13, 9/29/78.
17. Bar-Siman-Tov 1994, p. 44; BESA, *National Security Decision-Making*, p. 45; Weizman 1981, p. 29; Motta Gur interview, 6/30/91.
18. BESA, *National Security Decision-Making*, p. 45; Gur, in *Davar*, 3/4/83; Gur interview, 6/30/91; Ben-Elissar confirms Gur's account, in Ben-Elissar interview, 6/10/91.
19. Ben-Meir 1986, p. 78.
20. Ibid.
21. Benziman 1981, pp. 40, 45; Haber et al. 1979, p. 64; Haber 1978, p. 129; Naor 1988, p. 116; Uzi Benziman, *Haaretz*, 12/20/77, pp. 1–2; Weizman 1981, p. 59; *Haaretz*, 12/2/77, p. 13; Friedlander 1983, pp. 89, 102, 105.
22. Dayan 1981, p. 95; Zeev Schiff, *Haaretz*, 12/9/77, p. 14; Uzi Benziman, *Haaretz*, 12/9/77, p. 14; and 10/1/78, p. 22; Bar-Siman-Tov 1994; *Haaretz*, 12/4/77, p. 1; Zeev Schiff, *Haaretz*, 12/16/77, p. 13.

23. Bar-Siman-Tov 1994, p. 62; Haber 1978, pp. 172–173; Dayan 1981, p. 93.

24. Bar-Siman-Tov 1994, p. 62; Weizman 1981, pp. 118–120; Benziman 1981, p. 87; Uzi Benziman, *Haaretz*, 12/21/77, p. 9; and 10/1/78, p. 22; Aryeh Naor interview, 12/2/89; Haber et al. 1979, pp. 172–173, 177; Haber 1978, pp. 175–176; Quandt 1986a, p. 155; Friedlander 1983, p. 115; Markus 1979, pp. 48–49; Sharon 1989, p. 402.

25. Benziman 1981, p. 125; A. Tamir 1988, p. 34; Weizman 1981, p. 129.

26. Zeev Schiff, in *Haaretz*, 1/11/78, p. 9; A. Tamir 1988, pp. 37–38.

27. Haber 1978, p. 301; A. Tamir 1988, pp. 48–49; Markus 1979, p. 88; Uzi Benziman, *Haaretz*, 9/1/78, p. 17; Sofer 1986, p. 42.

28. Bar-Siman-Tov 1994, p. 110; A. Tamir 1988, p. 48; Uzi Benziman, *Haaretz*, 9/22/78, p. 18; and 9/1/78, p. 17.

29. Bar-Siman-Tov 1994, pp. 108–109; Uzi Benziman, *Haaretz*, 7/20/78, p.1; *Maariv*, 8/9/78, p. 1; *Haaretz*, 8/1/78, p. 1; Haber 1978, pp. 298–300, 305; Weizman 1981, p. 341; Carter 1985, p. 43; Benziman 1981, pp. 149, 172; Sofer 1986, pp. 42–433.

30. Bar-Siman-Tov 1994. p. 115; Weizman 1981, p. 347; Markus 1979, pp. 12, 21, 86, 88; Benziman 1981, p. 166.

31. Markus 1979, p. 130; Benziman 1981, p. 177.

32. Sofer 1986, p. 43; Peleg 1987, pp. 95, 110–111; Gad Yaacobi interview, 3/24/91; Shimon Sheffer, *Jerusalem Post*, 12/15/78; Friedlander 1983, pp. 102, 105.

33. Naor 1988, p. 111.

34. Quandt 1986a, pp. 81, 109; Naor 1988, p. 11; Aryeh Naor interview, 12/2/89; Sharon 1989; Haber 1979, pp. 5, 109; Markus 1979, p. 34; Dayan 1981, pp. 47, 52 (Hebrew version); Haber 1978, p. 12.

35. Aryeh Naor interview, 12/2/89; Naor 1988, pp. 111–115; Quandt 1986a, p. 110; Haber 1978, p. 128; Markus 1979, p. 38; A. Tamir 1988, p. 40; Dayan 1981, p. 47 (English version) and p. 52 (Hebrew version).

36. Markus 1979, p. 44; Haber 1978, p. 49; Bar-Siman-Tov 1994, pp. 35–37; Weizman 1981, pp. 19, 23, 25, 35–37; Uzi Benziman, *Haaretz*, 11/8/78, p. 9.

37. Bar-Siman-Tov 1994, pp. 39, 57; Benziman 1981, pp. 40, 45; Haber 1979, p. 64; Friedlander 1983, p. 89; Naor 1988, p. 116; Uzi Benziman, *Haaretz*, 12/20/77, pp. 1–2; Weizman 1981; *Haaretz*, 12/2/77, p. 13.

38. Bar-Siman-Tov 1994, pp. 63–64; Dayan 1981, pp. 93, 95 (English version); Weizman 1981, p. 117; Haber et al. 1979, p. 84.

39. Bar-Siman-Tov 1994, pp. 63–64; Dayan 1981, p. 95 (English version); Zeev Schiff, in *Haaretz*, 12/9/77, p. 14; Uzi Benziman, *Haaretz*, 12/9/77, p. 14; and 10/1/78, p. 22; Haber 1978; *Haaretz*, 12/4/77, p. 1; Zeev Schiff, in *Haaretz*, 12/9/77, p. 14; and 12/16/77, p. 13.

40. Benziman 1981, p. 125; A. Tamir 1988, p. 34; Weizman 1981, p. 129.

41. Haber 1979, p. 201; Benziman 1981, p. 130; Weizman 1981, p. 126.

42. Bar-Siman-Tov 1994, p. 89; Uzi Benziman, *Haaretz*, 10/1/78, p. 22; and 3/26/79, p. 14; Zeev Schiff, *Haaretz*, 1/11/78, p. 9.

43. Benziman 1981, p. 130; A. Tamir 1988, p. 45.

44. Markus 1979, p. 142; Weizman 1981, p. 293; *Haaretz*, 4/27/78, p. 1; and 4/30/78, p.1.

45. Uzi Benziman, *Haaretz*, 6/19/78, p. 1; 6/23/78, p. 14; 7/28/78, p. 18; and 7/24/78, p. 1.

46. Uzi Benziman, *Haaretz*, 7/28/78, p. 18; and 7/24/78, p. 1; Benziman 1981, p. 156.

47. Bar-Siman-Tov 1994, pp. 108–109; Uzi Benziman, *Haaretz*, 7/20/78, p. 1; *Maariv*, 8/9/78, p. 1; *Haaretz*, 8/1/78, p. 1; Haber 1979, pp. 298–299.

48. Benziman 1981, p. 198; Markus 1979, pp. 173, 175; Quandt 1986a, pp. 226, 260, 316, 318.

49. Haber et al. 1979, pp. 338–340; Markus 1979, pp. 104, 146, 171; see Knesset speeches, *Maariv*, 10/1/78, p. 13; Federal Broadcasting Information Service, Middle East, 5929/1/13, 9/29/78.

50. Benziman 1981, p. 206; interview with Weizman in *Maariv*, Weekend Magazine, 12/13/91, p. 6.

51. Benziman 1981, p. 206; interview with Weizman in *Maariv*, Weekend Magazine, 12/13/91, p. 6.

52. Benziman 1981, pp. 196–197; Uzi Benziman, *Haaretz*, 11/1/91, p. B2; Markus 1979, pp. 177, 189; A. Tamir 1988, pp. 5–51.

53. Bar-Siman-Tov 1994, pp. 100, 110–111.

54. Weizman 1981, p. 152.

55. Ben-Elissar interview, 6/10/91; Gad Yaacobi interview, 3/24/91; Quandt 1986a, p. 155; and 2005, p. 192; -; Friedlander 1983, p. 115; Markus 1979, pp. 48–49, 177; Sharon 1989, p. 402; A. Tamir 1988, p. 45; Weizman 1981, pp. 142–147; Bar-Siman-Tov 1994, pp. 87–88, 110.

56. Benziman 1981, p. 199; Markus 1979, p. 166; A. Tamir 1988, pp. 9–70; Friedlander 1983, p. 226.

57. Ben-Elissar interview, 6/10/91; Gad Yaacobi interview, 3/24/91.

58. Bar-Siman-Tov 1994, p. 110; Ehud Olmert interview, 7/8/91; Ben-Elissar interview, 6/10/91.

59. Bar-Siman-Tov 1994, p. 107.

60. Dayan 1981, p. 76; Benziman 1981, pp. 37, 40, 45; Haber et al. 1979, p. 64; Haber 1978, p. 129; Friedlander 1983, p. 89; Naor 1988, p. 116; Uzi Benziman, *Haaretz*, 12/20/77, pp. 1–2; Weizman 1981, pp. 36, 59; *Haaretz*, 12/2/77, p. 13.

61. Bar-Siman-Tov 1994, pp. 66–68, 71; Dayan 1981, p. 93; Benziman 1981, pp. 86–87; Weizman 1981, p. 119; Haber 1978, pp. 176, 177, 179; Quandt 1986a, p. 155; and 2005, p. 192; Friedlander 1983, p. 115; Markus 1979, pp. 48–49; Sharon 1989, p. 402.

62. Bar-Siman-Tov 1994, pp. 95–96.

63. Uzi Benziman, *Haaretz*, 6/23/78, p. 14; Perlmutter 1977, p. 14; and 1985, p. 279; Markus 1979, pp. 30, 40, 191; *Haaretz*, 3/10/78, p. 2; Weizman 1981, p. 333.

64. Haber 1978, p. 279; *Haaretz*, 6/12/78, p. 1; Uzi Benziman, *Haaretz*, 6/13/78, p. 1; 6/15/78, p. 1; and 6/23/78, p. 14.

65. Uzi Benziman, *Haaretz*, 7/28/78, p. 18; and 7/24/78, p. 1; Benziman 1981, p. 156.

66. Benziman 1981, p. 206; interview with Weizman in *Maariv*, Weekend Magazine, 12/13/91, p. 6.

67. Weizman 1981, pp. 191, 284; Motta Gur interview, 6/3/91; Benziman 1981, p. 40.

68. Markus 1979, pp. 42–43; Aronson 1978, pp. 359–360; Weizman 1981, p. 333; Uzi Benziman, *Haaretz*, 6/23/78, p. 14; Perlmutter 1977, p. 14; and 1985, p. 279; Markus 1979, pp. 30, 40.

69. Markus 1979, p. 30; Benziman 1981, p. 146; Naor 1988, p. 108; Weizman 1981, p. 37; Bar-Siman-Tov 1994, p. 66.

70. Naor 1988, p. 109; A. Tamir 1988, p. 125; Haber 1978, p. 42.

71. Bar-Siman-Tov 1994, p. 57; Friedlander 1983, p. 34; Perlmutter 1977, p. 360, and 1987 p. 375; Rabinovich 1984, p. 129; Benziman 1981, p. 146; Peleg 1987, pp. 95, 110–111.

72. Quandt 1986a, p. 81; Naor 1988, p. 111; Aryeh Naor interview, 12/2/89.

73. Gad Yaacobi interview, 3/24/91; Gideon Sheffer, *Jerusalem Post*, 12/15/78.

74. See Weizman 1981.

75. Benziman 1981, p. 146; Naor 1988, p. 108; Weizman 1981, p. 37.

76. Weizman 1981; Bar-Siman-Tov 1994, p. 115.

## 4. The Makings of a Young Lion

1. State Comptroller, *Annual Report #37*, 1987, p. 1292; Zeev Schiff, *Haaretz*, 10/1/81; Moshe Arens, *Haaretz*, 1/19/82.

2. State Comptroller, *Annual Report #37*, 1987, p. 1292; Zakheim 1996, p. 4.

3. Tom Friedman, *New York Times*, 2/20/86.

4. General Accounting Office 1987, p. 9; Wolf Blitzer, *Jerusalem Post*, 5/30/86.

5. Hirsh Goodman, *Jerusalem Post*, 2/27/87; Brigadier General Eini, Head of LPA, quoted by Arkin in *Maariv*, 3/25/83; Moshe Blumkin, VP for Engineering, IAI, quoted by Reuven Podhazur, *Haaretz*, 9/7/83.

6. General Accounting Office 1987, p. 9; Wolf Blitzer, *Jerusalem Post*, 5/30/86.

7. Sharon 1988, p. 452.

8. *Aviation Week and Space Technology*, 7/28/86; A. Ginai, *Yediot Aharonoth*, 6/12/85; Motta Gur interview, 6/30/91; Interview with Motta Gur, *Maariv*, 1/9/87; State Comptroller, *Annual Report #37*, 1987, p. 1293; Zeev Schiff, *Haaretz*, 3/2/80; Menachem Meron interview, 11/22/90; General Accounting Office 1983.

9. Reuven Podhazur, *Haaretz*, 7/26/87. See also Arens's statement in D. Arkin, *Maariv*, 12/16/84; Clark and Cohen, *Al Hamishrnar*, 6/25/86; State Comptroller, *Annual Report #37*, 1987, p. 1294; *Davar*, 1/15/85; *Maariv*, 11/13/83; Zeev Schiff, *Haaretz*, 11/14/83; Menahem Meron interview, 11/22/90; *Jerusalem Post*, 1/31/86.

10. *Aviation Week and Space Technology*, 7/28/86; A. Ginai, *Yediot Aharonoth*, 6/12/86; Motta Gur interview, 6/30/91.

11. Dov Zakheim was a deputy under-secretary of defense.

12. Zakheim 1996, pp. 82–83; General Accounting Office 1987, pp. 1–6; *Aviation Week and Space Technology*, 2/10/86; State Comptroller, *Annual Report #37*, 1987, pp. 1295–1296, 1316; Zeev Schiff, *Haaretz*, 2/18/88; Gad Yaacobi interview, 3/24/91.

13. Reuven Podhazur, *Haaretz*, 12/385; Abraham Tal, *Haaretz*, 12/13/85 and 1/7/86.

14. Zakheim 1996, pp. 162–163; General Accounting Office 1987, p. 104.

15. Reuvern Podhazur, *Haaretz*, 6/11/86 and 9/14/86; Wolf Blitzer, *Jerusalem Post*, 6/18/86; *Maariv*, 5/13/86.

16. Zakheim 1996, pp. 205–206, 246; Glenn Frankel, *Washington Post*, 1/8/87, p. 29; Y. Walter, *Maariv*, 1/6/87; *Maariv*, 1/5/87; Zeev Schiff, *Haaretz*, 8/6/86; *Yediot Aharonoth*, 1/7/87: Hirsh Goodman, *Jerusalem Post*, 1/9/87; Ron Ben Yishai, *Yediot Aharonoth*, 5/11/87; Reuven Podhazur, *Haaretz*, 1/2/87, 2/4/87, and 5/31/87; Orly Azulai Katz, *Yediot Aharonoth*, 8/20/87.

17. Zeev Schiff, *Haaretz*, 6/26/87; Yoel Markus, *Haaretz*, 6/30/89; A. Ginat, *Yediot Aharonoth*, 7/2/87; *Maariv*, 3/4/87

18. Zeev Schiff, *Haaretz*, 2/18/80; State Comptroller, *Annual Report #37*, 1987, p. 1310; Reuven Podhazur, *Haaretz*, 2/13/84.

19. *Jerusalem Post*, 5/31/87; *Maariv*, 8/23/87; Akiva Eldar, *Haaretz*, 8/21/87; Reuven Podhazur, *Haaretz*, 3/8/87, 5/3/87, 5/25/87, and 5/31/87; *Al Hamishmar*, 3/3/87; Tali Zelinger, *Davar*, 4/3/87.

20. Reuven Podhazur, *Haaretz*, Weekend Magazine, 9/7/83, 12/13/84, and 6/24/86; Aryeh Egozi, *Yediot Aharonoth*, 12/14/78; Tali Zelinger, *Davar*, 9/26/84; State Comptroller, *Annual Report #37*, 1987, p. 1292.

21. Zeev Schiff, *Haaretz*, 5/9/77; *Haaretz*, 2/12/78 and 7/14/78; *Davar*, 3/1/78.

22. Yoram Peri and Amnon Neubach, *Al Hamishmar*, 8/5/84; *Haaretz*, 7/10/78; Tom Friedman, *New York Times*, 7/20/86.

23. D. Arkin, *Maariv*, Special Supplement on the Lavi, 2/15/87; State Comptroller, *Annual Report #37*, 1987, pp. 1293, 1300; Yuval Elizur, *Maariv*, 7/18/80; Yoram Peri and Amnon Neubach, *Al Hamishmar*, 8/5/84; Shlomo Nakdimon, *Yediot Aharonoth*, 8/21/87.

24. Shlomo Nakdimon, *Yediot Aharonoth*, 8/21/87; State Comptroller, *Annual Report #37*, 1987, pp. 1300, 1302; David Ivri interview, 5/27/91; Zeev Schiff, *Haaretz*, 2/18/80 and 3/2/80.

25. C. Liber, *Ksafim*, 9/13/81; Reuven Podhazur, *Haaretz*, 9/1/83; *Jerusalem Post*, 2/2/80; Gad Lior, *Yediot Aharonoth*, 7/8/80; State Comptroller, *Annual Report #37*, 1987, pp. 1293, 1299–1301; Zeev Schiff, *Haaretz*, 3/2/80; David Ivri interview, 5/27/91.

26. Zeev Schiff, *Haaretz*, 7/7/81 and 10/1/81; Shlomo Nakdimon, *Yediot Aharonoth*, 8/21/87.

27. State Comptroller, *Annual Report #37*, 1987, pp. 1292, 1304; Zeev Schiff, *Haaretz*, 7/7/81, 1/2/82, and 1/15/82; *Haaretz*, 6/4/81; Reuven Podhazur, *Haaretz*, 9/7/83 and 12/13/84.

28. State Comptroller, *Annual Report #37*, 1987, pp. 1293, 1307; Shlomo Nakdimon, *Yediot Aharonoth*, 8/21/87; D. Arkin, *Maariv*, Special Supplement on the Lavi, 2/15/87; *Haaretz*, 6/2/81 and 8/22/85.

29. Zeev Schiff, *Haaretz*, 1/1/5/82 and 1/22/82; State Comptroller, *Annual Report #37*, 1987, pp. 1293–1294; Hirsh Goodman, *Jerusalem Post*, 2/19/82; Shlomo Nakdimon, *Yediot Aharonoth*, 1/28/87; *Jerusalem Post*, 12/18/81; *Davar*, 1/22/82; Yuval Elizur, *Maariv*, 1/25/82; *Haaretz*, 2/4/82.

30. Shlomo Nakdimon, *Yediot Aharonoth*, 8/28/87; P. Shachar, *Hadashot*, 7/29/87.

31. Zeev Schiff, *Haaretz*, 2/18/82 and 3/2482; Shlomo Nakdimon, *Yediot Aharonoth*, 8/28/87; State Comptroller, *Annual Report #37*, 1987, pp. 1294, 1310–1311.

32. Clark and Cohen, *Al Hamishmar*, 6/25/86; State Comptroller, *Annual Report #37*, 1987, p. 1294; *Davar*, 1/1/585; *Maariv*, 11/13/83; Zeev Schiff, *Haaretz*, 11/14/83; Menahem Meron interview, 11/22/90; Reuven Podhazur, *Haaretz*, 7/26/87; *Jerusalem Post*, 1/31/86.

33. Gad Yaacobi interview, 3/24/91; *Maariv*, 12/11/84; Hirsh Goodman, *Jerusalem Post*, 12/7/84 and 2/26/85; Reuven Podhazur, *Haaretz*, 10/2/84 and 12/6/84; *Haaretz*, editorial, 7/3/87; State Comptroller, *Annual Report #37*, 1987, p. 1316; Zeev Schiff, *Haaretz*, 3/1/85.

34. Gad Yaacobi interview, 3/24/91; *Maariv*, 12/11/84; Hirsh Goodman, *Jerusalem Post*, 12/7/84 and 2/26/85; Reuven Podhazur, *Haaretz*, 10/2/84, 12/6/84, 3/2/72, and 3/8/87; *Haaretz*, editorial, 7/3/87; A Temkin, *Jerusalem Post*, 12/31/87; *Davar*, 3/22/87.

35. Reuven Podhazur, *Haaretz*, 3/8/87, 5/3/87, 5/25/87, and 5/31/87; *Al Hamsihmar*, 3/3/87; Tali Zelinger, *Davar*, 4/3/87.

36. Zeev Schiff and Reuven Podhazur, *Haaretz*, June 26, 1987; Yoel Markus, *Haaretz*, 8/18/87; Ami Levitsky, *Koteret Rashit*, 9/18/87.

37. Reuven Podhazur, *Haaretz*, 7/8/87 and 7/23/87; S. Mekel, *Maariv*, 5/7/87 and 8/17/87.

38. *Jerusalem Post*, 8/31/87; *Maariv*, 8/23/87; Akiva Eldar, *Haaretz*, 8/21/87.

39. Akiva Eldar, *Haaretz*, 7/11/87; Yossi Melman, *Davar*, 7/6/87.

40. Hirsh Goodman, *Jerusalem Post*, 12/10/78.

41. *New York Times*, 10/1/87.

42. *New York Times*, 8/16/87.

43. Mina Tzemach poll, *Davar*, 5/26/87; Tom Friedman, *New York Times*, 8/16/87.

44. Hirsh Goodman, *Jerusalem Post*, 2/19/82 and 12/7/84; *Haaretz*, 1/6/82 and editorial on 1/27/88; *Maariv*, 8/19/83.

45. Reuven Podhazur, *Haaretz*, Weekend Magazine, 9/7/93.

46. A. Arad, *Davar*, 1/4/87; *Shaar*, 5/6/87; *Yediot Aharonoth*, 6/29/87; Vinkler, *Haaretz*, 8/25/87; Hirsh Goodman, *Jerusalem Post*, 2/19/82 and 12/7/84; *Haaretz*, 1/6/82 and editorial on 1/27/82; *Maariv*, 8/19/83; Zeev Schiff, *Haaretz*, 4/8/83; Gad Yaacobi interview, 3/24/91.

47. Hirsh Goodman, *Jerusalem Post*, 12/7/84 and 1/31/86; State Comptroller, *Annual Report #37*, 1987, p. 1295; Reuven Tessitura, *Haaretz*, 9/17/86.

48. State Comptroller, *Annual Report #37*, 1987, p. 1301; Shlomo Nakdimon, *Yediot Aharonoth*, 8/21/87; Zeev Schiff, *Haaretz*, 7/7/81.

49. State Comptroller, *Annual Report #37*, 1987, pp. 1292, 1301.

50. Ibid., p. 1295; *Haaretz*, 8/22/85; T. Preuss, *Davar*, 1/6/86; *Maariv*, 1/6/86; *Haaretz*, 1/6/86; Hirsh Goodman, *Jerusalem Post*, 5/30/86 and 7/21/86.

51. Zakheim 1996, pp. 136, 164.

52. Z. Alush, *Yediot Aharonoth*, 5/20/87; Reuven Podhazur, *Haaretz*, 5/21/87, 5/25/87, 5/31/87, and 6/4/87; *Shaar*, 6/5/87; *Yediot Aharonot*, 5/20/87 Gad Yaacobi interview, 3/24/91.

53. State Comptroller, *Annual Report #37*, 1987, pp. 1299–1300, 1303–1304; Reuven Podhazur, *Haaretz*, 2/13/84; C. Lieber, *Ksafim*, 9/13/81.

54. Quoted by Shlomo Nakdimon, *Yediot Aharonoth*, 8/21/87, with partial corroboration of the text in State Comptroller, *Annual Report #37*, 1987, p. 307.

55. State Comptroller, *Annual Report #37*, 1987, p. 1305; Reuven Podhazur, *Haaretz*, Weekend Magazine, 9/7/83 and 2/13/84.

56. P. Shachar, *Hadashot*, 7/29/87; Lipschitz, *Al Hamishmar*, 11/30/84; *Haaretz*, 8/22/85; A. Avneri, *Yediot Aharonoth*, 8/7/87.

57. *Yediot Aharonoth*, 7/5/87; Reuven Podhazur, *Haaretz*, 7/4/88; *Jerusalem Post*, 1/31/86, 8/5/81, and 5/16/83; *Maariv*, 8/19/83; *Haaretz*, 1/19/82 and 6/1/182; *Defense New*, 1/19/87; Roni Shaked, *Yediot Aharonoth*, 1/5/87; *Davar*, 1/27/82.

58. Zakheim 1996, p. 12; *Jerusalem Post*, 3/15/83; D. Arkin, *Maariv*, Special Supplement on the Lavi, 2/15/87; Zeev Schiff, *Haaretz*, 4/8/83; Reuven Podhazur, *Haaretz*, 2/14/84; Lipschitz, *Al Hamishmar*, 11/30/84; Doron Suslik interview, 10/1/90.

59. Reuven Podhazur, *Haaretz*, Weekend Magazine, 9/7/83; Yuval Elizur, *Maariv*, 4/21/78; Zeev Schiff, *Haaretz*, 5/9/77 and 1/12/82; A. Arad, *Davar*, 1/4/87; Zeev Schiff, *Haaretz*, 5/9/77; *Davar*, 3/1/78; *Haaretz*, 2/12/87.

60. State Comptroller, *Annual Report #37*, 1987, p. 1293; *Haaretz*, 2/12/78; *Maariv*, 3/8/78; Yizthak Rabin interview, 6/11/91; A. Arad, *Davar*, 1/4/87; Tali Zelinger, *Davar*, 9/6/84.

61. Gad Yaacobi interview, 3/24/91.

62. State Comptroller, *Annual Report #37*, 1987, pp. 1299–1302.

63. Ibid., p. 1301; Zeev Schiff, *Haaretz*, 7/7/81 and 10/1/81; Shlomo Nakdimon, *Yediot Aharonoth*, 7/21/87.

64. P. Shachar, *Hadashot*, 7/29/87; Hirsh Goodman, *Jerusalem Post*, 2/19/82; Ron Ben-Yishai, *Yediot Aharonoth*, 3/20/87; State Comptroller, *Annual Report #37*, 1987, pp. 1308, 1310–1311; Doron Suslik interview, 10/1/90.

65. *Davar*, 3/1/78; *Haaretz*, 2/12/78; *Maariv*, 3/8/78.

66. State Comptroller, *Annual Report #37*, 1987, p. 1307.

67. *Haaretz*, 6/4/81.

68. State Comptroller, *Annual Report #37*, 1987, pp. 1294–1298, 1318; *Maariv*, 1/29/85; *Haaretz*, 2/26/84; I. Tomer, *Yediot Aharonoth*, 8/10/87.

69. Yaron London, *Hadashot*, 4/25/86; A. Arad, *Davar*, 7/18/86.

70. David Ivri, in *Bitaon Hel Haavir* (IAF Journal), 4/86; Moshe Blumkin, IAI Deputy VP, quoted by A. Oren in *Davar*, Weekend Magazine, 5/15/81; *Jerusalem Post*, 5/5/87.

71. Reuven Podhazur, *Haaretz*, 1/3/85 and 5/25/87; *Yediot Aharonoth*, 2/4/86 and 6/5/87; *Jerusalem Post*, 3/20/86; *Shaar*, 6/5/87; Z. Alush, *Yediot Aharonoth*, 5/31/87.

72. Reuven Podhazur, *Haaretz*, 3/29/87 and 5/25/87; D. Arkin, *Maariv*, 5/29/87; *Davar*, 6/26/87.

73. *Jerusalem Post*, 8/21/87; Glenn Frankel, *Washington Post*, 7/1/87; *Haaretz*, 12/18/87; H. Raviv, *Hadashot*, 6/10/86; Menahem Meron interview, 11/22/90; Zeev Schiff, *Haaretz*, 3/1/85 Tali Zelinger, *Davar*, 8/8/86 and 5/20/87; Hirsh Goodman, *Jerusalem Post*, 1/27/86; Reuven Podhazur, *Haaretz*, 1/4/87; Ron Ben-Yishai, *Yediot Aharonoth*, 5/11/87; Abraham Tal, *Haaretz*, 8/14/87; Y. Walter, *Maariv*, 6/1/87.

74. *Haaretz*, 1/15/86, 1/17/86, and 2/9/86; *Davar*, 2/9/86; Hirsh Goodman, *Jerusalem Post* (international ed.), 11/28/87; *Jerusalem Post*, 7/21/86; Z. Alush, *Yediot Aharonoth*, 1/28/87.

75. Reuven Podhazur, *Haaretz*, 5/5/87 and 5/31/87; Menachem Meron interview, 11/22/90.

## 5. The Invasion of Lebanon, 1982

1. Rabinovich 1984, pp. 116–118, 122; Sharon 1989, pp. 426, 429; Schiff and Yaari 1982, pp. 22, 68.

2. Schiff and Yaari 1982, p. 68; Shiffer 1984, pp. 75–76; Zeev Schiff, *Haaretz*, 7/13/82, p. 9; Eitan 1985, p. 209; A. Tamir 1988, p. 145.

3. *Haaretz*, 4/13/84, p. 1; Sharon 1989, p. 426.

4. Schiff 1983, p. 77; Schiff and Yaari 1982, pp. 29–30; Sharon 1989, p. 430.

5. Sharon 1989, p. 433; A. Tamir 1988, p. 143; Yaniv and Lieber 1983, p.133; Rubinstein 1983, p. 12; Schiff and Yaari 1982, pp. 125–128; Eitan 1985, p. 197.

6. Haig 1984, pp. 321–322; Yaniv and Lieber 1983, p. 134.

7. Y. Porat, *Haaretz*, 6/25/82, p. 14; Rabinovich 1984, p. 128.

8. *Haaretz*, 9/9/81, p. 9; 9/15/81, p. 11; 9/16/81, p. 13; 11/3/81, p. 1; 11/17/81, p. 1; 11/22/81, p. 1; 12/20/81, p. 1; Schiff and Yaari 1982, pp. 80–81; Sharon 1989, p. 451.

9. Yossi Melman, *Haaretz*, 1/4/98; Shiffer 1984, pp. 72, 82; A. Tamir 1988, pp. 151, 223; Schiff 1983, p. 79; Haig 1984, p. 327; Benziman 1985, p. 34; Gideon Samet, in *Haaretz*, 2/11/82, pp. 1–2.

10. Gideon Samet, *Haaretz*, 2/21/82, p. 1; *Haaretz*, 2/26/82, pp. 1–2; Yossi Melman, *Haaretz*, 1/4/98; Haig 1984, p. 335; Sharon 1989, pp. 451, 487; Schiff 1983, pp. 80–81; Schiff and Yaari 1982, p. 89; Shiffer 1984, pp. 87, 89–90; Rabinovich 1984, pp. 92, 126; A. Tamir 1988, p. 159; Yaniv 1987, p. 137.

11. Schiff and Yaari 1982, pp. 75, 82, 90–91; Schiff 1983, pp.78, 81–82, 91; Naor 1986, p. 42.

12. Haig 1984, p. 318; Schiff and Yaari 1982, pp. 75, 82, 206; Schiff 1983, pp. 78, 91; Gideon Samet, *Haaretz*, 9/9/82, p. 1; Rabinovich 1984, p. 135; Shiffer 1984, p. 98; Yoel Markus, *Haaretz*, 6/11/82, p. 13.

13. Haig 1984, p. 344; *Haaretz*, 7/2/82, p. 2; Shiffer 1984, p. 99; Schiff and Yaari 1982, p. 245; Naor 1986, p. 96; Sharon 1989, p. 487.

14. Perlmutter 1985, p. 317.

15. Schiff and Yaari 1982, pp. 97–8; Shiffer 1984, p. 87; Yaniv 1987, p. 107; A. Tamir 1988, pp. 145, 152–154, 158; Sharon 1989, p. 436.

16. Yaniv 1987, p. 107; A. Tamir 1988, p. 158; Schiff and Yaari 1982, pp. 97–98.

17. Zeev Schiff, *Haaretz*, 12/17/81, p. 9; Schiff and Yaari 1982, p. 94; Rabinovich 1984, p. 131.

18. A. Tamir 1988, p. 160; Rabinovich 1984, p. 122; Shiffer 1984, pp. 76–78, 87; Yaniv 1987, pp. 108–110; Sharon 1989, pp. 426, 450, 455; Yanosh Ben Gal quoted by Reuven Podhazur, in *Haaretz*, 6/2/87; Schiff and Yaari 1982, pp. 98, 115–117; Zeev Schiff, *Haaretz*, 5/11/82, p. 9.

19. Sharon 1989, p. 426; Rabinovich 1984, p. 122.

20. Benziman 1985, p. 241; Naor 1986, pp. 16–17; Schiff and Yaari 1982, p. 20; Uzi Benziman, *Haaretz*, 6/16/82, p. 11.

21. Naor 1986, pp. 66–67; Feldman and Reichnitz-Kijner 1984, p. 31; Yaniv 1987, pp. 113–114; Sharon 1989, p. 460; Uzi Benziman, *Haaretz*, 6/16/82, p. 147; Schiff and Yaari 1982, p. 147; Eitan 1985, pp. 204, 213, 215, 230; Ben-Meir, *Maariv*, Weekend Magazine, 8/7/87.

22. A. Tamir 1988, p. 161; Uzi Benziman, *Haaretz*, 6/11/82, p. 14; Uzi Benziman, *Haaretz*, 6/16/82, p. 11.

23. Naor 1986 p. 70; Feldman and Reichnitz-Kijner 1984, p. 32; Yaniv 1987, p. 114; Sharon 1989, p. 466; Schiff and Yaari 1982, pp. 149, 193, 201; Uzi Benziman, *Haaretz*, 6/16/82, p. 11; Eitan 1985, p. 213; David Ivri interview, 5/27/91; *Haaretz*, Weekend Magazine, 12/20/85.

24. Schiff and Yaari 1982, pp. 207, 223; Uzi Benziman, *Haaretz*, June 16, 1982, p. 11; Naor 1986, p. 90; Energy Minister Berman, quoted in Feldman and Reichnitz-Kijner 1984, p. 15; *Haaretz*, 6/16/82, p. 11.

25. A. Tamir 1988, p. 182.

26. The entire system was destroyed on the fourth day without loss of a single Israeli aircraft.

27. *Haaretz*, Weekend Magazine, 12/20/85; Naor 1986, p. 72.

28. Friedman 1989, p. 130; Yaniv 1987, pp. 120–124; A. Tamir 1988, p. 182; *Haaretz*, Weekend Magazine, 12/20/85; Schiff and Yaari 1982, pp. 24, 262; Interview with Minister Zvulun Hammer, in *Haaretz*, Weekend Magazine, 12/2/0/85.

29. Friedman 1989, p. 144; Perlmutter 1985, p. 315; *Haaretz*, 12/18/81; Yoel Markus, *Haaretz*, 5/11/82, p. 11; and 12/25/81, p. 13; Yaniv 1987, p. 99.

30. Matti Golan, *Haaretz*, 9/15/81, p. 11; Gilmour 1983, p. 159; Randal 1983, p. 232; Shiffer 1984, pp. 42, 47, 50.

31. Schiff and Yaari 1982, p. 31; Yaniv 1987, pp. 89, 92.

32. Sagie 1998, p. 102; Perlmutter 1985, p. 375; Ehud Olmert interview, 7/8/91.

33. Schiff and Yaari 1982, p. 18.

34. Sharon 1989, p. 457; Yanosh Ben-Gal, quoted by Reuven Podhazur, *Haaretz*, 6/2/87; Schiff and Yaari 1982, pp. 223, 240, 262; Shiffer 1984, pp. 107–108; Interview with Ezer Weizman, *Maariv*, Weekend Magazine, 12/13/91.

35. Schiff and Yaari 1982, p. 98.

36. Naor 1986, p. 30; Yaniv 1987, p. 109; Schiff and Yaari 1982, pp. 97–98; Zeev Schiff, *Haaretz*, 5/12/82, p. 9.

37. Naor 1986, p. 44.

38. Naor 1986, pp. 48–49; Schiff and Yaari 1982, p. 98.

39. Naor 1986, pp. 50, 81; Yanosh Ben Gal, as quoted by Reuven Podhazur, *Haaretz*, 2/2/87; Schiff and Yaari 1982, pp. 18–19, 149, 185; Sharon 1989, pp. 426, 456; Yaniv 1987, pp. 111, 114; Benziman 1985, p. 238; Uzi Benziman, *Haaretz*, 6/11/82, p. 14; and 6/16/82, p. 11.

40. Sagie 1998; Naor 1986, pp. 38, 59; Eitan 1985, p. 233; Schiff and Yaari 1982, pp. 149, 193, 201; Uzi Benziman, *Haaretz*, 6/16/82, p. 11.

41. Naor 1986, pp. 66–67; Feldman and Reichnitz-Kijner 1984, p. 31; Yaniv 1987, pp. 113–114; Sharon 1989, pp. 426, 458, 460; Uzi Benziman, *Haaretz*, 6/16/82, p. 11; Schiff and Yaari 1982, pp. 20, 147; Eitan 1985, pp. 204, 213, 215, 230; Ben-Meir, in *Maariv*, Weekend Magazine, 8/7/87.

42. *Haaretz*, Weekend Magazine, 12/20/85; Schiff and Yaari 1982, pp. 24, 262; Interview with Minister Zvulun Hammer, in *Haaretz*, Weekend Magazine, 12/20/85.

43. Schiff and Yaari 1982, p. 279.

44. Ehrlich would later say, remarkably, that he had intended to vote against the invasion but was so tense when the vote was called that he inadvertently raised his hand in abstention. Ehrlich ultimately supported the invasion publicly in the strongest terms.

45. Janis 1983; Schulze 1998a.

46. Zeev Schiff, *Haaretz*, 7/2/82, pp. 13, 16; *Haaretz*, Weekend Magazine, 6/25/82, p. 8; Interview with Minister Zvulun Hammer, *Haaretz*, Weekend Magazine, 12/20/85.

47. Schiff and Yaari 1982, p. 32; Shiffer 1984, pp. 92, 160; Naor 1986, pp. 22, 47.

48. Randal 1983, p. 230; Shiffer 1984, pp. 28–30; Schiff and Yaari 1982, pp. 58, 67, 68; A. Tamir 1988, p. 182.

49. Weizman interview, *Maariv*, Weekend Magazine, 12/13/91; Zeev Schiff, *Haaretz*, 12/17/81, p. 9; Shiffer 1984, p. 161; Eliahu Ben-Elissar interview, 6/10/91; Shiffer 1984, p. 9.

50. Yehoshua Saguy interview, 4/25/91; Eliahu Ben-Elissar interview, 6/10/91; Perlmutter 1987, pp. 375, 383; Yoel Markus, *Haaretz*, 7/26/82, p. 9; Shiffer 1984, pp. 103, 162; Naor 1986, pp. 50, 81; Reuven Podhazur, *Haaretz*, 6/2/87; Schiff and Yaari 1982, pp. 149, 185.

51. *Haaretz*, Weekend Magazine, 6/25/82, p. 8; Shiffer 1984, p. 13; Schiff and Yaari 1982, p. 37; Zeev Schiff, *Haaretz*, 4/7/82, p. 11; Benziman 1985, p. 231; Feldman and Reichnitz-Kijner 1984, p. 3.

52. Naor 1986, pp. 29–32; Yaniv 1987, pp. 100–101; Feldman and Reichnitz-Kijner 1984, pp. 3, 19; Friedman 1989, p. 13; Dan Margalit, *Haaretz*, 12/14/89, p. 11; Naor 1988, p. 42; Mack 1983, pp. 3, 5; Schiff and Yaari 1982, pp. 38, 383–384; Yoel Markus, *Haaretz*, 4/13/82; Zeev Schiff, *Haaretz*, 5/23/82 and 7/2/82; Gideon Samet, *Haaretz*, 6/13/82; Randal 1983, p. 244.

53. Perlmutter 1985, p. 315; Aronson 1982–1983, p. 18.

54. Naor, in Erez 2003, p. 82; *Yediot Aharonoth*, 1/7/88; A. Tamir 1988, p. 300.

55. Sagie 1998, pp. 99–100.

56. Schiff and Yaari 1982, pp. 24, 25, 99, 101, 110; A. Tamir 1988, pp. 19, 35, 67, 110, 116, 154, 157, 382; Naor 1986, pp. 53–54; Ben-Meir, in *Maariv*, Weekend Magazine 8/7/87; and in *Haaretz*, 6/2/87; Shiffer 1984, pp. 95–96.

57. Shiffer 1984, pp. 95–96; Yehoshua Saguy interview, 4/25/91; Ehud Olmert interview, 7/8/91; Naor 1986, pp. 53–54; Ben-Meir, in *Maariv*, Weekend Magazine, 8/7/87; and in *Haaretz*, 6/2/87; Schiff and Yaari 1982, pp. 19, 35, 67, 110, 116, 382.

58. Sagie 1998, pp. 99–100; Yaniv 1987, p. 109; Reuven Podhazur, *Haaretz*, 5/31/85; Zeev Schiff, *Haaretz*, 2/22/85; Schiff and Yaari 1982, pp. 35, 97–98, 382; Naor 1986, pp. 30, 53, 69; A. Tamir 1988, pp. 145; Zeev Schiff, *Haaretz*, 5/12/82, p. 9; and 2/22/85.

59. Shiffer 1984, pp. 95–96; State of Israel, *Commission of Inquiry into the Events at the Refugee Camps in Beirut*, 1983, pp. 6–7, 40; Schiff and Yaari 1982, pp. 98, 110–11, 382; Yoel Markus, *Haaretz*, 5/11/82, p. 11; Zeev Schiff, *Haaretz*, 2/22/85.

60. Perlmutter 1987, pp. 380, 383.

61. Yaniv 1987, p. 116.

62. *Haaretz*, 7/9/82, p. 3; Schiff and Yaari 1982, p. 33; Shiffer 1984, p. 93; Eitan 1985, p. 333.

63. *Haaretz*, 7/9/82, p. 3; Schiff and Yaari 1982, p. 33; Shiffer 1984, p. 93; Eitan 1985, p. 333.

64. Eitan 1985, pp. 204, 213, 215, 218, 241–242; Naor 1986, p. 70; Reuven Podhazur, *Haaretz*, 6/2/87; Zeev Schiff, *Haaretz*, 7/23/82, pp. 13, 20; A. Tamir 1988, p. 157; Ben-Meir 1995, p. 62; Schiff and Yaari 1982, p. 115.

65. Reuven Podhazur, *Haaretz*, 5/31/85; Zeev Schiff, *Haaretz*, 2/22/85; Schiff and Yaari 1982, pp. 35, 382; Naor 1986, pp. 30, 53, 69; A. Tamir 1988, p. 145.

## 6. Leaving Lebanon

1. Matthews 2008, p. 11.
2. Harel and Issacharoff 2008, p. 41.
3. Author's personal knowledge.
4. Kaye 2002–2003, p. 567; Matthews 2008, p. 9; Luft 2000, p. 15; Alex Fishman, *Yediot Aharonoth* supplement *24 Hours*, 6/24/99, p. 5; Nahum Barnea, *Yediot Aharonoth*, Weekend Magazine, 2/4/00, p. 2; Eitan Glickman, *Yediot Aharonoth*, 2/8/00, p. 4; and 2/10/00, p. 2.
5. Kaye 2002–2003, p. 567; Luft 2000, p. 17.
6. Luft 2000, p. 17; Sela 2007, p. 65; Harel and Issacharoff 2008, p. 30; Nachum Barnea, *Yediot Aharonoth*, 9/3/99, p. 2.
7. Harel and Issacharoff 2008, p. 35; Zvi Barel, *Haaretz*, 4/2/00; *Yediot Aharonot*, 11/11/09, p. 7.
8. Harel and Issacharoff 2008, p. 41; Dan Margalit, *Haaretz*, 2/21/00; Ron Ben-Yishai, *Yediot Aharonoth*, Weekend Magazine, 9/17/99, p. 4.
9. Premier Barak, as cited by Harel and Issacharoff 2008, p. 41; Ehud Barak, Testimony before the Winograd Commission, 11/28/06, p. 9; Aluf Benn, *Haaretz*, 3/23/00.
10. Ynet (*Yediot Aharonoth* website), 5/25/00; Aluf Benn, *Haaretz*, 3/6/00; Amos Harel, *Haaretz*, 3/13/00; Barak, Testimony before the Winograd Commission, 11/28/06, p. 9.
11. Ron Ben Yishai, *Yediot Aharonoth*, 3/17/00, p. 8; Aluf Benn, *Haaretz*, 4/28/00; Amos Harel, *Haaretz*, 3/16/00.
12. Alex Fishman, *Yediot Aharonoth*, 10/10/99, p. 16; and Weekend Magazine, 10/15/99, p. 13; Zeev Schiff, *Haaretz*, 10/5/99; Ron Ben Yishai, *Yediot Aharonoth*, 2/7/00, p. 7; Amos Harel, *Haaretz*, 3/26/00.
13. Amos Harel, *Haaretz*, 3/27/00, 4/4/00, and 4/12/00; Alex Fishman, *Yediot Aharonoth*, 3/23/00, p. 6.
14. Amos Harel, *Haaretz*, 3/27/00, 4/4/00, and 4/12/00; Alex Fishman, *Yediot Aharonoth*, 3/23/00, p. 6.
15. Aluf Benn, *Haaretz*, 3/29/00.
16. Aluf Benn, *Haaretz*, 3/29/00; Amos Harel, *Haaretz*, 3/20/00, 4/3/00, 4/12/00, and 5/4/00; Shimon Shiffer and Alex Fishman, *Yediot Aharonoth*, 3/23/00, p. 6.
17. Ron Ben Yishai, *Yediot Aharonoth*, Weekend Magazine, 9/17/99, p. 4; Amos Harel, *Haaretz*, 4/12/00; Itamar Eichner, *Yediot Aharonoth*, 5/1/00, p. 2.
18. Ron Ben Yishai, *Yediot Aharonoth*, Weekend Magazine, 9/17/99, p. 4; Amos Harel, *Haaretz*, 3/26/00 and 5/8/00; Shimon Shiffer and Itamar Eichner, *Yediot Aharonoth*, 2/13/00, p. 2.
19. Matthews 2008, p. 8; Harel and Issacharoff 2008, pp. 15, 21.
20. Matthews 2008, p. 8; Harel and Issacharoff 2008, pp. 15, 21.
21. Sela 2007, pp. 19, 67; Kaye 2002–2003, pp. 562, 566, 572; Harel and Issacharoff 2008, p. 22.
22. Kaye 2002–2003, p. 571; Sela 2007, pp. 53, 54, 68.
23. Kaye 2002–2003, p. 564, 566; Luft 2000, p. 14; Dalia Shcory, *Haaretz*, 3/15/98; Zvi Barel, *Haaretz*, 3/20/98; David Makovsky and Zvi Barel, *Haaretz*, 11/29/98 and 12/27/98; Shimon Shiffer, *Yediot Aharonoth*, 3/3/99, p. 2.
24. *Yediot Aharonoth*, Weekend Magazine, 3/5/99, p. 10; Zvi Barel, *Haaretz*, 3/20/98, 5/4/98, and 5/5/98; Kaye 2002–2003, pp. 562–579; Itamar Eichner and Shimon Shiffer, *Yediot Aharonoth*, 3/2/99, p. 4.
25. Harel and Issacharoff 2008, pp. 18, 31; Drucker 2002, p. 130; Kaye 2002–2003, p. 581; Nechama Duek and Yuval Karni, *Yediot Aharonoth*, 3/3/99, p. 3; Sela 2007, p. 19.
26. Kaye 2002–2003, pp. 576–577; Ron Ben Yishai, *Yediot Aharonoth*, 2/7/00, p. 7; *Yediot Aharonoth*, 2/11/00, p. 11; Nechama Duek, *Yediot Aharonoth*, 11/11/99, p. 9.
27. Ron Ben Yishai, *Yediot Aharonoth*, 3/17/00, p. 9; Alex Fishman, *Yediot Aharonoth*, 12/26/99, p. 2.
28. Aluf Benn and Amos Harel, *Haaretz*, 2/27/00; Itamar Eichner, *Yediot Aharonoth*, 2/27/00, p. 5.
29. Aluf Benn and Amos Harel, *Haaretz*, 2/27/00; Itamar Eichner, *Yediot Aharonoth*, 4/27/00, pp. 2, 5; Shimon Shiffer, *Yediot Aharonoth*, 5/23/00, p. 2.

30. Itamar Eichner, *Yediot Aharonoth*, 2/12/00, p. 4; Akiva Eldar, *Haaretz*, 6/1/00.

31. Harel and Issacharoff 2008, pp. 26, 32, 41, 567–568; Drucker 2002, p. 131; Amir Oren, *Haaretz*, 1/1/99; Zeev Schiff, *Haaretz*, 3/6/00; Amos Harel, *Haaretz*, 4/12/00; Aluf Benn, *Haaretz*, 4/28/00; Chaim Shibi, *Yediot Aharonoth*, 4/12/00, p. 3; Kaye 2002–2003, pp. 561, 568.

32. Amir Oren, *Haaretz*, 1/1/99; Drucker 2002, p. 131.

33. Harel and Issacharoff 2008, pp. 26, 32, 41, 567–568; Drucker 2002, p. 131; Amir Oren, *Haaretz*, 1/1/99; Zeev Schiff, *Haaretz*, 3/6/00; Amos Harel, *Haaretz*, 4/12/00; Aluf Benn, *Haaretz*, 4/28/00; Chaim Shibi, *Yediot Aharonoth*, 4/12/00, p. 3; Kaye 2002–2003, p. 561.

34. Aluf Benn and Amos Harel, *Haaretz*, 2/27/00; Itamar Eichner, *Yediot Aharonoth*, 2/27/00, p. 5.

35. Drucker 2002, p. 131; Harel and Issacharoff 2008, p. 26; Uzi Benziman, *Haaretz*, 4/14/00.

## 7. Camp David II

1. Uzi Benziman, *Haaretz*, 10/8/99, p. B5; Aluf Benn, *Haaretz*, 6/20/00, p. B3; Akiva Eldar, *Haaretz*, 5/15/00, p. B3; Sher 2001, p. 22.

2. Amos Harel, *Haaretz*, 11/2/99, p. A3; Ross 2004, p. 593; Drucker and Shelah 2005, pp. 16, 85; Ben-Ami 2006, pp. 247, 251–252, 264; Ben-Ami 2004, p. 107; Sher 2001 pp. 34, 49, 56, 146; Aluf Benn, *Haaretz*, 7/23/00, p. A2.

3. Ross 2004, pp. 498, 500; Aluf Benn, *Haaretz*, 9/28/00, p. B3.

4. Ross 2004, p. 508.

5. Ibid.

6. Aluf Benn, *Haaretz*, 6/24/99, p. A1, and 7/29/99, p. A1; Ben-Ami 2006, p. 241; Sher 2001, pp. 64–66.

7. Ben-Ami 2006, p. 246.

8. Sher 2001, pp. 33, 112; Ben-Ami 2006, p. 265.

9. Ben-Ami 2004, pp. 92–94, 102.

10. Aluf Benn, *Haaretz*, 7/21/00, p. B2.

11. Sher 2001, pp. 171, 193; Mayer and Mourad 2008, p. 307.

12. Sher 2001, p. 160; Ben-Ami 2006, p. 264; Ben Ami 2004, p. 153.

13. Sher 2001, p. 166.

14. Ben-Ami 2006, pp. 262–263; Ben-Ami 2004, pp. 92–94, 152; Sher 2001, pp. 130, 168.

15. Dan Margalit, *Haaretz*, 9/2/99, p. B1.

16. Sher 2001, pp. 74–75, 80; Gilead Sher interview, 12/23/09.

17. Aluf Benn, *Haaretz*, 7/15/99.

18. Sher 2001, pp. 5, 41, 53, 160; Ben-Ami 2004, pp. 28–29, 85; Dalia Shechory, *Haaretz*, 4/1/0/00, p. A2; Aluf Benn, *Haaretz*, 6/28/00, p. A1.

19. This meant an interim agreement by February 2000 and a final one by October.

20. Ben-Ami 2004, p. 23.

21. Uzi Benizman, *Haaretz*, 10/22/99, p. B3; Aluf Benn and Nitzan Horvitz, *Haaretz*, 10/21/99, p. A1.

22. Sher 2001, p. 63.

23. Ben-Ami 2004, pp. 25–27; Sher 2001, pp. 69, 71.

24. Sher 2001, pp. 31, 84, 96, 99–105.

25. Ibid., p. 106; Aluf Benn, *Haaretz*, 6/20/00, p. A1, and 6/21/00, p. A3; Ben-Ami 2004, p. 133; Amir Oren, *Haaretz*, 7/18/00, p. A1; Ben-Ami 2004, p. 114.

26. Zeev Schiff, *Haaretz*, 4/28/00, p. B1; Drucker and Shelah 2005, pp. 21–22; Aluf Benn, *Haaretz*, 5/16/00, p. B3, 7/13/00, p. A6, and 7/14/00, p. A1; Tomer Shedmi, *Haaretz*, 77/00; Ben-Ami 2004, p. 55; Indyk 2009, p. 353.

27. Sher 2001, pp. 41, 60, 72, 106.

28. Ben-Ami 2004, p. 173; Aluf Benn, *Haaretz*, 7/28/00, p. B2; Sher 2001, pp. 75–76.

29. Ben-Ami 2004, p. 160; Sher 2001, pp. 163, 165–166.

30. Sher 2001, p. 79.

31. Ibid., pp. 127, 175–181.

32. Ben-Ami 2004, p. 155; Ben-Ami 2006, pp. 251, 256.

33. Sher 2001, p. 121; Aluf Benn, *Haaretz*, 7/16/00, p. A2.

34. Aluf Benn, *Haaretz*, 12/7/99, p. B3; Yoel Marcus, *Haaretz*, 8/3/99, p. B1.

35. Uzi Benziman, *Haaretz*, 7/16/99, p. B3; Sher 2001, p. 27; Aluf Benn, *Haaretz*, 7/12/99, p. A1, 7/19/99, p. A1, and 8/18/99, p. A6.

36. Aluf Benn and Nitzan Horvitz, *Haaretz*, 7/18/99, p. A2.

37. Sher 2001, pp. 56, 99; Aluf Benn, *Haaretz*, 7/29/99, p. A1, 9/1/99, p. A1 9/2/99, p. A3, and 9/5/99, p. A1; Klein 2003, pp. 40–42.

38. Klein 2003, pp. 40–42; Aluf Benn, *Haaretz*, 11/3/99, p. A2, 12/13/99, p. A1, and 1/17/00, p. A4.

39. Aluf Benn and Amira Hess, *Haaretz*, 3/9/00, p. A1; Nitzan Horvitz, *Haaretz*, 3/21/00, p. A5; Aluf Benn and Amnon Barzilai, *Haaretz*, 3/20/00, p. A3; Sher 2001, p. 68; Ross 2004, p. 615; Aluf Benn and Nitzan Horvitz, *Haaretz*, 4/27/00, p. A1.

40. Sher 2001, p. 80; Aluf Benn, *Haaretz*, 6/2/00, p. A1, and 6/13/00, p. B3.

41. Ross 2004, pp. 628, 674, 688, 705, 707, 708, 710, 712, 768; Indyk 2009, pp. 322, 325, 374; Miller, Miller, and Zetouni 2002, pp. 297, 298, 301; Sher 2006, pp. 99, 101, 106.

42. Sher 2001, p. 255. For a detailed summary of the Israeli positions at Camp David, see Sher 2001; Ross 2004; and Ben-Ami 2004 and 2006.

43. Ben-Ami 2006, pp. 248, 270.

44. Hana Kim, *Haaretz*, 8/6/99, p. B3.

45. Aluf Benn, *Haaretz*, 10/12/99, p. B3; Klein 2003, p. 46; Aluf Benn and Yossi Verter, *Haaretz*, 4/30/00, p. A3; Sher 2001, pp. 57, 60, 134; Indyk 2009, p. 344.

46. Ben-Ami 2006, p. 255.

47. Ross 2004, p. 591; Sher 2001, pp. 64–66; Uzi Benziman, *Haaretz*, 7/28/00, p. B5.

48. Ross 2004, p. 622; Sher 2001, pp. 86, 97; Ben-Ami 2004, p. 88.

49. Drucker 2002, p. 185; Sher 2001, pp. 37, 121; Klein 2003, p. 150; Gideon Alon, *Haaretz*, 7/18/00, p. A3.

50. Sher 2001, pp. 66, 68.

51. Nadav Shragai, *Haaretz*, 3/28/00, p. A1.

52. Ross 2004, p. 602; Ben-Ami 2004, p. 65; Uzi Benziman, *Haaretz*, 5/12/00, p. B3, and 5/14/00, p. B1; Gideon Allon and Aluf Benn, *Haaretz*, 5/16/00, p. A1.

53. Sher 2001, p. 32; Aluf Benn, *Haaretz*, 5/15/00, p. B3; Uzi Benziman, *Haaretz*, 5/12/00, p. B3.

54. Sher 2001, pp. 42, 120; Yossi Verter and Gideon Allon, *Haaretz*, 6/8/00, p. A1; Yossi Verter and Shachar Ilan, *Haaretz*, 6/22/00, p. A1, 6/25/00, p. A4, and 6/21/00.

55. Ben-Ami 2006, p. 96.

56. Uzi Benziman, *Haaretz*, 6/21/00, p. B1; Tomer Shadmi, Ynet, 6/26/00; Aluf Benn, *Haaretz*, 6/28/00, p. A3; Ross 2004, p. 641; Uzi Benziman, *Haaretz*, 6/30/00. p. B4; Drucker and Shelah 2005, p. 21.

57. Tomer Shadmi, Ynet, 7/11/00; Ben-Ami 2006, p. 129; Sher 2001, pp. 55, 151; Indyk 2009, p. 288; Yossi Verter, *Haaretz*, 7/19/00, p. A3; Sher 2001, p. 134.

58. Yossi Verter, *Haaretz*, 7/25/00, p. A3; Drucker 2002, pp. 216, 224; Sher 2001, p. 60; Dani Rubenstein, *Haaretz*, 10/4/99, p. B1; Drucker 2002, p. 192; Ben-Ami 2004, p. 66.

59. Sher 2001, p. 70.

60. Aluf Benn, *Haaretz*, 9/14/99, p. A1.

61. Klein 2003, pp. 46, 51; Ben-Ami 2004, pp. 62, 72, 124; Aluf Benn, *Haaretz*, 7/28/00, p. B2.

62. Sher 2001, p. 81.

63. Drucker 2002, pp. 212–213; Klein 2003, pp.50–52; Akiva Eldar, *Haaretz*, 7/20/00, p. B3; Ben-Ami 2004, p. 72; Klein 2003, p. 141; Sher 2001, pp. 25, 85.

64. Ben-Ami 2004, p. 107; Uzi Benziman, *Haaretz*, 6/16/00, p. B3; Aluf Benn and Nitzan Horvitz, *Haaretz*, 6/18/00, p. A6.

65. Sher 2001, p. 52; Akiva Eldar, *Haaretz*, 9/5/99, p. B1; Dalia Schory, *Haaretz*, 9/6/99, p. A3.

66. Uzi Benziman, *Haaretz*, 5/21/00, p. B1; Dani Yatom, in Shamir and Maddy-Weitzman 2005, p. 36; Akiva Eldar, *Haaretz*, 1/13/00, p. B1; Ben-Ami 2004, pp. 49–52; Sher 2001, p. 91; Sher interview, 12/23/09; Indyk 2009, p. 267.

67. Drucker 2002, p. 232.
68. Amir Oren, *Haaretz*, 7/18/00; Drucker and Shelah 2005, p. 21.
69. Sher 2001, p. 131; Ross 2004, pp. 629, 634; Sher interview, 12/23/09.
70. Ben-Ami 2004, pp. 88, 138; Sher 2001, p. 121; Sher interview, 12/23/09.
71. Sher 2001, p. 185; Drucker 2002, p. 244.
72. Aluf Benn, *Haaretz*, 7/8/99, p. A5, 7/12/99, p. A1, 7/15/99, p. A1, and 8/18/99, p. A6.
73. Aluf Benn, *Haaretz*, 12/7/99, p. B3.
74. Sher 2001, pp. 20–21; Aluf Benn, *Haaretz*, 7/7/99, p. A2, and 8/4/99, p. A1; Ben-Ami 2004, p. 96.
75. Ben-Ami 2006, p. 255.
76. Sher 2001, p. 86.
77. Ross 2004, p. 677.
78. Sher 2001, p. 247; Zeev Schiff, *Haaretz*, 1/22/99, p. B1.
79. Ben-Ami 2006, p. 272; Ben-Ami 2002, p. 459.

## 8. Disengaging from Gaza, 2005

1. Tsur 2006, pp. 30–32, Arieli and Sfard 2008, p. 39; Jacoby 2007, p. 21.
2. Tsur 2006, pp. 34–36, 78; Aluf Benn, *Haaretz*, Weekend Magazine, 12/29/06, pp. 34–40.
3. Tsur 2006, p. 34; Aluf Benn, *Haaretz*, Weekend Magazine, 12/29/06, pp. 34–40; Aluf Benn, *Haaretz*, 8/29/02; Amir Oren, *Haaretz*, 1/21/05 and 8/29/05; Drucker and Shelah 2005, p. 383.
4. Tsur 2006, pp. 70, 72.
5. Ibid., p. 70; Zelnick 2006, p. 32.
6. Zelnick 2006, pp. 26, 37; Bar-Siman-Tov 2001, pp. 264–265; Pressman 2006; Weisglass interview with Ari Shavit, *Haaretz*, 10/10/04.
7. Rynhold and Waxman 2008, pp. 27–29; Hefez and Bloom 2006, pp. 434, 436; Aluf Benn, *Haaretz*, 2/26/04 and 8/20/04; Uzi Benziman, *Haaretz*, 3/19/04; Nachum Barnea, *Yediot Aharonoth*, Weekend Supplement, 4/2/04; Sharon interview with Nachum Barnea and Shimon Shiffer, *Yediot Aharonoth*, Passover Supplement, 4/5/04, pp. 2–3; Sharon interview with Nachum Barnea and Shimon Shiffer, *Yediot Aharonoth*, Holiday Supplement, 4/22/05; Aluf Benn, *Haaretz*, 9/29/02; Weisglass interview with Ari Shavit, *Haaretz*, 10/10/04; Bar-Siman-Tov 2001, pp. 264–265; Aluf Benn, *Haaretz*, 8/29/02.
8. Rynhold and Waxman 2008, pp. 28–29.
9. Uzi Benziman, *Haaretz*, 3/19/04; Sharon interview with Nahum Barnea and Shimon Shiffer, *Yediot Aharonoth*, Holiday Supplement, 4/22/04, p. 2; Dov Weisglass interview with Ari Shavit, *Haaretz*, 10/10/04; Nir Hason et al., *Haaretz*, 4/6/05; Sharon interview with Nahum Barnea and Shimon Shiffer, *Yediot Aharonoth*, Passover Supplement, 4/5/04, pp. 2–3.
10. Aluf Benn, *Haaretz*, 12/17/04.
11. Weisglass interview with Ari Shavit, *Haaretz*, 10/10/04.
12. Nahum Barnea and Shimon Shiffer, *Yediot Aharonoth*, Holiday Supplement, 9/15/04, p. 2; Aluf Benn, *Haaretz*, Weekend Magazine, 12/29/06, pp. 34–40; Ben-Ami 2006, p. 307.
13. Sharon interview with Alex Fishman, *Yediot Aharonot*, Weekend Magazine, 12/26/03; Tsur 2006, p. 60; Amos Harel, *Haaretz*, 7/25/05, p. B6.
14. Pressman 2006; Tsur 2006, p. 89; Bar-Siman-Tov 2001, pp. 264–265.
15. Zelnick 2006, p. xiii; Pressman 2006; Drucker and Shelah 2005, p. 358; Shimon Shiffer, *Yediot Aharonoth*, 5/23/05, p. 2; Aluf Benn and Yossi Verter, *Haaretz*, Passover Supplement, 4/22/05, p. B2; Bar-Siman-Tov 2001, pp. 264–265, 275; Pressman 2006; Aluf Benn, *Haaretz*, 2/2/05. p. B1; Tsur 2006, p. 222; Rynhold and Waxman 2008, pp. 24–25, 31.
16. Pressman 2006; Bar-Siman-Tov 2001, pp. 275–276.
17. Bar-Siman-Tov 2001, pp. 275–276.
18. Brig. Gen. Eival Giladi, in Tsur 2006, p. 308.
19. Aluf Benn, *Haaretz*, Weekend Magazine, 12/29/06, pp. 34–40; Nahum Barnea and Shimon Shiffer, *Yediot Aharonoth*, Weekend Magazine, 3/3/06, p. 2; Aluf Benn, *Haaretz*, 2/6/04;

Nathan Guttman, *Haaretz*, 2/9/04; Akiva Eldar, *Haaretz*, 2/2/4/04; Ynet, 3/2/04; Aluf Benn, Nathan Guttman, and Mazal Muallem, *Haaretz*, 2/27/04.

20. Orly Azulai and Itamar Eichner, *Haaretz*, 3/28/04, p. 4; Itamar Eichner and Nechama Duek, *Haaretz*, 4/15/04; Nathan Guttman, *Haaretz*, 3/3/04; Nahum Barnea and Shimon Shiffer, *Yediot Aharonoth*, Passover Holiday Supplement, 4/5/05, pp. 2–3; Pressman 2006; Uzi Benziman, *Haaretz*, 3/19/04; Aluf Benn, *Haaretz*, 2/22/04, 3/28/04, 8/20/04, and 4/26/05, p. B1; Bar-Siman-Tov 2001, pp. 264–265.

21. Nachum Barnea, *Yediot Aharonoth*, Passover Supplement, 4/5/05, pp. 2–3; Itamar Yaar, former deputy national security adviser, lecture in Tel Aviv University, 1/12/06; Aluf Benn, *Haaretz*, 2/16/04 and 3/11/04; Nathan Guttman, *Haaretz*, 2/9/04; Akiva Eldar, *Haaretz*, 2/24/04 and 3/9/04; Pressman 2006.

22. Aluf Benn, *Haaretz*, 3/6/04 and 8/22/05, p. A1; Shimon Shiffer, *Yediot Aharonoth*, Weekend Supplement, 5/28/04, pp. 4–5; Smadar Perry, *Yediot Aharonoth*, 2/6/05; Sima Kadon, *Yediot Aharonoth*, Weekend Supplement, 5/21/04; Amos Harel, *Haaretz*, 3/11/05; *Yediot Aharonoth*, 7/27/05, p. 4.

23. *Haaretz*, 12/18/05.

24. Author's knowledge; Moshe Yaalon interview, 7/20/06; Sharon interview with Aluf Benn, *Haaretz*, 4/5/04; Hefez and Bloom 2006.

25. Ari Shavit, *Haaretz*, 6/4/06.

26. Aluf Benn, *Haaretz*, 2/6/04 and 2/18/04; Aluf Benn and Arnon Roglar, *Haaretz*, 2/9/04; Alex Fishman, *Yediot Aharonoth*, 2/16/04, p. 2; *Yediot Aharonoth*, Weekend Supplement, 3/19/04, p. 2; Tsur 2006, pp. 215–216.

27. Shimon Shiffer, *Yediot Aharonoth*, 2/18/04, p. 2.

28. Akiva Eldar, *Haaretz*, 2/2/4/04; Zvi Zinger, Ynet, 6/29/05; Uzi Benziman, *Haaretz*, 3/12/04; Nahum Barnea, *Yediot Aharonoth*, Weekend Supplement, 3/12/04, p. 21; Amos Harel, *Haaretz*, 3/3/04 and 3/30/04; Yaalon 2008, pp. 156, 160; Aluf Benn, *Haaretz*, 3/18/04; Aluf Benn, Sharon Sadeh, and Nathan Guttman, *Haaretz*, 3/7/04; Zeev Schiff, *Haaretz*, 2/3/04; Alex Fishman and Itamar Eichner, *Yediot Aharonoth*, 3/18/04, p. 6; Alex Fishman, *Yediot Aharonoth*, 2/20/04, Weekend Magazine, p. 6.

29. *Haaretz*, 6/7/04.

30. Aluf Benn, *Haaretz*, Weekend Magazine, 12/29/06, pp. 34–40; Nachum Barnea, *Yediot Aharonoth*, Weekend Supplement, 4/2/04.

31. Ari Shavit, *Haaretz*, 6/4/06; Aluf Benn, *Haaretz*, Weekend Magazine, 12/29/06, pp. 34–40; Itamar Eichner and Tova Zimucki, *Yediot Aharonoth*, 1/11/04.

32. Aluf Benn, *Haaretz*, 2/6/04, 2/8/04, and 2/18/04; Ari Shavit, *Haaretz*, 6/4/06.

33. Drucker and Shelah 2005, p. 370; Gideon Allon, *Haaretz*, 2/3/04.

34. Aluf Benn, Sharon Sadeh, and Nathan Guttman, *Haaretz*, 3/27/04; Aluf Benn and Amos Harel, *Haaretz*, 3/25/04; Aluf Benn, *Haaretz*, 3/18/04; Mazal Mualem and Aluf Benn, *Haaretz*, 3/22/04; Uzi Benziman, *Haaretz*, 3/19/04; Nathan Guttman, *Haaretz*, 3/3/04.

35. Alex Fishman and Itamar Eichner, *Yediot Aharonoth*, 3/18/04, p. 6; Nahum Barnea, *Yediot Aharonoth*, Weekend Supplement, 3/12/04, p. 21; Amos Harel, *Haaretz*, 3/11/05; Alex Fishman, *Yediot Aharonoth*, Weekend Supplement, 3/19/04, p. 4.

36. Uzi Benziman, *Haaretz*, 5/21/04; Aluf Benn, *Haaretz*, 5/23/04; Mazal Muallem, *Haaretz*, 5/23/04; *Yediot Aharonoth*, 5/3/04, p. 2.

37. Aluf Benn and Mazal Muallem, *Haaretz*, 5/23/04.

38. Aluf Benn, *Haaretz*, 11/22/04; Moshe Yaalon interview, 7/20/06; Ari Shavit, *Haaretz*, 6/4/06.

39. Amos Harel and Nir Hasson, *Haaretz*, 4/7/05, p. 2; Oded Shalom, *Yediot Aharonoth*, Weekend Supplement, 4/23/04, p. 8; Uzi Benziman, *Haaretz*, 5/15/05, p. B1; Aluf Benn and Motti Basuk, *Haaretz*, 2/28/05, p. A1; Gideon Allon, *Haaretz*, 6/21/05, p. A4.

40. Uzi Benziman, *Haaretz*, 5/15/05, p. B1.

41. Aluf Benn, *Haaretz*, Weekend Magazine, 12/29/06, pp. 34–40.

42. Aluf Benn, *Haaretz*, Weekend Magazine, 12/29/06, pp. 34–40; Hefez and Bloom 2006, p. 434; Aluf Benn, *Haaretz*, 2/8/04 and 4/5/04; Aluf Benn and Mazal Mualem, *Haaretz*, 3/21/04; Shimon Shiffer, *Yediot Aharonoth*, 3/14/04, p. 6.

43. Sima Kadmon, *Yediot Aharonoth*, Weekend Magazine, 12/19/04; Uzi Benziman, *Haaretz*, 4/23/04; Mazal Muallem and Aluf Benn, *Haaretz*, 3/22/04.

44. Uzi Benziman, *Haaretz*, 5/14/04; Aluf Benn, *Haaretz*, 5/19/04.

45. Nechama Duek, *Yediot Aharonoth*, 5/31/05, 6/1/00, and 6/1/04; Shimon Shiffer, *Yediot Aharonoth*, 5/31/04, p. 3; Itamar Eichner, *Yediot Aharonoth*, 5/31/04, p. 4.

46. Shimon Shiffer, *Yediot Aharonoth*, Weekend Supplement, 5/28/00, pp. 4–5; Itamar Eichner, *Yediot* Aharonoth, 6/6/04, p. 7.

47. Sima Kadmon, *Yediot Aharonoth*, Weekend Supplement, 5/21/04, p. 4; Aluf Benn and Mazal Muallem, *Haaretz*, 5/27/04; Aluf Benn, *Haaretz*, 5/28/04 and 5/30/04; Yossi Verter, *Haaretz*, 6/7/04; Shimon Shiffer, *Yediot Aharonoth*, Weekend Supplement, 5/28/00, pp. 4–5; Nechama Duek, *Yediot Aharonoth*, 6/7/04, p. 5.

48. Chaim Shibi and Nechama Duek, *Yediot Aharonoth*, 6/7/04, p. 5, and 6/8/04, p. 4; Nechama Duek, *Yediot Aharonoth*, 6/9/04, p. 3; Itamar Eichner et al., *Yediot Aharonoth*, 6/14/04, p. 4.

49. Chaim Shibi and Nechama Duek, *Yediot Aharonoth*, 7/6/04, p. 6, and 7/13/04, p. 4; Nechama Duek, *Yediot Aharonoth*, 7/14/04, p. 2; 7/26/04, p. 7, and 8/19/04, p. 2; Sima Kadmon, *Yediot Aharonoth*, Weekend Supplement, 7/16/04, p. 4; Nahum Barnea and Shimon Shiffer, *Yediot Aharonoth*, Weekend Supplement, 7/30/04, pp. 1–2.

50. Nahum Barnea and Shimon Shiffer, *Yediot Aharonoth*, 7/31/04, p. 2, and 9/14/04, p. 2; *Yediot Aharonoth*, 9/13/04, p. 4; Bar-Siman-Tov 2001, p. 271; Tsur 2006, p. 222.

51. Nahum Barnea and Shimon Shiffer, *Yediot Aharonoth*, 10/28/04, p. 6; Nechama Duek and Chaim Shibi, *Yediot Aharonoth*, 10/28/04, p. 7, and 11/9/04, p. 9; Tsur 2006, p. 222; Sima Kadmon, *Yediot Aharonoth*, Weekend Supplement, 10/22/04, pp. 4–5; Nechama Duek, *Yediot Aharonoth*, 10/27/04, pp. 4, 6, 11/9/04, p. 11, 11/10/04, 11/30/04, p. 4, 12/2/04, p. 4, and 12/09/04, p. 2; Chaim Shibi, *Yediot Aharonoth*, 11/30/04, p. 5; *Yediot Aharonoth*, 12/26/04, p. 5; *Yediot Aharonoth*, 1/6/05, p. 2, and 12/21/04.

52. Yossi Verter, *Haaretz*, 2/18/05, p. B3, and 2/21/05, p. B3; Gideon Allon and Aluf Benn, *Haaretz*, 2/21/05, p. A2; Itamar Eichner, *Yediot Aharonoth*, 2/21/05, p. 4; Chaim Shibi and Itamar Eichner, *Yediot Aharonoth*, 3/22/05, p. 2; Chaim Shibi et al., *Yediot Aharonoth*, 2/9/05, p. 9, 2/10/05, 2/17/05, p. 9, and 3/29/05, p. 4; Tsur 2006, pp. 231–233; Zvi Zarachia, *Haaretz*, 3/22/05, p. A1; Gideon Allon, *Haaretz*, 3/29/05, p. A2; Nadav Shragai, *Haaretz*, 3/29/05, p. A1.

53. Sever Plotzker and Gad Lior, *Yediot Aharonoth*, Holiday Supplement, 5/11/05; Itamar Eichner and Nechama Duek, *Yediot Aharonoth*, 7/4/05, p. 2; Sima Kadmon, *Yediot Aharonoth*, Weekend Supplement, 7/22/05, p. 10; Gideon Allon and Mazal Muallem, *Haaretz*, 7/2/05, p. A4; Mazal Muallem, *Haaretz*, 7/3/05, p. A1; Gideon Allon, *Haaretz*, 8/8/05, p. A4; Rynhold and Waxman 2008, p. 33.

54. Aluf Benn, Sharon Sadeh, and Nathan Guttman, *Haaretz*, 3/27/04; Aluf Benn and Amos Harel, *Haaretz*, 3/25/04; Aluf Benn, *Haaretz*, 3/18/04; Mazal Mualem and Aluf Benn, *Haaretz*, 3/22/04; Uzi Benziman, *Haaretz*, 3/19/04; Alex Fishman, *Yediot Aharonoth*, Weekend Supplement, 3/19/04, p. 4; Aluf Benn and Motti Basuk, *Haaretz*, 2/28/05, p. A1.

55. Aluf Benn, *Haaretz*, Weekend Magazine, 12/29/06, pp. 34–40.

56. Aluf Aluf Benn, *Haaretz*, Weekend Magazine, 12/29/06, pp. 34–40; Pressman 2006.

57. Yosi Yehoshua, Ynet, 12/22/03; Guy Meital, Ynet, 1/2/04; *Haaretz*, 1/6/05, p. 4; Nadav Shragaie, *Haaretz*, 4/20/04.

58. Nadav Shragai, *Haaretz*, 4/29/04; Oded Shalom, *Yediot Aharonoth*, Weekend Supplement, 4/16/04, p. 6; Nadav Shragai and Nir Chason, *Haaretz*, 7/27/04; *Yediot Aharonoth*, 12/20/04; Guy Meital and Chanan Greenberg, Ynet, 10/27/04; Bar-Siman-Tov 2001, p. 270.

59. Nadav Shragai, *Haaretz*, 1/11/05, p. A3, and 5/16/05, p. A1; *Haaretz*, 1/31/05, p. 1; *Haaretz*, 2/13/05, p. 4, and 2/14/05, p. 1; Roni Shaked, NRG, 2/22/05, p. 5; Itamar Eichner, *Yediot Aharonoth*, 2/28/05, p. 2; Nir Chason, *Haaretz*, 4/28/05; *Yediot Aharonoth*, 5/28/05, p. 5.

60. *Yediot Aharonoth*, 7/7/05, p. 7; Amir Ben David, *Yediot Aharonoth*, 7/18/05, p. 2; *Yediot Aharonoth*, 7/19/05, p. 1, 7/20/05, p. 2, 7/27/07, pp. 2–3, and 8/4/05, p. 4; Nadav Shragai, *Haaretz*, 7/19/06, p. A1; Nir Chason, *Haaretz*, 7/20/05, p. 20; *Haaretz*, 8/3/05, p. A1, 7/7/05, 8/15/05, p. A1, 8/12/05, p. A4; Amos Harel and Aluf Benn, *Haaretz*, 6/28/05, p. A1; Yuval Azulai, *Haaretz*, 6/30/05, p. A2; Guy Meital, Ynet, 6/24/04, p. 6.

61. Efraim Yaar and Tamar Herman, *Haaretz*, 8/10/04, 6/14/05, p. B3, 7/7/05, p. B3, and 8/8/05, p. B5; *Haaretz*, 1/4/05, p. B3, and 10/26/04, p. 11; *Haaretz*, Weekend Supplement, 1/7/05, p. 10; Sima Kadmon, *Yediot Aharonoth*, Weekend Supplement, 3/4/05, p. 8; Sima Kadmon, *Yediot Aharonoth*, Weekend Supplement, 8/12/05, pp. 6–7; *Haaretz*, 8/10/05, p. A1.

62. Nahum Barnea and Shimon Shiffer, *Yediot Aharonoth*, Weekend Magazine, 3/3/06, p. 2; Aluf Benn, *Haaretz*, Weekend Magazine, 12/29/06, pp. 34–40.

63. *Haaretz*, 3/23/01 and 4/13/01; Aluf Benn, *Haaretz*, 5/4/04; Aluf Benn, *Haaretz*, Weekend Magazine, 12/29/06, pp. 34–40; Zelnick 2006, p. 31; Pressman 2006.

64. Rynhold and Waxman 2008, p. 27; Tsur 2006, p. 29; Aluf Benn, *Haaretz*, 4/5/04; Aluf Benn, *Haaretz*, Weekend Magazine, 12/29/06, pp. 34–40; Nahum Barnea, *Yediot Aharonoth*, Weekend Supplement, 4/2/04.

65. Zeev Schiff, *Haaretz*, 3/12/04; Aluf Benn, *Haaretz*, 12/17/04; Nahum Barnea and Shimon Shiffer, *Yediot Aharonoth*, 5/23/04, p. 2.

66. Rynhold and Waxman 2008, p. 26; Pressman 2006.

67. Nahum Barnea, *Yediot Aharonoth*, Weekend Supplement, 4/2/04; Nahum Barnea and Shimon Shiffer, *Yediot Aharonoth*, Passover Supplement, 4/5/04, pp. 2–3; Aluf Benn, *Haaretz*, 4/5/04.

68. Uzi Benizman, *Haaretz*, 1/1605, p. B1; Aluf Benn, *Haaretz*, 1/23/05, p. A1; Arnon Rogler, *Haaretz*, 4/21/05, p. A3.

69. *Haaretz*, 1/14/04, p. 1, and 1/22/04, p. 1; *Haaretz*, Weekend Magazine, 1/23/04, p. 4, and 8/28/05, p. A5; Yaalon 2008, pp. 157, 160.

70. Uzi Benziman, *Haaretz*, 3/19/04; Ari Shavit, *Haaretz*, 6/1/05, p. A1; Alex Fishman, *Yediot Aharonoth*, Weekend Supplement, 3/19/04, p. 4.

71. Zvi Zinger, Ynet, 6/29/05, p. 2; Uzi Benziman, *Haaretz*, 3/12/04; Nahum Barnea, *Yediot Aharonoth*, Weekend Supplement, 3/12/04, p. 21; Drucker and Shelah 2005, p. 371; Amos Harel, *Haaretz*, 3/30/04.

72. Yaalon 2008, p. 171; Drucker and Shelah 2005, p. 371; Yossi Yehoshua et al., Ynet, 3/9/05, p. 5; Uzi Benziman, *Haaretz*, 3/12/04.

73. Yaalon 2008, pp. 156, 160; Deputy CoS Gaby Ashkenazi interview with Ariela Ringle Hoffman, *Yediot Aharonoth*, Weekend Supplement; MI chief Farkash, quoted in Haim Shibi, *Yediot Aharonoth*, 2/11/04, p. 4; Amos Harel, *Haaretz*, 3/3/04; Tsur 2006, pp. 187, 308; Aluf Benn, *Haaretz*, 3/18/04; Drucker and Shelah 2005, p. 3; Aluf Benn, Sharon Sadeh, and Nathan Guttman, *Haaretz*, 3/7/04; Zeev Schiff, *Haaretz*, 2/3/04; Uzi Benziman, *Haaretz*, 3/12/04; Tsur 2006, p. 186; Alex Fishman and Itamar Eichner, *Yediot Aharonoth*, 3/18/04, p. 6; Alex Fishman, *Yediot Aharonoth*, 2/20/04, Weekend Magazine, p. 6; Tsur 2006, p. 308; Nahum Barnea, *Yediot Aharonoth*, Weekend Supplement, 3/19/04, p. 2.

74. Aluf Benn, *Haaretz*, 3/18/04 and 5/13/04; Uzi Benziman, *Haaretz*, 3/12/04; Nahum Barnea, *Yediot Aharonoth*, Weekend Supplement, 3/19/04, p. 2; Alex Fishman, *Yediot Aharonoth*, Weekend Supplement, 3/19/04, p. 4; Sima Kadmon, *Yediot Aharonoth*, Weekend Supplement, 5/21/04, p. 8; Amir Oren, *Haaretz*, 3/9/04.

75. Drucker and Shelah 2005, p. 382; Aluf Benn, *Haaretz*, 2/6/04, 2/11/04, and 2/18/04; Zeev Schiff, *Haaretz*, 8/19/05, p. B1.

## 9. Back Again

1. Harel and Issacharoff 2008, p. 15; Amos Harel and Avi Issacharoff, *Haaretz*, July 14, 2006.

2. Shelah and Limor 2007, p. 148; Makovsky and White 2006, p. 10; Harel and Issacharoff 2008, p.142.

3. Harel and Issacharoff 2008, p. 75; Dov Weisglass, Testimony before the Winograd Commission, 1/11/07, p. 17; Ben-Israel 2007, p. 1; National Public Radio, 9/22/06.

4. Shaul Mofaz, Testimony before the Winograd Commission,12/6/06, p. 21; Kfir 2006, p. 150; Harel and Issacharoff 2008, pp. 75, 127; Rapoport 2007, pp. 95–96; Farkash, in Brom and Elran 2007, p. 81; Yaalon 2008, p. 204.

5. See, inter alia, Avi Dichter, Testimony before the Winograd Commission, 11/23/06, pp. 2, 5; Shelah and Limor 2007, pp. 46–49; Aluf Benn, *Haaretz*, 7/13/06.

6. Aluf Benn, *Haaretz*, 7/26/06.

7. Shelah and Limor 2007, p. 49.

8. Harel and Issacharoff 2008, p. 165; Kfir 2006, pp. 32, 228; Shelah and Limor 2007, pp. 53, 88, 277. Regarding "political time," see Amir Peretz, Testimony before the Winograd Commission, 1/24/07, p. 35; Amos Harel and Avi Issacharoff, *Haaretz*, 7/28/06; Anat Tal-Shir and Tzadok Yechezkeli, *Yediot Aharonoth*, 8/18/06; Ynet, 7/15/06 and 7/27/06; Rapoport 2007, pp. 32–33; David Cloud, *New York Times*, 7/22/06.

9. Ynet, 7/1/7/06; Shelah and Limor 2007, p. 121; *Haaretz*, editorial, 7/28/06; Shmuel Rosner and Aluf Benn, *Haaretz*, 7/28/06; *Haaretz* 7/17/07, Harel and Issacharoff 2008, p. 362.

10. Abdel Monem Said-Aly, Middle East Brief #2, October 2006, Crown Center for Middle East Studies; Ynet, 7/24/06; Susser and Heller, in Brom and Elran 2007, pp. 177, 210–211.

11. Rapoport 2007, pp. 24–25; Harel and Issacharoff 2008, p. 75; Dov Weisglass, Testimony before the Winograd Commission, 1/11/07, p. 17.

12. Amos Harel and Avi Issacharoff, *Haaretz*, 4/2/07; Shelah and Limor 2007, pp. 43–44, 55.

13. Judge Winograd, in Testimony of Benjamin Ben Eliezer before the Winograd Commission, 11/28/06, p. 27, and in Testimony of Ehud Olmert, 2/1/07, p. 39; Professor Gabison, in Testimony of Benjamin Ben Eliezer, 11/28/06, pp. 23, 29; General Nadal, in Testimony of Ehud Olmert, 2/1/07, p. 36, Testimony of Shaul Mofaz,12/6/06, p. 43; Testimony of Amir Peretz, 1/24/07, p. 44; State of Israel, *Winograd Commission: Interim Report*, 2007b (hereafter cited as *Winograd Commission: Interim Report*), pp. 111, 115–116, 120–121, 135.

14. Shelah and Limor 2007, p. 23; Kfir 2006, p. 21.

15. Harel and Issacharoff 2008, p. 163; Rapoport 2007, pp. 27–28; Shelah and Limor 2007, pp. 49–51; Amos Harel and Avi Issacharoff, *Haaretz*, 4/2/07.

16. Shelah and Limor 2007, pp. 49–51; Harel and Issacharoff 2008, pp. 163–164; Rapoport 2007, pp. 29, 30.

17. Shelah and Limor 2007, p. 54; Kfir 2006, p. 22; Rapoport 2007, pp. 34–35.

18. Yoram Turbovich, Testimony before the Winograd Commission, 12/27/06, p. 24; Rapoport 2007, pp. 33, 35.

19. Ofir Pinnes-Paz, Testimony before the Winograd Commission, 1/7/07, pp. 4, 13, 25;Yitzhak Herzog, Testimony before the Winograd Commission, 1/18/07, p. 39; *Winograd Commission: Interim Report*, pp. 121, 124; Avi Dichter, Testimony before the Winograd Commission, 11/23/06, pp. 4, 12; Eli Yishai, Testimony before the Winograd Commission, 11/8/06, p. 7; Shaul Mofaz, Testimony before the Winograd Commission, 12/6/06, p. 29.

20. Official website of the Premier's Office, www.pmo.gov.il/PMO/Government/Decisions.

21. *Winograd Commission: Interim Report*, pp. 119, 131; Justice Winograd in Dan Halutz, Testimony before the Winograd Commission, 12/28/07, p. 29.

22. Harel and Issacharoff 2008, p. 171; Rapoport 2007, p. 38.

23. An alternative account of the IDF document presents a different picture, though it is unclear whether the differences reflect errors in the accounts or were simply drawn from different parts of the document. Both versions strengthen the impression of ambiguously defined objectives. According to this version, they were (1) inflicting a *severe* blow to Hezbollah; (2) *preparing* for *extraction* of the abducted soldiers; (3) *preparing* for the destruction of Hezbollah targets near the border; and (4) acting to *disrupt* rocket fire. Later versions of the document further called for "*reducing* Iran's involvement in Lebanon," preventing Hezbollah's reconstruction, and eliminating its leadership. Harel and Issacharoff 2008, pp. 187–188; Rapoport 2007, p. 41; Zeev Schiff, *Haaretz*, 10/20/06.

24. Rapoport 2007, pp. 127–129.

25. Shelah and Limor 2007, p. 122.

26. State of Israel, *Winograd Commission: Final Report*, 2008 (hereafter cited as *Winograd Commission: Final Report*), p. 83.

27. Shelah and Limor 2007, pp. 163–164.

28. *Winograd Commission: Final Report*, part 1, p. 86; Shelah and Limor 2007, pp. 163–164.

29. *Winograd Commission: Final Report*, pp. 89, 92; Shelah and Limor 2007, p. 177; Matthews 2008, pp. 48, 50.

30. Official website of the Premier's Office, www.pmo.gov.il/PMO/Archive/Decisions; *Winograd Commission: Final Report*, p. 185.

31. Shelah and Limor 2007, pp. 41, 49–51, 54; Yoram Turbovich, Testimony before the Winograd Commission, 12/27/06, p. 25; Yitzhak Herzog, Testimony before the Winograd Commission, 1/18/07, pp. 9, 34; Harel and Issacharoff 2008, pp. 163–164; Rapoport 2007, pp. 29, 34–36; Amos Harel and Avi Issacharoff, *Haaretz*, 4/2/06; Kfir 2006, p. 22; Eiland, in Brom and Elran 2007, p. 29.

32. *Winograd Commission: Final Report*, pp. 100, 115; Shelah and Limor 2007, pp. 88, 167; Aluf Benn and Akiva Eldar, *Haaretz*, 10/1/06; Rapoport 2007, pp. 201–202; Harel and Issacharoff 2008, pp. 184–186.

33. *Winograd Commission: Final Report*, p. 524; Harel and Issacharoff 2008, p. 390; Rapoport 2007, p. 126.

34. Aluf Benn, *Haaretz*, 7/28/06.

35. *Winograd Commission: Final Report*, pp. 180, 182–184, 520; Shelah and Limor 2007, pp. 313–314; Harel and Issacharoff 2008, pp. 390, 393.

36. *Winograd Commission: Final Report*, pp. 252, 521, 397, 524–527, 538, 545.

37. Harel and Issacharoff 2008, p. 172.

38. *Winograd Commission: Interim Report*, pp. 118, 121.

39. Ibid., p. 124.

40. Shelah and Limor 2007, pp. 55, 57–58, 60–61, 87; Kfir 2006, pp. 24–25; *Winograd Commission: Interim Report*, p. 122; Justice Winograd in Ofir Pinnes-Paz, Testimony before the Winograd Commission, 1/7/07, p. 11; Dan Halutz, Testimony before the Winograd Commission, 1/28/07, p. 21; Ehud Olmert, Testimony before the Winograd Commission, 2/1/07, pp. 4, 23–24; *Winograd Commission: Final Report*, p. 521; Rapoport 2007, p. 123.

41. Halutz interview with Nahum Barnea and Shimon Shiffer, *Yediot Aharonoth*, 8/25/06; *Yediot Aharonoth*, Yom Kippur Magazine, 10/1/06; *Haaretz*, 4/25/07; Harel and Issacharoff 2008, pp. 173, 188; Rapoport 2007, p. 131.

42. *Winograd Commission: Final Report*, p. 100; Shelah and Limor 2007, pp. 88, 90, 167.

43. Kfir 2006, pp. 35, 37.

44. *Winograd Commission: Final Report*, pp. 96–98; Harel and Issacharoff 2008, p. 186; Rapoport 2007, p. 202; Shelah and Limor 2007, pp. 119, 167.

45. *Winograd Commission: Final Report*, pp. 89, 92; Shelah and Limor 2007, p. 177; Matthews 2008, pp. 48, 50.

46. Shelah and Limor 2007, p. 307; Harel and Issacharoff 2008, p. 312; Rapoport 2007, p. 190; Kfir 2006, p. 230.

47. Harel and Issacharoff 2008, p. 302.

48. Shelah and Limor 2007, p. 293; Ronen Bergman, *Yediot Aharonoth*, 8/8/06; *Winograd Commission: Final Report*, p. 112.

49. Shelah and Limor 2007, pp. 350–351; *Haaretz*, 8/9/06 and 8/10/06; Kaplinski interview, *Yediot Aharonoth*, Weekend Magazine, 10/12/07; *Yediot Aharonoth*, 8/11/06.

50. *Winograd Commission: Final Report*, p. 192; Shelah and Limor 2007, pp. 307, 345, 414.

51. *Winograd Commission: Final Report*, p. 191; Harel and Issacharoff 2008, p. 409; Kfir 2006, pp. 285–286; Shelah and Limor 2007, pp. 350–351; Benjamin Ben-Eliezer, Testimony before the Winograd Commission, 11/28/06, p. 29.

52. Olmert interview with Aluf Benn and Yossi Verter, *Haaretz*, 9/22/06.

53. Rapoport 2007, p. 133.

54. Shaul Mofaz, Testimony before the Winograd Commission, 12/6/06, p. 43; Shelah and Limor 2007, p. 55.

55. Verter, *Haaretz*, 7/13/06; *Winograd Commission: Interim Report*, p. 118.

56. Israel Ministry of Foreign Affairs website; Shelah and Limor 2007, p. 125; *Yediot Aharonoth*, Weekend Magazine, 8/11/06; *Haaretz*, 7/20/06; Ynet, 8/12/06; Ben-Meir, in Brom and Elran 2007, pp. 90–91.

57. Shelah and Limor 2007, p. 210.

58. Ibid., p. 266.

59. Yaalon interview, in Ari Shavit, *Haaretz*, 9/14/06.

60. Harel and Issacharoff 2008, p. 390; Shelah and Limor 2007, pp. 303, 349; Yaalon 2008, p. 210.

61. *Winograd Commission: Interim Report*, pp. 119, 123–124, 133; Gabison, in Amir Peretz, Testimony before the Winograd Commission, 1/24/07, p. 75, and in Ehud Barak, Testimony before the Winograd Commission, 1/28/06, p. 19; Winograd in Amir Peretz, Testimony before the Winograd Commission, 1/24/07, pp. 33–34; Rapoport 2007, p. 36.

62. *Winograd Commission: Final Report*, 100, 160; *Winograd Commission: Interim Report*, pp. 111, 115; Judge Winograd, in Testimony of Benjamin Ben Eliezer before the Winograd Commission, 11/28/06, p. 27, and in Testimony of Ehud Olmert, 2/1/07, p. 39; Professor Gabison, in Testimony of Benjamin Ben Eliezer, 11/28/06, pp. 23, 29; General Nadal, in Testimony of Ehud Olmert, 2/1/07, p. 36, and Testimony of Shaul Mofaz, 12/6/06, p. 43.

63. Amos Harel and Aluf Benn, *Haaretz*, 7/13/06; Aluf Benn, Ilan Gideon, and Amos Harel, *Haaretz*, 7/13/06; Aluf Benn, *Haaretz*, 7/16/06; Ehud Olmert, Testimony before the Winograd Commission, 2/1/07, p. 36; Chaim Nadal, in Ehud Olmert, Testimony before the Winograd Commission, 2/1/07, p. 36; *Winograd Commission: Interim Report*, p. 123.

64. *Winograd Commission: Final Report*, p. 121; Ynet, 7/24/06.

65. Halutz interview with Nahum Barnea and Shimon Schiffer, *Yediot Aharonoth*, 8/25/06; *Haaretz*, 8/9/06.

66. *Winograd Commission: Interim Report*, pp. 118, 127, 141–142; Dan Halutz, Testimony before the Winograd Commission, 1/28/07, p. 18; Shelah and Limor 2007, pp. 56–58.

67. Dan Halutz, Testimony before the Winograd Commission, 1/28/07, p. 18; *Yediot Aharonoth*, Yom Kippur Magazine, 10/1/06; *Haaretz*, 8/16/06; *Winograd Commission: Interim Report*, pp. 117, 141–142; Yaalon interview with Ari Shavit, *Haaretz*, 9/14/06; Yaalon 2008, pp. 204, 206; Rapoport 2007, p. 126.

68. *Winograd Commission: Interim Report*, pp. 119–120.

69. *Haaretz*, 8/13/06; Halutz on Israel Channel 10, 8/12/06; Sima Kadmon, *Yediot Aharonoth*, 8/18/08; Ben-Israel, 2007, p. 10.

70. Dan Meridor, State of the Nation Conference, INSS, 10/17/07.

71. Olmert interview with Aluf Benn and Yossi Verter, *Haaretz*, 9/22/06; *Winograd Commission: Final Report*, p. 161; Rapoport 2007, p. 64; Yaalon 2008, pp. 204, 206.

72. Shelah and Limor 2007, pp. 55, 57–58, 60–61; Kfir 2006, pp. 24–25; Harel and Issacharoff 2008, p. 175.

73. *Winograd Commission: Interim Report*, pp. 115, 123, 127; *Winograd Commission: Final Report*, p. 411; Yoram Turbovich, Testimony before Winograd Commission, 12/27/06, p. 27; Harel and Issacharoff 2008, pp. 163–164; Rapoport 2007, pp. 27–30, 33; Shelah and Limor 2007, pp. 49–51, 56; Amos Harel and Avi Issacharoff, *Haaretz*, 4/2/07.

74. *Winograd Commission: Final Report*, p. 161; *Haaretz*, 8/5/06; Shelah and Limor 2007, p. 167; Olmert interview, Aluf Benn and Yossi Verter, *Haaretz*, 9/2/06; *Winograd Commission: Interim Report*, pp. 96–98; Harel and Issacharoff 2008, p. 186; Rapoport 2007, p. 202; Aluf Benn and Akiva Eldar, *Haaretz*, 10/1/06; Scott Wilson, *Washington Post*, 10/22/06.

75. Shelah and Limor 2007, pp. 60–61, 215; Ben-Israel 2007, p. 22; Ronen Bergman, *Yediot Aharonoth*, Weekend Magazine, 8/18/06; *Winograd Commission: Interim Report*, p. 116; Harel and Issacharoff 2008, pp. 312, 409; Yuval Azulay, *Haaretz*, 11/11/07; Yaalon 2008, p. 213.

76. *Winograd Commission: Interim Report*, p. 133; Shelah and Limor 2007, pp. 233–234.

77. Tzipi Livni, Testimony before the Winograd Commission, 1/23/07, p. 25; Shelah and Limor 2007, p. 230, 346; *Winograd Commission: Final Report*, pp. 87–88, 90, 98, 563;.

78. Aluf Benn and Akiva Eldar, *Haaretz*, 10/10/06; Ofir Pinnes-Paz, Testimony before the Winograd Commission, 1/7/07, p. 31.

79. Eiland, in Brom and Elran 2007, p. 31.

80. *Winograd Commission: Final Report*, p. 572.

81. Shelah and Limor 2007, p. 304; Harel and Issacharoff 2008, pp. 388–389; Yaalon 2008, p. 205.

82. Amir Peretz, Testimony before the Winograd Commission, 1/24/07, p. 79.

83. Shelah and Limor 2007, pp. 313–314; Kfir 2006, pp. 231–234, 286–286; *Haaretz*, 8/10/06; Aluf Benn, *Haaretz*, 8/11/0606; Sima Kadmon, *Yediot Aharonoth*, Weekend Magazine, 8/11/06; Harel and Issacharoff 2008, p. 390.

84. *Winograd Commission: Interim Report*, p. 123; Shelah and Limor 2007, p. 115; Ehud Olmert, Testimony before the Winograd Commission, 2/1/07, p. 53; personal communication, senior INSC official, May 2008.

85. *Winograd Commission: Interim Report*, pp. 129, 139; Shelah and Limor 2007, p. 119.

## Conclusions and Recommendations

1. Dror 1992; Senior Officer, 6/24/08; Moshe Arens interview, 6/21/06; Moshe Yaalon interview, 7/20/06; Yossi Beilin interview, 8/12/06; Amnon Lipkin-Shahak interview, 6/15/06; David Ivri interview, 6/4/06; Gideon Sheffer interview, 6/21/06. Uzi Dayan generally concurs but is less emphatic (interview, 5/23/05).

2. Dayan, in Erez 2006, pp. 26–27; Miztna, in Erez, 2006, p. 57.

3. *Yediot Aharonoth*, 9/1/05.

4. Dan Meridor interview, 5/30/06.

5. Giora Eiland, lecture, Jaffee Center, Tel Aviv University, 10/31/06; Eiland, in Brom and Elran 2007; Harel and Isascharoff 2008, p. 394; Peri 2006, p. 59; Dayan interview, 5/23/06.

6. Dan Meridor interview, 9/1/11; Gilead Sher interview, 12/23/09.

7. Jones 2002, p. 128; Shlaim 1975, pp. 214–215; Shlaim 1976, pp. 368–369; Ben-Meir 1986, pp. 103–104; Dan Margalit, in *Haaretz*, 10/7/77; Dror 1978, p. 116.

8. Dror 1989, p. 170.

9. Ben-Meir 1986, p. 123; Tamir 1988, p. 302.

10. Dror 1989, pp. 67, 170.

11. State of Israel, *The Public-Professional Committee for a General Assessment of the Civil Service and Institutions Supported by the National Budget*, 1989; BESA 1992, p. 36.

12. Knesset Bill #2030, 1/15/91; Yaari 2004, p. 37; State Comptroller, *Report on the National Security Council*, 2006, p. 19.

13. Jones 2002, p. 129.

14. *Yediot Aharonoth*, 1/29/99; Gideon Sheffer interview, 6/21/06, David Ivri interview, 6/4/06; Netanyahu, Testimony before the Winograd Commission, 1/11/07, pp. 14–15; Cabinet Decision 4889, 3/3/99. Hebrew version of the law is available at http://www.google.com/url ?sa=t&rct=j&q=&esrc=s&source=web&cd=1&cts=1331743478615&ved=0CCUQFjAA&url= http%3A%2F%2Fwww.nsc.gov.il%2FNSCWeb%2FDocs%2Fgoverndecision4889.doc&ei= 9MpgT-2ZM8PVgQfTrNiaCA&usg=AFQjCNFcN5wf8G1XMQYHXFzMeKECN02Z5A&sig2= HPn-mWWfQy4oCQ-ZdfSDKw.

15. State Comptroller, *Report on the National Security Council*, 2006, pp. 28–30, 32–36, 40.

16. National Security Staff Law, enacted by the Knesset on 7/29/08 and published in *Reshumot*, 8/7/08.

17. The following section is a composite picture of the INSC's status today, drawing on the author's understanding of a series of interviews conducted with cabinet ministers and former and present INSC officials. The interviewees include Ministers Isaac Herzog, 1/10/10; Dan Meridor, 9/1/11; and Moshe Yaalon, 11/1/11; NSA Yaacov Amidror, 8/24/11; former NSA Dani Arditi, 7/21/09; Deputy NSA Eran Lerman, 8/30/11; Deputy NSA Sima Shine, 7/21/09; former INSC legal adviser Roy Dick-Keidar, 8/11/11; and former head of the IDF Strategic Planning Division, Udi Dekel, 6/24/07. State Comptroller, *Report on the Implementation of the INSC Law and the Turkish Flotilla*, 2012.

18. State Comptroller, *Report on the Implementation of the INSC Law and the Turkish Flotilla*, 2012.

19. Uzi Dayan interview, 5/23/06.

20. Interview with Israel Michaeli, Policy and Strategy Institute, Interdisciplinary Center, Herzliya, 2004; author's personal involvement as member of the INSC staff; Aluf Ben, *Haaretz*, 6/26/03, p. B1; and 3/8/03; Moshe Yaalon interview, 7/20/06; Amnon Lipkin-Shahak interview,

6/15/06; Amir Oren, *Haaretz*, 7/28/00; 9/17/00; and 11/29/01; cabinet minister, private communication, Fall 2011.

21. State Comptroller, *Report on the National Security Council*, 2006, p. 42.

22. Destler 1972, pp. 100–102; Destler et al. 1984, pp. 166, 186–187; Thayer 1971, p. 555; Johnson 1969, p. 719.

23. For example, see interview with former acting NSA Gideon Sheffer, 6/21/06.

24. Http://www.newamerica.net/node/7806.

25. The following section draws on Arian 1997; Carmon 2009; Presidential Committee on Governmental Reform, Report, 2007, available at http://www.ceci.org.il/_Uploads /dbsAttachedFiles/finalreport.pdf and http://www.knesset.gov.il/allsite/mark02/h0203382 .htm#TQL.

# Bibliography

Akehurst, M. 1981. "The Peace Treaty between Egypt and Israel." *International Relations* 7 (l): 1035–1052.

Akzin, B., and Dror, Y. 1966. *National Planning in Israel* [in Hebrew]. Tel Aviv: Administrative Seminar Press. [Originally published in English as *Israel: High-Pressure Planning*. Syracuse: Syracuse University Press.]

Allison, G. T. 1969. "Conceptual Models of the Cuban Missile Crisis." *American Political Science Review*, September, 689–718.

———. 1971. *The Essence of Decision*. Boston: Little, Brown.

Allison, G. T., and Halperin, M. H. 1972. "Bureaucratic Politics." *World Politics* 24 (Spring): 40–79.

Allison, G. T., and Szanton, P. 1976. *Remaking Foreign Policy: The Organizational Connection*. New York: Basic Books.

Amidror, B. 1982. "Governmental System of National Security" [in Hebrew]. *Maarachot*, August, 14–22.

Arens, M. 1995. *Broken Covenant* [in Hebrew]. Tel Aviv: Yediot Aharonoth.

Arian, A. 1997. *The Next Elections: How Will We Vote?* [in Hebrew]. Jerusalem: Israel Democracy Institute.

———. 2002. *Government Changes in Israel: Influences on the Structure and Workings of Government* [in Hebrew].

———. 2005. *Politics in Israel*. Washington, DC: Congressional Quarterly Press.

Arian, A., Nachmias, D., and Amir, R. 2002. *Executive Governance in Israel*. New York: Palgrave.

Arieli, S., and Sfard, M. 2008. *The Wall of Folly* [in Hebrew]. Tel Aviv: Aliat Hagag.

Aronson, S. 1978. *Conflict and Bargaining in the Middle East*. Baltimore: Johns Hopkins University Press.

———. 1982–1983. "Israel's Leaders, Domestic Order and Foreign Policy." *Jerusalem Journal of International Relations* 6 (4): 1–29.

Art, R. J. 1985. *Reorganizing America's Defense*. Washington, DC: Pergamon.

Avineri, S. 1978. "Peacemaking: The Arab-Israel Conflict." *Foreign Affairs* 57 (Fall): 51–69.

———. 1982. "Beyond Camp David." *Foreign Policy* 46 (Spring): 19–36.

———. 1986. "Ideology and Foreign Policy." *Jerusalem Quarterly* 37:3–13.

Baehr, P. R. 1973. "The Foreign Policy of the Netherlands." In R. P. Barston, ed., *The Other Powers*. London: Allen and Unwin.

Ball, D. 1974. "The Blind Men and the Elephant: A Critique of Bureaucratic Politics Theory." *Australian Outlook* 28 (1): 71–92.

Barak, O., and Sheffer, G. 2006. "Israel's Security Network and Its Impact." *International Journal of Middle East Studies* 38:235–261.

———. 2007. "The Study of Civil-Military Relations in Israel: A New Perspective." *Israel Studies* 12 (1): 1–27.

Bar-Joseph, U. 1995. *Intelligence Intervention in the Politics of Democratic States: The United States, Israel, and Britain*. University Park: Pennsylvania State University Press.

———. 1999. "Towards a Paradigm Shift in Israel's National Security Conception." *Israel Affairs* 6 (3–4): 99–114.

———, ed. 2001. *Israel's National Security towards the 21st Century*. Portland, OR: Frank Cass.

———. 2004–2005. "The Paradox of Israeli Power." *Survival* 46 (4): 137–156.

Bar-Or, A. 2006. "Political-Military Relations in Israel, 1996–2003." *Israel Affairs* 12 (3): 365–375.

Bar-Siman-Tov, Y. 1988. "Bar Lev Line Revisited." *Journal of Strategic Studies* 2 (2): 149–76.

———. 1994. *Israel and the Peace Process, 1977–1982*. Albany: State University of New York Press.

———. 2001. "Peace Policy as Domestic and Foreign Policy." In S. Sofer, ed., *Peacemaking in a Divided Society*. London: Frank Cass.

———. 2007. *The Israeli-Palestinian Conflict: From Conflict Resolution to Conflict Management*. New York: Palgrave.

Bar-Tal, D. 1983. *Masada Syndrome*. International Center for Peace in the Middle East, Discussion Papers 3.

———. 1999. *Security Concerns: Insights from the Israeli Experience*. London: JAI Press.

Bar-Zohar, M. 2007. *Shimon Peres: The Biography*. New York: Random House.

Barnett, M., ed. 1996. *Israel in Comparative Perspective*. Albany: State University of New York Press.

Barzilai, G. 1987. *Democracy at War* [in Hebrew]. Doctoral dissertation, Hebrew University.

Ben-Ami, S. 2004. *A Front without a Rearguard* [in Hebrew]. Tel Aviv: Yediot Aharonoth.

———. 2006. *Scars of War, Wounds of Peace*. Oxford, Oxford University Press.

Ben-Eliezer, U. 1998. *The Making of Israeli Militarism*. Bloomington: Indiana University Press.

Ben-Israel, Y. 2007. *The Missile War Israel-Hizballah: Summer 2006* [in Hebrew]. Tel Aviv: Tel Aviv University, School of Government.

Ben-Meir, Y. 1986. *National Security Decision Making: The Israeli Case*. Boulder, CO: Westview Press.

————. 1995. *Civil-Military Relations in Israel*. New York: Columbia University Press.

Benn, A. 2002. "The Last of the Patriarchs." *Foreign Affairs* 81 (3).

Ben Porat, Y. 1981. *Talks* [in Hebrew]. Jerusalem: Eidanim.

Benziman, U. 1981. *Premier under Siege* [in Hebrew]. Tel Aviv: Adam Press.

————. 1985. *Sharon: An Israeli Caesar*. New York: Adama Books.

Bercovitch, J. 1985. "An Analysis of Negotiations." *Crossroads* 17:83–106.

————. 1986. "A Case Study of Mediation as a Method of International Conflict Resolution." *Review of International Studies* 12:43–65.

Bergman, R. 2002. *Authority Given* [in Hebrew]. Tel Aviv: Miskal.

BESA [Begin-Sadat Center for Strategic Studies]. 1992. *National Security Decision Making in Israel* [in Hebrew]. Israel: BESA Center, in Cooperation with the IDF Command and Staff College.

————. 2007. *The Second Lebanon War and Its Aftermath*. Discussions on National Security #22, March.

Bilski, R., ed. 1980. *Can Planning Replace Politics?* The Hague: Martinus Nijhoff.

Brandriss, M. G. 1982. *Internal Politics and Foreign Policy in Israel: The Search for Peace, 1967–1973*. Ann Arbor: University of Michigan Press.

Brecher, M. 1973. *The Foreign Policy System of Israel: Setting, Images, Process*. New Haven: Yale University Press.

————. 1974. "Inputs and Decisions for War and Peace: The Israeli Experience." *International Studies Quarterly* 18 (12): 131–177.

————. 1975. *Decisions in Israel's Foreign Policy*. New Haven: Yale University Press.

————. 1980. *Decisions in Crisis*. Berkeley: University of California Press.

Brom, S., and Elran, M., eds. 2007. *The Second Lebanon War: Strategic Perspectives*. Tel Aviv: INSS.

Brownstein, L. 1977. "Decision Making in Israeli Foreign Policy: An Unplanned Process." *Political Science Quarterly* 92 (2): 259–279.

Byman, D. *A High Price: The Triumphs and Failures of Israeli Counterterrorism*. New York: Oxford University Press, 2011.

Carmon, A. 2009. *Reinventing Israeli Democracy: A Proposal for Correcting Governance in Israel*. Jerusalem: Israel Democracy Institute, http://www.idi.org.il/PublicationsCatalog/Documents/BOOK_7101/Book_7101.pdf [in Hebrew].

Carter, J. E. 1982. *Keeping Faith*. Toronto: Bantam.

————. 1985. *The Blood of Abraham*. Boston: Houghton Mifflin.

————. 1987. "Middle East Peace: New Opportunities." *Washington Quarterly* 10 (3): 5–14.

Caspit, B., and Kfir, I. 1997. *Netanyahu: The Road to Power* [in Hebrew]. Tel Aviv: Alpha.

Clarke, D. L., and Cohen, A. S. 1986. "The United States, Israel and the Lavi Fighter." *Middle East Journal* 40 (1): 16–32.

Clawson, P., and Eisenstadt, M., eds. 2000. *The Last Arab-Israeli Battlefield? Implications of an Israeli Withdrawal from Lebanon*. Monographs and Special Studies. Washington, DC: Washington Institute for Near East Policy.

Clinton, W. J. 2005. *My Life*. London: Arrow.

Coffman-Wittes, T., ed. 2005. *How Israelis and Palestinians Negotiate: A Cross-Cultural Analysis of the Oslo Peace Process*. Washington, DC: United States Institute of Peace Press.

Cohen, R. 1994. "Israel's Starry-Eyed Foreign Policy." *Middle East Quarterly* 1 (2).

Cohen, S. A. 2006. *The IDF's Over-Subordination: Changing Patterns of Relations between the Civil and Military Echelons in Israel*. Ramat Gan: BESA Center.

Cordesman, A. H. 2002. *Peace and War*. Westport, CT: Praeger.

———. 2006. *Arab-Israeli Military Forces in an Era of Asymmetric Wars*. Westport, CT: Praeger Security International.

Dayan, M. 1981. *Breakthrough: A Personal Account of the Egypt-Israel Peace Negotiations*. New York: Knopf. (Hebrew version: 1981. Jerusalem: Eidanim.)

Destler, I. M. 1972. *Presidents, Bureaucrats, and Foreign Policy*, Princeton, NJ: Princeton University Press.

Destler, I. M., Gelb, L. H., and Lake, A. 1984. *Our Own Worst Enemy: The Unmaking of American Foreign Policy*. New York: Simon and Schuster.

Diskin, A., and Galnoor, I. 1982. "Political Distances and Parliamentary Government: Debates over the Peace Agreement with Egypt" [in Hebrew]. *State Government and International Relations* 18:5–26.

Dowty, A. 1980. "In Defense of Camp David." *Commentary* 69 (4): 59–68.

———. 1997. *The Role of Domestic Politics in Israeli Peacemaking*. Jerusalem: Leonard Davis Institute, Hebrew University of Jerusalem.

———. 2005. *Israel and Palestine*. Cambridge: Polity.

Dromi, U. 2005. *The Israel Defense Forces and the National Economy of Israel*. Jerusalem: Israel Democracy Institute.

Dror, Y. 1971. *Ventures in Policy Sciences*. New York: Elsevier.

———. 1978. *Improving Policymaking and Administration in Israel* [in Hebrew]. Tel Aviv: Sifriat Haminhal.

———. 1982a. *Improvement of Policy Making in Israel*. Haifa: Neeman Institute.

———. 1982b. *Public Policymaking Reexamined*. New Brunswick, NJ: Transaction Books.

———. 1984. *Policymaking under Adversity*. New Brunswick, NJ: Transaction Books.

———. 1989a. *Grand Strategy for Israel* [in Hebrew]. Jerusalem: Academon.

———. 1989b. *Memorandum to the Prime Minister. Book 2: To Build a State* [in Hebrew]. Jerusalem: Academon.

———. 1992. *Memorandum for the Prime Minister A: Situation of the Nation*, [in Hebrew]. Jerusalem: Academon.

———. 2005. *Epistle to an Israeli Jewish-Zionist Leader* [in Hebrew]. Jerusalem: Carmel.

———. 2006. *A Take Off Politico-Military Grand Strategy for Israel* [Manuscript, August].

———. 2011. *Israeli Statecraft: National Security Challenges and Responses*. Milton Park, UK: Routledge.

Drucker, R. 2002. *Harakiri-Ehud Barak: The Failure* [in Hebrew]. Tel Aviv: Yediot Aharonoth.

Drucker, R., and Shelah, O. 2005. *Boomerang: The Failure of Leadership in the Second Intifada* [in Hebrew]. Jerusalem: Keter.

Eban, A. 1977. *Autobiography*. Tel Aviv: Steimatzky.

———. 1978. "Camp David—The Unfinished Business." *Foreign Affairs* 57 (Winter): 343–354.

Edelist, R. 2003. *Ehud Barak: Fighting the Demons* [in Hebrew]. Or Yehuda: Kinneret.

Eiland, G. 2007. *The Defense Budget* [in Hebrew]. INSS report, Strategic Focus, 6, June 1.

Eitan, R. 1985. *A Soldier's Story* [in Hebrew]. Tel Aviv: Maariv.

Eran, O. 1979. *A Comparative Analysis of Foreign and Defense Policy Oriented Research Establishments*. Jaffee Center for Strategic Studies, Tel Aviv University, #1, May.

Erez, R., ed. 2006. *Relations between the Civil and Military Echelons in Israel* [in Hebrew]. Jaffee Center for Strategic Studies, Memorandum 68, November 2003 and Memorandum 82.

Feldman, S. 1997. "Israel's National Security: Perceptions and Policy." In S. Feldman and A. Toukan, eds., *Bridging the Gap: A Future Security Architecture for the Middle East*. New York: Carnegie.

Feldman, S., and Reichnitz-Kijner, H. 1984. *Deception, Consensus, and War: Israel in Lebanon*. Jaffee Center for Strategic Studies, Tel Aviv University, Paper #27, October.

Freedman, R. O., ed. 1982. *Israel in the Begin Era*. New York: Praeger.

———, ed. 2000. *Israel's First Fifty Years*. Gainesville: University of Florida Press.

Freilich, C. D. 2006. "National Security Decision Making in Israel: Processes, Strengths and Pathologies." *Middle East Journal* 60 (4): 635–663.

Friedlander, M. A. 1983. *Sadat and Begin: The Domestic Politics of Peacemaking*. Boulder, CO: Westview Press.

Friedlander, S., and Cohen, R. 1975. "The Personality Correlates of Belligerence in International Conflict." *Comparative Politics* 7 (June): 155–186.

Friedman, T. L. 1989. *From Beirut to Jerusalem*. New York: Farrar, Straus & Giroux.

Garfinkle, A. 2000. *Politics and Society in Modern Israel*. 2nd ed. Armonk, NY: M. E. Sharpe.

Gazit, M. 1981. "The Role of the Foreign Ministry." *Jerusalem Quarterly* 18:3–14.

———. 2002. *Israeli Diplomacy and the Quest for Peace*. London: Frank Cass.

Gazit, S. 2003. *Trapped Fools: Thirty Years of Israeli Policy in the Territories*. London: Frank Cass.

George, A. L. 1969. "The Operational Code." *International Studies Quarterly* 13 (2): 190–222.

———. 1980. *Presidential Decision Making in Foreign Policy: The Effective Use of Information and Advice*. Boulder, CO: Westview Press.

Gilmour, D. 1983. *Lebanon: The Fractured Country*. Oxford: Martin Robertson.

Gilon, C. 2000. *Shin-Beth between the Schisms* [in Hebrew]. Tel Aviv: Yediot Aharonoth.

Golan, G. 1982–1983. "The Soviet Union and the Israeli Action in Lebanon." *International Affairs* 59 (1): 7–16.

———. 2004. "The Israeli Disengagement Initiative." *Middle East Policy* 11 (4): 64–71.

———. 2008. *Israel and Palestine: Peace Plans and Proposals from Oslo to Disengagement*. Princeton, NJ: Markus Wiener Publishers.

Goldberg, G. 2006. "The Growing Militarization of the Israeli Political System." *Israel Affairs* 12 (3): 377–394.

Gorenberg, G. 2006. *The Accidental Empire: Israel and the Birth of the Settlements*. New York: Henry Holt.

Guttmann, E. 1983. "Begin's Israel." *International Journal* 38 (4): 690–699.

Haber, E. 1978. *Menachem Begin: The Legend and the Man*. New York: Delacorte.

Haber, E., Schiff, Z., and Yaari, E. 1979. *The Year of the Dove*. New York: Bantam. (Hebrew version: 1978. *Shnat Havonah*. Tel Aviv: Zmora Bita.)

Haig, A. M. 1984. *Caveat: Realism, Reagan, and Foreign Policy*. New York: Macmillan.

Halevy, E. 2006. *Man in the Shadows*. New York: St. Martin's Press.

Handel, M. I. 1973. *Israeli Political-Military Doctrine*. Cambridge, MA: Center for International Affairs, Harvard University.

Har, E. 1987. *Today, War Will Break out* [in Hebrew]. Tel Aviv: Eidanim.

Harel, A., and Issacharoff, A. 2004. *The Seventh War* [in Hebrew]. Tel Aviv: Yediot Aharonoth.

———. 2008. *Spider's Web* [in Hebrew]. Tel Aviv: Yediot Aharonoth.

Harkabi, Y. 1977. *Arab Strategies and Israel's Response*. New York: Free Press.

———. 1983. *Bar Kochba Syndrome: Risk and Realism in International Politics*. Chappaqua, NY: Rossel Books.

———. 1984. "The Intelligence-Policymaker Tangle." *Jerusalem Quarterly* 30:125–131.

———. 1988. *Israel's Fateful Decisions*. London: I. B. Tauris.

Hartz, L. 1955. *The Liberal Tradition in America*. New York: Harcourt.

Hasdai, Y. 1982. "Doers and Thinkers in the IDF." *Jerusalem Quarterly* 24 (Summer): 13–25.

Hazony, Y. 2001. *The Jewish State: The Struggle for Israel's Soul*. New York: Basic Books.

Hefez, N., and Bloom, G. 2006. *Ariel Sharon: A Life*. New York: Random House.

Heller, M. 1979–1980. "Begin's False Autonomy." *Foreign Policy* 37 (Winter): 111–132.

———. 2000. *Continuity and Change in Israeli Security Policy*. London: Adelphi Papers, 335, International Institute for Security Studies.

Hilsman, R. 1959. "The Foreign Policy Consensus." *Journal of Conflict Resolution* 3:361–382.

Horowitz, D., and Lissak, M. 1984. "Democracy and National Security in a Protracted Conflict." *Jerusalem Quarterly* 51 (Summer): 3–40.

———. 1989. *Trouble in Utopia: The Overburdened Polity of Israel*. Albany: State University of New York Press.

Hoxie, R. G. 1982. "The National Security Council." *Presidential Studies Quarterly* 12 (1): 108–113.

Hurewitz, J. C. 1982. *Middle East Politics: The Military Dimensions*. Boulder, CO: Westview Press.

Inbar, E. 1983. "Israeli Strategic Thinking." *Journal of Strategic Studies* 6 (1): 36–59.

———. 1994. "Israel's Strategic Environment." *Strategic Review*, 34–40.

———. 1998. *Israeli National Security, 1973–1996*. BESA, Security and Policy Studies #38.

———. 2007. "How Israel Bungled the Second Lebanon War." *Middle East Quarterly* 14 (3): 57–65.

Indyk, M. 2009. *Innocent Abroad: An Intimate Account of American Peace Diplomacy in the Middle East*. New York: Simon and Schuster.

Jackson, H., ed. 1965. *The National Security Council*. New York: Praeger.

Jacoby, T. A. 2007. *Bridging the Barrier: Israeli Unilateral Disengagement*. Aldershot, UK: Ashgate.

Janis, I. L. 1983. *Groupthink*. Boston: Houghton Mifflin.

Jervis, R. 1968. "Hypotheses on Misperception." *World Politics* 20 (3): 454–479.

———. 1976. *Perception and Misperception in International Politics*. Princeton, NJ: Princeton University Press.

———. 1982–1983. "Deterrence and Perception." *International Security* 7 (3): 3–30.

Jervis, R., Lebow, R. N., and Gross, J. 1985. *Psychology and Deterrence*. Baltimore: Johns Hopkins University Press.

Johnson, R. H. 1969. "The National Security Council: The Relevance of Its Past to Its Future." *Orbis*, Fall, 709–735.

Jones, C. 2002. "The Foreign Policy of Israel." In R. Hinnebusch and A. Ehteshami, *The Foreign Policies of Middle East States*, 115–136. Boulder, CO: Lynne Rienner.

Jureidini, P. A., and McLaurin, R. D. 1981. *Beyond Camp David*. Syracuse: Syracuse University Press.

Kaarbo, J. 1996. "Power and Influence in Foreign Policy Making: The Role of Junior Coalition Partners in German and Israeli Foreign Policy." *International Studies Quarterly* 40: 501–530.

Kalb, M., and Kalb B. 1974. *Kissinger*. New York: Dell.

Karsh, E. 1996. *Between War and Peace: Dilemmas of Israelis Security*. London: Cass.

Katz, S. 1981. *The Hollow Peace*. Tel Aviv: Dvir.

Kaye, D. D. 2002–2003. "The Israeli Decision to Withdraw from Lebanon: Political Leadership and Security Policy." *Political Science Quarterly* 117 (4): 561–585.

Kfir, I. 1998. *Barak: Autobiography* [in Hebrew]. Tel Aviv: Alpha.

———. 2006. *The Earth Trembled*. Tel Aviv: Maariv.

Kissinger, H. A. 1966. "Domestic Structure and Foreign Policy." *Daedalus* 95 (Spring): 503–529.

———. 1969. *American Foreign Policy*. New York: Norton.

———. 1979. *White House Years*. Boston: Little, Brown.

———. 1982. *Years of Upheaval*. Boston: Little, Brown.

Klein, M. 2003. *The Jerusalem Problem*. Gainesville: University of Florida Press.

Klieman, A., and Levite, A. 1993. *Deterrence in the Middle East: Where Theory and Practice Converge*. Boulder, CO: Westview Press.

Klieman, A. S. 1978–1979. "Zionist Diplomacy and Israeli Foreign Policy." *Middle East Review* 11 (2): 11–17.

———. 1990. *Politics In Israel: Israel and the World after Forty Years*. New York: Pergamon Brassey.

———. 2005. "Israeli Negotiating Culture." In T. Cofman-Wittes, *How Israelis and Palestinians Negotiate*. Washington, DC: US Institute for Peace Press.

Lanir, Z. 1985. *Israeli Security Planning in the 1980s*. New York: Praeger.

Lapidot, R. 1979. "The Camp David Agreements: Some Legal Aspects." *Jerusalem Quarterly* 10:14–27.

Laqueur, W. 1978. "The View from Tel Aviv." *Commentary* 66 (1): 29–36.

Levite, A. 1989. *Offense and Defense in Israeli Military Doctrine*. Boulder, CO: Westview Press.

Linowitz, S. M. 1981. "Prospects for the Camp David Peace Process." *SAIS Review*, Summer, 93–100.

Lissak, M., ed. 1984. *Israeli Society and Its Defense Establishment*. London: F. Cass.

Luft, G. 2000. "Israel's Security Zone in Lebanon—A Tragedy?" *Middle East Quarterly*, September, 13–20.

Luttwak, E. N. 1979. "Strategic Implications of the Camp David Accords." *Washington Quarterly*, Spring, 38–43.

Mack, A. 1983. "Israel's War in Lebanon." *Australian Outlook* 37 (1): 1–9.

Mahler, G. S. 2004. *Politics and Government in Israel*. Lanham, MD: Rowman and Littlefield.

Makovsky, D. 1996. *Making Peace with the PLO: The Rabin Government's Road to the Oslo Accord*. Boulder, Co: Westview Press.

Makovsky, D., and White, J. 2006. *Lessons and Implications of the Israeli-Hizballah War*. Washington Institute for Near East Policy, Policy Focus #60, October.

Maman, D., Ben-Ari, E., and Rosenhek, Z. 2001. *Military, State, and Society in Israel*. New Brunswick, NJ: Transaction Publishers.

Maoz, Z. 2006. *Defending the Holy Land*. Ann Arbor: University of Michigan Press.

Marantz, P., and Stein, J. G., eds. 1985. *Peace Making in the Middle East*. London: Croom Helm.

Marcus, J. 1999. "Israel's Defense Policy at a Strategic Crossroads." *Washington Quarterly* 22 (1): 33–48.

Markus, Y. 1979. *Camp David: The Opening to Peace* [in Hebrew]. Tel Aviv: Shocken.

Matthews, M. 2008. *We Were Caught Unprepared: The 2006 Hezbollah-Israeli War*. Occasional Paper 26, US Army Combined Arms Center, Ft. Leavenworth.

Mayer, T., and Ali Mourad, S., eds. 2008. *Jerusalem: Idea and Reality*. London: Routledge.

Meir, Y., and Rahav-Meir, S. 2006. *Days of Disengagement* [in Hebrew]. Tel Aviv: Miskal.

Meital, Y. 2006. *Peace in Tatters: Israel, Palestine, and the Middle East*. Boulder, CO: Lynne Rienner.

Merom, G. 1999. "Israel's National Security and the Myth of Exceptionalism." *Political Science Quarterly* 114 (3): 409–434.

Michael, K. 2007. "The Dilemma behind the Classical Dilemma of Civil-Military Relations." *Armed Forces and Society* 33 (4): 518–546.

Miller, A., Miller, J., and Zetouni, S. 2002. *Sharon: Israel's Warrior-Politician*. Chicago: Academy Chicago.

Ministry of Defense. 2004. *Intelligence and Decision Makers* [in Hebrew]. Tel Aviv: MoD Press.

Nakdimon, S. 1993. *Tamuz in Flames*. Jerusalem: Eidanim.

Naor, A. 1986. *Government at War* [in Hebrew]. Tel Aviv: Lahav.

———. 1988. *Writing on the Wall* [in Hebrew]. Tel Aviv: Eidanim.

———. 2003. "Lessons of the Holocaust versus Territories for Peace, 1967–2001." *Israel Studies* 8 (1): 130–152.

Naveh, D. 1999. *Government Secrets* [in Hebrew]. Tel Aviv: Yediot.

Neumann, R. 1979. "The Middle East after Camp David." *Washington Quarterly*, Spring, 29–37.

O'Brien, W. V. 1982–1983. "Israel in Lebanon." *Middle East Review*, Fall–Winter, 5–14.

Ofer, Z., and Kober, A. 1987. "Intelligence and National Security" [in Hebrew]. Tel Aviv: .Maarachot.

Oren, M. 2003. *Six Days of War: June 1967 and the Making of the Modern Middle East*. New York: Presidio.

Parkinson, B. R. 2007. "Israel's Lebanon War: Ariel Sharon and Operation Peace for Galilee." *Journal of Third World Studies* 24 (2).

Pedatzur, R. 2003. "Israel's 'Security Culture': Origins and Influence on Israeli Democracy" [in Hebrew]. *Politika* 10:87–117.

Peleg, I. 1987. *Begin's Foreign Policy, 1977–1983*. New York: Greenwood Press.

Peres, S. 1995. *Battling for Peace*. London: Weidenfeld.

Peretz, D., and Doron, G. 1997. *The Government and Politics of Israel*. Boulder, CO: Westview Press.

Peri, Y. 1981. "Political-Military Partnership in Israel." *International Political Science Review* 2 (3): 303–315.

———. 1983. *Between Battles and Ballots: The Israeli Military in Politics*. Cambridge: Cambridge University Press.

———. 2002. *The Israeli Military and Israel's Palestinian Policy*. Peaceworks No. 47. Washington, DC: United States Institute of Peace.

———. 2005. "The Political-Military Complex: The IDF's Influence over Policy Towards the Palestinians since 1987." *Israel Affairs* 11 (2): 324–344.

———. 2006. *Generals in the Cabinet Room*. Washington, DC: United States Institute of Peace Press.

Perlmutter, A. 1977. "Begin's Strategy and Dayan's Tactics: The Conduct of Israeli Foreign Policy." *Foreign Affairs* 56 (2): 357–372.

———. 1978. *Politics and Military in Israel*. London: Frank Cass.

———. 1985. *Israel, the Partitioned State*. New York: Scribner's.

———. 1987. *The Life and Times of Menachem Begin*. New York: Doubleday.

Presidential Committee on Governmental Reform. 2007. Report. Available in Hebrew at http://www.ceci.org.il/_Uploads/dbsAttachedFiles/finalreport.pdf.

Pressman, J. 2006. "Israeli Unilateralism and Israeli-Palestinian Relations, 2001–2006." *International Studies Perspectives* 7:360–376.

Preuss, T. 1984. *Begin: His Regime* [in Hebrew]. Jerusalem: Keter.

Quandt, W. B. 1986a. *Camp David*. Washington, DC: Brookings.

———. 1986b. "Camp David and Peacemaking in the Middle East." *Political Science Quarterly* 101 (3): 357–377.

———. 2005. *Peace Process: American Diplomacy and the Arab-Israeli Conflict since 1967*. 3rd ed. Washington, DC: Brookings.

Rabin, Y. 1979. *The Rabin Memoirs*. Boston: Little, Brown.

Rabinovich, I. 1984. *The War for Lebanon*. Ithaca, NY: Cornell University Press.

Rahat, G., and Hazan, R. Y. 2005. "Israel: The Politics of an Extreme Electoral System." In M. Gallagher and P. Mitchell, eds., *The Politics of Electoral Systems*. Oxford: Oxford University Press.

Randal, J. C. 1983. *Going All the Way*. New York: Viking.

Rapoport, A. 2007. *Friendly Fire* [in Hebrew]. Tel Aviv: Maariv.

Ravenal, E. C. 1978–1979. "Walking on Water in the Middle East." *Foreign Policy*, Winter, 151–160.

Reich, B., and Keival, G. R., eds. 1988. *Israeli National Security Policy*. New York: Greenwood Press.

Rodman, D. 2003. "Israel's National Security Doctrine." *Israel Affairs* 9 (4): 115–140.

———. 2005. *Defense and Diplomacy in Israeli National Security Experience*. Brighton, UK: Sussex Press.

Ross, D. 2004. *The Missing Peace: The Inside Story of the Fight for Middle East Peace*. New York: Farrar, Straus & Giroux.

Rubenstein, D., Malley, R., and Agha, H. 2003. *Camp David 2000: What Really Happened There* [in Hebrew]. Tel Aviv: Yediot Aharonoth.

Rubin, B. 1979. "Egypt and Israel: The Politics of Conciliation." *Washington Quarterly*, Spring, 51–59.

Rubin, B., and Keaney, T. A. 2002. *Armed Forces of the Middle East: Politics and Strategy*. Portland, OR: Frank Cass.

Rubinstein, C. L. 1983. "The Lebanon War: Objectives and Outcomes." *Australian Outlook* 37 (1): 10–17.

Rynhold, J., and Waxman, D. 2008. "Ideological Change and Israel's Disengagement from Gaza." *Political Science Quarterly* 123 (1): 11–37.

Sachar, H. M. 1981. *Egypt and Israel*. New York: Marek.

Sagie, U. 1998. *Lights within the Fog* [in Hebrew]. Tel Aviv: Miskal-Yediot Aharonoth.

Said-Aly, Abdel Monem. 2006. Middle East Brief #2, October. Waltham, MA: Crown Center for Middle East Studies.

Saunders, H. H. 1982. "An Arab-Israel Peace." *Foreign Affairs* 61 (1): 100–121.

———. 1985a. "Arabs and Israelis: A Political Strategy." *Foreign Affairs* 64 (2): 304–325.

———. 1985b. *The Other Walls*. Washington, DC: American Enterprise Institute.

Schiff, Z. 1983. "The Green Light." *Foreign Policy* 50 (Spring): 73–85.

———. 1985. *The Israeli Army*. New York: Macmillan.

Schiff, Z., and Yaari, E. 1982. *Israel's War in Lebanon* [in Hebrew]. Tel Aviv: Schocken.

Schulze, K. E. 1998a. "Israeli Crisis Decision Making in the Lebanon War: Group Madness or Individual Ambition?" *Israel Studies* 3 (2): 215–237.

———. 1998b. *Israel's Covert Diplomacy in Lebanon*. New York: St. Martin's Press.

Segev, T. 2005. *1967: Israel, the War, and the Year That Transformed the Middle East*. New York: Henry Holt.

Sela, A. 2007. "Civil Society, the Military and National Security: The Case of Israel's Security Zone in South Lebanon." *Israel Studies* 12 (1): 53–78.

Seliktar, O. 1986. *New Zionism and the Foreign Policy System of Israel*. London: Croom Helm.

Shamir, S., and Maddy-Weitzman, B., eds. 2005. *The Camp David Summit: What Went Wrong?* Brighton, UK: Sussex Academic Press.

Shamir, Y. 1994. *Summing Up: An Autobiography*. Boston: Little, Brown.

Sharkansky, I. 1997. *Policy Making in Israel*. Pittsburgh: University of Pittsburgh Press.

Sharon, A. 1989. *Warrior*. New York: Simon and Schuster.

Shashar, M. 1996. *The Lebanese Swamp*. Jerusalem: Shashar.

Shavit, A. 2006. *Partition: Disengagement and Beyond* [in Hebrew]. Jerusalem: Keter.

Sheffer, G. 1975. *Dynamics of a Conflict*. Atlantic Highlands, NJ: Humanities Press.

———. 1996. "Has Israel Really Been a Garrison State? Sources of Change in Israel's Democracy." *Israel Affairs* 3 (1): 13–38.

Shelah, O. 2003. *The Israeli Army: A Radical Proposal* [in Hebrew]. Or Yehuda: Kinneret.

Shelah, O., and Limor, Y. 2007. *Captives of Lebanon* [in Hebrew]. Tel Aviv: Miskal.

Sher, G. 2001. *Just Beyond Reach: The Israel-Palestinian Peace Negotiations, 1999–2001*. New York: Routledge. (Hebrew version: 2001. *Bemerkhak Negia*. Tel Aviv: Maskal.)

Shiffer, S. 1984. *Snowball*. Tel Aviv: Yediot Aharonoth Books.

Shiffer, Z. 2007. "The Debate over the Defense Budget in Israel." *Israel Studies* 12 (1): 193–214.

Shlaim, A. 1975. "Crisis Decision Making in Israel: The Lessons of October 1973." In P. James, ed., *International Yearbook of Foreign Policy Analysis, 1975*. New York: Wiley.

———. 1976. "Failures in National Intelligence Estimates: The Case of the Yom Kippur War." *World Politics* 26:348–380.

Shlaim, A., and Tanter, R. 1978. "Decision Process, Choice and Consequence: Israel's Deep Penetration Bombing in Egypt 1970." *World Politics* 30:483–516.

Shlaim, A., and Yaniv, A. 1980. "Domestic Politics and Foreign Policy in Israel." *International Affairs* 56:242–262.

Silver, E. 1984. *Begin: The Haunted Prophet*. New York: Random House.

Simes, D. 1979. "Camp David: The Soviet View." *Washington Quarterly*, Spring, 44–50.

Sofer, S. 1986. *Menachem Begin at the Camp David Conference: A Chapter in the New Diplomacy* [in Hebrew]. Van Leer Institute, Policy Papers #15, Hebrew University, Jerusalem.

———, ed. 1997. *The Role of Domestic Politics in Israeli Peacemaking*. Jerusalem: Leonard Davis Institute.

Spulber, N. 1983. "Israel's War in Lebanon through the Soviet Looking Glass." *Middle East Review* 15 (Spring–Summer): 18–24.

State Comptroller, State of Israel. 1987. *Annual Report #37*. June. Jerusalem: State Comptroller.

———. 1995. *Annual Report #46*. Jerusalem: State Comptroller.

———. 2001. *Annual Report #51*. Jerusalem: State Comptroller.

———. 2002a. *Annual Report #52*. Jerusalem: State Comptroller.

———. 2002b. *Annual Report #53*. Jerusalem: State Comptroller.

———. 2005. *Annual Report #56a*. Jerusalem: State Comptroller.

———. 2006. *Report on the National Security Council*. September. Jerusalem: State Comptroller.

———. 2007. *Preparation and Functioning of the Home-Front in the Second Lebanon War*. July. Jerusalem: State Comptroller.

———. 2012. *Report on the Implementation of the INSC Law and the Turkish Flotilla*. June. Jerusalem: State Comptroller.

State of Israel. 1983. *Commission of Inquiry into the Events at the Refugee Camps in Beirut*. Final Report, reprinted by the *Jerusalem Post*, February 9.

———. 1989. *The Public-Professional Committee for a General Assessment of the Civil Service and Institutions Supported by the National Budget*. August, Jerusalem.

———. 2007a. *Recommendations of the Steering Committee for the Implementation of the Interim Report of the Winograd Commission* ["Shahak Committee"]. Prime Minister's Office, June 26, Jerusalem.

———. 2007b. *Winograd Commission: Interim Report*. April, Jerusalem.

———. 2008. *Winograd Commission: Final Report*. January, Jerusalem. [Note: See also website listings for individual testimony before the Winograd Commission at the end of this bibliography.]

State of Israel, Knesset, Foreign and Defense Affairs Committee. 2007. *Report on Lessons from the Second Lebanon War*. December, Jerusalem.

State of Israel, Prime Minister's Office. 2007. *Committee to Examine the Defense Budget* ["Brodet Committee"]. May 17, Jerusalem.

Stein, J. G. 1977–1978. "Can Decision Makers Be Rational and Should They Be? Evaluating the Quality of Decisions." *Jerusalem Journal of International Relations* 3 (2–3): 316–339.

———. 1982a. "Intelligence Failure: A Reconsideration." *Jerusalem Quarterly* 24:41–54.

———. 1982b. "Leadership in Peacemaking." *International Journal* 37 (4):517–542.

———. 1983. "The Alchemy of Peacemaking." *International Journal* 38 (4):531–555.

Stein, J. G., and Tanter, R. 1976. *Rational Decision Making: Israeli Security Choices in 1967*. Columbus: Ohio State University Press.

Steiner, M. 1983. "The Search for Order in a Disorderly World." *International Organization*, Summer, 373–413.

Tal, I. 1996. *National Security: The Few versus the Many* [in Hebrew]. Tel Aviv: Dvir.

Tamir, A. 1988. *Soldier in Search of Peace* [in Hebrew]. Tel Aviv: Eidanim.

Tamir, I. M. 1986. "The Camp David Decision Making Process" [in Hebrew]. *Baayot Beinleumiyot* [International Problems] 25 (1–2): 11–29.

Tamir, K., and Bar-Siman-Tov, Y. 2007. *The Disengagement from Gaza and the Northern Shomron* [in Hebrew]. Jerusalem: Jerusalem Institute for the Study of Israel.

Telhami, S. 1990. *Power and Leadership in International Bargaining: The Path to the Camp David Accords*. New York: Columbia University Press.

Telhami, S., and Barnett, B., eds. 2002. *Identity and Foreign Policy in the Middle East*. Ithaca, NY: Cornell University Press.

Thayer, F. C. 1971. "Presidential Policy Processes and 'New Administration.'" *Public Administration Review* 31:552–561.

Torgovnik, E. 1978–1979. "Accepting Camp David: The Role of Party Factions in Israeli Policy Making." *Middle East Review* 11 (2): 18–25.

Tsur, N. 2006. *Disengaging from the Strip: Ariel Sharon and Israel's Withdrawal from the Gaza Strip* [in Hebrew]. Jerusalem: Tzivonim Press.

Tucker, R. W. 1978. "The Middle East: For a Separate Peace." *Commentary* 65 (3): 25–31.

U.S. Government, General Accounting Office. 1983. *Report by the Comptroller of the United States, U.S. Assistance to the State of Israel*. GAO ID-83-51, June 24.

———. 1987. *Analysis of Cost Estimates for Israel's Lavi Program*. GAO/NSIAD-87-76, January.

———. 1989. *US Funds Used for Terminating Israel's Lavi Aircraft Program*. GAO/NSIAD-90-3, October.

Van Creveld, M. 1998. *The Sword and the Olive: A Critical History of the Israel Defense Forces*. New York: Public Affairs.

Wagner, A. R. 1974. *Crisis Decision Making; Israel's Experience in 1967 and 1973*. New York: Praeger.

Wald, E. 1987. *The Curse of the Broken Instruments* [in Hebrew]. Jerusalem: Shocken.

———. 1991. *The Gordian Knot*. Tel Aviv: Yediot Aharonoth.

Weizman, E. 1981. *The Battle for Peace*. Toronto: Bantam.

Wurmser, D. 1984. "Egypto-Centrism in Israeli Strategic Planning." *SAIS Review* 4 (2): 67–76.

Yaacobi, G. 1982. *The Government of Israel*. New York: Praeger.

Yaalon, M. 2008. *The Long Short Way* [in Hebrew]. Tel Aviv: Miskal Yediot Aharonoth.

Yaari, A. 2004. *Civil Control of the Military in Israel*. Jaffee Center of Strategic Studies, Memorandum 72, October.

———. 2006. *Whom Does the Council Advise? A New Model for the National Security Council*. Jaffee Center of Strategic Studies, Memorandum 85, September.

Yaniv, A. 1983. "Moral Fervor vs. Strategic Logic." *Middle East Review* 15 (Spring–Summer): 5–10.

———. 1987. *Dilemmas of Security: Politics, Strategy and the Israeli Experience in Lebanon.* New York: Oxford University Press.

———. 1993. *National Security and Democracy in Israel.* Boulder, CO: Lynne Rienner.

———. 1994. *Politics and Strategy in Israel* [in Hebrew]. Tel Aviv: Sifriat Hapoalim.

Yaniv, A., and Lieber, R. J. 1983. "Personal Whim or Strategic Imperative." *International Security* 8 (2): 117–143.

Yishai, Y. 1987. *Land or Peace.* Stanford, CA: Hoover Institution Press.

Zakheim, D. S. 1996. *Flight of the Lavi.* Washington, DC: Brassey's.

Zalmanovitch, Y. 1998. "Transitions in Israel's Policymaking Network." *The Annals* 555 (1): 193–208.

Zelnick, R. 2006. *Israel's Unilateralism.* Stanford, CA: Hoover Institution Press.

## Testimony before the Winograd Commission

Ehud Barak, 11/28/06
http://www.vaadatwino.gov.il/pdf/%D7%A2%D7%93%D7%95%D7%AA%20
%D7%90%D7%94%D7%95%D7%93%20%D7%91%D7%A8%D7%A7.pdf

Benjamin Ben-Eliezer, 11.28/06
http://www.vaadatwino.gov.il/pdf/%D7%AA%D7%9E%D7%9C%D7%99%D7
%9C%20%D7%91%D7%9F%20%D7%90%D7%9C%D7%99%D7%A2%D7%96
%D7%A8.pdf

Avi Dichter, 11/23.06
http://www.vaadatwino.gov.il/pdf/%D7%AA%D7%9E%D7%9C%D7%99%D7
%9C%20%D7%90%D7%9C%D7%99%20%D7%99%D7%A9%D7%99.pdf

Dan Halutz, 1/28/07
http://www.vaadatwino.gov.il/pdf/%D7%AA%D7%9E%D7%9C%D7%99%D7
%9C%20%D7%93%D7%9F%20%D7%97%D7%9C%D7%95%D7%A5.pdf

Tzachi Hanegbi, 1/21/07
http://www.vaadatwino.gov.il/pdf/%D7%A2%D7%93%D7%95%D7%AA%20
%D7%A6%D7%97%D7%99%20%D7%94%D7%A0%D7%92%D7%91%D7%99
.pdf

Yitzhak Herzog, 1/18/07
http://www.vaadatwino.gov.il/pdf/%D7%AA%D7%9E%D7%9C%D7%99%D7
%9C%20%D7%99%D7%A6%D7%97%D7%A7%20%D7%94%D7%A8%D7%A6
%D7%95%D7%92.pdf

Tzipi Livni, 1/23/07
http://www.vaadatwino.gov.il/pdf/%D7%AA%D7%9E%D7%9C%D7%99%D7
%9C%20%D7%A6%D7%99%D7%A4%D7%99%20%D7%9C%D7%91%D7%A0
%D7%99.pdf

Amos Malka, 11/2/06
http://www.vaadatwino.gov.il/pdf/%D7%9E%D7%A1%D7%9E%D7%9A%20
%D7%91-%20%D7%A2%D7%9E%D7%95%D7%A1%20%D7%9E%D7%9C%D7
%9B%D7%90.pdf

Shaul Mofaz, 12/6/06
http://www.vaadatwino.gov.il/pdf/%D7%AA%D7%9E%D7%9C%D7%99%D7
%9C%20%D7%A9%D7%90%D7%95%D7%9C%20%D7%9E%D7%95%D7%A4
%D7%96.pdf

Yitzhak Mordechai, 1/2/07
http://www.vaadatwino.gov.il/pdf/%D7%AA%D7%9E%D7%9C%D7%99%D7
%9C%20%D7%90%D7%99%D7%A6%D7%99%D7%A7%20%D7%9E%D7%A8
%D7%93%D7%9B%D7%99.pdf

Benjamin Netanyahu, 1/11/07
http://www.vaadatwino.gov.il/pdf/%D7%AA%D7%9E%D7%9C%D7%99%D7
%9C%20%D7%91%D7%A0%D7%99%D7%9E%D7%99%D7%9F%20%D7%A0
%D7%AA%D7%A0%D7%99%D7%94%D7%95.pdf

Ehud Olmert, 2/1/07
http://www.vaadatwino.gov.il/pdf/%D7%AA%D7%9E%D7%9C%D7%99%D7
%9C%20%D7%90%D7%95%D7%9C%D7%9E%D7%A8%D7%98.pdf

Shimon Peres, 11/7/06
http://www.vaadatwino.gov.il/pdf/%D7%9E%D7%A1%D7%9E%D7%9A%20
%D7%91-%20%D7%A9%D7%9E%D7%A2%D7%95%D7%9F%20%D7%A4%D7
%A8%D7%A1.pdf

Amir Peretz, 1/24/07
http://www.vaadatwino.gov.il/pdf/%D7%AA%D7%9E%D7%9C%D7%99%D7
%9C%20%D7%A2%D7%9E%D7%99%D7%A8%20%D7%A4%D7%A8%D7%A5
.pdf

Ofir Pinnes-Paz, 1/7/07
http://www.vaadatwino.gov.il/pdf/%D7%AA%D7%9E%D7%9C%D7%99%D7
%9C%20%D7%90%D7%95%D7%A4%D7%99%D7%A8%20%D7%A4%D7%96
%20%D7%A4%D7%99%D7%A0%D7%A1.pdf

Chaim Ramon, 1/10/07
http://www.vaadatwino.gov.il/pdf/%D7%AA%D7%9E%D7%9C%D7%99%D7
%9C%20%D7%97%D7%99%D7%99%D7%9D%20%D7%A8%D7%9E%D7%95
%D7%9F.pdf

Yoram Turbovich, 12/27/06
http://www.vaadatwino.gov.il/pdf/%D7%AA%D7%9E%D7%9C%D7%99%D7
%9C%20%D7%99%D7%95%D7%A8%D7%9D%20%D7%98%D7%95%D7%A8
%D7%91%D7%95%D7%91%D7%99%D7%A5.pdf

Dov Weisglass, 1/11/07
http://www.vaadatwino.gov.il/pdf/%D7%AA%D7%9E%D7%9C%D7%99%D7
%9C%20%D7%93%D7%91%20%D7%95%D7%99%D7%99%D7%A1%D7%92
%D7%9C%D7%A1.pdf

Eli Yishai, 11/8/06
http://www.vaadatwino.gov.il/pdf/%D7%AA%D7%9E%D7%9C%D7%99%D7
%9C%20%D7%90%D7%9C%D7%99%20%D7%99%D7%A9%D7%99.pdf

# Index

# DATE DUE

| JUN 1 0 2015 | |
|---|---|
| | |
| | |
| | |
| | |
| | |
| | |
| | |
| | |
| | |
| | |
| | |
| | |

BRODART, CO.                                    Cat. No. 23-221